Criminology
FOR
DUMMIES®

by Steven Briggs
with Joan Friedman

WILEY

Wiley Publishing, Inc.

Criminology For Dummies®

Published by
Wiley Publishing, Inc.
111 River St.
Hoboken, NJ 07030-5774
www.wiley.com

For general information on our other products and services, please contact our Customer Care Department within the U.S. at 877-762-2974, outside the U.S. at 317-572-3993, or fax 317-572-4002.

For technical support, please visit www.wiley.com/techsupport.

Wiley also publishes its books in a variety of electronic formats. Some content that appears in print may not be available in electronic books.

Library of Congress Control Number: 2009933756

ISBN: 978-0-470-39696-4

Manufactured in the United States of America

10 9 8 7 6 5 4 3 2

WILEY

About the Author

Steven Briggs has spent most of his legal career as a criminal prosecutor, working at the local, state, and federal levels. He has handled cases from petty theft to organized crime and capital murder. Several of his cases have been broadcast on national TV and have become the subjects of true crime books. Mr. Briggs also oversaw his state's criminal division, where he managed the organized crime, financial crime, and criminal intelligence units, as well as the state anti-terrorism and crime victim's programs. In addition, Mr. Briggs managed his state's district attorney assistance prosecution unit and special agents unit, which targeted complex crime, including Internet predators, social security fraud, and narcotics traffickers. An accomplished trainer, Mr. Briggs has regularly instructed state, national, and international audiences on a variety of criminal justice topics. A graduate of Dartmouth College and the University of Oregon School of Law, Mr. Briggs was a college football coach before pursuing his legal career.

Dedication

For Marla and Elena.

Author's Acknowledgments

I would like to give a big thanks to my agent, Barbara Doyen, as well as Development Editor Joan Friedman for their excellent work and guidance in preparing this book. Technical Editor Ken Rueben was, as always, a great resource and friend. Internationally recognized juvenile justice expert David Koch was very gracious with his time, as was Cynthia Stinson, the most knowledgeable person I know on the topic of crime victim services. Copy Editor Amanda Gillum and Project Editor Natalie Faye Harris worked very hard on improving this book's readability. I must also acknowledge the lingering influence of Blinker Black and all his fraters. Finally, I would like to thank the men and women of the criminal division, who were not only the source of many great examples in this book, but whose sacrifice of personal interest in the pursuit of justice has been a constant inspiration to me.

Publisher's Acknowledgments

We're proud of this book; please send us your comments at http://dummies.custhelp.com. For other comments, please contact our Customer Care Department within the U.S. at 877-762-2974, outside the U.S. at 317-572-3993, or fax 317-572-4002.

Some of the people who helped bring this book to market include the following:

Acquisitions, Editorial, and Media Development

Project Editor: Natalie Faye Harris

Acquisitions Editor: Michael Lewis

Copy Editor: Amanda M. Gillum

Assistant Editor: Erin Calligan Mooney

Editorial Program Coordinator: Joe Niesen

Technical Editor: Ken Rueben

Editorial Manager: Christine Meloy Beck

Editorial Assistants: Jennette ElNaggar, David Lutton

Art Coordinator: Alicia B. South

Cartoons: Rich Tennant (www.the5thwave.com)

Composition Services

Project Coordinator: Sheree Montgomery

Layout and Graphics: Melissa K. Jester, Mark Pinto, Christine Williams

Proofreader: Laura L. Bowman, David Faust, John Greenough

Indexer: Potomac Indexing, LLC

Publishing and Editorial for Consumer Dummies

Diane Graves Steele, Vice President and Publisher, Consumer Dummies

Kristin Ferguson-Wagstaffe, Product Development Director, Consumer Dummies

Ensley Eikenburg, Associate Publisher, Travel

Kelly Regan, Editorial Director, Travel

Publishing for Technology Dummies

Andy Cummings, Vice President and Publisher, Dummies Technology/General User

Composition Services

Debbie Stailey, Director of Composition Services

Contents at a Glance

Table of Contents

Chapter 6: Hitting You in the Pocketbook: Property Crimes 77

Chapter 7: Dressing Sharp and Stealing Big: White-Collar Crimes 93

Introduction

Crime is fascinating. How else can you explain why, as I'm writing this book, six of the top ten TV shows focus on criminal investigations (and right in the heart of the *American Idol* and *Dancing with the Stars* seasons, too!)? But the study of crime is not only fascinating, it's also terribly important. The U.S. government (and, in turn, every U.S. taxpayer) spends hundreds of billions of dollars every year combating crime. Are the government's efforts smart? Are they enough?

I've spent most of my career fighting crime at the local, state, and federal levels. I've worked with just about every category of law enforcement professional there is, from detectives to probation officers to terrorism experts to judges. And of the thousands of people I've known, I can count on one hand the number of people who weren't committed to something larger than themselves — to serving their fellow human beings. If you're considering joining these men and women in their fight against crime, you've picked up the right book.

In this book, I explore both the world of crime and society's response to it. Both topics are fascinating, exciting, and extremely vast. From the gang banger who sells eight balls of crack on the street corner to the cop who's just trying to get home to his wife, I try to explain what people do and why they do it.

About This Book

Criminology For Dummies isn't a textbook (although, if you're a student, it may help you actually understand your criminology textbook). It's meant to give you an insider's look into the world of crime and criminal justice. Throughout the book, I try to make the concepts and principles of criminology come alive because nothing is more real than personally experiencing crime.

I try very hard to avoid the use of complex terms in this book. As a prosecutor who has stood in front of numerous juries, I know that the secret to communicating is using straightforward language. Some of the ideas in criminology are complex, but their explanations don't have to be.

If you're considering a career in criminal justice, you should know that I don't pull any punches in this book. If I think a job is tough, I tell you so and give you the reasons why. But I also try to explain the job objectively so that you can decide for yourself whether it's the right move for you.

If you picked up this book simply because you're fascinated by crime, you may want to set this book on the nightstand next to your collection of works by Ann Rule, Sue Grafton, Patricia Cornwell, James Patterson, or the hundreds of other writers who make crime — at least the fictional kind — fun.

Conventions Used in This Book

Whenever I introduce a word or phrase that may not be familiar to you, I put that word in *italics*. You can rest assured that a definition or explanation is nearby.

On occasion, I include URLs for Web sites that I think may interest you. Those Web addresses appear in `monofont`, which helps them stand out from the rest of the text.

And speaking of Web addresses: When this book was printed, some Web addresses had to break across two lines of text. When that happened, rest assured that I didn't put in any extra characters (such as hyphens) to indicate the break. So, when you're using one of these Web addresses, just type in exactly what you see in this book, pretending that the line break doesn't exist.

What You're Not to Read

Given the amount of work that goes into writing a book, it may seem strange that I'm now suggesting that you don't have to read the whole thing! But my goal is to make sure you use the book to your full advantage, which may mean skipping over text that isn't crucial to your understanding of the subject at hand. In this book, you find two types of text that fall into this category:

- ✔ **Paragraphs accompanied by the Technical Stuff icon:** As I explain in a moment, this icon highlights text that goes into details that you may find unnecessary.
- ✔ **Sidebars:** These gray boxes contain anecdotes or explanations that I think you may find interesting but that aren't essential to your criminology education.

Foolish Assumptions

This book covers such a wide array of information that I truly can't assume I know why you're reading it. Here are some wild guesses:

- You're a college student taking an introductory course in criminology, and you picked up this book to help you interpret some of the jargon in your 600-page textbook.

- You've always thought about becoming a police officer or other law enforcement professional and are trying to gauge what the job entails and where it fits into the big picture of criminal justice.

- You're thinking about going to law school to become a prosecutor or public defender, and you want to know what you'd be in for.

- You have a friend or relative entangled in the criminal justice system, and you want to be able to talk the talk so you can distinguish an arraignment from an appeal.

- You're addicted to *CSI: Crime Scene Investigation* or any number of other criminal investigation shows.

Whatever your motivation, I hope you find what you're looking for in this book. And I hope you're inspired to find out even more about the specific area of criminology that interests you because there's much more to explore than I could possibly fit in these pages.

How This Book Is Organized

I've grouped the chapters in this book into six parts, each one focusing on a particular aspect of criminology. I've written the book so you can dive into any chapter without getting lost — just pick the topic that interests you most and start reading!

Part 1: Defining and Measuring Crime

Chapter 1 offers a broad overview of the book's contents so you can gain a better sense of what's covered and where to find it.

Starting with Chapter 2, I delve into some tough questions. The first question is: What is crime? When you think about it, someone has to define crime, right? Actually, it's most often defined by a group of someones whom folks like you and me elect to state and federal offices. The decisions these elected officials make about criminal law have far-reaching effects; they influence what actions are prosecuted and punished and, perhaps, how long punishments can last.

Another tough question I address in this part is: How much crime is there? Measuring crime can be a bit like measuring water with a sieve. In Chapter 3, I explain why.

No matter how you measure crime, almost every crime has one thing in common — a victim. In Chapter 4, I describe the various ways crime affects victims, and I explore recent efforts to secure victims' rights throughout the criminal justice process.

Part II: Identifying Types of Crime

The crimes that get the most attention on TV are violent in nature, so I start this part by defining and explaining the different types of violent crime in Chapter 5. But far more people are victims of property crime than violent crime; thus, I devote Chapter 6 to that topic.

Chapter 7 focuses on the unique nature of white-collar crime, and Chapter 8 explores the fascinating and frightening world of organized crime (including gangs).

I round out this part by devoting a chapter each to two topics that make front-page news all too frequently these days: the drug trade and terrorism.

Part III: Figuring Out Who Commits Crimes and Why

The heart of criminology is trying to figure out why people commit crime. After all, if you can answer that fundamental question, you may have a chance of reducing crime.

Obviously, no one claims to have a single answer. In this part, I explore several theories that seem to offer insights, from the rational choice theory (which holds that criminals make rational decisions based on the costs and benefits of their actions) to the theory of labeling (which holds that people labeled as criminals early in life have limited opportunities and, therefore, can't break free from lives of crime).

Part IV: Fighting Crime

TV producers sure love this stage of the criminal justice process — the stage that involves chasing and apprehending the bad guys. The chase may involve either local law enforcement officials or federal agencies, so I devote a chapter to explaining each. I then explore the processes that law enforcement officers use to try to solve crimes.

Part V: Prosecuting and Punishing Crime

Although the chase and apprehension of a suspect are exciting, what happens next can be equally riveting (hence the appeal of *Law & Order*). After all, when someone is arrested, that person's experience with the criminal justice system is just beginning.

In this part, I introduce the people who carry a criminal case through the courtroom phase. I explain what accepting a plea bargain means and what happens when a case goes to trial (which relatively few cases do).

When the prosecution is done and the accused person is sentenced, that person enters the punishment phase of the criminal justice system. In Chapter 21, I explore theories of why society punishes people and explain how punishment typically occurs in the United States.

I round out this part with a chapter that focuses on juvenile offenders, whose crimes may be similar to those of adults but whose experience with the criminal justice system is likely to be very different.

Part VI: The Part of Tens

Every *For Dummies* book contains this part, which features short chapters of easily digestible material. You get two chapters in this part: one on ten jobs to consider in the criminal justice field and one on ten notorious, unsolved crimes.

Icons Used in This Book

In the margins of this book, you find the following icons — mini graphics that point out paragraphs containing certain types of information:

This icon points out hints to help you better understand the concepts I cover in this book.

This icon sits next to paragraphs that contain real-life examples and anecdotes — most often from my years of experience in the criminal justice field.

This icon points out material that's important enough to put into your mental filing cabinet.

When you see this icon, you know the information in the accompanying paragraph encourages a note of caution.

On a few occasions, I include information that I consider worth knowing but that you may not. If you're looking for strictly big-picture information, feel free to skip these paragraphs.

Where to Go from Here

The beauty of this book is that you can start anywhere and understand it. If you're the type of person who likes to eat your dinner one food at a time, perhaps you want to start with Chapter 1 and read straight through. But if you're most interested in the theories about why people commit crime, skip straight to Part III and sink your teeth in. If you're most interested in how the criminal justice system treats juveniles, head to Chapter 22. Where you go next is your call!

Part I
Defining and Measuring Crime

The 5th Wave   By Rich Tennant

In this part . . .

*W*hat exactly is crime? When you think about it, you realize it's not such an easy question to answer. After all, someone has to decide that a specific action is criminal and, therefore, worth prosecuting and punishing. To complicate matters, the actions that the law labels *criminal* change as time goes by — new laws are added and old ones are revised.

Here's another tough question: How much crime is there? No one knows the exact amount. The methods for measuring crime are imperfect, partly because police reporting is imperfect and partly because crime stats depend on a victim's willingness to come forward.

In this part, I offer my best answers to these two questions and explain some of the nuances that color those answers. I also describe how crime impacts victims and explore a few recent movements to try to support and empower them.

Chapter 1

Entering the World of Crime

. . . .

. . . .

*E*ntering the world of crime — and I mean really *entering* it — seriously affects a person. Working in a world of violence and deceit is a hard and trying business. Nonetheless, criminologists and criminal justice professionals devote their lives to studying crime and criminals with the ultimate goal of keeping people safe. In this chapter, you get a brief overview of the criminal world — from what causes crime to what society can do about it.

Defining the Terms: What Crime Is and How You Measure It

Technically, a crime is what your legislature says it is. If legislators want to outlaw riding a horse over 10 mph, they can. (It's against the law to do so in Indianapolis, for example.)

But just outlawing an activity doesn't make it a crime. For example, running a red light is illegal, but it isn't a crime. A *crime* is something you can get locked up for.

Taking away a person's liberty is what separates criminal conduct from illegal conduct. And when the possibility of going to jail is involved, you have a number of constitutional rights that you don't have when you're caught for a traffic violation, including the following:

- ✔ The right to an attorney
- ✔ The right to a jury, which can convict you only if the evidence is beyond a reasonable doubt
- ✔ The right to remain silent and not have your silence used against you

Identifying elements of criminal behavior

Crime isn't as simple as it seems at first blush. If I signed my credit card receipt in a store and accidentally walked away with the pen, did I commit theft? Of course not. I didn't intend to steal the pen. To be guilty of a crime, I must have some *mental culpability,* such as criminal intent. Taking a pen is a crime only if a prosecutor can prove that I intended to deprive the owner of his pen.

In addition, committing a crime requires a physical act. It's not illegal just to think about committing a crime; you must physically *do* something. (Of course, a few exceptions exist. For example, not paying your taxes can constitute a crime.) I explore the elements of a *criminal law* (which is a law that defines a crime) in greater detail in Chapter 2.

Not all crimes are equal. The law breaks down crimes into two categories, according to seriousness:

- ✔ **Misdemeanor:** This type of crime includes the least serious offenses. Historically, misdemeanor crimes were crimes that couldn't be punished by more than a year in jail. Today, however, because overcrowding in jails is a serious problem, people convicted of misdemeanors, especially first-time offenders, aren't likely to get much jail time at all.
- ✔ **Felony:** This type of crime is usually more serious and is punishable by more than a year in custody. Serious violent crimes like murder, rape, kidnapping, and robbery are felonies that can result in lengthy prison sentences.

Gathering crime statistics

You may think that determining the amount of crime in a given city, state, or country is a pretty simple task. But, in reality, it's very challenging. For example, how do you gather statistics about illegal drug sales? Neither the seller nor the buyer is going to report a heroin deal. And wives who are beaten by their husbands don't usually call the cops. In fact, less than 50 percent of violent crimes and less than 40 percent of property crimes are ever reported to the police.

The Federal Bureau of Investigation (FBI) has developed a system called the *Uniform Crime Report* for gathering basic statistics about nine serious felonies, known in the crime business as *Part 1 crimes*. Whenever one of the roughly 17,000 police agencies in the United States gets a report that one of these crimes has been committed, that agency passes the information on to the FBI. If the agency ends up making an arrest, it passes that information on, as well. The FBI incorporates this information in its annual crime report.

Recognizing the limits of crime reports and arrest statistics in measuring crime, the federal government created the National Crime Victimization Survey, which canvasses 76,000 households every year to ask whether members of those households have been victimized by crime. The idea is that this survey can gather information about crimes that aren't reported to the police. This survey paints a pretty good picture of national crime trends, but the sampling just isn't large enough to allow for an accurate assessment of crime trends at the state or local level. In Chapter 3, I get into the crime statistics business in much greater detail.

Recognizing the Various Costs of Crime

While criminologists try to gather accurate statistics about the amount of crime, economists focus on the financial costs of crime. And, of course, no one can forget the life-changing impact crime has on victims.

Noting the financial impact

The most obvious cost of crime to society is the money it takes to run the criminal justice system, including the following big-ticket items:

- Police
- Jails, prisons, and the staff to run them
- Prosecutors
- Judges and court staff
- Defense attorneys to represent charged defendants at trial and on appeal
- Probation officers
- Juvenile justice counselors

Plus, in the United States, each of the three levels of government — local, state, and federal — may run its own justice system, which may include some or all of the preceding expenses.

In addition to governmental costs, society bears many other financial impacts of crime. For example, think of the lost productivity and lost tax revenue that occurs when a person decides to sell drugs rather than earn wages lawfully. Or think of the costs of providing medical care to victims of violence or the costs of developing cybersecurity for a corporation to protect its computer systems. The financial impact of crime is quite startling when you dive into it. In Chapter 3, I provide more details on the true cost of crime to all of society.

Respecting the price a victim pays

Crime doesn't just carry an economic cost, however. Every day, thousands of lives are turned upside down by criminal violence and theft. Think of the impact on a senior citizen who's defrauded out of her life savings or on a battered spouse who's isolated from her friends and family and lives in constant fear of upsetting her husband. There's simply no way to quantify the human toll of crime.

Until about 30 years ago, crime victims were pretty much left to fend for themselves. But in the early 1980s, a movement that brought help to victims began. Today, in every state, a victim of violent crime can get financial help with medical bills, grief counseling, lost wages, and other economic losses. Victims can also get help understanding the criminal justice system.

Significantly, within the last ten years, a movement to grant rights to victims has gathered tremendous momentum. In most states today, victims have at least the following rights:

- The right to be notified of all important hearings
- The right to speak at release hearings where criminal defendants seek to be released from jail
- The right to obtain a "no contact" order, which prohibits the defendant from contacting the victim
- The right to prevent the defendant from getting the victim's address
- The right to demand a blood test of the defendant if there's a possibility that a disease, such as HIV or hepatitis, was transferred to the victim during the crime
- The right to receive restitution for financial impact from a crime
- The right to give a statement to the judge explaining the impact of the crime on the victim at the time of sentencing the defendant

For much more information about what the criminal justice system does to protect victims, see Chapter 4.

Considering Categories of Crime

Law enforcement professionals often group crimes into the following two categories:

- ✔ Violent crimes (also called *person crimes*)
- ✔ Property crimes

But a careful study of crime reveals that *organized crime,* in which groups engage in a business of crime, is a whole different animal worthy of separate analysis.

Studying individual crimes

When police respond to a 9-1-1 call, they're almost always responding to an individual crime. Someone was assaulted or burglarized, for example. Typically, police treat violent crimes much more seriously than they do property crimes. For example, although a murder investigation may have ten or more cops assigned to it, police may not even respond in person to investigate a burglary at a home. Obviously, this discrepancy occurs because protecting personal safety is the number one job of people in law enforcement; plus, police resources are finite.

Here are the crimes you most likely think of when you consider individual crimes:

Violent Crimes	*Property Crimes*
Murder and manslaughter	Theft (including shoplifting, embezzlement, Internet fraud, identity theft, and car theft)
Assault and battery (including domestic abuse, child abuse, and vehicular assault)	Burglary
Sexual crimes (rape, sodomy, and child molestation)	Arson
Robbery	

Obviously, the punishment for violent crime is much more severe than it is for property crime. A person who shoplifts from a convenience store (a property crime) will get a much lighter sentence than someone who sticks a gun in the store clerk's face and demands cash (the violent crime of robbery).

Among different violent offenses, the punishment can vary depending on whether a weapon was used, how much harm was caused, and whether the bad guy *intended* to cause harm. For example, a drunk driver who crashes and kills his passenger will receive a much shorter prison sentence than a woman who knowingly poisons her mother-in-law. The drunk driver didn't intend to kill anyone, but the evil daughter-in-law surely did. (For more info, check out Chapter 5 on violent crimes and Chapter 6 on property crimes.)

Focusing on organized crime

Despite what you see on TV, organized crime is much more than the Italian mob. In fact, the mafia is really only a very small part of the organized crime threat in the United States today. *Organized crime* refers to the groups of individuals who organize themselves in a hierarchical structure, usually for the purpose of engaging in the business of crime. These groups are set up in such a way that even when police arrest one or two members, the organization continues to operate. This structure is what makes fighting organized crime so difficult.

Organized crime groups are traditionally set up along ethnic lines, in large part, because members of the same ethnic group are more likely to know and trust one another. (However, a group called the *United Nations gang*, known for its ethnic diversity, was taken down in May 2009 for a large-scale drug-smuggling operation between Canada and the United States.)

Some common organized crime groups include

- Motorcycle gangs
- Drug-smuggling operations
- Prison gangs
- Street gangs
- White-supremacist organizations

These groups usually gravitate toward the types of criminal activities that provide the most income. Obviously, much of this activity includes illegal drugs. But it also includes tobacco smuggling, trafficking in counterfeit goods, and Internet fraud. Plus, you can't forget the more traditional, localized organized crime activities, such as extortion, loan sharking, and robbery. And some groups, like white-supremacist criminal organizations, aren't as interested in making money; they're actually closer to being terrorist organizations. In Chapter 8, I go into much greater detail about the organized crime threat and how law enforcement is dealing with it.

Spotlighting terrorism

Throughout the world, and here in the United States, organized groups are using violence and the threat of violence to achieve political and social goals. These groups are called *terrorists,* and, today, criminal justice professionals are on the front lines in the fight against terrorism. Most known terrorist plots in the United States have been first identified or foiled by local police. As a result, it's standard practice for cops throughout the country to be trained in identifying signs of terrorist activity.

Terrorism experts generally categorize the terrorist threat into two groups: international terrorist organizations and domestic organizations. But, in reality, hundreds of international groups have many different agendas, and numerous domestic terrorist groups tout principles ranging from animal rights to white supremacy.

While law enforcement tends to investigate terrorists using the same methods used to attack organized crime, a significant threat continues to be the "lone wolf" actor, who goes at it alone (or perhaps works with a buddy). Timothy McVeigh and Terry Nichols, who killed 168 people by bombing the federal building in Oklahoma City, are prime examples. Such lone wolf attacks are very challenging to detect because the attackers don't communicate their plans to accomplices.

In Chapter 10, I discuss the major international and domestic terrorist threats that the United States faces today.

Figuring Out What Makes Someone Commit a Crime

One significant branch of criminology focuses on determining the causes of crime. Why do some people become life-long criminals while others become productive members of society? If criminologists — or anyone for that matter — can answer this question, maybe they can figure out some ways to prevent crime.

The following sections just skim the surface of the major theories criminologists have developed for why people commit crime. For a much more detailed discussion of the various causes of crime, check out Chapters 12 through 15.

Making a rational decision

Underlying society's current response to crime is the *rational choice theory,* which says that people generally make rational decisions about choices in their lives, including decisions to commit crime. This theory holds that when deciding whether to commit an illegal act, a person assesses the potential rewards and risks and then acts accordingly. If society provides enough punishment, a rational actor will decide not to commit crime. Thus, the threat of punishment acts as a deterrent to committing crime.

Of course, not everyone acts rationally. Human beings are prone to doing stupid things, even when they know they're stupid. And then, of course, you can't forget the impact of drugs and mental illness. A person high on methamphetamine probably won't do a very good job of analyzing potential risks and rewards.

Pointing the finger at society

Sometimes people make rational choices to engage in crime because their values are significantly different from those of normal society. For example, a gang banger may rationally choose to commit assault to gain status within his gang. How does a person develop such antisocial values?

Criminologists have developed a number of theories to explain society's role in crime. *Social disorganization theory,* for example, asserts that the structure of a neighborhood is strongly correlated to the amount of crime in that neighborhood. Where social structures are in decay, more crime is likely to occur. Poor schools, high unemployment, and a mix of commercial and residential property are some of the indicators of social disorganization.

Strain theory contends that everyone in society has generally the same goals and ambitions. But some people aren't able to achieve those goals because they lack opportunity, attend poor schools, or have few positive role models, for example. In response, they resort to crime to achieve their goals. In other words, the frustration, or *strain,* of not achieving their goals leads them to commit crime. A variety of strain theories focus on different causes of frustration.

Yet another theory, called the *social learning theory,* contends that criminals learn the skills, attitudes, and behaviors that lead to crime from the people they hang out with. Under this theory, a person's peer group and family are instrumental in shaping the values that lead them to criminal or law-abiding behavior.

Other explanations for crime come from a collection of theories known as *social control theories.* Generally, these theories argue that crime is exciting and fun and provides immediate gratification, so most people would become criminals if not for a variety of "controls" that restrain the urge to commit crime. These controls may be external, such as family, schools, church, and the social bonds related to these organizations. Or, they may be internal, such as self-discipline and strong self-esteem. In neighborhoods where institutional controls are weak, more crime occurs.

Blaming mental and physical defects

It's increasingly clear that genetics, diet, brain chemistry, and even the environment can play a role in causing a person to commit crime.

Adoption studies have confirmed a genetic link between criminal parents and criminal conduct by their offspring. But these same studies also show that the environment created by the parents raising the children has an impact on the children's criminal conduct. Thus, criminologists recognize that genetics are just part of the picture.

Other studies have shown that a poor diet can lead to learning disabilities, attention deficit/hyperactivity disorder, and depression, all of which are linked to greater potential for criminal behavior.

And, of course, personality disorders and mental illnesses may create a greater likelihood of criminal behavior. For example, a large percentage of people in prison have an *antisocial personality disorder,* which generally means they've engaged in a pattern of behavior that violates the rights of others.

Waging a War against Crime

Society fights crime with three levels of police: Local, state, and federal. Each level has different responsibilities, but they all join forces when it comes to fighting organized crime.

Policing the streets

Of the 17,000 police agencies in the United States, most of them are local agencies, which means they're city police or county sheriffs. These agencies handle most of the emergency calls for police services. In addition to responding to 9-1-1 calls, however, local police patrol the streets and enforce traffic laws. In fact, the only interaction most people have with a cop is getting pulled over for a traffic violation.

Although local agencies can range in size from one officer to thousands, most departments have the following categories of cops:

- ✔ **Patrol officers:** Respond to 9-1-1 calls and drive the streets to try to discourage crime with their presence.
- ✔ **Sergeants:** Typically supervise five to ten officers.
- ✔ **Detectives:** Conduct criminal investigations. Rather than just responding to a 9-1-1 call and writing a report, a detective typically is assigned more

complex cases that require longer-term investigations. A smaller police department may have just a general detective unit, while a larger department may have detectives who specialize in specific types of crime, such as homicide.

✔ **Management:** Includes lieutenants, captains, and the chief of police or sheriff.

In Chapter 16, I discuss the functions of all these cops in detail.

Getting the feds involved

Although the federal government has over 65 different federal agencies with law enforcement personnel, the vast majority of federal officers work for agencies I'm sure you've heard of, including the following:

✔ Federal Bureau of Investigation (FBI)

✔ Drug Enforcement Administration (DEA)

✔ Bureau of Alcohol, Tobacco, Firearms and Explosives (ATF)

✔ Immigration and Customs Enforcement (ICE), which used to be the INS and the Customs Service

✔ Secret Service

✔ U.S. Marshal's Service

✔ Internal Revenue Service (IRS)

These agencies enforce *federal criminal laws,* which are criminal laws passed by the U.S. Congress. (Local police agencies typically enforce local or state laws.) Each of these agencies focuses on its area of specialty, with the FBI having broader authority to get into more types of crime. An officer with a federal agency is usually called a *special agent* and conducts complex, long-term investigations. Special agents don't respond to 9-1-1 calls or enforce traffic laws. If you're intrigued by life as a fed, look at Chapter 17 where I give you a brief overview of the major federal law enforcement agencies.

Working together in task forces

Because organized crime frequently crosses the territorial boundary of one police agency, local, state, and federal cops often come together to form *task forces,* which fight a specific type of crime. Most commonly, officers from different agencies work together on drug or gang task forces. For example, when a drug mule carries dope from one city into another, the task force has authority in each town to conduct surveillance and make arrests.

One of the greatest benefits of task forces is that they encourage information sharing between different agencies. When agencies combine their information about a particular organized crime group, they often create a much better picture of the threat and are then able to devise a strategy to investigate and eliminate that threat. Because so many different police agencies are working toward the same goal of public safety, cooperation among them is crucial, and task forces help to foster that cooperation.

Bringing Criminals to Justice

When police catch a criminal, that person enters a large, complex system that is set up to make sure that individual's constitutional rights are protected at the same time that society as a whole is protected.

Prosecuting crime

After police make an arrest, a prosecutor must determine whether or not to file criminal charges. (At the local level, a prosecutor is usually known as an *assistant district attorney* or *county prosecutor.* At the federal level, prosecutors are called *assistant U.S. attorneys.*) After reading a police officer's report, if a prosecutor decides to file charges, he drafts a charging document, sometimes called an *information* or an *indictment,* which lists all the criminal charges against the defendant.

At the *arraignment,* the defendant hears the charges against him and has the chance to apply for a court-appointed attorney. (Most defendants can't afford to hire their own lawyers.) Thereafter, the prosecutor and the defense attorney engage in plea negotiations. The vast majority of criminal cases are resolved by negotiations and don't go to trial. But if the lawyers can't agree, they do go to trial, where a jury decides whether or not the defendant is guilty. (A defendant can choose to waive his right to a jury and let a judge decide the case.) I discuss the responsibilities of prosecutors, defense attorneys, and judges in Chapter 19, and I walk you through all the steps of a typical criminal trial in Chapter 20.

Determining punishment

If a defendant is convicted, the judge decides what punishment to impose, although many states have taken away most of a judge's discretion by passing laws that provide for mandatory sentences for certain serious crimes. Low-level offenses often don't result in any jail time. Rather, a defendant may just receive a fine, some community service, and probation. But serious offenses can result in lengthy sentences.

A person sentenced to do time can go to either a local jail, usually run by a county sheriff, or a prison, run by a state or the federal government. Jail is usually reserved for shorter sentences, and prison often involves sentences of a year or more.

After serving their time, convicted persons are often placed on *probation* or *parole,* which means they have to comply with certain conditions imposed by the judge or else be sent back to jail or prison. Here are some typical probation conditions:

- ✔ Pay all court costs and fines
- ✔ Complete community service
- ✔ Attend all ordered treatment, such as drug treatment, anger management, or sex offender treatment
- ✔ Obey all laws (of course!)

In Chapter 21, I talk about the U.S. *corrections system,* which is made up of the jails, prisons, and probation services that house convicted defendants and attempt to get them back on a law-abiding track.

Giving juveniles special attention

What do you do with a kid who commits a crime? In the United States, the system for dealing with juvenile offenders is different from the one dealing with adults. The primary reason for having a separate system is that society recognizes that because kids aren't yet mature, society shouldn't hold them fully responsible for their misconduct. Recent science supports the idea that until children's brains are fully developed (at around the age of 25), they're more likely to be impulsive and exercise poor judgment. Thus, it's no wonder that roughly half of all crimes are committed by people under the age of 25.

When a juvenile is arrested, he's assigned a juvenile counselor who works closely with him to get him back on the law-abiding track, which means identifying problems at home, drug use, or other environmental factors that are causing difficulty.

Most juveniles are given the chance to avoid formal trials and, thus, avoid creating permanent records by handling their cases *informally.* In other words, they admit their conduct to the juvenile counselor and are given some form of light punishment, such as community service.

For more serious offenses, or for chronic offenders, the system may treat the juvenile *formally.* This means he has the right to an attorney and a trial before a judge. If he's found *responsible* (kids aren't found *"guilty"*), the judge can sentence him to do some time in a local juvenile facility or even a state-run youth correctional facility — the equivalent of an adult state prison. However, recognizing that incarcerating kids is often counterproductive, there's a strong bias against ordering kids to do time. Usually judges don't incarcerate kids unless they repeatedly violate their probation.

For very serious offenses, such as murder or rape, all states have laws that allow judges to waive the kid into adult court. In other words, the kid is tried like an adult and, if found guilty, sentenced like an adult. So in most states, a 16-year-old murderer can be sentenced to life in prison. If you're interested in more details about the juvenile justice system, turn to Chapter 22.

Chapter 2

What Is Crime?

*I*n Oregon, threatening to kill someone in the future is legal, but preventing a pregnant pig from lying down is illegal. Seriously.

The good news is that if you choose to make a pregnant pig unhappy in Oregon, you're breaking the law but not committing a crime. What's the difference? Well, *criminal* activities carry the possibility of jail time with them, but not all illegal activities are criminal. (For example, messing with a pregnant pig may be punished only with a fine — what a relief!)

In this chapter, I explain how laws are created and why they change over time. I also show you the essential elements of a criminal law, which are important to know because the way in which criminal laws are written largely determines whether they achieve their goals in the long run.

Understanding the Two Categories of Criminal Activity

At the simplest level, you can break criminal activity into two categories:

✔ Acts that are inherently bad

✔ Acts that aren't bad but need to be regulated

Check out the following sections for more details on these categories.

Violating natural laws: Acts that are inherently bad

When you think of criminal activity, you likely think first of violent acts, such as murder, rape, kidnapping, theft, and assault. Crimes like these are known as *mala in se*, which is Latin for "wrong by itself." (A few lawyers, myself included, still like to throw around Latin phrases — it makes us sound smart, right?)

Mala in se crimes are bad acts that people instinctively know are crimes. A general consensus in society says that these acts should be illegal because they're immoral. This consensus didn't just spring up overnight — it has been developing as part of English and U.S. common law over the last 600 years.

The term *common law* refers to laws created by court decisions rather than by legislative bodies.

Today, legislatures in most states have passed laws making *mala in se* acts criminal, which means that the justice system no longer relies on the common law to convict someone of this type of crime. (However, common law continues to play an important role in *appellate* decisions — court decisions made during appeals after people are convicted of crimes. See Chapter 19 for a detailed discussion of appellate courts.)

How the common law developed

In England prior to the 1600s, private citizens or government officials brought cases before judges, who would then decide whether certain acts were illegal. The judges wrote *opinions* that contained the reasoning behind their decisions. Over time, judges came to rely on the consensus that emerged from these opinions. The collection of these written opinions came to be known as the *common law*. By the 1600s, the judges — not the English Parliament — had defined crimes such as murder, theft, rape, and assault.

Of course, clever citizens repeatedly found new ways to commit immoral acts, so society continued to call on judges to refine the common law by defining new crimes. For example, in the 1700s, judges concluded that inciting rebellion against the government should be criminalized; thus, they created the crime of *sedition*.

Sometimes judges didn't criminalize certain conduct, such as incest, and, as a result, the English Parliament stepped in to pass a law (known as a *statute*) that made familial sex a crime.

Today, common law plays a less important role than it did centuries ago. In the United States, people are prosecuted when they violate *statutes* — laws enacted by legislatures — rather than when they violate the common law. But, like in England centuries ago, human beings still find new ways to commit immoral acts, so legislatures must constantly refine and add to their criminal statutes.

Violating manmade laws: Acts that aren't inherently bad

Although some acts are clearly wrong, many others aren't naturally evil, but, nonetheless, they need to be regulated. These acts are known as *malum in prohibitum,* meaning "wrong because prohibited." Preventing a pregnant pig from lying down, for instance, clearly falls within this category. In fact, a large percentage of criminal laws today are *malum in prohibitum.* Following are some other examples of *malum in prohibitum* crimes:

✔ Driving under the influence of intoxicants

✔ Driving without a license

✔ Hunting without a license

✔ Carrying a concealed weapon

✔ Selling a drugged horse (in Oregon)

✔ Catching fish with your bare hands (in Indiana)

✔ Throwing snow "missiles" (in certain parts of Missouri)

The line between *mala in se* and *malum in prohibitum* crimes isn't always crystal clear. For example, some *malum in prohibitum* crimes involve conduct that's arguably immoral. I wouldn't argue that driving without a license is immoral. However, the law against selling a drugged horse exists because unscrupulous horse traders used to sedate horses to make them more attractive to purchasers. The courts decided to regulate this conduct because society considers cheating the buyer an immoral act.

As you can see, laws can punish acts that are moral or immoral. But keep in mind that not all immoral acts are punished by laws. Legislatures don't want to try to control every facet of human life through regulation. For example, most people agree that sleeping with your best friend's spouse is immoral, yet doing so is completely legal.

Identifying Elements of a Criminal Law

The U.S. justice system includes many types of law, such as property law, contract law, tort law, and administrative law. These examples all fall under the broad heading of *civil law.* Civil law generally governs the affairs between private parties. For example, civil law decides the fault in a car accident and interprets the terms of a contract in a dispute. For a law to be considered *criminal,* on the other hand, it must contain certain elements and characteristics, which I explain in this section.

Distinguishing civil from criminal law

Most civil and criminal laws alike are created to redress wrongs or to compel good behavior. However, civil law and criminal law have unique characteristics that distinguish them from each other. For example,

- A civil lawsuit is almost always between private parties, but only the government can bring a criminal proceeding.

- Only in criminal law can a person lose his freedom and be sent to jail or prison. When a *plaintiff* (the person bringing the case) wins a civil lawsuit, he typically gets an award of money, but he can't put the other party in jail.

- In criminal law, the defendant has certain constitutional rights that a defendant in a civil lawsuit doesn't have. The following rights are some of the more important constitutional rights a defendant has in a criminal case:

  - The right to have a jury decide guilt

  - The right to confront witnesses and cross-examine them

  - The right to have a lawyer represent the defendant

  - The right to "remain silent" without that silence being used against the defendant in court (In other words, no one can force the defendant to take the witness stand.)

  - The right to have a speedy trial

  - The right to be found guilty only by a standard of "beyond a reasonable doubt"

Criminal versus civil law in the O. J. Simpson case

A memorable example of how criminal and civil laws work in the real world is the O. J. Simpson murder case. Simpson was tried in a criminal case for the murders of his ex-wife Nicole Brown Simpson and Ron Goldman. When the jury found Simpson not guilty, the families of Ron Goldman and Nicole Brown Simpson filed a civil suit against Simpson for causing the deaths. As a result of that civil suit, a jury found Simpson *liable* (not *guilty*) for causing the deaths of Ron Goldman and Nicole Brown Simpson. Because the verdict came from a civil suit, Simpson couldn't be put in prison. Rather, the jury ordered him to pay over $30 million to the family of Ron Goldman and to Nicole Brown Simpson's two children.

In the civil trial (unlike in the criminal trial), Ron Goldman's family (the plaintiffs) forced Simpson to testify, and they didn't have to prove "beyond a reasonable doubt" that Simpson committed the murders. Rather, the plaintiffs had to prove only that "more likely than not" (in other words, that there was at least a 51 percent chance) Simpson committed the murders.

Defining felonies and misdemeanors

To be considered criminal, an act has to carry the possibility of a jail sentence as punishment. Criminal laws are categorized according to the punishments they impose. Generally, a criminal law may be either a felony or a misdemeanor. The difference between the two is as follows:

- ✔ A *misdemeanor* is a minor offense, and its maximum sentence usually can't exceed one year. However, if someone is convicted of three misdemeanors, he can conceivably serve up to three years in jail. Petty larceny, such as shoplifting some cigarettes from a local convenience store, is usually a misdemeanor, and the punishment may be very light.

- ✔ A *felony* is the more serious offense, and someone who commits a felony can be punished with more than a year in jail or prison. Theft of an expensive item, such as a 52-inch plasma HDTV, can rise to the level of a felony and be subject to serious punishment.

You can look at your state's criminal statutes to find out exactly which crimes your state considers misdemeanors and which ones it considers felonies. After all, an act that's a misdemeanor in New York may be a felony in Alaska and vice versa.

I describe the main elements or requirements of a criminal law in the following sections. If an act doesn't include these elements (and doesn't include the possibility of jail time as punishment), it probably isn't considered a crime. (But there are always exceptions, which is why people have to hire lawyers.)

Requiring a physical act

A criminal law almost always requires a physical act. Simply thinking bad thoughts can't be the basis for a violation of criminal law. Also, the act must be *voluntary*. In other words, the person committing the crime must have acted of his own free will. You can best understand this requirement by looking at acts that the courts *don't* deem voluntary, such as

- ✔ Reflexive motions, such as a sneeze that accidentally causes a person to discharge a gun

- ✔ Acts that occur during sleep, such as sleepwalking

- ✔ Acts that occur under the effects of hypnosis

- ✔ Acts committed under orders and at gunpoint

In most cases, the failure to act can't constitute a crime. For example, refusing to jump into a river and save a drowning child doesn't constitute homicide.

However, in some limited circumstances, when a *legal duty* to act is involved, the failure to act can constitute a crime. A great example is the legal duty of all citizens to pay their taxes. Failure to act — to write a check to the government, for example — can result in a criminal prosecution. Similarly, parents have an obligation to care for their children. The failure to feed or care for kids may constitute the crime of child neglect.

Having a guilty mind

Along with requiring a physical act, a crime also requires a *culpable mental state.* This phrase is law-school talk that means the act wasn't an accident and the offender had some moral responsibility. For example, a person can be considered morally culpable if he planned or *intended* to commit the criminal act. Aside from intent, however, most states recognize three other mental states, which I describe in the following list, that can result in criminal responsibility.

You can find detailed descriptions of these culpable mental states in the Model Penal Code, which the American Law Institute drafted in the 1960s as a model for states as they reformed their antiquated criminal laws. Many states adopted the Model Penal Code's definitions of the four mental states required to prove criminal responsibility, which I paraphrase in the following list. In almost every criminal case, the jurors have to find that the defendant committed the crime in one of these four ways:

- **Intentionally (or purposely):** A person acts intentionally when he has the conscious objective of engaging in criminal conduct.

- **Knowingly:** A person acts knowingly when he's aware that his conduct is of a certain nature that is an element of the crime. (For example, a thief acts knowingly when he steals a TV, *knowing* that it belongs to someone else.)

- **Recklessly:** A person acts recklessly when he consciously disregards a substantial and unjustifiable risk that a particular result will occur. The risk must be of such a nature and degree that disregard of the risk is a gross deviation from the standard of conduct that a law-abiding citizen would observe.

- **Negligently:** A person acts negligently when he should be aware of a substantial and unjustifiable risk that a particular result will occur. The risk must be of such a nature and degree that his failure to perceive it is a gross deviation from the standard of conduct that a reasonable person would observe.

I list these mental states in order of responsibility, so a person who acts intentionally is usually held more accountable and, thus, punished more severely than a person who acts negligently.

Using homicide as an example (although this principle applies to many crimes), an *intentional* killing is murder and can result in a life sentence in prison or even a death sentence. A *reckless* killing may be considered murder in the second degree or manslaughter and results in a lesser sentence of 10 to 20 years. A *negligent* killing, such as when a drunk driver kills his own passenger in a crash, can result in five years or less in prison.

In rare circumstances, a jury can hold a person liable for a crime without proof of any of these culpable mental states, a situation called *strict liability*. A great example of strict liability has to do with the crime of driving under the influence of intoxicants. When it comes to driving under the influence, most states don't require any proof that the offender acted intentionally, knowingly, recklessly, or negligently. The prosecutor just has to prove that the defendant drove while he was intoxicated. Although strict liability is somewhat common in civil law, it's almost unheard of in criminal law, except for the crime of driving while intoxicated because society doesn't want to lock people up unless they have some moral responsibility for what they did.

Linking Criminal Behavior to Cultural Mores

In a democratic society, in which laws are passed by elected representatives (or even directly by citizens through public votes called *initiatives*), criminal laws generally reflect the values of society. In this section, I explain the influence that society has on the development and implementation of criminal laws.

Understanding that crimes change over time

As society's values change over time, the passage of new criminal laws and the repeal of old criminal laws reflect these changes. For example, until the early 1900s, you could legally possess and use both cocaine and marijuana in the United States. In 1914, Utah became the first state to criminalize marijuana. That same year, the federal government passed the Harrison Act, which treated cocaine like other illegal drugs, such as morphine and heroin.

Consider a more recent change: In 1994, the federal government began requiring that convicted sex offenders register their addresses with their state government after their release from prison. As a result, the failure to register constituted a crime. Thereafter, states began to enact laws requiring that the addresses of these sex offenders be made available to the public. These various state laws are known collectively as *Megan's Law,* named after a 7-year-old girl who was raped and killed by a sex offender who lived across the street from her. Megan's parents never even knew the sex offender was there.

Sometimes laws change not because of a legislature, but because of a court system. For example, in 1972, many states had laws that made performing an abortion a crime. But, in 1973, in the famous case of *Roe v. Wade,* the U.S. Supreme Court held that a woman has a constitutional right to an abortion. This ruling effectively repealed laws criminalizing the performance of an abortion.

Here's another example of how the courts affect criminal law: In 2003, the U.S. Supreme Court in *Lawrence v. Texas* ruled that laws in Texas criminalizing sexual acts between persons of the same sex were unconstitutional, effectively repealing those laws. Just 17 years earlier, in 1986, the Supreme Court had ruled in *Bowers v. Hardwick* that Georgia could have criminal laws prohibiting sexual acts between members of the same sex. So, you can see how laws can change with the times.

Recognizing the impact of location

The *Lawrence v. Texas* and *Bowers v. Hardwick* cases demonstrate how different cultural values across the United States manifest themselves in criminal laws. For instance, Texas and Georgia criminalized sodomy between consenting males even though such conduct was legal in many other states. On this topic, at least, you can reasonably conclude that the cultural values of Texas and Georgia probably differ from those of Massachusetts or Vermont.

Each state has its own electoral process and its own court system, so each state may develop laws (including criminal laws) that reflect the will and values of its people.

Outside of the United States, criminal laws are even more diverse, which reflects the fact that dramatic cultural differences exist among different countries. For example, some Islamic countries, such as Iran and Saudi Arabia, follow a code of laws based on their religion, known as *sharia law.* Based on this law, these countries allow the death penalty for homosexual acts in some circumstances. Also under sharia law, someone guilty of a crime such as theft may be punished by imprisonment and by amputation of hands — if the person has a very serious criminal history. Clearly, the cultures — as well as some of the laws — of these countries differ greatly from those of the United States.

In some provinces of Russia, where alcohol consumption has been a cultural norm, driving under the influence of alcohol isn't a crime unless the driver crashes and causes an injury. This leniency contrasts sharply with the United States, where the permissible blood alcohol content (BAC) for adults dropped from 0.10 percent in some states to 0.08 percent in all 50 states in 2005. (In other words, driving with a BAC of more than 0.08 percent now constitutes a crime in the United States.)

How various states define *theft*

To show the diversity of laws among the 50 U.S. states, I present three states' efforts to define the crime of theft:

California Penal Code Section 484 — Theft

Every person who shall feloniously steal, take, carry, lead, or drive away the personal property of another, or who shall fraudulently appropriate property which has been entrusted to him or her, or who shall knowingly and designedly, by any false or fraudulent representation or pretense, defraud any other person of money, labor or real or personal property, or who causes or procures others to report falsely of his or her wealth or mercantile character and by thus imposing upon any person, obtains credit and thereby fraudulently gets or obtains possession of money or property or obtains the labor or service of another, is guilty of theft.

New York Penal Law Section 155.05 — Larceny

A person steals property and commits larceny when, with intent to deprive another of property or to appropriate the same to himself or to a third person, he wrongfully takes, obtains or withholds such property from an owner thereof.

Louisiana Code Title 14 Section 67 — Theft

Theft is the misappropriation or taking of anything of value which belongs to another, either without the consent of the other to the misappropriation or taking, or by means of fraudulent conduct, practices, or representations. An intent to deprive the other permanently of whatever may be the subject of the misappropriation or taking is essential.

Realizing that politics play a role

Theoretically, laws in the United States reflect the will of the people, as carried out by their elected representatives in the legislature. But the passage of laws doesn't always play out so neatly. Criminologists fall into at least two different camps on the issue of what influences the passage of laws in the United States:

- ✔ One group believes that, generally speaking, criminal laws reflect a consensus of the values of the citizens.

- ✔ Another group contends that the legislative process isn't so clean and that the passage of criminal laws actually reflects conflicts between different interest groups.

Criminologists in the second group point to the scarcity of laws regulating large businesses or the wealthy because those interest groups wield a lot of political power. These criminologists see conflict, rather than consensus, as the method by which criminal laws are passed. They argue that the more powerful and wealthy a group of people is, the less likely that group is to be regulated.

Having witnessed the passage of criminal laws firsthand, I argue that both views are partially right. With *mala in se* crimes — the crimes that most of us agree are evil (such as murder and rape) — the political process usually reflects the will of the people. However, in terms of *malum in prohibitum* acts (the ones that aren't necessarily evil but do need to be regulated), powerful and wealthy interest groups can sometimes sway legislators who are debating those acts.

Consider gun-control laws as an example: The National Rifle Association (NRA) devotes a good deal of time and money to influencing these laws. Depending on your personal views, you may see this fact as either good or bad. If you're an NRA member, you may argue that the organization tries to ensure that individuals maintain their Second Amendment rights to own guns, hunt, and protect personal property. If you're not an NRA member, you may consider the NRA an aggressive political advocacy group that prevents the reasonable regulation of firearms.

Almost every industry commits significant resources to protecting its corporate interests by *lobbying* (or influencing) legislators. And lobbying can sometimes mean trying to prevent the passage of criminal laws that may punish industry misconduct.

Nonetheless, U.S. society is far more regulated through criminal laws today than it was just 50 years ago. In a society that continues to grow more and more complex, new laws are often necessary to protect food and drug sources, the environment, civil rights, and personal safety.

Chapter 3

How Crime Is Measured and Why It Matters

● ●

In This Chapter

▶ Gathering crime stats and determining how many crimes occur

▶ Realizing how crime stats affect public policy

▶ Calculating the costs of crime

● ●

Documenting how much crime occurs in the United States and calculating its impact on society is an incredibly difficult — some would say impossible — task. Yet, understanding how crime statistics are gathered and how reliable those statistics are is essential because politicians and other policymakers rely heavily on crime stats to make decisions that impact the rest of society.

Should money be diverted from social services to build more prisons? Should inmates be released early from prison to free up money to solve a state budget crisis? Should schools develop Internet safety programs to protect kids from sexual predators? Crime stats, even imperfect ones, help people answer tough questions like these.

People who rely on statistics without really understanding them can make serious policy mistakes that waste money and may even risk lives. Reading this chapter is a great first step toward truly understanding where crime stats come from and what their flaws may be.

Gathering Crime Stats: How Much Crime Is There?

Knowing about every crime that occurs is impossible because many crimes go unreported. For example, a typical cocaine sale involves two willing parties, and neither party is likely to share news of the exchange with the police.

Even with a violent crime, the victim doesn't always report it. For example, rival gang members involved in a fight aren't likely to call the police, and victims of domestic violence often don't report their abuse. (See Chapter 5 for more info about why domestic violence victims often keep quiet.) Similarly, rape victims may not want to endure the emotional trauma of making a report to police.

Fraud and property crimes present other challenges. For instance, you probably don't call the police every time you receive a fraudulent e-mail that asks you to cash a large check for a "Nigerian official." (See Chapter 6 for a discussion of the infamous Nigerian scams.) And you may not even call the police when someone steals your wallet or purse. After all, many people believe that, at least for property crimes, filing a police report simply doesn't do any good.

Even though many crimes don't get reported to the police, crime reports are still one of the most important sources for gathering crime stats.

Relying on crime reports

More than 17,000 police agencies operate in the United States, and about 93 percent of those agencies participate in a voluntary program that reports statistics to the Federal Bureau of Investigation (FBI). The compiled statistics are published annually in the Uniform Crime Report (UCR). You can access the most recent UCR report at the FBI's Web site: http://www.fbi.gov/ucr/ucr.htm.

The UCR contains information about only certain types of serious crimes, known as *Part 1* crimes:

- ✔ Murder
- ✔ Manslaughter
- ✔ Forcible rape
- ✔ Robbery
- ✔ Aggravated assault
- ✔ Burglary
- ✔ Larceny-theft
- ✔ Motor vehicle theft
- ✔ Arson

Because Part I crimes are so serious in nature, experts believe that they're reported more reliably than less-serious crimes. The UCR purposely excludes crimes that people aren't likely to report, such as drug offenses or embezzlement, as well as crimes that occur infrequently, such as kidnapping.

But even for crimes that you think a victim would report, the actual report rate is quite low. According to the U.S. Bureau of Justice Statistics, fewer than half of violent crimes and property crimes are ever reported to police (see Figure 3-1).

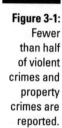

Figure 3-1: Fewer than half of violent crimes and property crimes are reported.

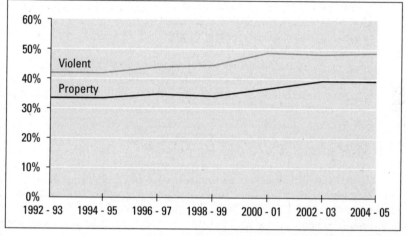

Source: U.S. Bureau of Justice Statistics

Besides not receiving reports for every crime, another significant problem with the UCR is that a police agency must pick only the *most serious* crime from a criminal incident to report to the FBI. In other words, the police can't report multiple crimes that occurred during a single incident. So, if a man steals a car and then later sets the car ablaze to conceal his first crime, the investigating police agency reports only the arson, not the motor vehicle theft.

But, despite its problems, the UCR provides a solid, nationwide picture of long-term crime trends and allows for year-to-year comparisons among each of the Part 1 crimes because its problems are generally consistent from year to year.

The following list compares the overall violent crime rates over the past two decades (provided by the UCR). The numbers reflect how many violent crimes occurred per 100,000 people in the United States.

1988: 641   1991: 758

1989: 667   1992: 758

1990: 730   1993: 747

1994: 714	2001: 505
1995: 685	2002: 494
1996: 637	2003: 476
1997: 611	2004: 463
1998: 568	2005: 469
1999: 523	2006: 474
2000: 507	2007: 467

Figure 3-2 illustrates the overall reduction in violent crime since 1991.

Keep in mind that an effort to improve the UCR is in the works and has been partially implemented. This effort, called the National Incident-Based Reporting System (NIBRS), is designed to more efficiently and accurately gather more information on more crimes from police agencies' computerized record management systems. An improved reporting system like the NIBRS can resolve some of the problems with the UCR; however, building the necessary electronic systems costs money for police departments. As a result, progress has been slow, and NIBRS is still far from reaching its eventual potential. For more information on NIBRS, you can check out the U.S. Department of Justice's Web site: http://www.ojp.usdoj.gov/bjs/nibrs.htm.

Tallying the number of arrests

In addition to the number of crime reports, the UCR also collects information on the number of arrests. For these statistics, the UCR looks at not only the Part 1 crimes I mention in the preceding section, but also 21 other crimes, including simple assault and driving under the influence of intoxicants.

Obviously, arrest statistics don't give a full picture of crime. (Arrest doesn't necessarily mean guilt, and no nationwide statistics show the percentage of arrested persons who are found guilty in state court.) Even so, arrest statistics do help evaluate police effectiveness by showing *clearance rates* — the percentage of reported crimes that end in arrests. Obviously, the higher the clearance rate, the more effective the police are at catching the bad guys.

Table 3-1 shows the 2007 national clearance rates for various crimes.

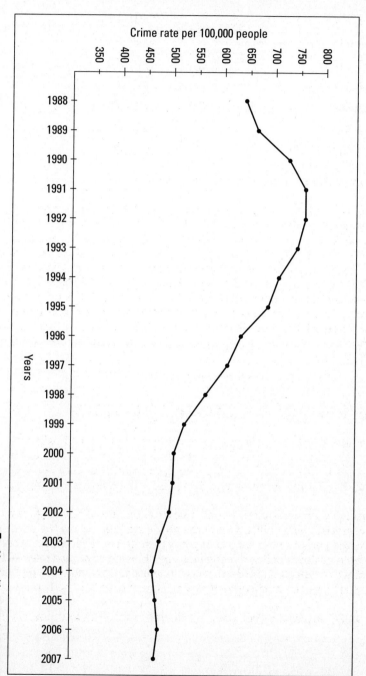

Figure 3-2:
The U.S.
violent
crime rate
has dropped
fairly
steadily
since 1991.

Source: Federal Bureau of Investigation

Table 3-1 U.S. Clearance Rates for Various Crimes in 2007		
Type of Crime	*Number of Crimes Reported*	*Percent of Reported Crimes That Led to Arrest*
Violent crime	1,227,330	44.5%
Murder and nonnegligent manslaughter	14,811	61.2%
Forcible rape	78,740	40.0%
Robbery	383,749	25.9%
Aggravated assault	750,030	54.1%
Property crime	8,716,315	16.5%
Burglary	1,946,803	12.4%
Larceny-theft	5,774,598	18.6%
Motor vehicle theft	994,914	18.3%
Arson	62,248	18.3%

Source: Federal Bureau of Investigation

You can see that police are much more likely to solve violent crimes than they are to solve property crimes, which is largely a result of the greater resources that police commit to solving violent crimes. Another important factor that leads to the increased clearance rate for violent crime is the fact that violent crimes often leave eyewitnesses who can help identify the perpetrators. In contrast, property crimes often happen in the absence of witnesses.

Arrest statistics provide another tool for evaluating crime rates: Tracking the number of arrests helps track certain crime trends for crimes that people usually don't report, such as driving under the influence of intoxicants. Yet, tracking the number of arrests has its shortcomings. For instance, a decrease in the number of arrests for a certain crime may have several explanations, including the following:

✔ Fewer people are committing the crime.

✔ Police are putting fewer resources into investigating the crime.

✔ Criminals have figured out ways to commit the crime without being caught.

A decrease in a certain crime can have some other explanations, too, so you can't draw many conclusions from these arrest statistics alone. For example, from 2003 to 2007, arrest statistics for the crime of fraud decreased by more than 19 percent. I highly doubt that the incidences of fraud actually decreased that much in those four years. More likely, fraudsters have moved to the Internet, where investigation and arrest are much more difficult. (See Chapter 6 for a discussion of Internet fraud.)

Spotlighting unreported crime: Victimization surveys

How do researchers get around the problem that so many crimes go unreported? The best answer is the National Crime Victimization Survey (NCVS). Each year, the U.S. Bureau of the Census, in cooperation with the Bureau of Justice Statistics (a part of the U.S. Department of Justice), conducts a survey of 76,000 households and asks people 12 and older questions about crimes they experienced in the previous year. Based on this sampling, the Bureau of Justice Statistics then estimates rates for a variety of crimes. (The survey excludes uncommon crimes, such as kidnapping, because the sampling isn't large enough.) The questionnaire is quite detailed with about 27 pages of questions. To see the 2006 version of the survey, you can visit the following Web site: `http://www.ojp.usdoj.gov/bjs/pub/pdf/ncvs104.pdf`.

As expected, the NCVS shows that many crimes aren't reported to the police. For example, the number of rapes reported to census workers for the NCVS is more than twice the number of rapes reported to police. (Women often don't report rape for a variety of reasons, such as shame, embarrassment, fear of a process that can seem degrading, and a concern that the report won't do any good. See Chapter 5 for more information about violent crimes, including rape.)

Like the other forms of measuring crime, victimization surveys have their shortcomings, too. Primarily, they're very expensive. Because of their high cost, the NCVS sampling of 76,000 households is just not large enough to draw meaningful conclusions at the state and local levels. For instance, a criminologist in Pueblo, New Mexico, can't draw any conclusions about rape trends in his home state or town from this national survey. Thus, the NCVS data isn't very helpful in planning to provide resources to local domestic violence and rape shelters.

Separate from the NCVS, local and state governments, nonprofit agencies, and universities sometimes conduct their own localized surveys. Such surveys aren't just limited to victims, however. Researchers rely heavily on surveys of youth alcohol and drug use to identify new and dangerous trends, for example. Since about 2006, local surveys have helped researchers identify an emerging trend among kids for using and abusing prescription drugs.

Accepting the shortcomings of crime statistics

As I explained previously, none of the three primary methods of gathering crime stats — crime reports, number of arrests, or victimization surveys — is perfect.

But despite the shortcomings of each approach, together (and combined with other observations) they provide a decent picture of crime in the United States, in general. And, in the future, if more police agencies move to the National Incident-Based Reporting System (which I describe in the "Relying on crime reports" section), this system will automatically take statistical reports from police agencies' computer systems — as a result, crime report stats will become even more valuable.

Putting Crime Stats to Use

Analyzing crime stats isn't just an intellectual exercise. Criminologists don't stand around sipping glasses of Chateau Margaux with their pinky fingers extended, saying (in their best British accents), "Reginald, tell us your theory about why child homicides have risen." Analyzing crime stats is too important to be a parlor game.

Rather, U.S. citizens ask — and deserve informed answers to — questions such as how can we do a better job protecting ourselves and our neighbors, how can we improve services for victims, and how can we prevent kids from choosing a life of crime? Crime stats help law enforcement agencies deal with these questions by helping them correct mistaken approaches and point the way to improvement.

The U.S. Congress, along with every state legislature, faces the challenge of not having enough resources to fight crime. As a result, congressmen and congresswomen must look for information to help them decide how best to spend tax dollars — often they turn to statistics for help. If statistics show that a particular program is successful, a legislature is more likely to fund that program in the future. Conversely, a lack of evidence to support a particular program's success more or less dooms it to termination.

Unfortunately, policymakers often use statistics without sufficiently understanding their limitations. Like guns, statistics in the hands of untrained users can be dangerous. All too frequently, statistics can be subject to enough differing interpretations that they end up being of little value. I've seen policymakers spend more time arguing over the value of a set of statistics than the actual merits of the program they're trying to justify.

The wisest course for policymakers to follow is to take advantage of all relevant sources of information, including crime stats, arrest stats, and surveys. I recently attended a meeting to discuss drug trends in my home state. Although some people wanted to rely just on arrest stats, the group eventually agreed to gather information from each of the following sources:

Controversy over crime reduction

One of the larger criminology controversies arose in the late 1990s. Crime rates through the 1970s and 1980s had risen to all-time highs, but in the late 1990s, as states began to implement much tougher sentencing laws, crime rates began to plunge. As Figure 3-2 shows, violent crime began to decrease dramatically in 1992 and was almost cut in half by 2003.

Proponents of tougher sentencing laws pointed out the dramatic coincidence of crime dropping at the same time that sentences were lengthening. But others saw different potential causes. For example, Steven Levitt and John Donohue concluded that the drop in crime that began in the mid-1990s was, to a large extent, the result of the legalization of abortion, which occurred in

1973. Their theory was that unwanted children from unplanned pregnancies, who are more likely than children of planned pregnancies to be involved in crime when they become adults, were aborted and, thus, never lived to commit crimes. A potential criminal who was aborted in 1973 would've become an adult in 1991 if she'd lived. Other criminologists have challenged the methodology of Levitt and Donohue's analysis, questioning the assumption that unwanted children are more likely to commit violent crime.

This controversy shows that, with the inherent weaknesses in the ways criminologists currently gather statistics, the value of crime statistics in helping guide policy choices continues to be somewhat limited.

✔ Arrest stats

✔ A youth drug and alcohol survey

✔ Amounts of drugs seized by police drug task forces

✔ Studies of drug residue amounts in a city's sewage system (which is an increasingly valuable tool for measuring drug use)

✔ A survey of drug cops

Through careful analysis of the information from these five sources, policymakers may be able to establish an accurate picture of illegal drug use. However, this approach takes a lot more work than just relying on arrest stats.

Considering the Costs of Crime

In the United States, the government devotes billions of dollars to public safety. From arrest to prosecution to jail to probation, the costs mount up fast. But crime has other costs, as well, including a plethora of economic costs, insurance costs, and, of course, the personal losses that millions of crime victims and their families face. Knowing how much crime occurs and how much it costs can help policymakers make smarter decisions in fighting crime.

Funding the justice system

The most obvious costs of crime are the ones incurred through the government's efforts to control it. And, of course, the largest cost of these efforts comes from compensating the law enforcement personnel who fight crime and incarcerate criminals. As I explain in Chapter 19 in more detail, the number of people necessary to resolve one criminal case is astonishing. Here are just some of the steps — and the people — involved:

1. Police officers make an arrest.

2. A jail staff member *books* the suspect (in other words, he fingerprints and documents who the suspect is).

3. Another jail staff member moves the suspect into jail.

4. A police officer writes a report of the crime and sends it to the district attorney.

5. The district attorney decides whether to file charges against the suspect.

6. A secretary drafts an *indictment,* which is the charging document that lists the crimes.

7. A grand jury decides whether to indict the suspect.

8. The district attorney files an indictment with court staff.

9. Jail staff bring the defendant to a judge for *arraignment* (an initial appearance where the defendant is informed of the charges).

10. The judge appoints a defense attorney.

11. If the defendant wants a trial, the case is given to another judge.

12. The district attorney and the defense attorney select a jury.

13. The judge conducts the trial.

14. The defense attorney and district attorney bring their witnesses to court.

15. If the jury convicts the defendant, the defendant may go to jail or prison.

16. Corrections officers transport the defendant to jail or prison, move the defendant into a cell, and provide ongoing security.

17. A probation officer later oversees the defendant's release from jail or prison.

Generally, you can break the functions that I describe in the preceding list into three categories:

- ✔ Police (including detectives, patrol officers, and other police staff)
- ✔ Judicial (including district attorneys and defense attorneys)
- ✔ Corrections (including jail, prison, and probation personnel)

Figure 3-3 shows an estimate of criminal justice costs in the United States, broken down by these three categories (using data from the U.S. Bureau of Justice Statistics).

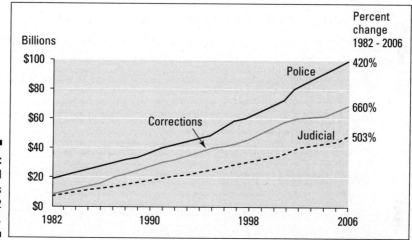

Figure 3-3:
U.S. criminal justice costs from 1982 to 2006.

Source: U.S. Bureau of Justice Statistics

This figure shows a clear trend upward, even as the overall rate of violent crime in the United States has decreased significantly since the early 1990s.

Keep in mind that each of the three primary units of government — local, state, and federal — has separate criminal justice responsibilities. A local government, such as a city or county, has a police force, a court system, and a jail. A state government may also have its own police, courts, and prison system. And, of course, the feds have their own completely separate system of criminal justice. Figure 3-4 shows how costs are spread among these three levels of government.

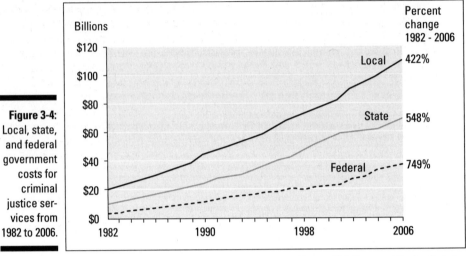

Figure 3-4:
Local, state,
and federal
government
costs for
criminal
justice ser-
vices from
1982 to 2006.

Source: U.S. Bureau of Justice Statistics

As you can see, state and local governments bear the lion's share of the costs of fighting crime.

Measuring the costs to society and victims

In addition to the direct costs of administering a criminal justice system, you have to keep in mind numerous other, less obvious costs. Quantifying these costs is an ongoing challenge for economists and criminologists alike.

For example, the cost of preventing crime throughout society can be quite large. Many retail stores have loss-prevention units. Many businesses and homes have security cameras and systems, and some also employ private security patrols. Some economists even include costs such as security lighting and locks in their estimates of how much crime costs society. They reason that these costs are ones that a crime-free society wouldn't have to pay. And, of course, in addition to physical security, every business must have high-quality computer security to protect against Internet hackers and criminals.

After a crime occurs, all kinds of additional costs come into play. For example, a woman who had $100 stolen is obviously out $100. (Some economists argue that this loss isn't a net loss to society because it's just a transfer of wealth from a victim to a criminal.) But the woman may also lose wages or vacation time if she calls the police and ultimately has to go to court.

Property crimes (such as vandalism) and drug manufacturing can dramatically impact the value of a home or even a neighborhood. During the methamphetamine manufacturing epidemic in recent years, meth labs sprang up seemingly everywhere in the West and Midwest. The chemical residue from a meth lab is so toxic that any house with a lab has to be completely scrubbed — the cleanup costs alone can sometimes reach up to $100,000.

Assessing the costs of violent crimes can be even more complex. A victim of a violent crime may incur costs for medical treatment and mental health counseling. Often victims themselves don't bear the full cost of medical treatment; taxpayers, insurance companies, or hospitals pick up a significant portion.

A study by Philip Cook, Ted Miller, and Bruce Lawrence examined the medical cost of the 138,000 gun-shot injuries that occurred in the United States in 1994. The medical cost was more than $2.3 billion (or about $17,000 per injury), and the taxpayer picked up 49 percent of that cost. The U.S. Centers for Disease Control and Prevention estimated that the 2003 medical and mental health costs stemming only from domestic violence crimes totaled $4.1 billion.

A victim's emotional trauma may be so extensive that it impacts his ability to earn a wage, resulting in a lower-paying job. Economists conclude that the emotional damage from rape and sexual assaults has the greatest economic impact of any crime (next to murder, of course). Another part of the economic impact of crime is the reduction in the quality of life that a victim endures from the injury itself. Some economists have used "pain and suffering" judgments from civil lawsuits to estimate the financial impact of a similar injury on the victim of a crime.

Economists may also consider the productivity loss to society when a person becomes a criminal rather than a positive, contributing member of society. The failure of a criminal to earn a wage and pay taxes is a net loss to society. Drug crime helps demonstrate this fact. After all, a drug dealer doesn't pay taxes, and he sells a product that makes other people less productive in their legitimate jobs. Drugs also lead to social welfare costs because drug abusers often can't care for their children or themselves and usually require several rounds of drug abuse treatment.

When you combine all these factors, you see how complex the cost analysis is, and you see how far-reaching and expensive the impact of crime is. At the high end, one study concluded that the annual economic cost of crime in the United States exceeds $1.5 trillion. A 1996 study placed the annual cost at a more conservative $450 billion, or $1,800 for every person in the United States (in 1996 dollars).

Chapter 4

Helping Those in the Wake of Crime: Victims

T he human toll of crime is enormous. Victims often suffer dramatic personal loss, tremendous pain, and a lot of economic hardship. While the entire U.S. court system was originally set up to protect a *defendant's* rights, historically, victims have received no institutionalized assistance at all. They've been left to fend for themselves, sometimes with no way to pay medical bills or even to get someone to explain how the justice system works. But thanks to some forward-thinking folks in the 1970s and 1980s, a victims' rights movement has swept across the United States. Today, victims are front and center in the minds of politicians and policymakers.

In this chapter, I discuss the historical treatment of victims in the criminal justice system. I discuss victimization, starting with the different types of harm that a victim can suffer. I also help you get a better idea of who is more likely to become a victim of crime. Then I address how far U.S. society has come and describe the types of services that are available to victims today.

Looking at the Historical Treatment of Victims

Prior to the 1970s, if you were the victim of a crime, you were essentially just another witness for the government. Sure, people were sympathetic to you, but sympathy only goes so far. No one helped you get medical care, let alone reimbursed you for that medical care. A victim of domestic violence didn't have a shelter she could take her family to. A rape victim had no one to provide counseling services. No one explained how the criminal justice system worked or provided any of the myriad of victim services that exist today.

In the 1970s, this situation slowly started to change as individual communities began to take action. District attorney offices in Philadelphia, Brooklyn, and Milwaukee got the ball rolling with some rudimentary victim assistance programs. Soon thereafter, private advocacy groups sprang up to advocate for victims in Congress and in state legislatures. For example, Mothers Against Drunk Driving (MADD) formed in 1980 to advocate against drunk driving and to support its victims.

In 1982, President Ronald Reagan commissioned a task force to look at victims' rights. The task force came up with 68 recommendations for how to provide better service to victims of crime. The next year, Reagan created the Office for Victims of Crime within the U.S. Department of Justice to implement these recommendations. And in 1984, Congress passed the Victims of Crime Act (VOCA), which called for the money from fines and assessments levied against federally convicted criminals to be used to provide services to victims of crime all across the country. Together, these actions became the springboard for dramatic improvements in how society and the court system treat victims of crime. Today, society goes to much greater efforts — both inside and outside the courtroom — to help victims deal with the many painful effects of crime.

Identifying the Impact of Crime on Victims

Being the victim of a crime can leave painful, permanent scars. These scars can be physical, emotional, and financial.

Physical scars

According to the National Crime Victimization Survey (a survey administered annually by the Bureau of Justice Statistics as a way to measure crime), approximately 6.3 million violent crimes occurred in the United States in 2005. That's 21 victims for every 1,000 citizens over the age of 12, which makes for a lot of crime victims suffering physical injury. (For more on the National Crime Victimization Survey, check out Chapter 3.)

Many of the injuries resulting from crime — which range from bruises to death — require medical care. The physical pain can last for months, years, or even a lifetime. For example, you've no doubt seen news reports of gang members or armed robbers firing their weapons at particular people (like rival gang members) and hitting innocent bystanders. Such victims may suffer life-long debilitating injuries. But sometimes physical injuries are just a small part of the total story.

Emotional effects

Crime creates ongoing fear in people who are victimized. Out of fear, victims often alter their lifestyles dramatically, and a life lived in fear isn't a full life. Imagine a rape victim who becomes so afraid of another attack that she won't leave her home at night or go anywhere without a companion.

Beyond fear, victims may suffer very serious psychological effects, including post-traumatic stress disorder (PTSD). Someone suffering from PTSD may endure bouts of depression, severe anxiety, and difficulty with relationships.

Kids and spouses who are victimized by people they love are particularly susceptible to this psychological pain, often because of their dependence on the abuser. The psychological effects of abuse over a long period of time can sometimes exceed those of a one-time assault by a stranger.

In addition to the fear and psychological pain that many victims of violence feel, I must also mention the grief that victims' family members endure as their loved ones suffer serious injury or death. I personally have shed tears with families of murder victims who miss their loved ones and struggle to make sense of the tragedies. They face a torrent of emotions from anger to despondency, and sometimes there's no way to console them.

Another mental stressor comes from entering the criminal justice system as a victim. The vast governmental bureaucracy can seem cold and impersonal to someone who has already suffered a great deal. Take a rape victim, for example. Police may ask her to submit to a rape exam to look for DNA evidence, including semen, blood, and pubic hair. They may also ask her to describe the assault in detail. The defense attorney may even assert a defense of *consent* in which he argues that she was a willing participant in sex and not the victim of a violent crime.

Although I've known some exceptional victim advocates, they can only do so much to help a victim deal with the lengthy, harsh reality of the criminal justice system (see the "Support of victim advocates" section later in this chapter for more info). Some of the greatest acts of courage I've seen have come from crime victims who were willing to endure the long process so that others wouldn't be victimized like they were.

Economic loss

In the United States, the cost of crime tops $450 billion annually, which comes out to be about $1,800 per citizen. Some criminologists refer to this cost as a "crime tax" because of its negative effect on the economy. This $450 billion figure includes lost wages and productivity, property loss, medical bills, an estimate of the cost of pain and suffering, and long-term disability costs.

If the cost of crime in the aggregate is too overwhelming, consider the cost to an individual such as a victim in a convenience store robbery who takes a bullet in the chest. He may not have health insurance to cover the hundreds of thousands of dollars in medical bills. He probably doesn't have disability insurance to keep providing an income while he's in the hospital, either. If his wife has a job, she may have to take time off to care for him, which means they'll lose some, if not all, of her income, too. Thanks to crime, a family can quickly suffer economic disaster through no fault of their own.

Pinpointing Who Is Likely to Be Victimized

Not surprisingly, who you are, where you live, and what kinds of activities you engage in play a huge part in whether you're likely to become a crime victim. For instance, the following personal characteristics have been linked to victimization in some way or another:

- ✔ **Age:** Your age is a significant factor primarily because so many crimes are committed by young men (see Chapter 11 for more on the link between age and criminality). Thus, people who hang out in the same places that young men do are much more likely to be victimized. Someone between the ages of 20 and 24 is more than *four times* as likely to be the victim of a violent crime as a person between the ages of 50 and 64. Generally speaking, the older you get, the safer you are.

    However, as people become elderly, they do become more susceptible to property crimes, such as fraud and theft. Scam artists throughout the world focus their energy on identifying older folks whom they can easily confuse and defraud. (For a more detailed discussion of property crimes, turn to Chapter 6.)

- ✔ **Race:** Here are some facts about the link between race and victimization:

    - For all crimes, African Americans are more likely to be victimized than whites.
    - Native Americans are far more likely than anyone else to experience violence.
    - In terms of property crimes, Hispanics are the most likely to be victimized.
    - Asians are the least likely to be victimized.

Most criminologists agree that these stats reflect a number of complicated factors. For example, each community where certain racial or ethnic groups are more likely to live has its own characteristics. And each racial and ethnic group experiences its own cultural trends regarding two-parent homes, income disparities, identification with gangs, and so on.

In Chapter 13, I discuss societal factors that can lead to greater crime.

✔ **Gender:** Although the crime victim movement often emphasizes crimes that mostly affect women, such as rape and domestic violence, the truth is that except for sex crimes, men are much more likely to become crime victims than women. Also, men are more likely to be victimized by strangers, while women are more likely to be victimized by people they know.

✔ **Income:** As you may expect, the lower your household income, the greater your chances of being the victim of a crime. Again, this link between income and victimization is likely a reflection of the community you live in. As I discuss in Chapter 13, the poorer the neighborhood, the higher the crime rate generally is.

✔ **Lifestyle choices:** Perhaps even more than your age, skin color, gender, or income, the way you live your life impacts your vulnerability to crime. Hanging out with street gangs, drug dealers, or even heavy-drinking sorority sisters creates a greater risk of victimization.

Expanding Victim Services in the 21st Century

Today most communities provide a variety of services to victims of crime, including some or all of the ones I discuss in this section. Note that although far more people are victims of property crime than violent crime, the majority of crime victim services are set up primarily to provide help to the victims of violent crime.

Crime victim compensation

After a convenience store clerk is shot during a robbery, how does he pay his medical bills? Today every state has a crime victim compensation program that helps victims pay their bills and cope with the aftermath of the crime. Typically, victim compensation programs are *payers of last resort,* meaning that a victim must exhaust his own personal health insurance first. Here are just a few of the expenses victim compensation programs can reimburse victims for:

✔ Medical care

✔ Lost wages

✔ Grief counseling

✔ Funeral expenses

✔ Injury rehabilitation

✔ Counseling for kids who witness crime

To be eligible for compensation, a person must be an *innocent* victim, meaning that he didn't contribute to the criminal activity in any way. Also, he must fully cooperate with law enforcement. Victim service providers employ compensation officers to make sure victims' claims are valid. (You may not be surprised to learn that people try to defraud the victim compensation system — which is about as low as stealing from an offering plate.)

Because the amount of funds in these programs is limited, so, too, is the amount of compensation a victim can get. Typically, reimbursement for medical costs is limited to $20,000 or $25,000. Reimbursement for counseling services, funeral costs, and rehabilitation is also limited.

Money to support compensation programs comes from a variety of sources. One of those sources is the criminals themselves — federal and state governments collect fines and fees from all criminal defendants when they're found guilty. In addition, if a defendant causes a victim's injury and that injury receives some compensation from the state's victim compensation program, the judge can make the defendant pay back the costs to the program.

For example, when the robber who shoots the convenience store clerk is found guilty, the judge can order him to repay the compensation program for any money forwarded to the clerk for his medical costs. In addition, the clerk has the legal right to file a civil lawsuit against the robber for the full amount of his medical costs and for all his pain and suffering. As a practical matter, however, most robbers don't have any money to pay large judgments; plus, they usually end up in prison for awhile, where they don't earn enough to repay the costs. Nonetheless, some states employ collection officers to go after criminals and collect these funds if they're available.

Support of victim advocates

In the immediate aftermath of a violent crime, a victim may be traumatized and unable to make even the most basic decisions. To provide help to victims of violence, many police departments employ *victim advocates,* who offer the victims the support and resources they need to take the first steps of their recoveries.

Imagine a woman who was beaten up by her boyfriend. After the police haul him away, what will she do about her injury? Who will take care of her kids while she's in the hospital? What if her boyfriend gets out of jail because of overcrowding (a common occurrence) and comes back? An advocate can help the abused woman answer these tough questions. For example, the advocate may help her think of family members who can take care of her children. Or the advocate may recommend a domestic violence shelter where she and her children can live temporarily to protect themselves against the abuser in case he comes back home.

If a police department doesn't employ advocates, often police officers are in the position of trying to help victims cope with these challenges. The department may also call on trained volunteers.

Prosecutor offices usually employ victim advocates, as well. Like advocates in police departments, these advocates may help victims get emergency services. In addition, they help explain the court process to victims, often sitting with them through hearings. After all, sitting in a courtroom with the man who raped you can be very intimidating. Having an advocate hold your hand can make a big difference. Another important service an advocate in the prosecutor's office provides is explaining to the victim what rights she has. (I discuss these rights in the "Observing the Laws That Protect Victims' Rights" section.)

Another type of victim advocate helps victims after the court case is done. For instance, this person may notify the victim when the criminal is set to be released from jail or prison. Some states have a statewide automated victim notification system that allows a victim to call a phone number and find out if and when a criminal is scheduled to be released. Victims, however, often don't know about this system or don't know how to use it, so advocates help them. Advocates also may help victims deal with unwanted contact from criminals while they're on probation or parole.

Because each state is different, all these services may be performed by a variety of people in different agencies, or perhaps by just one overworked person in a small police department. These government advocate positions often rely heavily on private organizations and volunteers for the bulk of services.

Direct help from private, nonprofit groups

Although government-run victim programs are the conduit for providing services to victims, nonprofit organizations provide the day-in and day-out crucial help that victims need.

For instance, private organizations almost always run the domestic violence shelters that government-employed victim advocates send abused woman to. These private, nonprofit organizations are made up of citizens who care passionately about victims of crime. They fund their efforts with private donations, public and private grants, and contracts with the government.

Without these private services, a victim advocate often would have nowhere to refer a victim. Note, however, that nonprofit care providers (and government-run victim assistance offices) have little money and rely heavily on volunteers to provide services such as the following:

- ✔ Answering phone hotlines (such as rape, domestic violence, or suicide lines)
- ✔ Providing *crisis response* — immediate, in-the-field care to victims
- ✔ Helping with victim compensation
- ✔ Accompanying a victim to court
- ✔ Accompanying police or other officials when notifying a family member of a death
- ✔ Helping to run the service provider's office
- ✔ Securing address confidentiality for the victim to make sure a criminal doesn't learn the victim's new address

Observing the Laws That Protect Victims' Rights

All the victim services I discuss in the previous section are offered, for the most part, outside of the court system. In recent years, however, a movement has developed to help ensure that a victim's interests are considered *inside* the courtroom, too. Every state has passed laws that create victims' rights, and 29 states have even made such laws part of their state constitutions.

Invoking victims' rights

The victims' rights movement that has recently swept across the United States seeks to give the victim a voice in the criminal justice process. For instance, most states have enacted laws that require the court system or the prosecutor to notify victims of all release hearings related to their attackers and to give the victims the right to be heard at those hearings.

Imagine that your ex-boyfriend (or ex-girlfriend) has been stalking you and recently set your car on fire. He was arrested, but what happens next? Will he get out? Will he come back to hurt you? Thanks to the victims' rights movement, if your ex-boyfriend requests a release hearing, you have the right not only to be present but also to tell the judge why your ex shouldn't be released.

Here are some of the victims' rights that most states have enacted:

- **Notification of all hearings:** A victim has the right to know what's going on at every step of a case she's involved in. This notification applies to appeal hearings, too.

- **Opportunity to speak at a release hearing:** If the victim wants to comment, the judge must listen to the victim's concerns before deciding whether to release a defendant pretrial. Victims can speak in person or just write out a statement and give it to the prosecutor to read to the court.

- **Option to obtain a "no contact" order:** If the victim wants the defendant to stay away from her, the judge has the power to issue a "no contact" order, which prohibits the defendant from contacting the victim. Violation of the order can mean the defendant is arrested and placed back in jail.

- **Address confidentiality:** A defendant has the right to all police reports involving his case. However, the prosecutor must black out all references to where the victim is living if the victim requests such an action.

- **HIV and disease testing:** If the crime involved the exchange of bodily fluids, the victim can have the defendant tested to see whether he has a disease.

- **Consultation about plea offers:** The victim can request that the prosecutor confer with her about any deals the state plans to offer the defendant. This right doesn't mean the prosecutor has to do what the victim wants, however.

  It's important to note that prosecutors are *not* the victims' lawyers (they represent the state). Sometimes victims don't want the defendant to be prosecuted (a situation that frequently occurs in domestic violence cases). But the prosecutor can go ahead with the case anyway.

- **Option to refuse to be interviewed by the defense attorney or investigator:** Although anyone can refuse to be interviewed, victims can make this declaration early in the process and, theoretically, not be bothered at all by the defendant's representatives.

- **Opportunity to give a statement at sentencing:** One of the most important victims' rights is known as the *victim impact statement,* which means that, at the time of sentencing, the victim gets to tell the judge how the crime impacted her. The victim can address the court directly or have the prosecutor read a statement.

- **Restitution:** If a victim suffered financial loss, she has a right to a court order that requires the defendant to pay the money back. Typically, the defendant makes monthly payments to the court, which then distributes the money back to the victim.

Enforcing victims' rights

What happens when someone in the justice system violates one of these rights? In many states, the answer is nothing. Victims' rights often don't have any teeth. However, a number of states have begun to enact laws to give victims some recourse in the event that they believe their rights have been violated. Even so, protecting victims' rights can quickly become complicated.

Picture this scenario: A victim is notified that the defendant who attacked her is about to be arraigned. She doesn't attend the hearing because the victim advocate told her that nothing significant usually happens at an arraignment. But at the arraignment, the defendant receives the plea offer and decides to take the deal and be sentenced. The victim clearly hasn't been notified of the sentencing proceeding.

Should the judge go forward with the case? Or should the judge slow down the whole system and schedule a new hearing so that the victim can be notified and given the right to be present? The judge faces a choice between achieving greater efficiency and notifying the victim. In an overburdened system, the temptation to quickly resolve the case is great. If the judge decides to go forward with the case, the victim doesn't have much recourse.

A few states, however, have created mechanisms through which victims can file complaints about violations of rights. For example, for certain serious crimes in Colorado, if a victim feels her rights were violated, she can file a complaint with a committee responsible for enforcing victims' rights. The committee may conduct a hearing to assess the facts. If it determines that a violation occurred, it may issue recommendations to resolve the complaint. For instance, if a prosecutor failed to notify a victim of an important hearing, the prosecutor's office may be required to create a formal policy for victim notification and to train its staff on how to notify victims. Although these kinds of repercussions may not do an individual victim much good, they do help to improve the overall system.

Although just about everyone in the criminal justice system is in favor of protecting victims, in reality, the system sometimes sees victims as complicating factors. After all, they can slow down the process and create extra political pressure on judges and prosecutors. However, given the fact that victims were ignored for so long, the fact that they now have some power in the courtroom is a great step forward. After all, an innocent victim who is forced into the criminal justice system against her will is entitled to have the system slow down a little to make sure she receives justice.

Part II
Identifying Types of Crime

In this part . . .

Not all crimes are the same, of course. Some involve physical attacks on people, and some involve damage or misuse of people's property. Some crimes are committed by people acting alone, and some require a coordinated effort by organized crime groups. Many crimes these days involve drugs, and others are designed to evoke terror. In this part, I describe all these types of crimes and more.

Chapter 5

Getting Violent: Crimes of Force

....

In This Chapter

▶ Labeling various types of homicide

▶ Looking at other violent crimes, including assault, rape, robbery, and kidnapping

▶ Considering some causes of violence

....

*E*ver since Cain snuck up behind his brother Abel, violence has been a part of the human condition. This fact isn't exactly a source of pride, but you can't deny it — any more than you can deny the fact that, as humans, you and I experience anger, jealousy, acne, and bad breath.

No human character trait has caused more misery and grief than mankind's propensity for violence. In this chapter, I show you how violence manifests itself in criminal activity, and I walk you through the most common causes of that violence.

Identifying Types of Violent Crimes

When one person physically harms another, that person's violent conduct is generally (but not always) punishable as a crime. Through laws enacted by state legislatures and Congress, society uses the following criteria to rank the seriousness of violent crimes:

✔ The type of violence

✔ The severity of the violence

✔ The harm the violence caused

✔ Whether the offender intended to cause harm

In the following sections, I offer an overview of various types of violent crimes, including what each crime entails, who's most likely to commit each crime, and how severe the punishment for each crime is.

Defining Homicide

The most serious type of violent crime is *homicide,* which is the killing of one human being by another. But not all homicides are equal. There's a big difference, for example, between capital murder and assisted suicide. Here, I explain the labels that the law uses to characterize homicides, and I note the circumstances in which each label is applied.

Homicide tends to be a young man's crime. Over the last 30 years, persons between the ages of 18 and 24 have been much more likely to commit homicide than any other age group, and men are about ten times more likely than women to commit homicide.

Murder

Murder is a type of homicide that most states once defined as the killing of another human being with "malice aforethought." Because that's such a tough phrase to crack, many states have nixed it from their laws. Hence, murder is now more commonly defined as the *intentional* killing of another human being.

Some states require proof of premeditation or deliberation to convict someone of murder. *Premeditation* means that the killer not only intended to kill the victim, but also made a cool-headed, thoughtful decision to do so. A typical sentence for murder may be anywhere from 20 years to life in prison.

Although the word *murder* is more specific than *homicide,* it often isn't specific enough for today's criminal justice system. Thus, you hear terms like first-degree murder and capital murder. Keep reading to find out how the law distinguishes between the different types of murder.

First- and second-degree murder

Instead of just using the word *murder,* some states refer to an intentional killing as *first-degree murder.* Those states use the term *second-degree murder* to describe a murder in which the killer didn't intend the death but nonetheless exhibited behavior that demonstrated "extreme indifference to human life" or "wanton disregard" for the life of the victim. For example, a gang member who drove by the home of a rival gang member and fired a shot into the home that killed someone may be convicted of second-degree murder because he manifested extreme indifference to human life.

In the states that have laws ascribing degrees to the different types of murder, first-degree murder is the most serious and receives the most serious sentence.

Generally, a person who commits first-degree murder receives 25 years to life in prison. Second-degree murder (also called manslaughter in some states) can net a prison sentence of 10 to 25 years.

Felony murder

In many states, if a death occurs during the commission of a serious felony (such as a robbery or a kidnapping), all participants in that felony can be charged with murder, hence the term *felony murder*.

For example, a gang decides to rob a bank. During the course of the robbery, one of the robbers shoots and kills a bank guard. Under a felony murder statute, the driver of the getaway car — who never even set foot inside the bank — can also be charged with felony murder.

The sentence for a felony murder conviction is usually similar to the sentence for regular murder — anywhere from 20 years to life in prison.

Capital murder

The most serious type of murder is that which can be punished by a death sentence. Because the death sentence is also known as capital punishment, this type of murder is sometimes called *capital murder*. Although most industrialized nations have abolished capital punishment, the United States has not — 36 states still allow for some form of capital punishment.

The U.S. Supreme Court has significantly limited the cases in which someone can be sentenced to death. Most importantly, there must be "aggravating circumstances" above and beyond the murder itself. In other words, there must be additional factors that make the murder worse than just an intentional killing. Some common aggravating circumstances include the following:

- More than one person was murdered.
- The person murdered was a child.
- The murder took place during the course of another serious felony being committed. (Unlike felony murder, only the killer who personally committed the murder can be charged with capital murder.)
- The victim was tortured before the murder.
- The person murdered was a government official, a police officer, or a witness in a criminal or civil trial.

In addition to requiring aggravating circumstances, many states also require the prosecutor to show *deliberation* by the defendant — meaning that he thought about his actions before committing them. Many states also require the prosecutor to prove there's a likelihood that the killer will commit future acts of violence.

U.S. Supreme Court rulings have required that during a capital murder trial, the defendant be given the chance to present evidence to persuade the jury that he should *not* be sentenced to death. Such evidence can include the following:

- ✔ Proof that he was raised by negligent parents
- ✔ Proof that he has no previous history of violence
- ✔ Proof of the positive contributions he has made to society

Adults who are legally insane (see Chapter 20 for more on this term) or mentally retarded aren't eligible for a death sentence. People under the age of 18 can't receive the death sentence, either. For a detailed discussion of the death penalty, turn to Chapter 21.

Manslaughter

Manslaughter refers to the *non-intentional* killing of another person, but the killer still has some moral responsibility for the death. For example, a severely intoxicated driver who runs a red light while talking on his cellphone probably doesn't intend to crash his car and kill his passenger. But the state can still call his conduct *reckless,* which justifies a manslaughter charge. (See Chapter 2 for an explanation of the difference between intentional and reckless conduct.)

Often in a homicide in which the intent to kill is difficult to prove, prosecutors choose to negotiate a guilty plea to a charge of manslaughter. A sentence for manslaughter typically ranges from 1 to 15 years.

As you may have guessed, manslaughter appears very similar to second-degree murder. In fact, they're essentially the same. Some states have first- and second-degree murder, and some states have murder and manslaughter.

Negligent homicide

In criminal law, a person who engages in *negligent conduct* is considered less responsible than someone who is reckless. (In case you ever want to go to law school, know that conduct is *negligent* if the actor should've been aware of a substantial risk of doing harm. Conduct is *reckless* if the actor was aware of the substantial risk of doing harm but chose to engage in the activity anyway.) However, in some states, even negligently causing someone's death can result in a charge of *negligent homicide.* For example, an intoxicated driver who is *not* talking on his cellphone and who does *not* run a red light can still be charged with negligent homicide if he crashes his car and kills his passenger.

A sentence for negligent homicide may range from probation to five years in prison.

Assisting a suicide

Technically, suicide isn't a homicide because it doesn't involve the killing of *another* human being. However, in many countries (such as India), attempted suicide is a crime. (I'm not aware of any states in the United States that punish attempted suicide.)

In the United States, helping *another* person commit suicide — an act known as *euthanasia* — can be punished as homicide. Most famously, Dr. Jack Kevorkian, who claimed to have assisted 130 people in committing suicide, was convicted of second-degree murder in Michigan and served eight years in prison before being paroled in 2007.

As of this writing, Oregon and Washington are the only states that have legalized physician-assisted suicide. Washington passed its law in 2009. And Oregon's Death with Dignity Act, which took effect in 1997, allows Oregon citizens with terminal medical conditions to get prescriptions from their doctors for self-administered, lethal doses of "medication."

Attacking or Threatening Someone: Assault and Battery

Although the words *assault* and *battery* are often used interchangeably, in many states, they mean two different things:

- ✔ **Battery:** This crime requires actual physical contact that is offensive in some way.

- ✔ **Assault:** This crime typically refers to just a threat of battery, or an attempted battery, without actual physical contact. However, in states that don't use the word "battery," an assault may mean actual physical contact that's offensive or causes injury. In other words, in those states, assault is the same thing as battery.

For example, if you pull out a gun and tell someone you're going to shoot him, you're committing an assault (among other offenses). If you actually shoot the person without killing him, you're committing a battery.

The seriousness of these types of crimes and the sentences they warrant in court generally depend on whether a weapon is used and on how severe the harm caused is. Here are two key distinctions:

- ✔ *Simple* assault or battery refers to conduct that results in low-level physical injury, not serious injury. It's typically punished as a misdemeanor with only a little jail time.

✔ *Aggravated* assault or battery refers to serious felony conduct that involves the use of a dangerous or deadly weapon or that results in serious injury. Aggravated assault or battery may result in a lengthy prison sentence of one to ten years (or even more, depending on the circumstances).

The types of conduct that can result in a criminal charge of battery (or assault) are almost limitless, but here are just a few examples:

✔ Punching or slapping

✔ Stabbing

✔ Shooting

✔ Using any object as a weapon to cause an injury

✔ Crashing a vehicle

I once prosecuted someone who repeatedly kicked another person using steel-toed boots. I charged the defendant with battery with a "dangerous weapon," a charge that resulted in a longer sentence than the defendant would've received with a simple battery charge.

In the following sections, I discuss the major crimes involving assault and battery.

Vehicular assault

Car crashes are the most common means of violent death or serious physical injury in the United States. Groups such as Mothers Against Drunk Driving (MADD) have helped elevate society's awareness of the damage that can be done by a speeding, three-ton pile of metal. As a consequence, many states have created offenses, such as *vehicular assault,* that criminalize dangerous driving that results in injury. However, just crashing a car and injuring someone isn't enough to constitute a crime. In most states, the driver must have driven recklessly to warrant a charge.

Although reckless driving can involve a number of behaviors, such as speeding or running a red light, intoxication is by far the primary factor prosecutors use in proving vehicular assault, in part because intoxication is involved in so many crashes. If a driver wasn't intoxicated during a crash, to win a conviction of vehicular assault, a prosecutor has to prove very bad driving judgment (such as drag racing on a busy street).

Sentences for vehicular assault often depend on the severity of the victim's injury. A sentence can range from probation with no jail to eight or more years in prison.

Spousal assault

Also known as *domestic assault* or *intimate partner violence, spousal assault* usually involves violence between domestic partners and is most often committed by men toward women. More than 21 percent of all nonfatal violence against women is inflicted by an intimate partner. (In contrast, only 3.6 percent of nonfatal violence against men is inflicted by an intimate partner.)

Female victims of such violence are usually emotionally attached and financially dependent on their abusers, which may lead them to go through what's known as the *cycle of domestic violence* (see Figure 5-1).

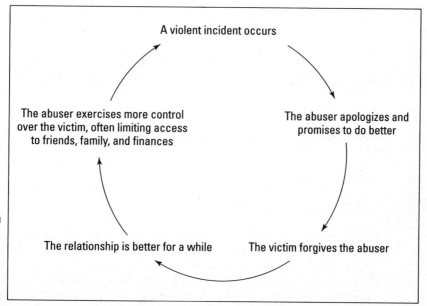

A violent incident occurs

The abuser exercises more control over the victim, often limiting access to friends, family, and finances

The abuser apologizes and promises to do better

The relationship is better for a while

The victim forgives the abuser

Figure 5-1:
The cycle of domestic violence.

In the past 15 years, domestic violence victim services have become much more commonplace. These services include short-term shelters for women and children fleeing from violence, along with counseling and employment services to help victims break the cycle. Perhaps not coincidentally, victimization survey results show that incidents of domestic violence in the United States have been steadily declining since 1993. (Check out Chapter 3 for more on victimization surveys and Chapter 4 for more on victim services.)

Keep in mind, though, that gathering a true statistical picture of the scope of intimate partner violence is difficult. By nature, this violence occurs within the home — away from witnesses — which makes arrest and prosecution difficult.

In cases of spousal assault, conflicts sometimes occur between law enforcement officers and victim service providers. Law enforcement officers are generally concerned with obtaining evidence to punish the violent offender. On the other hand, victim service providers want to protect the victim. In doing so, they may take actions that inhibit an investigation, such as refusing to disclose the victim's location to police.

Fortunately, as victims' rights have become a more significant part of the criminal justice system, such conflicts are becoming less common (see Chapter 4 for more on victims' rights). Nonetheless, finding a female domestic violence victim who is willing to cooperate with the prosecution against an offender is still unusual. Most often, the victim refuses to cooperate.

Because most domestic violence doesn't involve severe injuries, a typical sentence for a spousal assault charge involves probation and some jail time, along with requirements to complete anger management training and perhaps drug or alcohol treatment. Sometimes, however, spousal abuse does result in serious injury to the victim. When that occurs, the offenders may receive prison sentences of one to ten years or more.

Child abuse

Child abuse is a great concern to policymakers and the public. Today the term *child abuse* means more than just physical violence against children; it also includes neglect and mistreatment.

Traditionally, courts have shown great deference to parents with regard to child-rearing strategies, but criminal child abuse or child neglect is generally far beyond anything that can be considered "parenting." For example, in the homes of parents who are drug addicts, it's common to find pet and human feces throughout the house, garbage piled up so that the floor isn't even visible, and drug paraphernalia strewn about. Children may regularly watch their parents do drugs, and they may go without proper food or medical care for extended periods of time.

In addition to narcotics abuse, which is an issue in roughly 70 percent of all child abuse cases, parents may also abuse children because they learned the behavior from their own parents. If parents were abused as children, they may not know other skills for dealing with children and may resort to violence when they're angry or frustrated. Such violence can include physically beating a child, hitting a child with a belt or bat, burning a child's skin with a cigarette, and shaking a baby. (Because an infant's brain is so vulnerable, just one or two violent shakes can result in serious injury or even death — a situation called *shaken baby syndrome*.)

There are roughly 900,000 reported cases of child abuse in the United States each year, which means 12 out of every 1,000 children. However, this crime

often goes unreported, so the actual number of abuse cases has been estimated as high as 2.7 million. The majority of this abuse takes the form of
neglect rather than physical or sexual violence.

Sentences for child abuse can range from probation to lengthy prison sentences. Judges prefer to keep families intact — if doing so won't put the child
in danger — so probationary sentences that require the defendant to undergo
parenting education and drug or alcohol treatment are fairly common.

Forcing Sexual Contact: Rape, Sodomy, and Child Molestation

Sexual violence can take many forms, from improper sexual touching to
sodomy and rape, and most states have numerous laws that punish each and
every one. For example, a state may have several degrees of rape, sodomy,
and sexual abuse that vary based on the age and mental capacity of the
victim and on the offender's use of force.

In this section, I take a closer look at what constitutes rape, sodomy, and
child molestation, as well as what sentences these crimes carry with them.

Rape and sodomy

The crime of *rape* traditionally requires proof that someone (usually a man)
forcibly compelled someone else (usually a woman) to have sexual intercourse.
However, rape can also involve consensual sexual intercourse between an
adult and a partner under the age of 18 (a crime called *statutory rape*) or intercourse with someone whom the law deems incapable of consent because of a
mental handicap. The word *sodomy* refers to forced anal or oral sex or to those
same acts when they're done consensually between an adult and a juvenile.

Society once believed that rape and sodomy were offenses committed by
men unable to control their sexual desires. But in the past 30 years or so,
society has come to see crimes such as rape and sodomy as violent acts committed by both men *and* women that result in lasting physical and emotional
damage to the victim.

Today the most common type of rape is rape committed by a person the
victim knows. In fact, according to the 2006 National Crime Victimization
Survey, more than 70 percent of rape victims knew their offenders.

For example, *date rape,* a kind of rape that appears most often in campus
settings, is when someone you know forces you to have sexual intercourse,

usually at the end of a date or other social outing. One reason why date rape appears in campus settings is because a large percentage of all rapes are committed by men under the age of 25. Higher levels of alcohol and drug abuse, which are also common on campuses, likely play a role, too.

The media has paid a lot of attention to *date-rape drugs,* such as gamma-hydroxybutyric acid (GHB), that are put in a victim's drink to render that person more susceptible. Keep in mind, however, that alcohol consumption plays a much more significant role in making women vulnerable to sexual offenses.

The heavy consumption of alcohol or drugs by a victim not only makes the victim more susceptible to abuse but also makes prosecuting the offender more difficult. This is because the victim may have a poor memory of the events and may have engaged in conduct that the defendant will offer as evidence that the victim consented to the act.

Victims of rape experience a wide range of lasting physical and emotional effects. For example, for purposes of prosecution, women are encouraged to be examined by a doctor to obtain forensic evidence of rape (such as semen, pubic hairs, and blood). This experience can be frightening and embarrassing. Rape victims may also contract venereal diseases, become pregnant, suffer economic loss, and struggle with the significant emotional impacts. Fortunately, within the last 15 to 20 years, police and victim services workers have become much better at recognizing these challenges and helping victims through their ordeals.

Although each state is different, forcible rape and sodomy are usually punished by severe sentences, somewhere between 5 and 20 years, depending on the circumstances. Statutory rape, involving consensual sex between an adult and a minor, results in much shorter punishment and typically no prison time.

Child molestation

Few crimes provoke more public anger than *child molestation,* a sexual offense against a prepubescent child. And, yet, this type of crime occurs with alarming frequency. Statistics on the exact number of child molestation cases are difficult to come by. (One reason for this lack of stats is that the National Crime Victimization Survey, one of the most reliable measures of crime, reaches out only to people older than 12.) But you can get an idea of how many child molestation crimes occur by looking at a survey released in 1994 that tracked the actions of more than 9,600 convicted sex offenders after they were released from prison. The purpose of this survey was to measure how often convicted sex offenders committed more sex offenses after their release.

The results were alarming: The survey concluded that sex offenders were *four times* more likely than other violent offenders to be rearrested for sex crimes. But the most disconcerting number that came out of this survey is this: Almost 4,300 of the 9,600+ sex offenders involved in this study, or almost half, were child molesters.

Looking at who commits child molestation

Frequently, child molestation involves someone in the child's household. But other molesters may hold jobs or volunteer positions that place them in close proximity to children; they may be youth counselors or coaches, for example. Whoever the child molester is, he often "grooms" a child for the crime by trying to convince him or her that sex with an adult is okay.

I once prosecuted a case that provides a classic example of grooming. A man spent lots of time at a community swimming pool during the summer. Of all the kids who came swimming every day, he identified two susceptible 8-year-old boys and quickly befriended them, talking about video games, skateboards, and so on. He eventually persuaded one of the boys to engage in multiple acts of sodomy. (This man was convicted and sentenced to 15 years in prison.)

Molesters also separately groom adult parents and community members, seeking to gain their trust so they can have greater access to their children. They go to great lengths to persuade parents that they're trustworthy and reliable. Although offenders are almost always male, the child victims may be male or female.

Quite often, sentences for sexual molestation of a child are similar to sentences for forcible rape on adults (see the "Rape and sodomy" section for more details).

Considering the reasons why and the effects on victims

Why would someone molest a child? That's the million-dollar question. Clearly, some people have sex drives directed toward children — psychologists and psychiatrists call this condition *pedophilia.* But how this sex drive ultimately leads a person to actually violate a child is difficult to say.

Criminologists can certainly speculate that the increased use of the Internet has had a profound effect on the crime of child molestation. Just a few decades ago, a person with some sexual drive toward children would've had a tough time obtaining child pornography or finding like-minded people to associate with. Today, child molesters can use chat rooms to communicate with one another, discuss strategies, and generally encourage one another that their behaviors are okay. And, of course, child pornography flows across the Internet virtually unabated. The combination of chat-room support from like-minded people and stimulation from child pornography may lead some people down a path where they ultimately molest a child.

Perhaps even more significant is the fact that children who are sexually abused are much more likely to become abusers themselves. A 2001 study by Gene Abel, MD, and Nora Harlow found that more than 47 percent of child molesters admitted being similarly abused as children. Of children who were abused more than 50 times, 82 percent became pedophiles when they matured.

Along with the greater risk of becoming molesters themselves, victims of molestation can suffer dramatic, life-altering emotional damage and possibly even destroyed familial relationships. For example, if the molester is a family member or the boyfriend of the mother, the prosecution process may pit the child against his or her own relatives. For this reason, many children are reluctant or unwilling to cooperate with police. Detectives and prosecutors with specialized expertise often work with child sex victims to help conduct interviews and get the full story.

Taking Property under the Threat of Violence: Robbery

Robbery is essentially theft by force. Stealing a woman's purse from her closet is *theft*. Knocking her down and taking her purse directly off her shoulder is *robbery*. Unlike theft and burglary, which are both considered property crimes, robbery is considered a violent crime and is usually punished more severely because it involves a risk to the personal safety of the victim (see Chapter 6 for more on theft, burglary, and other property crimes).

The amount of punishment doled out for robbery generally depends on whether a weapon is used and, if so, the type of weapon used. Here are the basic distinctions among weapons:

- **Deadly weapons:** In most states, using a firearm during the commission of a robbery results in the most severe sentences. Using other weapons capable of causing death (called *deadly weapons*) may also result in severe punishment.

  Armed robbery, for example, may result in a sentence of one to ten years in state prison. Although most violent crimes are handled in state court, bank robbery is commonly prosecuted in the federal system where sentences can reach 20 years in prison if the robber was armed.

- **Dangerous weapons:** This category of weapons includes those that can cause significant injury, such as clubs, fists, and stun guns. Using a *dangerous weapon* during a robbery may result in a more severe sentence than a robbery without a weapon.

- **Pretend weapons:** Of course, I can't neglect to mention the robber with his hand in his pocket, pretending to have a gun. In many states, even *pretending* to possess a weapon may result in an enhanced sentence.

By far, most robberies happen to people in vehicles. For instance, *carjacking* is when a robber forces a person out of his car and then takes the car. In 2007, 20 robberies of people in vehicles were committed for every one bank robbery. Also, far more common than bank robberies are robberies of convenience stores and homes.

Unlike most other violent crimes, which peak during summer months, more robberies occur during the colder months. Some criminologists theorize that the reason behind this trend is the increased darkness in the colder months, which helps to conceal the crime. Also, wearing a mask and hat to cover your appearance without raising suspicions is much easier to do in the winter.

Robberies of drug dealers are extremely common, too, but few of these cases show up in statistics compiled by the Federal Bureau of Investigation (FBI). Obviously, drug dealers aren't likely to report being victimized, which is precisely what makes them such appealing targets to robbers.

Kidnapping

When you hear the word *kidnapping,* you likely think of the taking and holding of a person against her will for ransom purposes. Early in the 20th century, kidnappings of public or wealthy citizens happened regularly. The most famous case may have been the kidnapping of Charles Lindbergh's infant son from his bedroom.

Other well-known cases include the kidnappings of the granddaughter of newspaper magnate William Randolph Hearst in California and of the 9-year-old son of lumberman J. P. Weyerhaeuser from Tacoma, Washington.

These days, however, kidnapping for ransom is relatively rare in the United States. Much more common than kidnapping for ransom is kidnapping in conjunction with another crime. For example, in a rape case, if a person is transported or confined against her will, a prosecutor may charge the offender with both rape and kidnapping.

Recently, the United States is seeing cases where Mexican kidnappers snatch family members of other Mexicans who are in the country illegally and hold them for ransom. Kidnappers view this action as a low-risk crime because the victims aren't likely to contact police for fear of being deported.

Because kidnapping is relatively rare in the United States, the FBI doesn't gather statistics on the number of kidnappings that occur.

Sentences for kidnapping are often similar to those for other violent crimes, such as robbery, rape, or aggravated assault.

U.S. violent crime rates in recent decades

Here's a sampling of violent crime rates in the United States:

✔ **Homicide:** According to Uniform Crime Report statistics from the FBI, the homicide rate in the United States rose steadily from 1965 to 1980, when it peaked at more than ten homicides per 100,000 persons. The rate remained relatively high until it began to decline in 1993. In 1999, the homicide rate again stabilized, and it has since remained at roughly 5.6 homicides for every 100,000 persons.

✔ **Assault and battery:** According to the National Crime Victimization Study, the number of assaults and batteries in the United States peaked at about 12 aggravated assaults and 30 simple assaults for every 1,000 persons around 1993 and has

been dropping ever since. In 2005, the U.S. assault rate was around 1,700 assaults for every 100,000 persons.

✔ **Rape and other sexual assault:** According to the 2006 National Crime Victimization Survey, there were 192,320 rapes or attempted rapes that year in the United States and a total of 260,940 sexual assaults — roughly 90 incidents per 100,000 persons. From 1999 to 2006, there was a marked trend toward fewer rapes and sexual assaults; but, in 2006, an uptick in the number of rapes and sexual assaults occurred.

✔ **Robbery:** According to FBI statistics, the number of robberies has been declining in the United States since 1991, when more than 687,000 robberies were committed. In 2007, the number was down to 445,125.

Pinpointing Causes of Violence

Why does a man strangle his spouse? Why does a woman shake her infant son until he dies? Why does a street gang member unload a clip into the home of a rival gang member?

Although the specific reasons why people commit crimes of violence vary from case to case, criminologists study potential underlying causes with the hope that they may be able to reduce the amount of violence in society. Keep in mind that these studies aren't just academic exercises; policymakers base significant policy decisions on the conclusions that criminologists make from their studies. For example, does lengthening prison sentences deter some violent offenders from committing crimes? The answer to that question can lead to changes in the way judges hand down sentences. And do early family-intervention programs for juvenile delinquents help turn juveniles away from violent crime? The answer to that question can influence how much government money is or isn't funneled into such prevention programs.

There are at least five key factors that may play a part in someone's decision to engage in violence. I discuss these five factors in this section:

- ✔ Drugs and alcohol
- ✔ Family troubles
- ✔ Mental illness
- ✔ Society
- ✔ Personal choices

Struggling with drugs and alcohol

Are you ready for a shocking statistic? More than half of all persons arrested have illegal drugs in their systems.

Not surprisingly, studies have shown a strong correlation between drug and alcohol use and increased violence. For example, more than 25 percent of defendants facing domestic violence charges have substance abuse problems. Other studies have shown that kids who had used drugs in the previous year were more than twice as likely to engage in violence when compared with non–drug users. And the more drugs used, the greater the likelihood of violence. Of kids who had used more than three drugs in the previous year, more than 61 percent had engaged in violence. In contrast, only 26 percent of kids who hadn't used drugs had engaged in violence.

Drugs aren't the only mind-altering substances associated with increased criminal violence. A 1996 study revealed that almost 40 percent of violent acts involved the use of alcohol, 40 percent of fatal motor vehicle crashes involved alcohol, and 66 percent of domestic violence victims reported that alcohol was a factor in their assaults.

When substance abuse directly leads to violent conduct, criminologists refer to the connection as a *psychopharmacological* relationship. A clear-cut example of this kind of relationship can be found in a condition known as *methamphetamine psychosis.* This condition occurs in methamphetamine abusers and can result in extreme paranoia, delusions, panic, and a great propensity for violence. When a person suffering from methamphetamine psychosis commits an assault, there's a psychopharmacological relationship between the drug and the crime.

As I explore in detail in Chapter 9, even more violence results from the *business* of illegal narcotics. Drug traffickers commonly protect territory and trafficking routes by using murder, assaults, and kidnapping. For example, in 2008 and 2009, the Mexican side of the U.S. border experienced extreme violence. As the Mexican government cracked down on international drug traffickers, and as those same traffickers fought for control over the lucrative border region, more than 71 people were murdered in Tijuana, Mexico, in just a nine-day period in the fall of 2008. In the first five months of 2009, there were 671 murders in the city of Ciudad Juarez.

The drug business within the United States also commonly results in violence as dealers compete for markets and customers. Increasingly, violent offenders commit armed robberies (known as *rips*) on drug dealers, seeking to obtain drugs or cash. Drug dealers are particularly susceptible to violence because they're not likely to seek protection from law enforcement.

Feeling the lasting effects of family troubles

Proving that a particular family problem led to a particular act of violence is probably impossible. Nonetheless, some common issues within a family are associated with juvenile delinquency and future violence. For example, violence between parents (or between a parent and his or her partner) has been linked to future violence by children. For this reason, many state laws provide more severe punishment for domestic violence when it's committed in the presence of a child.

Similarly, physical and sexual abuse by adults *on* children may play a big part in leading those children to commit the same acts when they grow up. Kids who are constantly exposed to violence can come to view violence as an appropriate way to solve conflict. For example, a boy who regularly sees his mom's boyfriend physically and emotionally abuse his mom may copy the abusive behavior when he grows up because he never learned other skills for resolving arguments with others, especially women.

STRANGE BUT TRUE

Organized drug rips

In 2008, eight people from an organized gang were indicted in New York for a five-year crime spree in which the defendants allegedly impersonated police to take drugs and cash off of large-scale cocaine dealers. The crimes occurred across five states and netted more than $20 million worth of cocaine and $4 million in cash. More than 100 cocaine dealers were victimized.

According to court papers, the robbers sometimes conducted police-style traffic stops of cocaine dealers who were transporting drugs or money. In other cases, the robbers invaded cocaine dealers' homes and bound family members with duct tape and handcuffs, sometimes holding them hostage for days. One victim recounted how the robbers applied pliers to his testicles and threatened to squeeze if he didn't reveal the location of large caches of cocaine. Other victims reported being tortured, including having their heads held under water to force them to talk. After the cocaine was located, the gang sold the drugs on the streets of New York.

At the opposite end of the spectrum from physical abuse, some parents may not discipline their kids at *all*. If a child is never reigned in after misbehaving, he may be less likely to learn proper boundaries or decision-making skills. Later in life, that kid may be less able to conform to society's rules, including laws against violence.

Suffering from mental problems

Studies of groups of murderers have revealed that murderers are likely to have lower IQs than the average citizen. You might say that they have mental deficiencies.

Note that a mental *deficiency* is much different from a mental *disease,* which is a mental illness as defined by psychiatrists and psychologists. In court, a mental disease can be the basis of an insanity defense. A mental deficiency such as a decreased IQ, on the other hand, can't be part of an insanity defense; it simply helps explain, in part, why someone may have committed an act of violence.

One mental disease that prosecutors often encounter in criminal cases is *paranoid schizophrenia*. For example, a person who suffers from paranoid schizophrenia may experience a delusion in which he believes his television is telling him to kill his neighbor's dog. If he actually kills the dog, he'll likely be excused from criminal responsibility thanks to an insanity defense. (For a more detailed discussion of the insanity defense, see Chapter 20.)

A *personality disorder* is yet another mental problem that can be a cause of violence. Like a mental disease, a personality disorder is diagnosed by a psychologist or psychiatrist. But it's not considered as severe a disability as a mental disease and, therefore, can't be used for an insanity defense. Two of the best-known personality disorders in the criminal justice system are

- ✔ **Narcissistic personality disorder:** Someone with this disorder generally sees herself as very important, needs others to see her as important, and lacks the ability to experience empathy with others.

- ✔ **Antisocial personality disorder:** Someone with this disorder has a pattern of disregarding the rights of others that starts when she's a juvenile and progresses into adulthood.

Similar to antisocial personality disorder is a characteristic known as *psychopathy*. A psychopath is a predator who uses charm, manipulation, and violence to control others and achieve her own selfish needs without experiencing any guilt or remorse. Studies of psychopaths within prisons reveal that psychopaths are generally untreatable and may even become more cunning and manipulative *after* being subjected to treatment. Psychopaths are also considered much more likely to engage in future acts of violence than other inmates.

See Chapter 14 for a more detailed discussion of how a psychological or personality disorder can lead to criminal behavior.

Being influenced by society

Some criminologists look to cultural values within a society as a potential cause for violence. For example, the murder rate in Japan has been measured at less than 10 percent of that in the United States. For this reason, some people have theorized that the United States, which highly values independence and self-reliance, may have more violence, in part, because of these values. In contrast, Japan is a more socially organized country that places less value on independently resolving conflict and, thus, has less violence.

Today's society also offers people constant access to violent messages. Some people believe that relentless exposure to violence (through TV programs, movies, music, video games, and so on) may desensitize children, making them more likely to resort to violence to resolve conflicts. One analysis concluded that by the time the average child in the United States reaches the age of 8, she has seen 8,000 murders on TV, and by the time she reaches 18, she's seen more than 200,000 acts of violence on TV.

I devote Chapter 13 to exploring theories of how society may influence someone to become a criminal.

Making a personal choice

Drugs, mental health, and pop culture all may play a role in influencing someone to commit a violent crime, as I discuss earlier in the chapter. But another possibility is that criminal violence is, in part, a conscious, rational choice based on how an individual weighs the risks of committing a crime versus its potential rewards.

How else can you explain why two brothers raised in the same family environment and culture take radically different paths in life? Why does one become a drug dealer who commits capital murder while the other becomes a productive member of society? (I explore this theory in detail in Chapter 12.)

Chapter 6

Hitting You in the Pocketbook: Property Crimes

*N*o other crime affects more people than property crime. Odds are that you haven't been the victim of a serious violent felony, but I bet you've been the victim of at least one property crime. After all, three-fourths of all crime is property crime. The term *property crime* refers to all the types of crime that impact your property, including theft, fraud, burglary, arson, vandalism, Internet scams, car break-ins, and auto theft.

I've actually been the victim of property crime on more than one occasion. For instance, I had a pickup truck that thieves repeatedly broke into when I lived in San Francisco. Eventually, I decided to leave it unlocked so that the thieves could get inside without breaking the windows.

The amount of property crime in the United States dropped significantly between 1974 and 2003 and then began to rise again slightly. In 1974, more than 55 property crimes for every 100 households occurred annually in the United States! By 2003, the number had dropped to about 16 property crimes per 100 households.

In this chapter, I discuss various types of property crime, and I attempt to explain why people commit them.

Categorizing Types of Theft

You may be wondering, what exactly is *theft?* Well, legal definitions of the crime can be quite complicated (see Chapter 7 if you want proof), but everyone knows what theft is in its most basic sense: intentionally taking the property of another person without having that person's permission to do so.

I don't have enough space in this book to list all the ways you can commit theft, but I cover the most common ones in this section.

Shoplifting

Shoplifting occurs when a person enters a retail outlet during business hours and intentionally takes something without paying for it. According to the National Association for Shoplifting Prevention (NASP), a nonprofit organization that aims to raise awareness of the negative effects of shoplifting on the community, shoplifters steal approximately $35 million worth of goods from retailers every day (for more info on this association, check out its Web site at www.shopliftingprevention.org).

In my profession, I've prosecuted people for stealing cigarettes, beer, gum, meat, clothes, jewelry, yarn, razor blades, and even cat food. Usually, people don't steal because they actually need the items. More commonly, they want something but either don't want to or can't afford to pay for it.

Two of the most common defenses against theft charges are the following:

- ✔ **"It was an accident."** As in, "My daughter must have put those candy bars in my coat pocket before we left the store."

- ✔ **"The item is really mine."** As in, "I didn't take these sunglasses from the store. I bought them two years ago."

The impact of shoplifting is great — the cost of theft passes on to the law-abiding consumer, and some estimates indicate that shoplifting raises the retail cost of goods by 10 to 15 percent.

Although the vast majority of shoplifters aren't career criminals, a small percentage actually derives significant income from shoplifting. These people systematically identify and target high-value items that they can resell. Typically, shoplifters target small items that they can easily conceal, such as CDs, DVDs, and small electronics like MP3 players. But they also target expensive items, such as baby formula, perfume, and razor blades, which they can resell in flea markets or ship in volume overseas.

Letting the fear of lawsuits run amok

Once at a training conference, I was sitting outside a grocery store eating a sandwich with an off-duty police officer friend. We saw three separate teenagers enter the store, steal some beer, and leave without paying. (The officer didn't interfere because he was out of his jurisdiction.) We finally went inside and told the manager. The manager said he knew what was happening but that his corporate office told him to allow the thefts because the corporate office was afraid that if loss-protection officers chased the kids, one of them may get hit by a car in the parking lot and sue the store.

In the last ten years, the practice of moving through a region, stealing from numerous stores along the way, and sending the stolen goods to Mexico or another country has become increasingly more common among organized groups of thieves. The aggregate value of items stolen may be great, but each individual theft is small. As a result, when only one member of the gang is arrested, local authorities likely don't hold her in jail, and she can then rejoin her partners in the next town (where she continues to steal), never returning to court.

Most large retailers employ some antitheft security, including *loss-prevention officers* (store employees who look for thieves), surveillance cameras, and electro-magnetic devices that sound an alarm when a thief crosses the store's threshold with stolen merchandise. Sometimes retailers also lock high-value items in glass cases that only sales associates can open.

If a loss-prevention officer spies someone hiding an item for a possible theft, she follows the person outside (making sure the person doesn't pay for the item) and confronts him or her. The loss-prevention officer usually asks the thief to go back inside to wait for the police to arrive. The loss-prevention officer has no more authority than a private citizen, but, in most jurisdictions, private citizens are allowed to detain someone — making a *citizen's arrest* — and even use some minimum force if the person has committed a crime.

Increasingly, however, stores are discouraging their loss-prevention officers from making citizen's arrests out of fear of lawsuits by people wrongfully detained or injured in the process.

Scamming people out of their money

Enterprising criminals often come up with creative ways to separate people from their money. Have you ever had someone come to your home and try to sell you magazine subscriptions or frozen meat? Once a guy stopped me in my yard and said that he had some extra asphalt from another job and wanted to repave my driveway for next to nothing. Now, this offer for practically free asphalt or offers for magazines or frozen meat may be legitimate offers, but they can just as easily be *scams* — attempts to cheat you by selling you an inferior product or no product at all.

Although some people have little sympathy for people who get scammed, saying *caveat emptor* ("buyer beware"), scammers often pick on the most vulnerable people, including the elderly, who can least afford a loss.

Some of the most common scams are pyramid and ponzi schemes, which I distinguish here:

- ✔ *Pyramid schemes* take many forms, but, generally, they involve a promise of large profits to people who recruit others to join a program that sells a product. So, an initial investor may recruit five people, who, in turn, all recruit five more people, who take orders for the sale of a product from still other people. The money goes to the people higher up in the pyramid. Usually there's no product, or, at least, not enough product to fulfill all the orders, and the customers lose their money.

- ✔ *Ponzi schemes* are very similar but generally don't involve the sale of a product; they're investment scams. The initial "investor" recruits other investors, who all pay money to buy into the scheme. Each round of new investors pays previous investors until the scheme collapses and the people at the bottom of the pyramid lose their investments.

Both pyramid and ponzi scams have become much more common with the rise of the Internet.

Another common scam, with many variations, is the Nigerian or *419 scam*. An e-mail from a "Nigerian official" offers you the opportunity to share in millions of dollars if you help place the millions in bank accounts overseas. But, first, you have to front several thousand dollars because the Nigerian official can't yet access the millions. The label *419 scam* refers to section 419 of the Nigerian legal code, which addresses criminal fraud.

Scam artists often use Internet auction sites as hosts for scams and fraud because of their huge popularity. Typically, a person purchases an item and makes payment but never receives the goods. Some common indicators of a possible fraudulent transaction include the seller's request for you to send payment overseas or a request for you to wire money directly to the seller. Wire transaction payments are almost impossible to recover.

Internet sites are also hosts for selling stolen merchandise. For instance, burglars and organized theft rings often use Internet auction sites to sell stolen goods.

A Nigerian scam

Following is one of a series of e-mails that a victim of a Nigerian scam received. The e-mail appears as it was actually written, with all the original errors and crazy syntax (my editor didn't want you to think she was lazy). The goal of the e-mail is to convince the victim to keep making payments to the fraudsters with the promise that the victim will ultimately claim a $12 million inheritance. The victim in this case wired more than $100,000 to Nigeria.

I CHIEF OUSEGUN OBASANJO ,DCFR PRESIDENT AND COMMANDER IN CHIEF OF ARMED FORCES OF THE FEDERAL REPUBLIC OF NIGERIA. I WISH TO INFORM ALL OUR CONTRACTORS THAT AFTER MY MEETING WITH THE UNITED NATIONS AND WORLD BANK, IMF, INTERPOLE DIGNITARIES RECENTLY, THE FEDERAL HOUSE OF SENATE HAVE DECIDED TO RID OUR ECONOMY OF ENORMOUS DEBT BURDEN TO ENHANCE MORE INTERNATIONAL BUSINESS RELATIONSHIP BETWEEN MY GOVERNMENT AND THE INTERNATIONAL COMMUNITY.

SEQUEL TO MY LAST MEETING HELD IN THE WHITEHOUSE WITH PRESIDENT GEORGE BUSH, MY NEW SENATE PRESIDENT, MY VICE PRESIDENT, THE HONOURABLE MINISTER OF FINANCE AND ALSO THE ATTORNEY GENERAL OF THE FEDERATIONS (F.R.N.).

I HAVE DECIDED TO SETTLE ALL THE FOREIGN BENEFICIARY(S) FUNDS THROUGH MY OWN BLISSFUL WAY, FOR WE HAVE SENT OUT MEMEBRS LIKE MR PAUL MOSELY WHO HAS BEEN CONTACTING YOU LATELY. I AM PERSONALLY ASSURING YOU THAT YOUR FUNDS WHICH WAS INHERITED, IS NOW SET TO BE WIRED INTO YOUR ACCOUNT WITHIN SIX HOURS.

(VICTIM'S NAME) RIGHT NOW YOU HAVE TO CONTACT MY PERSONAL SECRETARY AND INCQUIRE FOR HIM TO GET YOU A BENEFICIARY FILE AND FORM SO YOU CAN FILL AND SEND BACK TO ME FOR MY APPROVAL SIGNATURE TO ORDER FOR THE RELEASE OF YOUR RIGHTFUL FUNDS TO YOUR DESIGNATED ACCOUNT VIA WASHINGTON MUTUAL WIRE.

YOU WILL FIND BELOW THE CONTACT OF MY PERMANENT SECRETARY AND MAKE SURE YOU CALL HIM IMMEDIATELY FOR YOUR REQUEST.

Taking personal and credit card information: Identity theft

The Internet has revolutionized many activities, including fraud. One of the most common types of Internet crime involves trying to obtain other people's personal information, such as credit card numbers, Social Security numbers, and bank account information. This type of crime is called *identity theft*.

If you have an e-mail account, I'm confident you've seen examples of *phishing:* phony e-mails that attempt to get you to divulge confidential information. In effect, the sender is "fishing" for your information. Often, the sender accomplishes this task by *spoofing:* sending you forged e-mails that purport to come from entities you do business with, such as banks or credit card companies. In reality, the "entity" sending the e-mails is some guy in Kerblakistan who, after he gets your credit card number, uses it to make purchases at will until he reaches your credit limit. Because so much Internet fraud originates overseas, you can't do much after you've been fooled.

The Internet isn't the only place where you find credit card theft. Some thieves who work in retail stores or restaurants use credit card readers to accumulate numbers and then charge items using those numbers, or they sell the numbers to other thieves via the Internet. I once prosecuted a man who was a barista in a high-end coffee shop. He retained a customer's credit card number so that he could purchase an airplane ticket to Mexico after he murdered his family.

Thieves can also get your credit card information through muggings or mail theft. Although this method is less common than it was five years ago, law enforcement still deals with organized groups that steal mail from mailboxes, looking for credit cards or credit card applications to exploit. Often, ring leaders pay the street-level thieves with drugs and use the credit card information to buy goods for themselves.

Most states have laws that specifically punish identity theft. These laws often carry greater punishment than other theft laws — including prison time.

Overcoming identity theft

If you're the victim of identity theft, you should follow these steps:

1. **Place a fraud alert on your credit report.** This alert warns other creditors to check your identity before opening any new credit accounts in your name.

2. **Review your credit report.** You have the right to a free review of your credit report from the following three agencies that track credit: Equifax (www.equifax.com), Experian (www.experian.com), and TransUnion (www.transunion.com). Even if your identity hasn't been stolen, following this step is a good way to stay on top of your credit history and to correct errors when they occur.

Know that you're liable for only up to $50 of any credit card fraud if you review your credit card statement in a timely fashion and notify the credit provider of any errors.

3. **Request that the three companies that maintain credit reports remove any records of fraudulent transactions from your report.**

If you're victimized, a good source of information to check out is http://www.ftc.gov/bcp/edu/microsites/idtheft/, a site maintained by the Federal Trade Commission.

Identity theft is one of the most widespread crimes in the world. A 2005 survey by the Federal Trade Commission (FTC) reported that in one year, 8.3 million American adults were victims of identity theft. The most common complaints to the FTC in 2005 were the following:

- ✔ Foreign money offers (such as the Nigerian scam)
- ✔ Prizes, sweepstakes, and lotteries
- ✔ Internet auctions
- ✔ Shop-at-home/catalog sales
- ✔ Telephone services
- ✔ Work-at-home offers

Stealing autos

Since the U.S. government started keeping auto theft statistics in 1973, they've never been lower than they are today, at about 8 thefts per 1,000 households each year. (See Figure 6-1, which shows data from the U.S. Bureau of Justice Statistics.)

Despite this downtrend, however, the stats still represent about 1.2 million stolen cars each year, with a total value of about $8 billion.

People steal autos for a variety of reasons, including the following:

- ✔ To go for a joy ride
- ✔ To sell the auto in another country (often Mexico)
- ✔ To strip the vehicle for parts, which the thief then sells domestically or overseas
- ✔ To use the auto in the commission of another crime, such as a bank robbery or a drive-by shooting

Many people have an interest in car theft rates, given that a car is the second most expensive item most people own (the first being a home). For one thing, the higher the frequency of car theft in your neighborhood, the higher your auto insurance rate is going to be.

Today ever-improving technology means that fewer cars are being stolen and more stolen cars are being recovered than ever before. For example, many cars (including most rental cars) are equipped with global positioning system (GPS) devices that track the exact locations of the vehicles.

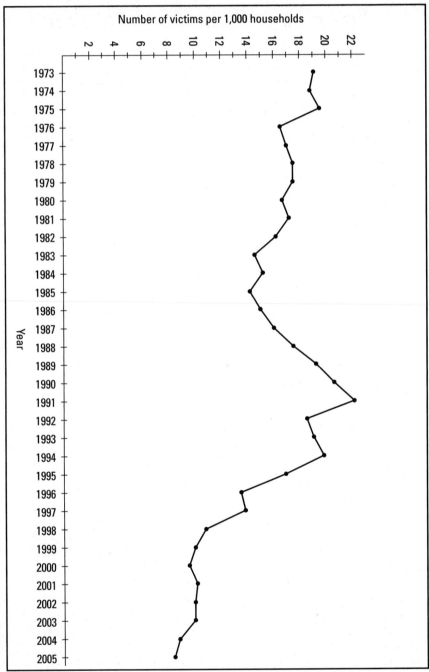

Figure 6-1: The rate of auto thefts per 1,000 households from 1973 to 2005.

Source: U.S. Bureau of Justice Statistics

Breaking and entering: Burglary

Burglary is the unlawful entering of a home or building to commit a crime therein. An *unlawful entry* means the person doesn't have permission or authority to enter — similar to the crime of trespassing. But what distinguishes a trespass from a burglary is that burglary includes the intent to commit another crime in the building. Normally people think of this secondary crime as theft: A person breaks into a home to steal jewelry, for example. However, a person who breaks into a house to commit a rape is also committing burglary.

In most states, the severity of punishment for burglary depends on several factors:

✔ Was the building a home (as opposed to an office building, for example)?

✔ If the building was a home, did the burglary happen at night (when residents may have been home)?

✔ Was anyone present at the time of the burglary?

✔ Did the burglar forcibly enter the building?

✔ Did the burglar have a weapon when he entered the building?

A burglary that includes all these factors — armed burglary that involves kicking in the door of an occupied dwelling at night — is the most serious type of burglary because it's most likely to result in violent harm to the victims. In most states, burglary with these elements results in a lengthy prison sentence.

The number of burglaries in the United States has been decreasing since 1974, although the decrease did level out in about 2001. Figure 6-2 demonstrates this decrease, using data from the U.S. Bureau of Justice Statistics.

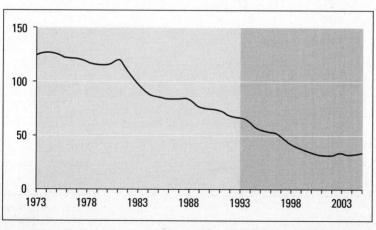

Figure 6-2: The burglary rate per 1,000 households from 1973 to 2005.

Source: U.S. Bureau of Justice Statistics

Professional criminals are much more likely to engage in burglary (and perhaps Internet fraud) than any other crimes. (By *professional,* I don't mean that the burglars wear coats and ties. Rather, they develop special burglary skills and commit repeated crimes, almost as if burglary is their job.) But more commonly, burglars are juveniles or people in their 20s who are seeking thrills or looking for money to buy their next drug or alcohol fix. Nonetheless, burglary can be a more challenging crime than shoplifting because it requires planning the entry in advance, targeting specific locations, and finding a market in which to sell the stolen goods.

You may assume that most burglars focus on homes, but, these days, burglars increasingly target retail establishments because they can lawfully visit the stores during the day, identify the locations of high-value items, and then return at night. Pharmacies, in particular, have become popular targets because burglars can easily sell (or use) prescription drugs. Burglars more commonly commit retail or office burglaries at night when the business is closed, but they more commonly commit residential burglaries during the day when residents are at work.

How does a burglar dispose of his ill-gotten gains? Historically, middlemen operated fencing operations. A *fence* would buy stolen items for a huge discount and then resell those items. Today, fences still exist, but burglars now have new ways to sell their goods. Internet sites, such as eBay and craigslist, are chock full of stolen items. Burglars also sell items to friends, family members, or pawn shops; some even exchange stolen items directly for drugs.

A burglar skilled in his trade may commit a hundred acts before being caught. And because the punishment for property crimes is typically mild, a person may spend several years as a burglar before he does any significant time behind bars.

Committing outdoor property theft

Commodity and metal theft has become a significant problem across the United States. Drug users, for instance, steal metal items, such as copper piping from buildings, and then sell them for scrap to get drug money. And highways in Hawaii are often in the dark because thieves repeatedly steal the wiring for the street lights. The cost to replace the wiring may be tens of thousands of dollars for the community. Ironically, the thief sells the wiring for $100 or less to buy drugs.

Construction materials and tools are frequent targets, too, because they're often left outside without any security. Some states have responded by passing laws requiring scrap metal dealers to record identify information from the people who sell them the metal.

Defining Property Damage

Property crime includes more than just theft; it also includes property damage. Two of the more common crimes involving property damage are arson and vandalism.

Committing arson

Arson typically refers to the intentional burning of a home, building, vehicle, aircraft, or personal property of another. In 2007, police agencies reported 64,332 arsons to the Federal Bureau of Investigation (FBI). The average dollar loss per arson event was $17,289.

People commit arson for many reasons, including the following:

✔ To collect insurance money

✔ To strike back at employers, ex-spouses, or business competitors

✔ To get perverse pleasure from burning things (which is a reason why emotionally disturbed juveniles or adults start fires)

✔ To cover up evidence of additional crimes

In the western United States, wildfires are a significant problem every summer, requiring thousands of firefighters and millions of dollars to put them out. Mounting evidence suggests that significant numbers of these fires are started intentionally by people — some of whom seek work fighting the very fires they start. (Of course, lightning strikes and careless humans start many wildfires, too.)

Police face daunting challenges in proving the crime of arson. After all, the fire destroys most of the evidence. Nonetheless, arson investigators, many of whom work for fire departments, are skilled at identifying the causes of fires. Arson investigators talk to the firemen who first arrived at the scene to find out whether they detected any clues about where the fire started, how it progressed, or what color the smoke was. Investigators can often detect the location where a fire originated because of evidence of the use of accelerants, such as gasoline-soaked rags or lighter fluid. Similarly, investigators look for signs of forced entry by the arsonist or even tampering with fire suppression systems. And, of course, the presence of a motive, such as burning a business that's failing, can be an important clue that eventually leads police to the arsonist who started the fire.

Vandalizing property

Some people don't choose to use violence to get back at someone else. Instead, they decide to damage the other person's property, a crime called *vandalism*. Perhaps the most common form of vandalism is graffiti (also known as *tagging* when committed by a street gang to mark its territory).

But vandalism also includes other damaging actions, such as breaking the windows of businesses or homes. For example, I once prosecuted a man for breaking the windshield of his girlfriend's car because he thought she was seeing another man. (In case you're curious, she wasn't.)

How vandalism is punished usually depends on the dollar value of the damage that was committed. If you throw a rock through your ex-girlfriend's window, you'll probably just be charged with a misdemeanor. But if you *key* someone's Maserati (meaning you used your key to significantly scratch the car's expensive paint job), you may be prosecuted for a more serious felony crime.

Looking at the Causes of Property Crime

You may be wondering, why do people steal or commit burglaries? Well, there are many reasons, but here I address some of the most common ones.

Wrestling with drug addiction

I can't emphasize enough that drugs (including alcohol) are the primary motivation behind *all* crime, including property crime. People who develop addictions have trouble holding jobs. As a result, they're frequently unemployed or underemployed. But they still need money to feed their drug habits, as well as to pay for food and shelter — many of them resort to financial property crime to do so.

The criminal justice system is full of property crime offenders with substance abuse problems. These offenders frequently cycle through the system in a pattern similar to the following:

1. A person begins using drugs (or alcohol) and develops an addiction.

2. The person buys drugs, perhaps sells drugs, and commits property crimes to pay for drugs.

3. Eventually, the person is arrested for a drug or property crime.

4. The person may do a little jail time, or none at all, depending on the crime.

5. If the court becomes aware that the crime was related to drugs (which doesn't always happen with property crimes), the court may order the offender to go through a drug treatment program as a condition of probation.

6. After getting out of jail (if the court included jail time in the sentence), the person again begins using drugs (because the person is an addict).

7. The person commits more property crimes to pay for drugs, and the cycle continues.

Breaking this cycle has become a significant challenge for policymakers, but they usually rely on two major approaches: focusing on drug treatment and locking up repeat offenders. Both approaches have some major drawbacks.

Focusing on drug treatment

Drug treatment programs are significantly underfunded in most parts of the country. And no single drug treatment plan works for all drugs. For example, treating marijuana addiction is significantly different from treating methamphetamine addiction.

In addition, oversight and evaluation of treatment programs is lax, which means that ineffective court-ordered treatment programs can continue to operate for years, doing little good and draining already-sparse funds. Of course, oversight costs money, and the truth is that it's very difficult to know what makes a good treatment program. Perhaps the most significant challenge to drug treatment, however, is that you can't treat someone who doesn't want to be treated. Frequently, drug users enjoy the partying lifestyle, and they're not willing to commit to overcoming their addictions until they have cycled through the justice system many times.

Politicians who philosophically oppose punishment often adopt a "treatment" mantra without committing resources to identifying good programs, evaluating existing programs, or developing strategies for treating people who are unwilling to be treated. Fortunately, some states are committing resources to identifying effective treatment programs, and, as the science of addiction develops, you're likely to see much improvement in the coming years.

Locking up offenders

A movement to put property criminals in prison when they repeatedly commit crimes has swept across the country. But putting a person in prison costs a lot of money. According to a study by the U.S. Bureau of Justice Statistics, the cost of housing an inmate in a state prison in 2001 averaged $22,650 a year, or

$62 a day. This amount doesn't include the societal loss of a person who isn't being productive in a job or paying taxes (assuming the person can be effectively treated for drug addiction and can hold a steady job).

Also, criminals serving time in prison are surrounded by a criminal culture that may teach them how to be more effective criminals in the future. This fact places them at high risk for *recidivism* — being sent back to prison after they're released.

One reason why some policymakers push to lock property criminals up is to make sure they can't commit more crimes while they serve their sentences. (For a discussion of the different theories of incarceration, see Chapter 21.) However, studies have shown that the dollar cost to society of reoffending property criminals is much less than the cost of reoffending violent criminals. In fact, some people argue that locking up property criminals costs more than what society saves by preventing their future crimes.

The treatment versus prison debate is one of the most significant public safety policy debates in every state. Most states settle on some combination of the two when dealing with property criminals.

Making a career choice

When your second-grade teacher asked you what you wanted to be when you grew up, I bet you didn't say, "I want to be a professional burglar." As a matter of fact, very few people who commit crimes end up as career criminals.

Property criminals are typically juveniles or people in their 20s who don't really view themselves as criminals. They may occasionally shoplift, forge a check, or *tag* a fence (in other words, spray paint graffiti), but generally they get along in society without causing serious harm. As they get older and punishment grows more severe for each subsequent offense, most low-level property offenders set aside their antisocial ways (often with the help of drug treatment) and conform to the law.

However, a very small subset of people continues committing crimes throughout their entire lives. I've seen criminals with more than 60 arrests — men in their fifties who don't know any other way to live. When they're hungry and don't have money, they shoplift food. They think nothing of burglarizing a house when they want something they can't afford. Often, these offenders have serious drug or alcohol problems, as well.

Beyond these low-level career criminals is an extremely small group of professional criminals, who are glorified in movies such as *To Catch a Thief* and

The Thomas Crown Affair. These professional burglars may develop special skills for identifying good targets, entering buildings, and selling stolen goods, but rarely do they look like Cary Grant or end up with Grace Kelly.

Being drawn to bright and shiny objects

In today's commercialized society, where advertisements constantly badger people to buy the newest toy or gadget, the temptation to have these shiny, new objects becomes too great for many people. They may not be able to afford the most decked-out iPods or the latest fashionable purses, but they want them so badly that they succumb to their impulsive feelings and steal them. These offenders don't typically view themselves as criminals, and they rationalize their conduct to themselves in a variety of ways. For example, a shoplifter may think stealing jewelry from a particular store is okay because the store makes a lot of money; plus, she has paid for many other items there. This kind of thievery may continue until these offenders are caught, but then they typically reform their ways and stay out of the criminal justice system in the future.

Battling kleptomania

A few people suffer from a mental disorder, known as *kleptomania,* which means they can't control the temptation to steal. They get great satisfaction and pleasure from the act of stealing, regardless of what they steal. This disorder explains why some very wealthy people get caught shoplifting. Being caught or even doing jail time doesn't dissuade people with kleptomania from stealing again, so treatment by a mental health professional is the only real solution.

Chapter 7

Dressing Sharp and Stealing Big: White-Collar Crimes

*W*hat does a person's shirt color have to do with crime? In the 1930s, highly regarded criminologist Edwin Sutherland coined the term *white-collar crime* to refer to crime committed by someone of "respectability and high social status in the course of his occupation." (Of course, *blue-collar* is a shorthand way of referring to people whose jobs involve physical labor.)

Criminologists devote significant effort to studying white-collar crime because doing so highlights the distinction in the criminal justice system between the haves and the have-nots. In this chapter, I explain what white-collar crime is, touch on the challenges of investigating and prosecuting this type of crime, and explore some of the controversy surrounding the punishment phase of white-collar trials.

Identifying Types of White-Collar Crime

White-collar crime has changed somewhat since the 1930s. And while criminologists and others debated a precise definition, the National White Collar Crime Center (NW3C) — a nonprofit corporation that Congress set up to help police departments investigate such crimes — came up with a pretty good one. According to the NW3C, white-collar crimes are

> *Illegal or unethical acts that violate fiduciary responsibility or public trust for personal or organizational gain*

This definition is broad, but it basically means that people in business or government who violate a trust for their own gain or for their business's gain are white-collar criminals.

How much white-collar crime is committed? Because the types of white-collar crime are so varied, I can't quote any good statistics to help you gauge how widespread the problem is. But because white-collar crime frequently results in the loss of millions of dollars, you need only a few cases to see that white-collar crime is a big problem. And you need only to scan the news to see frequent examples of misconduct by corporations, politicians, and wealthy people in society. In the sections that follow, I discuss some of the more common examples of white-collar crime.

Stealing from the boss: Embezzlement

In a nutshell, *embezzlement* is the act of stealing from your employer. Some people may debate whether embezzlement can really be considered a white-collar crime because it occurs so widely across the socioeconomic spectrum. Most commonly, embezzlement occurs when retail employees steal cash or merchandise. The U.S. Chamber of Commerce estimates that 75 percent of all employees have stolen from an employer at least once. And the National Retail Federation estimates that, in 2006, the amount of employee theft exceeded $19 billion — just among retail businesses!

But classic embezzlement goes far beyond just dipping into the till. Employees with special access to money, and in a position of trust, can systematically steal from their employers for years without being caught. For instance, a city finance director may divert a small amount of money every week into an innocuous-looking account, thus escaping the auditor's notice. But after five years, that director has embezzled over $1 million! Examples like this one are common in both the government and the private sector. In private companies, however, employers often don't report these crimes to police because they fear that disclosure may spook clients or customers and be a source of embarrassment.

Why do people violate the trust of their employers in this way? Sometimes they steal simply because they want to buy more stuff than they can afford with their legitimate salaries. But frequently, embezzlement follows this pattern:

- ✔ An employee has a significant financial problem.

- ✔ Intending to pay the money back, the employee takes the money as a loan.

- ✔ The loan quickly grows too big, and the embezzler can't repay it.

The legalization of gambling over the last 30 years — and the gambling addictions that have resulted — may have led to an increase in embezzlements. Also, as advertisers put greater pressure on people to have the latest and greatest products, more people succumb to this pressure, become shopaholics, run up their credit card debts, and then steal from their employers to bail themselves out.

In the 20th century, some criminologists identified middle-aged men as the most likely embezzlers. But today, in the 21st century, a significant number of embezzlement cases reported to the police involve middle-aged women. Perhaps this change reflects the greater role that women play in the modern workforce.

Evading taxes

You just can't avoid taxes — at least not lawfully. Everyone in the United States pays income taxes, sales taxes, estate taxes, employment taxes, tobacco taxes, alcohol taxes . . . and the list goes on. All levels of government collect taxes: local, state, and federal. So the opportunity for individuals and corporations to cheat on taxes is great.

In 2007, the Internal Revenue Service (IRS) found 37,566,699 federal tax violations and issued over $29 billion in civil penalties. But that same year, the IRS initiated only 4,211 criminal investigations, mainly because the vast majority of tax-cheating violations are handled through civil fines and not through criminal investigations. Why? Well, for one, the IRS has only 2,800 special agents who at the most could only investigate a fraction of all those violations in a year. (Tax investigations are usually very complex.) Also, criminal investigations aren't a cost-effective way to collect money. Finding an error in a tax form and simply issuing a fine is much easier than having a special agent try to prove beyond a reasonable doubt that a person *intentionally* cheated on her taxes. (For a more complete discussion of the difference between the civil justice system and the criminal justice system, see Chapter 2.)

Intentionally evading or defeating a tax is a federal felony. So, technically, each time a waiter purposely chooses not to report her tips as income, she's committing a federal felony. But the IRS usually saves criminal investigation and prosecution for the most egregious acts — the ones involving large dollar figures or blatant and repeated flaunting of the law.

If there was no possibility of a serious sanction, including prison time, many people would just ignore their tax obligations. The occasional high-profile prosecution serves as a deterrent, persuading people to pay their taxes rather than risk being arrested.

Selling phony investments: Securities fraud

In a capitalist system, the financial investment business provides a great opportunity for criminal exploitation, namely in the form of *securities fraud,* which, in its most simplistic sense, is the act of lying to get someone to make an investment. The list of potential fraud scams is limitless. However, some scams are more common than others. Selling stock in a phony company, for example, is one form of securities fraud.

I once investigated a man who bilked numerous investors by telling them he had created a sports nutrition bar. Investors gave him a total of over $1 million, which he used to travel around the country, visiting professional athletic events as part of a "marketing tour." He never manufactured any sports bars, and, as a result, he eventually went to prison.

Lying about the value of a business can also constitute securities fraud if the guilty party does so to induce people to invest in that business. At the individual level, this crime can involve a restaurant entrepreneur who lies to investors by telling them that her new chef is a highly regarded graduate of the Cordon Bleu school in France when he's never even been to France. On a larger scale, a corporation may manipulate the market by overstating earnings, which, in turn, may lead investors to believe the company is worth more than it really is.

Insider trading is another form of securities fraud. People with *inside* information about a company (stuff the public doesn't know about) aren't allowed to benefit from that information before the rest of the public can do so.

Most famously, Martha Stewart went to prison after she sold $230,000 worth of ImClone stock after ImClone executives leaked secret inside information to a few people that one of its experimental drugs was disapproved by the Food and Drug Administration. Stewart's conviction stemmed from obstructing justice and lying about her stock sale. The ImClone founder was convicted of securities fraud.

The U.S. Securities and Exchange Commission (SEC) investigates significant corporate securities fraud and has the ability to allege civil violations and settle them with monetary penalties and other civil sanctions. Often these settlements include no admission of wrongdoing by the offender. For example, the former CEO of United Health Group, Inc., was accused of backdating documents that set stock option dates to coincide with low prices. Although he didn't admit wrongdoing, he paid a $7 million penalty and agreed not to serve as a corporate officer or director for ten years.

The enforcement division of the SEC has about 1,200 employees and brought 671 enforcement actions in 2008. Given the hundreds of thousands of corporations that exist in the United States, you can see that corporate misconduct and securities violations have relatively little government oversight compared to other crimes, although it's worth noting that individual states often have their own agencies to investigate local securities fraud.

Dumping waste and endangering employees: Environmental crime

Almost every manufacturer creates some form of waste, and the temptation is great to cut corners and costs by illegally disposing of it. At the local level, thousands of different businesses must dispose of toxic chemicals.

For example, auto body shops have large amounts of chemical waste that are quite expensive to dispose of properly. And fish-processing plants produce millions of gallons of water containing fish guts when they clean their equipment; if these plants pump this water back into estuaries without filtering it, it can create algae blooms, deplete oxygen, and kill the streams' inhabitants.

The regulation of toxic materials and waste is extremely complex. At the federal level, the Environmental Protection Agency (EPA), created by Richard Nixon in 1970, has the authority to punish polluters. Most states have similar agencies to help protect the environment. At both the federal and state levels, most enforcement action takes place with civil fines and *injunctions* (court orders demanding that the illegal activity be stopped).

In 2008, the EPA Criminal Investigations Division opened 319 new cases. The EPA doesn't report the number of convictions in a given year, but it did report that, for all convictions for federal environmental crimes in 2008, the total number of years in prison was 57. This number seems extremely low for the entire United States, but keep in mind that EPA special agents sometimes participate in task forces with local and state law enforcement to try to maximize their resources. As a result, prosecutions for environmental crimes may occur in state courts rather than federal courts. Even so, in many states, the criminal enforcement of environmental laws lags far behind the enforcement of other crimes.

Other environmental misconduct occurs when companies fail to take precautions to protect employees from unsafe conditions, including exposure to chemicals. Companies may choose not to take these safety precautions because taking them can be expensive and can hurt the bottom line. Safety violations aren't usually treated as crimes but, instead, are regulated by a federal agency known as the Occupational Safety and Health Administration (OSHA) and by similar state agencies. OSHA typically issues fines and injunctions for safety violations and doesn't pursue criminal punishment.

For example, if an employee of a commercial landscaper believes that he's being overexposed to pesticides, he can make a complaint to his state OSHA, which may respond with an inspection or investigation. Unfortunately, however, employees aren't always aware of the dangers they face on the job, so the misconduct goes unreported. For example, a car painter may use an old, ineffective respirator from his employer. That employee may never realize that his health is being put at risk to save his company a little bit of money.

Cheating business and service clients

The part of the economy that involves business services for clients is so large that the fact that it's an area ripe for exploitation by white-collar criminals is no surprise. For example, doctors and dentists may systematically overcharge patients or bilk Medicaid, Medicare, or other insurance providers to make some extra money for themselves.

I've seen professional tax preparers take advantage of immigrant communities by creating phony tax credits and then having the money from the tax returns deposited with the preparer. I also know of a lawyer who once billed clients for more than 24 hours in a single day. (Yes, a dishonest lawyer — shocking!)

But despite being widespread, client fraud is difficult to prosecute. For one thing, clients often don't know they're being cheated. And if they do catch the fraud and confront the perpetrator, they may get their money back and chalk the whole thing up to a mistake, not knowing about all the other people who were also cheated.

When people do report such fraud, police are often hesitant to get involved. Proving beyond a reasonable doubt that a client was intentionally cheated — and not just the victim of a mistake — is very difficult. Police and prosecutors often explain why they refuse to begin such investigations by saying, "It's a civil dispute."

Cheating consumers: False advertising and price fixing

In the competitive business world, people sometimes resort to false advertising or other deceptive practices that defraud thousands of consumers to make a quick buck.

For example, you may have seen TV ads depicting a character known as "Smilin' Bob." Bob's constant smile implied that he had achieved some level of male enhancement by taking a supplement known as Enzyte, which, in fact, didn't provide any male enhancement. In 2008, federal prosecutors in Cincinnati, Ohio, convicted corporate officials from Berkeley Premium

Nutraceuticals, the company that produced and advertised Enzyte, of mail fraud and money laundering. The founder of the company was sentenced to 25 years in prison, and the company was ordered to forfeit $500 million.

The government frequently deals with false advertising matters through civil suits under a set of laws known as the *Unfair Trade Practice Act.* But Smilin' Bob had such a ubiquitous presence on TV that federal prosecutors made Berkeley Premium Nutraceuticals a criminal case — and a high-profile example.

Another criminal corporate practice is *price fixing,* which occurs when different corporations selling a product secretly agree to sell the product for an inflated price. Federal and state governments often deal with price fixing through civil antitrust lawsuits. But sometimes corporations are prosecuted criminally. Antitrust laws are meant to keep a corporation or a group of corporations from having a monopoly over a certain product.

In 2008, for example, the U.S. Department of Justice convicted Sharp Corp., LG Display Company, and some other businesses of conspiring to fix the prices of LCD panels. These companies secretly agreed among themselves to keep prices artificially high on LCD televisions and other electronic products, cheating consumers in the process. LG Display Company had to pay a criminal fine of $400 million, and Sharp Corp. had to pay $120 million. In total, this case produced the second-largest criminal antitrust fine ever obtained by the U.S. Department of Justice. A vice president of LG was also sentenced to seven months in jail.

Mixing politics and crime

A governor accused of selling a senate seat. A mayor accused of accepting bribes in exchange for steering a city's business to friends. The headlines these days are full of allegations of government corruption. And high-profile elected officials aren't the only ones committing crime. Even lower-level government employees get wrapped up in criminal activity.

Here's just one recent example: The attorney general of Florida convicted corporate officials from Stone Cold Chemicals, Inc., a cleaning supply business, of criminal racketeering (a law originally designed to attack organized crime) for developing a business plan that targeted low-level government employees and encouraged them to purchase the company's cleaning products. In exchange for buying the cleaning products at inflated prices, the low-level government employees received pro-sports merchandise and restaurant gift certificates. The scam reached across the nation and resulted in charges of bribe receiving against jailers, janitors, transportation workers, and other low-level government employees.

Committing white-collar crime: Why do it?

Criminologists have come up with several theories for why respectable businesspeople resort to crime. As I mention in this chapter, some people get themselves in personal financial binds and "borrow" from their employers until their borrowing reaches such levels that they can never repay their debts. Compulsive gamblers and shoppers, as well as people with overly expensive lifestyles, may fit this category.

A second theory holds that the competitive nature of corporate life itself turns some people into criminals. The corporate need to maximize profits and the intense pressure to move up the company ladder can lead some employees to cut corners or otherwise commit crimes. Doing so allows the perpetrators to receive social rewards, including bonuses and promotions. Ironically, negative conduct is rewarded.

A third theory holds that white-collar criminals are just like street criminals, only in a different environment. Some criminologists believe that what drives many criminals is laziness combined with a desire for finer things. White-collar criminals want to achieve greater social status and higher salaries from business success, but they don't want to work hard for these results. So they follow the easy road and cheat.

I think each of these theories — or a combination of them — provides a legitimate explanation for why otherwise respectable people turn into white-collar criminals.

Ideally, a government official accused of crime is treated like any other citizen and is investigated by the local police. Frequently, however, the potential impact of media and politics means that high-profile cases receive different treatment.

For example, a city police department probably wouldn't investigate the city's mayor (because she exercises authority over the department budget and could retaliate, among other reasons). So the chief of police would ask an outside law enforcement agency from another county, from the state government, or even from the Federal Bureau of Investigation (FBI) to conduct the investigation. And with intense media scrutiny, investigators must be sure to track down every lead, no matter how improbable, because some reporter is likely waiting to criticize the investigation when it's complete.

The Challenges of Investigating White-Collar Crime

The vast majority of police are equipped to deal with traditional crime, such as violent acts and property crime. They respond to 9-1-1 calls and enforce traffic laws. But police often lack the primary tools that are necessary to tackle white-collar crime — time and expertise.

Measuring the costs (in time and money)

White-collar crime is expensive to investigate. Consider this example: Investigating a robbery may involve interviewing a few witnesses and writing a police report, nothing too time-consuming. On the other hand, investigating even a simple embezzlement from a small business can involve a lot more work and, thus, a lot more time. Like with a robbery, the detective must interview the business's owner and all witnesses, of course. But he must also obtain copies of all relevant financial records and do a thorough analysis of those records. This process is slow, and, in law enforcement, time is money.

A police chief has only a finite number of detectives to handle all significant cases, so he's necessarily hesitant to devote one detective to a long-term financial case. Unfortunately, what often happens is that the detective simply declines to take the case, using the most common cop-out in law enforcement: "It sounds like a civil matter." Police use this phrase when the victim may have a chance at a remedy through a civil lawsuit and when the case seems too time-consuming and difficult to investigate and prosecute in a criminal court.

Facing a dearth of financial investigators

Probably the greatest impediment to attacking white-collar crime is the lack of cops qualified to conduct financial investigations. If an officer doesn't know how to manage a spreadsheet or doesn't know how to put basic accounting principles to use, trying to figure out a financial crime is next to impossible. Without any financial experience, an officer could spend six months staring at a box of financial records and never prove the case.

Why saying "It's a civil matter" isn't necessarily a cop-out

Although almost every crime could also be the basis for a civil suit — a victim of a criminal assault can also choose to sue the perpetrator, for example — sometimes a cop's decision to decline to investigate a matter as a crime because "it's a civil matter" makes sense. What the cop's really doing, although he may not know it, is conducting a cost/benefit analysis — weighing the likely success of an investigation along with the likely punishment to be achieved against the hours and expenses of conducting the investigation. Police agencies conduct this type of analysis all the time.

For this reason, as I explain in Chapter 17, many police departments greatly value IRS special agents. The special agents are trained in conducting financial investigations, which are often essential in proving white-collar crimes. However, the IRS has only 2,800 special agents for the whole United States, and their primary mission is tax enforcement.

The FBI has made white-collar crime its seventh priority (see Chapter 17 for the FBI's other priorities) and devotes considerable resources to the fight, but the bureau can take on only the most significant cases. Some large police departments or state agencies may have a couple of trained financial detectives, and a few other courageous detectives take on financial cases and try to figure them out as they go, despite not having any financial expertise. But all too often, law enforcement agencies and departments just can't investigate mid- to low-level white-collar crimes because they lack human resources.

Prosecuting and Punishing White-Collar Crime

If investigating white-collar crimes is tough, prosecuting the offenders is no walk in the park, either. Criminal cases involving white-collar crimes are often more complicated, more expensive, and more difficult to win than criminal cases involving violent crimes. In this section, I explain why. I also discuss why white-collar convictions often carry lighter sentences than other types of crime.

Equating good suits with good verdicts

Most criminal defendants can't afford to hire their own lawyers, so they receive court-appointed public defenders. I've known some very good public defenders, but, generally, you get what you pay for.

White-collar defendants, on the other hand, can usually afford to hire expensive lawyers with their own money. These defendants hire not only good lawyers but also private investigators and experts to testify on their behalf. So what may start out as a relatively simple prosecution can quickly turn into a battle against a large (and talented) defense team.

If a corporation or multiple defendants are involved, the complexity of the trial can grow quickly. For example, I once investigated a corporation for tax fraud and theft, among other crimes. The corporation quickly hired the state's best criminal defense lawyers to represent six different corporate employees, each of whom immediately asserted his Fifth Amendment right against self-incrimination. Although ultimately I could prove misconduct by the corporation itself, I couldn't hold any individual employees accountable because none of them would talk.

Testing the limits of corporate liability

Although individuals commit crimes, corporations can often be prosecuted in criminal cases. A corporation is a *legal fiction* — something created by law — but, in most jurisdictions, it can be prosecuted as a criminal defendant.

For a corporation to be held liable for a criminal action, a prosecutor usually has to prove criminal conduct by a corporate officer or a high-level manager. Take a case of toxic waste dumping. A dump site may have a barrel with "Acme, Inc." written on it, but unless the police can prove that a manager at Acme, Inc., ordered the waste dumping — in other words, that he *intended* to commit the crime — proving corporate criminal liability (at least in state court) can be difficult. (For a more thorough discussion of the need to prove intent in a criminal case, see Chapter 2.)

Proving a criminal case against a corporation can be challenging and expensive. For this reason, most corporate misconduct is regulated by civil or administrative law rather than criminal law.

Regulating businesses

Because of the difficulty of proving criminal cases against businesses or corporations, governments tend to rely on other means of regulation. For example, to regulate Wall Street and the securities business, the government has the Securities and Exchange Commission (SEC). The SEC doesn't have *criminal authority* — which means it can't arrest someone for a crime — but it can investigate and file civil suits against corporations for misconduct.

As you may know, in a criminal case, a prosecutor must prove *beyond a reasonable doubt* that the defendant committed the crime; on the other hand, in a civil suit, the plaintiff must only prove by a *preponderance of the evidence* (in other words, that it's more likely than not) that the defendant engaged in misconduct. Because the SEC files only civil suits, the SEC can more easily prove misconduct by corporations in civil suits and force settlements that bring financial punishment along with corrective action.

Corporate interests are powerful, however. Big businesses lobby hard to protect their interests, sometimes by controlling or reducing the budgets and resources of the very agencies that have regulatory authority.

Making punishments fit the crimes

In 2006, former Enron CEO Jeffrey Skilling was convicted of securities fraud and conspiracy, among other charges, and was sentenced to over 24 years in prison. (You didn't think I could talk about white-collar crime without mentioning Enron, did you?) For many people in the corporate world, this case was a signal event, marking a change in historic sentencing practices for white-collar criminals.

Previously, most people probably believed that the more common treatment of white-collar criminals resembled what Martha Stewart received for her convictions in 2004: five months in a federal "country club" and five months of home detention.

This common viewpoint is important because one significant reason why society imprisons criminals is to deter other people from committing similar crimes. (For a more detailed discussion of theories of punishment, see Chapter 21.) If the risk of serious punishment isn't real, people may be more likely to run the risk of conviction, especially when the payoff is millions of dollars in profit.

But there are legitimate reasons why white-collar criminals have received relatively light sentences in the past. Perhaps most importantly, such cases are often very difficult to prove. Sometimes law enforcement agencies make plea agreements to resolve cases instead of committing massive resources to lengthy and costly trials that may have uncertain outcomes. In addition, white-collar crimes often involve significant financial harm to victims, so prosecutors may be willing to negotiate away jail time in exchange for making the defendant pay money back to victims.

Sometimes the prosecutor doesn't agree to a short jail sentence, but the judge imposes the sentence on her own. One significant theory of punishment holds that jail or prison should be reserved only for people too dangerous to remain in society. The argument goes that, because white-collar criminals usually commit financial crimes, society shouldn't spend a lot of money incarcerating them. Instead, jails should house people who are violent risks to society. Judges who subscribe to this theory may also believe that the damage to the professional reputation of a white-collar criminal is sufficient punishment in itself, without sentencing the criminal to a lengthy prison sentence.

Chapter 8

A Group Effort: Organized Crime and Gangs

In This Chapter

▶ Defining organized crime

▶ Getting to know the Italian mob and other ethnic-based organizations

▶ Realizing what organized crime groups do

▶ Battling against organized crime

▶ Considering where criminal gangs fit in

Many people are fascinated by pop-culture depictions of organized crime (hence the popularity of films like *The Godfather* and TV shows like *The Sopranos*). But few really understand what organized crime is and how it truly impacts the world today. In this chapter, I discuss the various types of organized crime — including the mafia, street gangs, motorcycle gangs, and prison gangs — and I show you what they do. I also explain law enforcement's efforts to combat this significant challenge.

Grasping the Basics of Organized Crime

Organized crime doesn't refer to a group of criminal neat freaks who are so fastidious they segregate their socks by color. (In fact, organized crime figures are often very messy.) The phrase *organized crime* refers to groups of people who conspire together, generally, to make a business out of crime (although the attainment of power and companionship also plays a role).

Organized crime groups are usually *hierarchical* — in other words, they have leaders as well as low-level operatives — which means that when you arrest one member of the organization, the organization can replace that person and continue its "business" of crime. This structure is what makes organized crime so difficult to defeat.

Another important feature of organized crime groups is how they resolve conflict. Many groups use violence or the threat of violence as their primary mechanism for resolving disputes. Think about it: If two lawful businesses have a dispute, one can sue the other in court. But if both businesses are illegal, they can't call attention to themselves with a legal battle.

Note: In defining organized crime, some criminologists require a *formalized* hierarchical structure with leaders, lieutenants, and soldiers. I believe this requirement is too limiting, restricting the label "organized crime" to the mafia model and excluding significant criminal businesses that may use independent contractors or looser affiliations to commit crime.

Obsessing over the Italian Mafia

When you first read the title of this chapter, I bet you thought of some big Italian guys in suits — thanks to Hollywood's obsession with the mafia. From Godfather Vito Corleone to Tony Soprano to "Fat Tony" from *The Simpsons,* the predominant media image of organized crime is the Italian Mafia.

In this section, I explore the birth of the original Mafia and the extent of its U.S. operations today.

Tracing the growth and decline of the Sicilian mob

In the 21st century, following decades of consistent law enforcement attention, the Mafia is in decline. Frankly, it's a very small component of the overall organized crime problem in the United States today. Nonetheless, it continues to play a role in a few cities in the Northeast, Midwest, and South.

Historically, Italy was frequently the subject of invasions by outsiders. Secret societies formed among Italians to defend families and communities against the outsiders. These societies eventually became known as the *Mafia.* They turned into major organized crime entities in the early 20th century. Around the same time, a massive number of Italians, including *mafiosa,* immigrated to the United States. For more on the history of the mafia, you may want to check out *Conspiracy Theories and Secret Societies For Dummies* by Christopher Hodapp and Alice Von Kannon (Wiley).

At least four separate crime organizations with origins in Italy continue to be major criminal forces in Italy today. However, the Sicilian Mafia is the primary group that expanded into the United States, where it's known as *La Cosa Nostra* (which translates "our thing").

La Cosa Nostra is organized in the United States by family groups. In the 1940s, Charles "Lucky" Luciano (head of a major crime family in New York) helped end feuding between seven different families and organized them under a ruling body called the *Commission,* which ran La Cosa Nostra activities in the United States. At the Commission's height, these activities included the following:

- ✔ Narcotics trafficking

- ✔ Gambling

- ✔ Cigarette smuggling

- ✔ Extortion

- ✔ Infiltration of legitimate businesses

- ✔ Violence to enforce each of these money-making operations

The FBI estimates that roughly 3,000 members of La Cosa Nostra still live and work in the United States today, predominantly in New Jersey, New York, Chicago, Detroit, New England, and eastern Pennsylvania.

La Cosa Nostra continues to be heavily involved in narcotics trafficking, extortion, and other money-making operations. However, its influence is decreasing. Most of the old-school family leaders have been put in prison or are now dead. Younger members don't follow the strict *code of silence* that once forbade members from informing on others. Furthermore, the ethnic makeup of neighborhoods previously dominated by the Mafia has changed so that other ethnic organized crime groups exert more influence today.

Recognizing the Mafia's impact on public policy

The rise of La Cosa Nostra led to the development of some significant crime-fighting tools in the United States, such as the RICO laws. (RICO stands for *Racketeer Influenced and Corrupt Organizations.*) These laws allow law enforcement to target an entire organization by making its members punishable for offenses committed to further the organization's criminal activity.

For example, one guy is a lookout for street-corner drug deals for an organization. Another guy commits several assaults to collect drug debts for the same organization. A third guy uses some of these illegal proceeds to buy stolen cars and then sells the parts overseas. All three men can be prosecuted for the crime of *racketeering* because their crimes are furthering the criminal interests of the organization. The crime of racketeering can carry a much stiffer sentence than the simple crimes of aiding in the sale of drugs, assault, money laundering, or auto theft.

Fighting a narrow view of organized crime

The popular image of the mafia as *the* organized crime threat in the United States has had a negative impact on law enforcement's ability to attack other types of organized crime. As the former head of my state government's organized crime unit, I repeatedly heard declarations like, "We don't have organized crime in our state." What these people (including public leaders) were actually saying was that they didn't have the mafia, which was true.

But, like every other state, my state *does* have major drug traffickers, fraud rings, gangs, illegal gambling, tobacco smuggling, extortion, and kidnapping — all perpetrated by non-Italian groups of organized criminals.

Congress passed the first RICO law in 1970, and many states enacted their own RICO laws thereafter. The goal was to respond aggressively to the challenges posed by the Mafia. Before these laws were passed, when an organized crime figure was arrested, another person simply took his place, and the organization continued on without missing a beat. Now, with much greater RICO sentences, the entire infrastructure of an organization can be locked up, which leaves no one to recruit replacements. I must note, however, that many in law enforcement are hesitant to pursue RICO investigations because the laws are complicated, and a good investigation can take a year or more.

Identifying Other Ethnic-Based Organized Crime Groups

Many organized crime groups in the United States are organized along ethnic or racial lines for reasons of community, trust, and security. For example, infiltrating a Vietnamese gang can be almost impossible for law enforcement because few police speak Vietnamese and because members of the Vietnamese community tend to know everyone in their neighborhood.

Here are some of the ethnic organized crime groups that are most common in the United States:

- ✔ **Russian organized crime:** Calling this group *Eurasian organized crime* may be more accurate because it includes crime groups from Ukraine, Armenia, and other parts of the former Soviet Union. These groups are a dominant criminal presence in their home countries and, because of the Internet and the internationalization of commerce, now play a significant role in the United States. For example, these groups regularly use U.S. financial institutions to launder criminal proceeds from their home countries.

Russian organized crime is present on U.S. soil, but it's not very involved in traditional organized crime, such as drugs and gambling. Instead, it's involved in a broader array of crimes, such as credit card fraud, stock scams, auto theft, and healthcare fraud. Extortion among fellow Eurasians also occurs.

✔ **Chinese Triad groups:** These secret societies of Chinese had a significant presence in Hong Kong in the 1960s and 1970s. They're still active in China and a few major international cities, including San Francisco, Los Angeles, and New York in the United States. They're involved in human smuggling, the manufacture and sale of counterfeit goods, software piracy, narcotics trafficking, extortion, and tobacco smuggling.

✔ **Chinese Tongs:** These groups are fraternal organizations of Chinese in the United States, formed by Chinese immigrants after arriving. Some Tongs engage in criminal conduct, such as drug trafficking, prostitution, and illegal gambling, although many are more interested in the social-organization aspect of being a Tong. Tongs involved in crime may use street gangs as enforcers.

✔ **Other Asian organized crime:** This category includes Vietnamese and Korean groups in the United States that often start as street gangs. Such groups are often willing to work with or use criminals from other ethnic groups. (In contrast, Russian organized crime groups and the Italian Mafia are less likely to work with other ethnicities.) These organized crime groups are involved in drugs, extortion, human smuggling, the sale of counterfeit products, and all kinds of fraud. Some groups branch out into legitimate businesses, in part at least, to launder their money.

✔ **Mexican organized crime:** The Mexican Mafia, or *La Eme,* started as a California prison gang in the 1950s and today is one of the largest organized crime operations on the West Coast. A rival organization split off and is known as *La Nuestra Familia* or "our family." Leaders in these organizations are some serious, hardcore criminals. The Mexican Mafia has cultivated street gangs known as *Surenos,* which means "southerners" (these gangs are primarily from southern California). Meanwhile, La Nuestra Familia has built up street gangs known as *Nortenos,* which means "northerners" (not surprisingly, these gangs are mostly from northern California). Surenos and Nortenos engage in battles across the western United States for territory to distribute drugs and engage in other criminal acts. Proceeds then make their way to leadership within the Mexican Mafia or La Nuestra Familia.

Looking at What Organized Crime Groups Do

In this section, I discuss some of the most common organized crime activities for making money. Of course, criminals can be ingenious when it comes to figuring out ways to make money illegally. And leaders of organized crime groups tend to be some of the smartest criminals, so this list isn't comprehensive. But it does give you a good picture of what's going on.

Selling narcotics

There's so much money to be made in drug trafficking that it has been the primary organized crime business for the last 60 years. Because this type of crime is such a significant challenge for law enforcement and has such a profound impact on society, I devote Chapter 9 to a discussion of narcotics and touch only briefly on the subject here.

Selling drugs usually requires the support of an organization. Most illegal drugs are trafficked into the United States from other countries. At a bare minimum, the illegal drug business requires someone in an organization to do the following:

- ✔ Produce the drugs
- ✔ Transport the drugs
- ✔ Sell the drugs
- ✔ Move the money back to the organization's leaders

In other words, unless you're stealing Mom's prescription pills from the medicine cabinet and selling them to your friends (a growing problem in the United States, by the way), you probably require the help of a much larger organization to be part of the narcotics trade.

Marketing counterfeit and pirated products

In the last 20 years, counterfeit and pirated products have become huge business drivers for organized crime. But before I describe the nuts and bolts of this business, I need to explain what counterfeit and pirated products are:

- ✔ **Counterfeit goods:** Counterfeit goods are imitation products that infringe on someone's rights, such as patent or trademark rights. For example, a purse that bears the Gucci symbol but sells for $29.99 is probably counterfeit. (In case you aren't a purse aficionado, Gucci purses regularly go for $2,000 or more.)
- ✔ **Pirated goods:** Pirated goods are goods that have been illegally copied. The sale of pirated goods violates someone's copyright because the person pirating the goods doesn't have the legal right to make copies. For example, if you photocopied this book and then sold it, I could (and probably would) track you down and have you arrested.

The sale of counterfeit and pirated products is a multi-billion-dollar business, which explains why organized crime groups are involved. Today, almost anything can be counterfeited or pirated, from music and movies to clothing, golf clubs, cigarettes, car parts, and pharmaceuticals. In a very conservative estimate by the international Organization for Economic Co-operation and Development, the annual cost of counterfeit goods is $176 billion or 2 percent of the world economy.

More sophisticated criminal organizations counterfeit products to try to fool the consumer. Try shopping for golf clubs on e-Bay, for example. Do you know which clubs are the real deal? More dangerous than knock-off golf clubs are the counterfeit after-market car parts and pharmaceuticals that criminal organizations commonly sell to unsuspecting consumers. For example, counterfeit brake pads probably aren't made to the same standard as those made by the true manufacturer. When you jam on your brakes at an intersection, you don't want to discover that you bought a counterfeit, defective product.

In some parts of the United States, such as California, counterfeit cigarettes are very common. You may think you're buying Marlboros with North Carolinian tobacco, but you're really smoking tobacco grown in Southeast Asia. Making and marketing counterfeit cigarettes is a big business for organized crime groups because it allows them to avoid the federal and state tobacco taxes, which can add up to millions in profit from just one truckload.

Southeast Asia and China produce the vast majority of counterfeit and pirated products. The Chinese government has tacitly acquiesced in the activity because counterfeiting and piracy bring a huge influx of money to the country.

International organized crime groups may move counterfeit and pirated goods via the same international transportation routes they use to traffic drugs, or they may simply import goods via container ships by mislabeling ship manifests. (See Chapter 9 for more on the international drug trade.) For example, a container may be listed as possessing toys, but it's really filled with counterfeit DVDs.

After the goods arrive in the United States, distributors move the goods to flea market sellers, stores that mix counterfeit goods in with legitimate goods, and even normally honest citizens who hold house parties where they sell counterfeit goods.

Counterfeiting and piracy are attractive to organized crime groups not only because of their significant profit potential but also because the punishments for such crimes aren't great. For example, if you make counterfeit Calloway golf clubs in China, chances are the Chinese government won't do anything to you. Even in the United States, the punishment for selling $1 million of pirated DVDs is much less than it is for selling drugs. Plus, very few police have the time to work piracy or counterfeit cases, so the chances of getting caught aren't great.

Committing fraud

With the dramatic technological advances in recent years, *fraud* (the process of tricking people out of what's rightfully theirs) has become a relatively easy and cost-effective way to commit crime. I discuss fraud crimes in detail in Chapter 6. Here, I briefly touch on how organized crime groups engage in fraud.

Of course, not all fraud today is technologically based. Some organized crime groups still count on the old-fashioned kind of fraud to make a quick buck. For example, a motorcycle gang member reports his motorcycle stolen. He gets his insurance money, rebuilds his bike with a few new parts, and registers it as a newly built vehicle. Insurance fraud like this example is a constant challenge, which is why insurance companies have their own fraud investigators.

On the other hand, some organized crime groups have switched to a more sophisticated type of fraud. For example, in 1991, 13 members of a Russian organized crime group were arrested in California after stealing more than $1 billion through a false medical billing scheme. The ringleader was sentenced to 21 years in prison and had to pay back $41 million in restitution to the victims.

Internet fraud is becoming more and more common among organized crime groups because it's such an easy way to make money. A massive e-mail campaign can almost instantaneously solicit millions of people to be victimized. For a more detailed discussion of Internet fraud, see Chapter 6.

Credit card fraud has become a big business for organized crime groups, too. They exploit the fact that stores and banks would rather have fast credit transactions than confirm that fraudsters are who they say they are. Basically, organized crime groups commit credit fraud by stealing your credit information and then using it for their own purposes. Although the possible ways to commit credit fraud are innumerable, a real-life example may help explain how it can work.

I know of a criminal organization that worked a clever credit fraud operation: The organization included a person who worked in a hotel in Las Vegas. When a guest checked in to the hotel, that person swiped the guest's credit card in his own personal credit card reader as well as the hotel's reader. After he stole the guest's credit card number, he sent it to another member of the organization in another state. That person attached the number to a blank credit card and then quickly maxed out the card by buying Home Depot gift cards at a grocery store. A third person used the gift cards to purchase expensive items at Home Depot in the self-checkout line. A fourth person then returned the items to Home Depot for cash.

Loan sharking

Loan sharking, in a nutshell, is the act of illegally loaning money at extremely high interest rates. In some states, weak usury laws allow legitimate businesses to lawfully make such loans. These legitimate businesses are often known as "check-cashing" businesses. Although they cash your check for a fee, they make most of their money by charging you high interest in exchange for loaning you money, perhaps in advance of your paycheck or with your car as collateral.

In states where such practices are illegal, criminals known as *loan sharks* or *shylocks,* who work for organized crime groups, often step in and bankroll desperate people who are looking for cash. (The term *shylock* is a reference to one of the main characters in Shakespeare's *The Merchant of Venice.*) The interest rate that loan sharks charge can range from 5 percent a week to 20 percent or more, depending on the client. As practiced by the Mafia, if the people who borrow the money can't pay back the money, they must at least pay the interest . . . or else.

Old-fashioned loan sharking still exists today, particularly in bad neighborhoods where desperate people and drug addicts are willing to take on significant risks for immediate cash.

Extorting money

In essence, *extortion* is the process of getting something (usually money) from someone by using violence or threats. Organized crime groups have historically relied on the ol' shakedown tactic to extort money from others (and to avoid getting caught in the process). Essentially, this tactic involves threatening violence unless a person pays money.

Here are a few examples of common extortion tactics that organized crime groups still use today:

- A gang tells a store owner she needs to pay "protection money" to the gang to make sure nothing bad happens to her store.

- An organization sets up a politician in a compromising situation and then extorts political favors in exchange for not revealing the information.

- A Mexican citizen pays a *coyote* (a human smuggler) to smuggle her into the United States. After she arrives, the coyote holds her hostage until the Mexican citizen's family pays more money for her to be released.

Extortion is a difficult crime to prove because the victim is usually vulnerable and unwilling to report the crime out of fear of what the organized crime group may do in retaliation. So the risk of getting caught is low.

Committing violence to support the "business"

The threat of violence runs behind much of organized crime. Because criminals can't sue each other in court, they often settle disputes with violence. Organized crime groups also use violence to eliminate competition and grab market share. They may even use the threat of violence as part of their business plans to make money or collect money (see the preceding section).

For some organizations, such as street gangs, violence is even part of their rite of initiation. In some gangs, for example, a new member must be "jumped" in, which means other gang members join in a group assault on the new member.

Laundering money

Having a lot of money derived from crime is a double-edged sword. On one hand, it's the reason why people get into the business of crime in the first place. But, on the other hand, the existence of a lot of money creates suspicion, which can lead to criminal investigations. For example, when you see a young man who doesn't have a job driving a Mercedes and wearing a lot of bling around his neck, you probably assume he's either a trust-fund kid or a drug dealer.

Plus, everyone in the United States must pay taxes on their income, whether that income is legitimate or not. Failure to pay taxes — not bootlegging — is what landed Al Capone in prison.

To avoid creating suspicion and to avoid being prosecuted for tax crimes, organized crime groups try to *launder* their money — in other words, they try to make their income look legitimate. (A third reason to launder money is to prevent law enforcement from taking the money away through forfeiture, which I discuss in the "Taking back the money: Forfeiture" section later in this chapter.)

Common ways to launder money include the following:

- ✔ **Running legitimate businesses:** Sophisticated organized crime groups may own legitimate businesses that deal mostly in cash, such as car washes, night clubs, and restaurants. Because cash transactions have no records that can be traced, organized crime groups can declare their profits from criminal activities to be income from their legitimate businesses.

- ✔ **Sending money overseas:** Some organized crime groups send money overseas. Some criminals may then bring the money back to the United States in the form of a foreign currency or small amounts of U.S. currency. Others just keep the money in the foreign countries.

As I discuss later in this chapter, law enforcement sometimes tries to defeat organized crime by taking away the profits, but laundering schemes have become so sophisticated that seizing cash is often more a matter of luck than skill.

Fighting Organized Crime

Attacking organized crime is more difficult than dealing with ordinary crime. When you arrest a burglar, you take him off the street and, thus, stop his criminal activity (theoretically, at least). In contrast, when you arrest one person in an organized crime group, you don't stop the criminal activity — the organization recruits another person and continues on without missing a beat. Success in attacking organized crime means not only arresting and convicting individual suspects but also disabling entire criminal organizations so that the criminal activity ends. In this section, I outline a few of the ways law enforcement attempts to do just that.

Using criminal intelligence

Criminal intelligence is information that police keep about suspects or organizations as they work investigations. Intelligence is the primary tool police use to identify the members of an organization, as well as their roles in the organization. (Check out Chapter 16 for more details about intelligence-led policing.)

Imagine that you're a narcotics detective and an informant tells you that marijuana and cocaine are being sold at the house at 123 Easy Street. You set up surveillance at the house one afternoon and get the license plate numbers of about 20 cars that stop in front of the house. You approach one of the drivers and ask him whether you can search him for drugs. When you find a small baggy of marijuana, he admits that he bought it in the house and gives you the name of the dealer. Hoping to avoid arrest, he says the dealer gets a new delivery of marijuana every Sunday morning. You decide you want to go after the dealer's dealer, so you arrange for surveillance on the house next Sunday.

All the information you gathered in the preceding example is considered criminal intelligence. It tells you who's involved in the drug organization and what each person's role is. This information is absolutely essential to your investigation. By gathering intelligence about the drug organization at 123 Easy Street, you can devise a strategy for arresting two levels of dealers.

Overcoming jurisdictional boundaries: Task forces

Criminals don't necessarily stay within their own towns. They may travel across city, county, and state lines to commit crimes because they know that police often don't share information with officers in other jurisdictions. One way police combat this limitation is by forming task forces of officers from multiple agencies. Although I discuss task forces in detail in Chapter 16, it's important to note that task forces play a crucial role in attacking organized crime.

A *task force* is a group of police officers from different agencies who join together to target a particular type of crime. Usually, task forces target organized crime in the form of gangs or drug organizations. One advantage of creating a task force is that each participating officer shares intelligence with the other officers from different agencies. Also, the task force's members develop specialized investigative skills and knowledge for the type of crime they're focusing on. For example, a multijurisdictional gang task force develops relationships with informants who know about a gang's activity. With the help of these informants, the task force can learn the identities of the gang members and figure out what criminal activity the gang is involved in.

The criminal intelligence that the task force acquires is crucial to developing a strategy for taking out the organization. For example, if your city's police department doesn't have a gang task force (or isn't part of one), it will have trouble gaining the intelligence or expertise it needs to fight the gang's criminal conduct. As a result, patrol officers just respond to 9-1-1 calls of crime; they don't proactively attempt to eliminate the gang behind the crimes.

Proving conspiracy

An important concept in attacking organized crime is *conspiracy*. A conspiracy is an agreement between two or more people to commit a crime. In criminal law, conspiracy to commit a crime is a crime itself. Here's an example of conspiracy in action:

- Bob and Chuck discuss killing Ken.
- Bob obtains a gun and gives it to Chuck.
- Chuck agrees to use the gun to kill Ken.

In this example, Bob and Chuck commit the crime of conspiracy to commit murder. Often, using the crime of conspiracy is the best way for law enforcement to attack organized crime groups.

In essence, organized crime is one large, ongoing conspiracy. Each member of an organization agrees to do a particular job so that the organization can make money. One of the best ways to prove the existence of a criminal conspiracy is by listening to the criminals talk to each other, which is where wiretaps come in.

Setting up wiretaps

The U.S. Constitution prohibits searches without probable cause. In other words, law enforcement has to reasonably believe you're committing a crime before they can search your person, home, or other personal effects.

A *wiretap* is the tapping of a telephone or other device to get information secretly; it's considered the most intrusive type of search. After all, the police aren't just rummaging through your sock drawer; they're listening to everything you say. For this reason, extra strict rules apply to the use of wiretaps, and some states don't allow wiretaps at all. But for a cop, there's nothing like listening to two guys discuss their plans to commit a crime — and there's no better tool for defeating organized crime. So, if the case is important enough, police may be willing to jump through all the extra procedural hoops to wiretap a suspect.

To obtain a wiretap, a police officer has to write an *affidavit* (a sworn written statement) for a judge that shows that the police have met the requirements set out here:

- ✔ The police have probable cause to believe that the suspect is committing a crime.

- ✔ The crime being investigated is one for which a wiretap is permitted. (This varies from state to state, but, generally, you can't obtain a wiretap for most crimes. You can, however, obtain one for violent crimes, drug crimes, and a few others.)

- ✔ The police have exhausted every other investigative avenue for gathering enough information to arrest the suspects. In other words, police must show that they've tried and failed at techniques such as

  - • Using informants

  - • Using undercover officers

  - • Tailing the suspect

  - • Conducting aerial surveillance of the suspect

  - • Searching the suspect's garbage

Talking in crime code

Here's an example of a coded conversation between two drug dealers that police may intercept using a wiretap:

Rick: Dude, what do you got?

Manuel: I got a kitchen of nine.

Rick: How much?

Manuel: Eight.

Rick: That's too much.

Manuel: Alright. Let me call around.

What are they talking about? Out of concern that someone may be listening, criminals often talk in code. Here, Rick is checking to see what Manuel has to sell. Rick is a low-level dealer, and Manuel is Rick's source. Manuel has a "kitchen of nine," which is a corner of a brick of cocaine, or 9 ounces. Manuel is selling each ounce for $800, and Rick says that's too expensive. So Manuel offers to call around and see if he can buy some cocaine from someone else at a cheaper price. In effect, Manuel is acting as Rick's cocaine broker.

After acquiring a judge's permission to use a wiretap, the police must stop listening to any conversation when they determine the suspect isn't talking about crime but maybe is talking about dinner plans instead, for example. This technique is called *minimizing,* but doing so can be tricky because it may sound like the bad guy is just talking about what to have for dinner when he's really talking in code about how many drugs to order up.

Police can use different types of wiretaps. For instance, they may directly listen to phone calls, or they may install microphones in a suspect's home or vehicle. Police usually also have to obtain a wiretap order from a judge to tap into a suspect's text messages or Internet communications.

Wiretap investigations are extremely expensive to conduct. If police are tapping phone lines, they must pay the phone company for its time and expenses. If the suspects speak a foreign language, they must hire interpreters. Most organized crime is committed after hours, so officers usually have to work a lot of overtime during wiretap investigations, which means departments have to pay overtime. Because of these costs, police use wiretaps much less frequently than most people think.

Relying on informants

Before you can obtain a wiretap, you must try to use an informant. And because of the costs and difficulties of doing wiretaps, which I discuss in the preceding section, informants are one of the preferred tools for most organized crime investigators.

An *informant* is someone who gives information to police about criminal conduct. For example, a citizen who calls the police about his neighbor selling drugs is an informant. But, more commonly, informants are people who exist in the criminal world. They become informants because the police caught them and they want to work off charges or because they need some money.

In a simple narcotics investigation, for example, an officer may give an informant $50 and ask him to go to a drug dealer and buy drugs. The informant gives the drugs he buys to the officer, and the officer uses those drugs as evidence to write a search warrant for the drug dealer's home.

Informants may also work within an organization and decide to help the government. Usually, informants do this not because they're good citizens but because they may face criminal charges themselves and agree to work for the government in exchange for a reduced sentence. A good example is Sammy "The Bull" Gravano, a mafia underboss who turned state's evidence against Mafia kingpin John Gotti, Sr.

Although informants can be extremely helpful in organized crime investigations, the world of informants is often very murky and complicated. A member of one drug organization may become an informant for police against a rival drug-trafficking organization, trying to improve his own organization's market share. Some informants treat informing as a profession, moving around the country, trying to infiltrate criminal organizations in exchange for cash from the police. Not surprisingly, some informants are less than reliable, which can cause problems in an investigation. For instance, if an officer learns that an informant has lied in the past, she generally can't use information from that informant in her affidavit for a search warrant or a wiretap.

Going undercover

Another tactic for investigating organized crime is going undercover. To go undercover, a police officer pretends to be a criminal and seeks to obtain evidence from the organization without the organization knowing it's being investigated. This tactic may be as simple as doing a one-time drug buy or as difficult as going deep undercover and trying to infiltrate the organization. You can find an interesting depiction of life deep undercover in *Under and Alone* (Random House). Former ATF Special Agent William Queen wrote this book about his infiltration of the Mongols motorcycle gang.

Undercover work can be dangerous. Criminal organizations conduct *countersurveillance,* which means they look out for police who may be watching them. Outlaw motorcycle gangs, such as the Mongols and the Hells Angels, conduct extensive background investigations on anyone trying to join their gangs. Obviously, the purpose of these investigations is to weed out undercover cops.

Taking back the money: Forfeiture

The federal government and most states have laws that allow law enforcement to conduct *forfeiture* (or seize criminal assets). Generally, the government can do so in the following two circumstances:

- ✔ **When the assets are *proceeds* of criminal conduct:** For example, law enforcement can seize cash made from a drug deal or a car purchased with cash from a drug deal.

- ✔ **When the assets are an *instrumentality* of a crime:** In other words, the assets are an instrument used during the commission of the crime. For example, when a gun trafficker transports guns in a hidden compartment in an SUV, the police consider the SUV to be a tool used in the commission of a crime and can seize it.

As I discuss in the "Laundering money" section, criminals try to hide the money they make; they do so, in large part, to prevent the police from seizing it. Usually, the government conducts forfeiture by bringing a civil lawsuit against the owner of the asset. For example, after seizing an SUV that contained illegal firearms, the government files a suit against the owner of the SUV, alleging that the vehicle was an instrumentality of criminal conduct. The owner can choose to respond to the lawsuit, but, often, as part of a plea agreement in the criminal case against the owner, the owner gives up the right to the vehicle.

After the government obtains ownership of the SUV, it sells the vehicle. In most jurisdictions, it then distributes the money back to the police agencies that made the arrests. These agencies can use that money to help pay for the organized crime task force that made the arrest in the first place.

Getting an Inside Scoop on Criminal Gangs

People don't always think about gangs as being part of organized crime. And, sometimes, gangs — particularly street gangs — aren't really into organized crime as much as they're into basic delinquent behavior over turf, girls, and establishing a place in their neighborhood's social hierarchy. But then again, some gangs associate with and participate in organized crime. In this section, I briefly touch on the three types of criminal gangs: street gangs, motorcycle gangs, and prison gangs.

Youth and street gangs

A gang doesn't have to be criminal. Youths may join together, come up with a name for their group, and even engage in some level of delinquent behavior. Many youth gangs (also called street gangs) aren't much more than associations of friends who share tastes in music, drugs, and an antiauthoritarian view. Gangs may be a way for kids to make some income (through selling drugs, for example) or to establish some self-esteem and respect in their neighborhoods. For a discussion of what causes kids to join gangs or turn to lives of crime, turn to Chapters 12, 13, and 14.

In contrast, many street gangs are significantly involved in crime and pose a serious risk for cities all across the country. I discuss this risk in the following sections.

Some sizeable U.S. street gangs

Here are some larger street gangs in the United States, most of which have many smaller neighborhood cliques or sets associated with them:

✔ **18th Street:** Originally formed in Los Angeles, this gang is believed to have between 30,000 and 50,000 members in 20 states.

✔ **Fresno Bulldogs:** This gang is one of the few California Hispanic gangs not to claim allegiance to the Surenos or Nortenos.

✔ **Latin Kings:** This Chicago-based group consists of more than 160 cliques in 30 states and has as many as 35,000 members.

✔ **Mara Salvatrucha (or M.S. 13):** This violent Hispanic organization has origins in El Salvador. It has roughly 8,000 members in the United States and another 20,000 outside the United States.

✔ **Bloods:** With its roots in Los Angeles, this African American street gang exists in 123 cities and 33 states.

✔ **Crips:** Also founded in Los Angeles, this African American gang exists in 40 states and has 30,000 to 35,000 members.

✔ **Gangster Disciples:** This Chicago-based African American gang is active in at least 31 states and has more than 25,000 members.

✔ **Vice Lord Nation:** This Chicago-based African American gang has around 30,000 members in 28 states.

✔ **Asian Boyz:** One of the largest Asian street gangs, it has as many as 2,000 members in 14 states. Members are primarily Vietnamese or Cambodian.

Each of these large gangs is involved in street-level narcotics trafficking along with other crimes, such as assault, murder, fraud, identity theft, burglary, and money laundering.

Connecting with organized crime

In assessing a street gang's threat to society, knowing whether it's affiliated with other gangs or serious organized crime is important. For example, a street gang may go by the name "Tiny Locos." If the Tiny Locos aren't affiliated with other groups, they may not be much of a threat to society because they probably don't have access to large quantities of drugs or weapons. However, if they're associated with another larger gang, they may be part of a drug distribution network or other large-scale organized crime activities.

Like other organized crime groups, street gangs tend to form along racial lines, so the first step in assessing a street gang is looking at the ethnicity of the gang. For example, some gang cops may describe the affiliations of the Tiny Locos organization in the following ways:

- ✔ The Tiny Locos are mostly Mexican.
- ✔ They claim to be affiliated with the Surenos (a southern California gang). (Gang cops may say the Tiny Locos are a *clique* or *set* of the Surenos, which just means they're a smaller gang affiliated with a larger one.)
- ✔ The Surenos are affiliated with the organized crime group known as the *Mexican Mafia,* a serious organized crime prison gang.

Knowing these connections, a police chief may be concerned that the Tiny Locos are carving out territory in town to serve as part of a drug-distribution network for the Surenos and the Mexican Mafia. As a result, the police chief may try to form a specialized gang unit to fight this particular street gang.

Carving up territory

Another trait of gangs that can pose a threat to society is their tendency to carve out territory for themselves. Sometimes gangs claim territory for business purposes, such as to control the drug and prostitution markets in a particular area. For other gangs, asserting authority over territory is less a business move and more a way to establish hierarchy in relation to other gangs.

A street gang may establish its territory through *tagging,* which means spray painting gang graffiti. It may also do so by using violence.

Using violence

Gang violence can have a dramatic impact on neighborhoods and even entire cities. Periodic heavy violence may erupt as rival gangs exchange attacks, placing all city residents in fear. Street gangs use violence for a variety of reasons, such as the following:

- ✔ To protect territory.
- ✔ To enforce the collection of debts.

> ✔ To extort something, most likely money. (See the "Extorting money" section for more info on this common gang activity.)
>
> ✔ To respond to a perceived slight to a gang member or the entire gang.
>
> ✔ To protect the honor of a gang member's family or girlfriend.
>
> ✔ To prove a gang member's toughness and establish a prominent position in a gang.
>
> In fact, many gangs require an act of violence to gain membership. Skinheads, for example, may require a prospective member to assault someone before being allowed to join. Skinheads typically are white-supremacist youth (although some skinheads are nonracist) who are less involved in crime for profit and more interested in intimidation of minorities and gays.

Getting females involved

Lest you think gangs are just for males, female gangs have become an increasing problem in the past decade, although they're still nowhere close to the scope and size of male gangs.

An intelligence analyst I know recently helped solve a gang shooting in which female gang members called the victim on his cellphone and tricked him into coming outside so that a male gang member could shoot him.

Motorcycle gangs

Outlaw motorcycle gangs, or *OMGs* as they're known in law enforcement, are generally more organized than street gangs, with bylaws, officers, and strict hierarchies. Motorcycles are often ancillary to their criminal activity, but the love of bikes is one of the things that binds members of OMGs together.

The U.S. Department of Justice reports that there are more than 300 OMGs in the country but that the three most heavily involved in international drug smuggling are the Hells Angels, the Bandidos, and the Outlaws. Larger OMGs often affiliate with smaller ones and even use the smaller ones for recruiting purposes.

Aside from trafficking drugs, OMGs are involved in a variety of other crimes. They may engage in motorcycle thefts, extortion, prostitution, insurance fraud, weapons trafficking, assault, and murder.

As with street gangs, intense rivalries often exist among OMGs. For example, the Hells Angels and the Mongols are bitter rivals. In fact, the Mongols have created alliances with other OMGs, such as the Bandidos, the Outlaws, and the Pagans, against the Hells Angels.

Recently, a Mongol showed up at a chapel in Las Vegas to marry his girlfriend. How sweet, right? Unfortunately, the wedding turned ugly when a knife fight broke out after the groom discovered the person getting married in front of him was a member of the Hells Angels.

Recognizing an OMG member

Obviously, not everyone who rides a motorcycle and wears a leather jacket is involved in criminal activity. Several things distinguish OMGs from other groups that like to ride bikes.

First of all, to my knowledge, all OMGs in the United States require a member to ride an American-made motorcycle — either a Harley Davidson or an Indian. And most telling, OMGs wear distinctive patches, which consist of a rocker over the top, a symbol in the middle, and a rocker on the bottom, when they ride. (A rocker is a patch in the shape of the bottom part of a rocking chair.) This three-part patch is known as a biker's *colors*.

You may see a biker without the bottom rocker. This person may be a *prospect,* also known as a prospective member who hasn't yet earned full-patch membership.

OMG members take pride in being "1%ers," a term that supposedly refers to a quote from a former president of the American Motorcycle Association, who, in 1947, claimed that 99 percent of motorcyclists are law-abiding citizens. As a matter of fact, OMG members usually have a "1%" patch on their leather jackets.

In October of 2008, after a lengthy undercover investigation, the Bureau of Alcohol, Tobacco, Explosives and Firearms (ATF) arrested 61 members of the Mongols motorcycle gang across six states on a federal racketeering indictment. In a novel approach, the federal government has sought to take away the trademark rights for the Mongols name, which is displayed on their patch. (Yes, the Mongols trademarked their patch.) The idea is that if a police officer sees a Mongol wearing the group's patch, the police can seize it.

Living the biker life

OMGs have strict rules. Members must pay dues and attend regular meetings, which some clubs call "church." If a member fails to abide by the rules, he's punished with a fine, a beating, or forfeiture of property, such as his bike. Members may even be killed by other members for serious violations of rules, such as becoming informants for the police.

Most OMGs have strong racist, sexist, and homophobic views. They usually prohibit nonwhites, gays, and women from joining. (Hispanics are generally accepted, except in the Hells Angels.) Despite this exclusivity, OMGs have associates and *hangers-on,* or people who like to participate in the biker lifestyle but who aren't full-patched members. These associates may even help in the commission of crimes. For example, associates often carry members' weapons so that if police stop the members, the police won't find the weapons.

Despite not being allowed to join, women often associate with and participate in the OMG lifestyle. I know of a biker named Butch whose girlfriend proudly wore a jacket with a patch that read "Butch's Bitch."

Prison gangs

Prison is a tough place. To survive, inmates often band into groups, called *prison gangs,* usually according to ethnicity. When a gang member is assaulted, other members of his gang retaliate. Thus, prison gangs help provide protection for their members through deterrence.

Prison officials often refer to prison gangs as *security threat groups* because they stand in the way of the officials' job, which is to control violence within prisons.

A number of prison gangs have expanded beyond their original bases of operation to become interstate criminal enterprises that reach well outside of prison walls. They often have strict hierarchies, bylaws, and rules, and they enforce these rules through violence. Here are some of the larger prison gangs in the United States:

- **Mexican Mafia:** A group mostly made up of Hispanics from southern California

- **La Nuestra Familia:** A group mostly made up of Hispanics from northern California

- **Aryan Brotherhood:** A white-supremacist group

- **Nazi Lowriders:** A white-supremacist group

- **Public Enemy Number One (PEN1):** A white-supremacist group

- **Texas Syndicate:** A group mostly made up of Mexican Americans that operates both in Mexico and the United States

- **Barrio Azteca:** A group mostly made up of Mexican Americans that started in Texas and the Southwest

- **Mexicanemi:** A group that's also called the Texas Mexican Mafia

- **Neta:** A group made up of Puerto Ricans that started in Puerto Rico and is now prominent in the Northeast

- **Black Guerilla Family:** A group made up of African Americans that started in California and is now also in Maryland

How do these groups spread beyond their home prisons? Frequently, inmates are transferred to other states' prisons to keep them safe. For example, a Nazi Lowrider who has been targeted by the Mexican Mafia in a California prison may be moved to a Colorado prison. While in Colorado, that prisoner may start up a new Nazi Lowrider chapter.

Although these groups may have started for protection, they have grown into criminal enterprises that commit crimes inside and outside prison walls. Inside, members may engage in a variety of crime. For example, they may assault rival gang members or extort money from other prisoners who want to avoid being beaten — or worse. The smuggling of contraband, such as cigarettes and drugs, is very lucrative in prison, and prison gangs can be very adept at bringing contraband inside the walls.

But as dangerous as prison gangs can be inside prison walls, their expansion into vast drug-trafficking operations is an even bigger concern. Of particular concern are groups near the southwest border of the United States, where so much of the nation's illegal narcotics come from. Where drugs are, so, too, is violence as the gangs protect distribution routes and territory.

However, when they leave prison, many prison gang members step away from the formal criminal operations of their prison gangs. They may go back to their old street gang, or they may even leave the criminal lifestyle altogether.

Chapter 9

Tackling a Worldwide Problem: The Narcotics Trade

Drugs and the consequences of drug use and addiction are easily the largest criminal problems in the United States. Organized crime makes billions of dollars off of selling drugs, and drugs and the drug business ruin hundreds of lives every day (see Chapter 8 for more on organized crime).

When policymakers discuss how to tackle the drug problem, they use the analogy of a three-legged stool. The three legs of the stool are enforcement, treatment, and prevention. The argument is that unless all three legs receive proper funding, the antidrug effort will fail.

In this chapter, I discuss the challenges that law enforcement faces in tackling this global criminal business. I also discuss efforts to provide help to people who are addicted to drugs, as well as efforts to prevent kids from using drugs in the first place.

The Global Workings of Dealing Drugs

I bet you know someone who smokes an occasional joint of marijuana or even does a little cocaine. Maybe you knew the local dealers in your high school. All these people probably say, "What's the big deal?" Well, these low-level users — and even the public at large — generally don't honestly know what the drugs really are, why they're illegal, and where they come from. I explain all these details in this section.

Making drugs illegal

Just because a substance makes you high doesn't mean it's illegal. Kids may sniff glue to make themselves dizzy, and, although doing so is stupid, it isn't illegal. For a drug to be illegal, the U.S. Congress or your state legislature must pass a law that makes possession or sale of that particular substance illegal.

Congress passed the primary law governing drugs in the United States in 1970; it's known as the *Controlled Substances Act.* The act created five categories or *schedules* of drugs, based in part on their level of addictiveness and whether they're currently accepted for any medical uses. Here's a brief description of each schedule:

- ✔ **Schedule I:** Drugs in this category carry a high potential for abuse and have no currently accepted medical use in treatment in any circumstances. These drugs include heroin, ecstasy, marijuana, and psilocybin mushrooms. Possession of these drugs is illegal.

- ✔ **Schedule II:** These drugs carry a high potential for abuse, but each one is currently accepted as medical treatment in certain circumstances. These drugs are available legally only by prescription. Some commonly known drugs in this category are cocaine, opium, methadone (used for treating heroin addicts), morphine, amphetamines, and oxycodone.

- ✔ **Schedule III:** These drugs carry an abuse potential that's less than drugs in Schedules I or II and currently have accepted medical uses in treatment, but they're also legally obtainable only by prescription. Some Schedule III drugs include marinol (which contains the active ingredient in marijuana and helps control nausea and weight loss) and anabolic steroids.

- ✔ **Schedule IV:** These drugs carry a low potential for abuse relative to drugs in Schedules I through III. They have medically accepted uses and involve limited risk of physical or psychological dependence. Generally, these drugs also require a prescription. One Schedule IV drug is phenobarbital.

- ✔ **Schedule V:** These drugs carry a low potential for abuse and little chance of creating psychological or physical dependence. This category includes drugs like cough suppressants, which don't always need a prescription.

Outside of the Controlled Substances Act, some states have criminalized other drugs. For example, some states have made *pseudoephedrine* — a cold medicine — a substance for which a person must get a prescription because *pseudo* is a primary ingredient in methamphetamine (often referred to as meth). People used to buy cases of this cold medicine to make methamphetamine in their kitchens.

When I talk about illegal drugs in this chapter, I'm talking about Schedule I and II drugs — specifically heroin, cocaine, methamphetamine, marijuana, and ecstasy. Many other illegal substances also ruin lives, but these five drugs are trafficked the most heavily in the western world.

Growing plants for the drug trade

Just as the Cabernet Sauvignon grape reaches its greatest glory in the Bordeaux region of France, the plants that yield three of the most trafficked drugs in the world have their ideal climates, as well. Here I briefly discuss the three drugs that have an organic base; that is, they're grown just like any other agricultural crop. I note where they're grown and how they make their way to the United States.

Cocaine

Cocaine is made from the coca plant. Coca leaves are grown, converted into a paste, and put through complex chemical treatments before they become cocaine. The coca plant is indigenous to the Andes Mountains of South America and grows best between elevations of 1,500 and 5,000 feet. Thus, the vast majority of cocaine comes from this region, specifically from Peru, Bolivia, and Colombia. Production in Peru and Bolivia has been decreasing over the past few years, but it has been increasing in Colombia.

Today's generation of Colombian drug traffickers have become much more sophisticated than previous generations of drug cartel leaders, who directly confronted their nation's government. In the 1980s, drug cartel leaders regularly killed judges and political figures. Today, however, Colombian cartels reduce their risk by not antagonizing their own government and by stepping back from the retail distribution in the United States, which, they hope, saves them from the wrath of Washington, D.C.

To reduce their risk, Colombian cartels employ sophisticated technology as part of their drug trade, including the use of submarines. They move drugs from Colombia to Mexico, and, from there, Mexican cartels traffic the drugs into the United States.

For an interesting look at the lengths the U.S. government was willing to go to in order to track down the old-school Colombian cartel leader Pablo Escobar, check out *Killing Pablo: The Hunt for the World's Greatest Outlaw* by Mark Bowden (Atlantic Monthly Press).

Mexican cartels that control border crossings and distribution routes into the United States move the cocaine, along with other drugs, through the southwest land border region. They also move drugs into the Gulf states through water routes. Figure 9-1 shows a map of preferred drug routes from South America, including the percentage of drugs that follow each path.

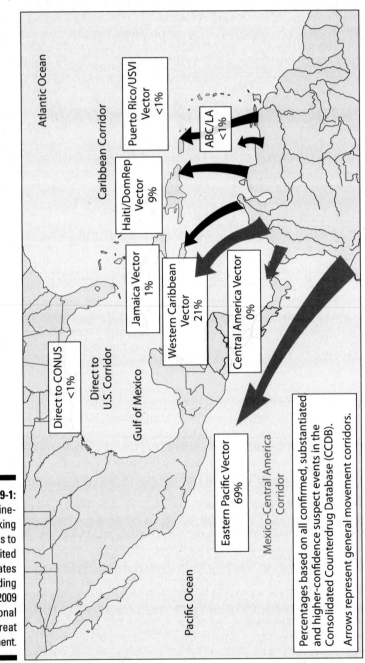

Figure 9-1:
Cocaine-
trafficking
routes to
the United
States
according
to the 2009
National
Drug Threat
Assessment.

Source: U.S. Department of Justice

Heroin

Heroin is synthesized from a specific type of poppy plant. Heroin is produced by slicing the poppy seed pod, gathering the resin that seeps out, and using various chemical processes.

The countries most responsible for producing heroin are Myanmar (in Southeast Asia), Afghanistan, Mexico, and Colombia. The majority of Afghan and Asian heroin moves to markets in Europe, Asia, and the Middle East. Increasingly, however, East Africa is becoming a *transfer zone* (a place where drugs are repackaged for shipping to their final destination) for heroin — as well as other drugs, such as marijuana and cocaine. Drugs that move from East Africa to the eastern United States generally do so in smaller quantities through human couriers on commercial flights.

For the most part, Mexican heroin supplies the western half of the United States, and Colombian heroin supplies the eastern United States. However, because heroin use is more prevalent in the eastern United States, Mexican groups are expanding their distribution to the East Coast. Transporting heroin from Mexico often involves human couriers, *go-fast* boats (high-performance boats that were originally designed for offshore racing), and concealment in vehicles or luggage.

Marijuana

The marijuana plant grows best in temperate, rainy climates, such as the Pacific Northwest and certain regions of Hawaii. Nonetheless, marijuana is grown worldwide because it can also be grown indoors under grow lights — an increasingly popular means of propagation.

Indoor grows can produce four crops per year of high-quality marijuana that sells for between $2,500 and $6,000 a pound. A small, 40-plant basement grow can gross almost $1 million in a year.

Like cocaine and heroin, marijuana is smuggled into the United States in large quantities by Mexican drug cartels along the same routes and with the same methods. The only difference is that marijuana is much bulkier. As a result, it's harder to get marijuana through border crossings. Traffickers may use airplanes and larger commercial vehicles to move significant quantities.

Interestingly, however, in recent years, Mexican organizations have started growing marijuana *in* the United States in forests and on land run by the U.S. Bureau of Land Management (BLM), which eliminates the main smuggling part of the drug-trafficking equation. In 2007, law enforcement found and cut down 4,791,838 marijuana plants in California alone. Undoubtedly, many more millions of plants weren't found and were harvested and sold. Usually, Mexican nationals living unlawfully in the United States tend these so-called gardens.

Law enforcement in several states, including California, Washington, and Oregon, sometimes become overwhelmed in summer months with locating and eradicating marijuana gardens. Imagine you're the sheriff of a five-person department in Washington, and you discover 10,000 marijuana plants growing on BLM land in your county. Some of these plants grow 8 feet tall or higher. As a sheriff, you can't just leave all that dope in the forest; you have to remove it. However, while you're addressing this problem, your office may be unable to handle other calls for service.

Marijuana is also trafficked into the United States from Canada, where Vietnamese organized crime groups and the Hells Angels (a criminal motorcycle gang) are heavily involved in cultivation and distribution (see Chapter 8 for more information on organized crime).

Incidentally, through genetic modifications and improvements in cultivation, the potency of marijuana, as measured by its *THC* content (the level of its main psychoactive substance), has been rising. In other words, marijuana carries a more powerful punch today than it did for the flower-power generation in the 1960s and 1970s (see Figure 9-2).

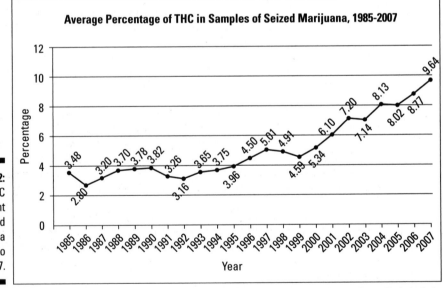

Figure 9-2: The THC content of seized marijuana from 1985 to 2007.

Source: University of Mississippi Potency Monitoring Project

Mixing chemicals for the drug trade

Here I discuss the two primary illegal substances that are made through mixing chemicals: methamphetamine and ecstasy.

Methamphetamine

Unlike cocaine, heroin, and marijuana, most methamphetamine isn't based on an organic plant but rather on a mix of various chemicals, which are known as *precursor chemicals.* One of the key ingredients is *pseudoephedrine,* which is a popular cold remedy.

In the late 20th century and early 21st century, people all across the western, midwestern, and southern United States were creating methamphetamine in their houses, apartments, and motel rooms. The chemicals used to make meth are extremely toxic, so these meth labs had to be cleaned up like toxic waste sites. (Interestingly, meth still hasn't caught on along the East Coast like it has elsewhere in the United States.)

Through the recent passage of federal and state laws that control the availability of pseudoephedrine, the number of meth labs in the United States has decreased dramatically. But because a large market for meth still exists, someone was bound to step in and fill the void. You guessed it: Mexican drug organizations have begun manufacturing large quantities of methamphetamine and trafficking it into the United States. Recently, the Mexican government passed a law ceasing all legal imports of pseudoephedrine into Mexico. This law has somewhat eased meth production in Mexico.

However, not to be deterred by importation limits on pseudoephedrine, Mexican drug organizations have begun to illegally import pseudoephedrine as well as the precursor chemicals for pseudoephedrine. In effect, Mexican drug cartels import chemicals to make chemicals to make methamphetamine. Mexican drug-trafficking organizations then move the meth into the United States using the same methods and routes they use for heroin, cocaine, and marijuana.

But meth isn't just made in Mexico. It's produced throughout the world, including in Southeast Asia in "super labs" that produce large quantities of the drug. While a kitchen lab in the United States may produce 200 doses in a single production cycle, a super lab can produce as many as 1 million doses in just one cycle.

From Southeast Asia, international drug-trafficking organizations move the methamphetamine along routes that they also use for heroin and other drugs. The drugs may move through several countries and be repackaged in a variety of disguises for smuggling. For example, a drug-trafficking organization in Hawaii hollowed out a piece of hydraulic equipment and used it repeatedly to smuggle meth and cash.

Ecstasy

Methylenedioxymethamphetamine (say that three times fast), also known as *MDMA* or *ecstasy,* is a source of significant drug abuse within the United States. It isn't based on a particular plant; rather, like meth, it's a mix of precursor chemicals. The final product is packaged in single-dose pill form. Unlike meth, however, ecstasy is primarily produced in Canada by Asian organized crime groups. (With its heavy emphasis on chemical production, China is one of the leading producers of the various precursor chemicals needed to make heroin, meth, cocaine, and ecstasy.) The ecstasy manufacturers in Canada import the precursor chemicals (legally and illegally) and then move the final product throughout the world.

Traffickers smuggle ecstasy into the United States from Canada every which way. Of course, most commonly, they use the standard smuggling tactics, such as hiding drugs in cars and commercial vehicles, flying it in airplanes, and mailing it.

Between 2003 and 2007, the amount of ecstasy seized at the Canadian border increased 900 percent. This fact reflects the greater production levels in Canada and the increased demand in the United States.

In a recent trend, ecstasy is being adulterated with more highly addictive chemicals, such as methamphetamine, which is cheaper to produce than MDMA. For instance, in a 2007 seizure of 135 kilos (2.2 pounds equals 1 kilo) of ecstasy in the state of Washington, half of the drugs had methamphetamine but no MDMA in them, and the other half had MDMA mixed with methamphetamine.

Moving dope to your neighborhood

From the poppy, marijuana, or coca fields (or the meth labs) to your neighborhood, drugs may pass through 20 different sets of hands. Drugs move from growers or manufacturers to distributors, who specialize in crossing the U.S. border, to organizations with distribution routes already set up within the United States. Finally, they reach the street-level dealers, who sell the drugs to individual drug users.

Trying to explain all the variables of drug distribution in the United States is nearly impossible, but, in general, the overall process of drug distribution is segmented, with different people handling each level of the distribution chain. With this setup, when police catch one person, other affiliates — including the main leaders — are insulated from arrest. This structure makes stopping the flow of drugs very difficult.

To better understand the drug distribution process, consider how it works with cocaine from Mexico.

From the field (or lab) to the U.S. border

Coca growers in Colombia harvest their leaves and turn them over to a Colombian cocaine cartel that processes the leaves into cocaine. The cartel transports the drugs in bulk by ship to the state of Michoacan in Mexico, just north of Acapulco. In Michoacan, the Columbian cartel sells the drugs to a Mexican cartel, which then drives a load of cocaine north on Mexican Interstate 15 close to the U.S. border. The cartel then offloads the drugs and places them into vehicles with hidden compartments called *traps* for driving across the border. Using their own sophisticated intelligence, Mexican cartels seek to minimize the risk of being caught by doing the following:

- ✔ Crossing when border patrol staffing is low to minimize the chance of inspection.

- ✔ Crossing when corrupt border patrol staff members, who agree not to inspect load cars, are working.

- ✔ Making crossings at unapproved crossing areas, such as in the desert where no border patrols are set up.

- ✔ Concealing drug loads inside large commercial loads of legal goods.

- ✔ Building underground tunnels that cross into the United States.

- ✔ Flying small private aircraft into the United States and landing at small airfields. (Thousands of little-used airfields are available in the United States, including 549 in Arizona alone.)

After the cocaine crosses the border in Arizona, other members of the cartel may ship it to a stash house in Tucson, where the drugs are offloaded. Here yet other members of the organization may load the drugs into another vehicle with hidden compartments. (Or, at this point the cartel may sell the drugs to another organized crime group that specializes in distribution.) This vehicle then moves the drugs along a specific route, perhaps dropping drugs off with wholesale dealers in Phoenix, Albuquerque, and Denver. These wholesale dealers may be part of the Mexican cartel, part of other organized crime groups, or just independent dealers.

Because most dealers handle multiple drugs, any combination of marijuana, heroin, cocaine, or methamphetamine may be added to the dealer's drug load at any stage of transport. (Remember, though, that most ecstasy moves to the United States via Canada, so dealers from the Southwest probably wouldn't have any ecstasy with them.)

From the U.S. border to your city

At this point, the wholesale dealer may have his own organization, which performs the following functions:

- ✔ Offloads and stores the drugs.

- ✔ Recruits buyers. (These buyers may be lower-level wholesalers, who buy 9 ounces of cocaine and 12 ounces of meth, for example, and then sell off 1-ounce blocks to street-level dealers, who sell user amounts.)

- ✔ Transports smaller loads to buyers. (A person who transports drugs is called a *runner*.)

- ✔ Performs security and countersurveillance duties (in other words, looks for cops).

In some cases, the wholesale dealer not only distributes to smaller independent dealers but also oversees the entire organization, right down to controlling a street gang that handles the street-level sale of the drugs.

From your city to your street corner

Eventually, the drugs are resold in smaller and smaller amounts. People who start selling drugs in fractions of ounces are often heavy users themselves, selling drugs as a means of raising money to feed their own addictions.

For example, a fraction of a gram of methamphetamine is enough to get a person high. So a low-level dealer may buy a half-ounce of meth, sell most of it to fund his next purchase, and keep the rest of the dope for his own use.

Common nicknames for drugs

I could probably fill this book with street names for different illegal drugs, but here are a few of the more common ones. Keep in mind that names are often regional and change with the times. And, of course, know that people in law enforcement often refer to any drug as *dope*.

Marijuana: Grass, weed, pot, reefer, chronic, cheeba, ganja, bud, leaf, Aunt Mary, gangsta, skunk, tobacco, nuggets, hooch

Cocaine: Coke, Charlie, snow, flake, blow, stash, stardust, Aunt Nora

Crack cocaine (a cheap, heavily addictive product that results from continued processing of powder cocaine): Black rock, purple caps, blotter, yam, base, bopper

Heroin: Smack, junk, horse, H, Aunt Hazel, ballot, Big Harry, black pearl, blanco, reindeer dust

Methamphetamine: Meth, crank, crystal, Cristina, Chris, ice, redneck coke, garbage, speed

Treating Drug Users

The drug problem is almost too big to comprehend. The economic impact of drug abuse is an estimated $181 billion annually. This cost includes the following:

- Healthcare, such as emergency room visits and treatment
- Investigation, prosecution, and incarceration of users and dealers
- Lost productivity for employers
- Welfare and unemployment payments
- Child services and foster care for children of drug users

But aside from the economic impact, alcohol and substance abuse problems are currently turning the lives of more than 23 million people in the United States upside down. (And their substance abuse problems affect the lives of their families, friends, and co-workers, as well.) That number — 23 million — is roughly 10 percent of the U.S. population over 12 years of age. Most of these people aren't yet full-fledged addicts, but their abuse still affects their relationships, employment, and health, and many of them have real potential to become addicted.

As a matter of fact, the numbers are so high that chances are you know someone who has suffered greatly from drug or alcohol abuse. (***Note:*** The National Institute on Drug Abuse, which compiles these statistics, includes alcohol as a large part of the nation's substance abuse problem. In fact, treatment admissions for alcohol account for 22 percent of all substance abuse treatment, followed by marijuana at 16 percent. Because alcohol use is legal, here I focus only on illegal drug abuse and treatment.)

So what can society do? Well, out of the 23 million abusers who could benefit from treatment, only about 10 percent receive treatment in a given year. One major obstacle to receiving drug treatment is that many people have a hard time recognizing that they have a problem in the first place. But another important barrier to treatment is the fact that the treatment capacity in the United States is well below the need for it.

In most states, policymakers debate whether prison funding should be diverted to treatment and whether drug abusers should be required to complete treatment rather than serve prison sentences. In reality, though, drug users (as distinguished from drug dealers) don't go to prison unless they commit other serious crimes, such as robbery or assault. Nonetheless, prison budgets are often seen as a potential source for funding to increase drug treatment programs. In Chapter 21, I explain the incarceration versus treatment debate in more detail.

Considering the medical marijuana movement

As of this writing, 14 states have passed laws legalizing the use of marijuana for medical purposes: Alaska, California, Colorado, Hawaii, Maine, Maryland, Michigan, Montana, Nevada, New Mexico, Oregon, Rhode Island, Vermont, and Washington. These states passed medical marijuana laws that allow marijuana use by people in chronic pain or by people suffering from certain diseases, such as glaucoma, that can be treated by marijuana. As a result, in most of these states, a person who gets a note from a physician saying that she benefits medically from the use of marijuana can't be convicted of crimes associated with possessing and using marijuana, as long as she follows the rules.

Interestingly, marijuana continues to be a Schedule I controlled substance and, as such, is still illegal to possess under federal law. Thus, law enforcement officials in these 14 states have the challenge and confusion of enforcing both state laws that legalize medical marijuana and federal laws that prohibit marijuana possession. (In the hierarchy of laws, federal law trumps state law, so, theoretically, a person who lawfully grows medical marijuana under Maine law could still be arrested by a federal special agent and prosecuted in federal court for marijuana possession. To date, however, the federal government hasn't aggressively enforced federal marijuana laws on medicinal users.)

Opponents to medical marijuana laws argue that patients can easily use *marinol,* a prescription pill that contains the active ingredient in marijuana (THC), to provide the necessary treatment. However, proponents of medical marijuana laws contend that marinol doesn't have the same effect as regular marijuana and that smoking the drug is a much better delivery mechanism than swallowing a pill.

In Oregon, medical marijuana has become a significant problem for law enforcement and people opposed to marijuana use, which includes most people in the business of treating drug addiction. (More people are admitted for drug treatment because of marijuana abuse than any other illegal drug.)

In 1998, Oregon voters approved of the law on the understanding that physicians would limit access to the drug to people in severe pain or people with other medical needs, such as people going through chemotherapy or suffering from glaucoma. But the law hasn't worked out that way. Today, roughly 1 out of every 185 people in Oregon has a medical marijuana card. Why? Because a few physicians in the state decided to grant a marijuana card to almost anyone who asked for it, and there's currently no oversight of these physicians.

Another kink in the law is the amount of dope a person can legally possess for medical use. In Oregon, a person can possess 6 full-grown marijuana plants and 18 juvenile plants. Many plants grow to be 6 feet or higher, and because a full-grown plant can easily produce a pound of dope, a person can lawfully possess way more marijuana than she can smoke in a year. Guess what happens to the extra marijuana? It often gets sold to others, which is illegal.

I strongly believe that medical marijuana laws — at least in their current forms — pose a serious threat to local communities by making marijuana much more available and lessening the social stigma attached to drug use, in general.

Examining types of treatment

Of the people who do receive drug treatment, most of them end up in drug-treatment facilities because they get arrested and a judge orders them to go. However, some people are confronted by friends and co-workers in "interventions" designed to make the drug abusers recognize their problems. Increasingly, doctors and hospitals are asking patients questions about drug use as a screening tool to see whether patients have any abuse problems.

Drug treatment occurs in the following two forms:

- **Inpatient treatment:** Inpatient treatment is generally for people who have developed serious addictions and who would easily relapse if they were allowed to leave the premises. The patient stays overnight in the treatment facility for a significant period of time, often six months or more. The treatment focus is on resocializing patients so they can reenter society without using drugs or committing crimes.

- **Outpatient treatment:** People in less severe circumstances, who need individual or group counseling about drug abuse, often take part in outpatient treatment. Increasingly, outpatient treatment attempts to address all aspects of a person's life, including family life. Family therapy can be particularly effective in helping families correct the behaviors that can increase the risk that a member, particularly a kid, will abuse drugs. For example, simply having a parent home after school decreases the likelihood that a child will be tempted to use drugs.

As the science of treatment progresses, professionals are learning that treatment must be tailored to individual circumstances because the factors that lead to drug abuse are so complex. Today, effective treatment may go well beyond just trying to stop drug use. It may also include a plan for providing a variety of services to treatment patients, such as the following:

- Skill instruction, such as instruction on parenting or conflict-resolution skills

- Help with daycare while the patient looks for a job

- Instruction on how to stay away from other drug users

- Mental health treatment (because drug abuse frequently goes along with mental illness)

In the last decade, science has begun to explore the physiological effects of drug use, and the evidence shows that drug abuse can significantly alter brain structure. For example, methamphetamine results in the release of large amounts of pleasure-causing chemicals, such as dopamine, in the brain, which explains why people get hooked so easily. Over time, an abuser needs more and more meth to experience the same pleasure. When a user is off the drug, normal events in life that used to give pleasure become meaningless.

One of my state's leading treatment providers told me how sad it was to watch a recovering meth addict mother experience no pleasure while playing with her infant. Another mother, who hasn't abused drugs, experiences great joy because of the small amount of dopamine released in her brain while she plays with her child.

Some of the physiological changes to the brain may reverse themselves after two years of abstinence from the drug, but other brain changes may never reverse.

Treatment of drug abuse often includes the use of medication, especially during the management of the initial stages of withdrawal from addiction. For example, heroin and morphine addicts are often prescribed methadone, which suppresses withdrawal symptoms. Medication may also help with mental illnesses, such as depression, anxiety, bipolar disorder, and schizophrenia, which sometimes accompany abuse or addiction.

Using drug courts

Many jurisdictions are setting up special courts for people arrested on drug offenses. Usually, these courts see low-level users or dealers — not high-profile drug traffickers. The idea behind these drug courts is that after an offender undergoes regular drug testing and completes a course of treatment, that person's crime is wiped off the books.

Drug courts can have significant success when they impose immediate sanctions for violations. For example, when someone's urine tests positive for drugs and she is immediately punished with a day in jail, she's much more likely to complete treatment eventually and remain drug free in the future. Drug courts that take a lenient approach to violations don't see as much success.

Like so many things in the justice system (and in life), a disciplined, well-run program is the key to success.

Shifting treatment goals

Historically, society didn't consider anything short of total abstinence to be a treatment success for a drug addict. Realistically, however, this expectation sets up recovering drug abusers for failure.

Today treatment providers are redefining successful treatment with more plausible goals. For instance, if a crack cocaine addict stops using but starts drinking six beers a night, is that situation a success? In the past, people may have viewed it as trading one addiction for another and, thus, as a failure.

But today, because the person can better function in society and hold a job (despite the daily six-pack), many treatment providers consider this situation to be a qualified success.

Working in the criminal justice system, I can honestly say it's easy to have a jaded view of court-ordered drug treatment. I regularly saw courts order drug treatment for people who didn't believe they had drug problems, and, as a result, they did the treatment only because the judge ordered it. They were often rearrested for more drug offenses.

My office recently investigated a gentleman who was selling cocaine *while* he was in an inpatient treatment center. At the same time, however, I've talked to an addict who said the only way he ever got clean was by getting sent back to treatment again and again. Eventually, he realized how he was wasting his life, so he worked hard to get clean. Remembering that drug users and addicts are human beings and not giving up on them is a significant challenge for most people in the criminal justice system.

Preventing Drug Use

How do you prevent kids from starting to use illegal drugs in the first place? The challenge is daunting. In 2005, one out of every five people between the ages of 18 and 25 admitted to using an illegal drug in the previous 30 days. These same statistics offer a sampling of marijuana use by high school seniors over the past 30 years:

- ✔ **1980:** 33.7 percent
- ✔ **1990:** 14.0 percent
- ✔ **1995:** 21.2 percent
- ✔ **2000:** 21.6 percent
- ✔ **2003:** 21.2 percent
- ✔ **2004:** 19.9 percent
- ✔ **2005:** 19.8 percent
- ✔ **2006:** 18.3 percent

Because marijuana is usually the first illegal drug that people use, it's a good measure of general drug use. These stats demonstrate that drug use by young people is quite variable. But what explains the dramatic decrease in marijuana use between 1980 and 1990? Why did marijuana use rise during the 1990s and then start to slowly drop in 2003? I take a look at a few possible answers to these questions next.

Educating the public

The primary tool in preventing drug use has always been education. Front and center in the education effort are dramatic TV ads. If you're old enough, you may remember an ad that first ran in 1987 in which a guy said, "This is your brain on drugs," while he showed the audience a picture of eggs frying in a pan. Today the federal government spends about $100 million on the National Youth Anti-Drug Media Campaign and obtains close to $3 billion worth of free air time from broadcasters for radio and TV messages that speak to the negative impacts of illegal drug use.

In recent years, these ads have focused on reducing the use of the most common first drugs of abuse: marijuana, alcohol, and tobacco. The idea is that if you can prevent or delay kids' experimentation with drugs until they're a little older, they're less likely to develop severe drug abuse problems down the road.

Recently, this type of advertisement has come under some criticism. Academic researchers have identified a curious result from these ads. Such ads can increase curiosity among some kids, which, in turn, can have the counterintuitive effect of actually encouraging some kids to try marijuana. Dr. Carson Wagner of the University of Texas concluded that edgy, impactful ads keep kids thinking about drugs, which can make them more likely to experiment. As an alternative ad campaign, Wagner suggests using ads that don't emphasize the negative effects of drug use itself but instead emphasize the positive effects of activities that don't involve drugs, such as sports, music, or even skateboarding.

However, other researchers strongly believe that impactful ads can decrease drug use. Hence, you can imagine the rigorous debate that continues to take place today about the effectiveness of different media campaigns to discourage drug use.

Aside from TV and radio, nonprofit organizations have expended significant efforts toward reaching kids in school, particularly in middle school and high school. These organizations sponsor antidrug efforts in schools, which include training parents, teachers, and community leaders in how to give an effective antidrug message. These organizations often lobby government agencies for resources to fight drug use.

Testing for drugs

Recently, the federal government has been encouraging random drug testing in schools as a means of preventing drug abuse. Usually, the testing is done through urine samples. The government and schools alike hope that if a student knows that he may be tested, he'll have a reason to say "no" to his friends who put peer pressure on him to try drugs. In addition, if the testing shows that a student has just started using drugs, the school can refer him to services to help prevent drug dependency.

Schools that do random drug testing usually do so for athletic participants or kids participating in other competitive extracurricular activities. The U.S. Supreme Court has upheld random drug testing of student athletes under the theory that athletes engage in dangerous activities that may make them more susceptible to injury if they're under the influence of drugs.

Does testing work? Consider this example: The U.S. military started mandatory drug testing after the Vietnam War, and a survey in 1981 showed that about 28 percent of military personnel had used an illegal drug in the previous 30 days. Since that time, the military has imposed a rigorous drug-testing program, and the results have been impressive. Today, less than 2 percent of military personnel test positive for recent drug use.

Aside from schools and the military, employers have a strong interest in keeping their employees off drugs. Drug and alcohol abuse decrease employee productivity and increase injuries and absenteeism. Workplaces that conduct drug testing can improve safety and performance. One study of construction companies that conducted drug testing showed that injury rates dropped 51 percent within the first two years after the companies began the testing programs.

Not surprisingly, some people object to drug testing. The National Organization for the Reform of Marijuana Laws (NORML) believes that drug testing in schools not only fails to deter drug use but also encourages binge drinking, undermines trust between students and educators, and is too expensive. Its Web site provides information about how to defeat such testing. The American Civil Liberties Union (ACLU) contends that drug-testing programs are ineffective and inaccurate. Some communities, such as San Francisco and Berkeley, have passed laws that prohibit workplace drug testing except for safety reasons.

Chapter 10

Front-Page News: Terrorism

*T*wenty years ago, you may not have thought of terrorism as a criminal justice issue. But since the bombing of the federal building in Oklahoma City in 1995 and the attacks on the World Trade Center and the Pentagon on September 11, 2001, law enforcement has been front and center in the battle against terrorism.

Terrorism is a crime that is intended to have a disproportionately large impact on a society through the creation of terror. Although hundreds of definitions of terrorism exist, the Federal Bureau of Investigation's (FBI's) definition is commonly used in law enforcement:

> *The unlawful use of force or violence against persons or property to intimidate or coerce a government, the civilian population or any segment thereof in furtherance of political or social objectives*

In other words, a crime becomes terrorism when it involves violence with the intent to achieve a political or social goal. Someone who burns down a building to get insurance money commits arson. But someone who burns down a meat-processing plant to stop cruelty to animals commits a crime of terrorism.

In this chapter, I look at both international terrorism and the home-grown kind. I then discuss how law enforcement agencies at the local, state, and federal levels are working to combat terrorist crimes.

Recognizing Types of Terrorist Threats

Terrorists may attack as part of an organizational effort or as lone actors. And their choice of weapons is no longer limited to conventional tools, such as guns and bombs. In this section, I take a look at the different types of terrorism, in terms of both the players and their weapons.

Striking as an organization

Most people think of terrorists as working within organizations to commit attacks. The international group Al Qaeda, for example, planned the 9/11 attack for years, breaking into groups (or *cells*) of four or five, obtaining flight lessons, and mapping out an intricate strategy to carry out multiple simultaneous hijackings. In fact, this type of simultaneous attack is almost a hallmark of an Al Qaeda operation. (See the "Facing International Terrorist Threats" section for more details about Al Qaeda.)

Domestic terrorists often follow the same strategy of forming cells (if not conducting simultaneous attacks). A cell may consist of various terrorists, each with a special responsibility. For example, in an attack on an animal research business, one cell member may get a job inside. Another may procure weapons and have expertise in building a bomb. A third may be responsible for conducting surveillance to determine facility security, and a fourth may have access to donors who can fund the costs, including lodging, food, travel, and tools to commit the act.

After the terrorist group strikes, the temporary organizational structure is broken and the cell disbands. In this way, terrorists try to take advantage of the benefits of organization while minimizing the risks — namely, infiltration and discovery by law enforcement.

Acting alone

Some individuals, perhaps inspired by the ideology of a particular terrorist organization, may choose to strike out on their own. In 2006, for example, Naveed Afzal Haq entered a Jewish social service organization in Seattle and opened fire with two pistols, killing one person and wounding five others. His apparent motivation was his anger toward Israel. Similar strikes have occurred in every region of the country.

Following the bombing of the Oklahoma City federal building, law enforcement in the United States stepped up efforts to identify people who may perpetrate similar acts. But identifying potential "lone wolf" terrorists, as they're called, has proved extremely difficult. (See the "Dealing with Domestic Antigovernment Groups" section for more info on the Oklahoma City bombing.)

Many terrorist organizations, including Islamic extremist groups, actively encourage individuals to strike out alone. Thus, a terrorist incident may not be *committed* by Al Qaeda, but it may be *inspired* by Al Qaeda.

Choosing a weapon

Keep in mind that the purpose of terrorism is to effect social or political change through *terror*. So to a terrorist, the choice of weapon is very important. Of course, for many, especially domestic terrorists, simplicity and ease of use are the most important considerations. For example, a gallon jug filled with gasoline may be sufficient to set a Hummer on fire — the ecoterrorist hopes that this act will dissuade others from buying gas-guzzling SUVs. Another increasingly common terrorist choice is putting white powder in an envelope, meant to simulate anthrax and scare the recipient.

But in the 21st century, scientific advances have taken weapons technology to a whole new level, exponentially increasing the potential damage from an attack. Until recently, terrorists weren't in a position to obtain the four most dreaded weapons, known in shorthand as *CBRN:*

- ✔ **Chemical:** Weapons made from nonliving toxic substances, such as ricin and mustard gas
- ✔ **Biological:** Weapons made from living pathogens, such as viruses and bacteria
- ✔ **Radiological:** Weapons formed from dangerous radioactive material
- ✔ **Nuclear:** Weapons made using nuclear energy (which is released during nuclear reactions), such as the atomic bomb

Today weapons made of these components are more easily obtained. For example, many countries, including some that consider the West their enemy, stockpile chemical and biological weapons. Radiological material is much more prevalent today (it can even be found in hospitals) and can be used in the creation of *dirty bombs* in which radioactive material is spread across populated areas by conventional explosions. And as countries that sponsor terrorism, such as North Korea and Iran, develop nuclear capabilities, the risk of a devastating nuclear strike grows.

Facing International Terrorist Threats

In nations throughout the world, thousands of terrorist groups pursue numerous causes. To achieve a designation by the U.S. government as a *foreign terrorist organization,* a group must meet these criteria:

- ✔ It must be a foreign organization.
- ✔ It must engage in terrorist activity.
- ✔ Its activity must threaten the security of U.S. nationals or the United States itself.

Based on their current level of exposure in the U.S. media, you may believe that the numbers of such groups are expanding and that their success is increasing. Believe it or not, however, the number of terrorist acts worldwide has dropped significantly since the 1980s. One reason for this drop is the breakup of the Soviet Union, which was infamous for sponsoring terrorism in its struggle against the West. Also, more countries are joining in the fight against terrorism.

But despite the decrease in numbers of terrorist acts, the terrorist *threat* as a whole has actually grown significantly in recent years as weapons of mass destruction have become more available to terrorists.

As of mid-2008, the U.S. Department of State had developed a list of 44 designated foreign terrorist organizations. You can review the latest information on this list at `http://www.state.gov/s/ct/rls/other/des/123085.htm`.

The majority of these groups fall into the following three categories:

- ✔ Islamic extremist groups
- ✔ Communist groups, such as the Communist Party of the Philippines
- ✔ Separatist groups interested in rebelling against their national government, such as the Real Irish Republican Army

Providing material support to any of these 44 organizations is a federal crime.

On the international scene, the United States is primarily concerned with Islamic extremist groups that have the capability and intent to attack U.S. interests. In this section, I focus on some of the most significant threats that confront criminal justice professionals in the Western world today.

Al Qaeda

Islam is essentially divided into two groups of believers: Sunni and Shiite. To find out about the differences between the two, take a look at *Islam For Dummies* by Malcolm Clark (Wiley). *Al Qaeda* is an extremist terrorist group of the Sunni branch of Islam.

Although Al Qaeda burst into the public consciousness on 9/11, it has existed since 1988, growing out of the Afghanistan resistance movement opposing the Soviet invasion in the 1980s. Al Qaeda is an international terrorist group that seeks to rid Muslim countries, such as Egypt and Saudi Arabia, of Western influences and to replace their governments with fundamentalist Islamic ones. Its long-term goal is to replace all governments worldwide with Islamic leaders who impose Islamic law, and it plans to do so by waging a holy war or *jihad*. Since its creation, Al Qaeda has been led by Osama Bin Laden.

After the 9/11 attacks, the U.S. military effectively eliminated Al Qaeda from its base of control in Afghanistan. Although Al Qaeda has operatives all over the world, today it appears that some of its leaders (including Bin Laden) have relocated to the mountainous region along the Pakistan-Afghanistan border, where they have regained some of their earlier operational capabilities.

Although Al Qaeda is best known for the 9/11 attacks, it has been linked to many others, including the following:

- The 1998 bombings of U.S. embassies in Tanzania and Kenya, which killed more than 220 people.

- The 2000 bombing of the USS *Cole,* which killed 17 U.S. sailors.

- The 2002 explosion near a synagogue in Tunisia, which killed 21 people.

- The 2003 car bomb attacks on buildings in Riyadh, Saudi Arabia, which killed 35 people.

- The 2004 bombings of trains in Madrid, Spain, which killed more than 190 people. (More than 300 Islamic extremists have been arrested in Spain since that attack.)

- The 2005 bombing of London's public transport system, which killed more than 50 people.

- The 2006 suicide bombing of the world's largest petroleum processing plant in Saudi Arabia. The plot was partially thwarted but nonetheless killed three Saudi security officers.

Because the U.S. military has repeatedly been successful at killing or capturing key Al Qaeda leaders, the organization has evolved accordingly. It now operates under a model that has become increasingly common for terrorist groups, in general, including U.S. domestic terrorists. Instead of a structured, centralized organization, Al Qaeda now appears to be a looser affiliation of individuals throughout the world who are connected by ideology. These individuals may come together for a specific action, but they also may take less direction from the organizational leaders. Nonetheless, formal Al Qaeda–directed plots, such as those carried out on 9/11, continue to be a source of worry for counterterrorism professionals.

Autonomous terrorist cells are often made up of individuals who have distinct skills that contribute to terrorist acts. Some valuable terrorist skills include

- ✔ Acquiring weapons
- ✔ Making bombs
- ✔ Conducting surveillance or obtaining jobs at target facilities
- ✔ Obtaining false identifications
- ✔ Learning different languages
- ✔ Raising funds and/or laundering money

As I note earlier in the chapter, even though the frequency of terrorist attacks has lessened in recent years, the prevalence of weapons of mass destruction makes the potential impact of a terrorist strike exponentially greater than it was 20 years ago, when conventional weapons were the primary threat. In an interview in 1999, when asked about using nuclear or chemical weapons, Osama Bin Laden answered that it was his "religious duty" to obtain such weapons.

Hezbollah

Hezbollah, which means the "party of God," is a terrorist group of the Shiite branch of Islam. It was formed in 1982 in response to the Israeli invasion of Lebanon. Hezbollah is closely allied with Iran and receives most of its support from that nation. The Syrian government (which is much more secular than Iran) also supports and encourages Hezbollah, mostly because Hezbollah serves its political interests, including the destabilization of Israel.

Much of the Islamic world views Hezbollah as a legitimate resistance operation. But aside from the 9/11 attacks by Al Qaeda, Hezbollah is responsible for more American deaths than any other terrorist group. If you're old enough, you may remember the Hezbollah-sponsored bombing attacks on Marine barracks in Lebanon in 1983 and on the U.S. Embassy there in 1983 and 1984. Numerous kidnappings and murders of U.S. citizens also occurred in Lebanon during the 1980s.

Hezbollah has terrorist cells throughout the world, including in the United States. Given that Iran has developed intercontinental ballistic missile capability, and given the increasing possibility that Iran may develop nuclear weapon capability, these terrorist cells have the potential to become active should the United States or Israel make a preemptive strike against Iran.

Hamas

Hamas was formed in 1987 as part of the Palestinian uprising against Israel known as the *Intifada*. It has political and military wings and is primarily concerned with representing extreme Palestinian interests in attacking and defeating Israel. A thorough description of Hamas activity could fill volumes, but this group has *not* made a point of directly targeting U.S. interests. However, it launches frequent suicide and rocket attacks on Israel without much concern for the presence of foreigners.

The impact of Hamas in the United States comes mostly from fundraising efforts, ostensibly for humanitarian needs, such as to take care of orphans. Most people don't realize that such donations are often promised to "martyrs" (suicide bombers, for example) to take care of their families after the bombers die. So a charitable contribution to take care of an orphan may do so, but the orphan may be the child of a suicide bomber. Hamas and other terrorist organizations use this money to induce young Palestinians to commit terrorist acts with the promise that their families will be provided for.

Dealing with Domestic Antigovernment Groups

When law enforcement officials refer to "antigovernment extremists," they generally aren't talking about Islamic extremists who are also U.S. citizens (who are an ongoing threat). Instead, they're typically referring to non-Islamic groups, such as militias and sovereign citizen movements, that reject the authority of the federal government or state and local governments. Antigovernment groups give action to their beliefs primarily in two ways — through violent crimes and through paper crimes. I discuss these crimes in more detail in the following sections.

Keep in mind that the United States has a long history of antigovernment movements. After all, the country was founded through a violent revolution against an oppressive British government.

Identifying violent threats

Any discussion of antigovernment domestic terrorism must begin with the April 19, 1995, truck bombing of the federal building in Oklahoma City that killed 168 people. Timothy McVeigh and Terry Nichols bombed the building to protest U.S. government intervention with right-wing groups at Ruby Ridge, Idaho, and Waco, Texas. Prior to 9/11, the Oklahoma City bombing was the deadliest terrorist act committed within the United States.

Some other antigovernment causes that lead people to violence include the fear that gun rights may be taken away and — believe it or not — the fear that the United Nations will take over the United States. (One county in my home state actually passed a law declaring itself a "UN-free zone.")

At least two types of antigovernment organizations pose significant threats for committing violent criminal acts:

- ✔ **Sovereign citizen organizations:** These groups often apply convoluted interpretations of the Constitution to deny federal and state governments any authority over individuals. They may create their own driver's licenses and license plates, and even their own passports. They may also resist the authority of law enforcement, refuse to pay taxes, and threaten public officials.

- ✔ **Militia organizations:** These groups pass themselves off as quasi-military or law enforcement. They may stockpile weapons, participate in "weapons training" in rural areas, wear uniforms, and claim to patrol the forest or even the U.S. border.

In addition to threatening the lives of U.S. citizens, such groups can cause significant damage in pursuit of their goals. For example, some antigovernment groups hoped that as the nation's computer system rolled over from the year 1999 to 2000, the governmental infrastructure would collapse. Some of these folks took direct action to help the process along by damaging phone lines and electrical infrastructure.

Although there seems to have been a decrease in antigovernment terrorist strikes since 2001, the FBI reports that of the 14 terrorist strikes prevented between 2002 and 2005, 8 were planned by right-wing antigovernment types — not by Islamic extremists.

Using paper crimes

By all definitions, terrorism requires an act of violence. Nonetheless, nonviolent crimes committed in preparation for terrorist strikes are still considered terrorism. For example, an antigovernment group that creates false IDs may be attempting to gain access to a secure facility like an airport or power station to commit a violent act, and, thus, the act of creating false IDs is considered a precursor crime to terrorism. Police are taught to look for precursor crimes so they can prevent the ultimate terrorist acts.

In addition, members of antigovernment groups may attempt to harass public figures (sheriffs or legislators, for example) by filing false liens or claims in which they assert that the public figure owes them money. Another common trick is for antigovernment types to file false documents with the IRS, asserting that the public figure received a multi-million-dollar income. (This last trick can wreak havoc on the public figure's tax situation.)

Starting around 1999, a movement called *redemption* swept across the country. This scheme is almost impossible to understand, but essentially, it asserts that you can create a second *you,* known as a fictional STRAW MAN (there's some kind of significance in using all capital letters), and the government is responsible for all the debts of your straw man. Some unscrupulous characters have made a lot of money pushing this scam, which is why it greatly appeals to antigovernment extremists. It continues to be very common today.

Focusing on Single-Issue Terrorists

Some domestic terrorist groups aren't necessarily considered antigovernment. Instead, they're consumed with a single cause, such as protecting animal rights, saving the environment, or preventing the murder of unborn children. These *single-issue terrorists* sometimes turn to violence in the hopes of achieving their social or political goals.

Committing crimes to save animals

Many groups advocate against cruelty to animals, but some people on the fringes of these groups resort to violence in the name of protecting animals. For example, the Animal Liberation Front (ALF) has taken credit for firebombs on facilities such as meat-packing plants and on federal wild-horse corrals. ALF, like other single-interest groups, is more of a movement than a real organization. It consists of loosely affiliated individuals who come together in cells to commit terrorist acts and then disband — a situation that makes observation and infiltration by law enforcement difficult.

Animal rights' terrorists often target mink farms, releasing minks and destroying breeding records. (They may also attempt to release other animals, such as rats and monkeys.) Ironically, massive mink releases usually result in the deaths of those minks because they're domesticated and can't survive in the wild.

Increasingly, animal rights' terrorists focus attention on businesses and schools that use animals for testing pharmaceuticals, cosmetics, pesticides, and the like. In 2008, for example, animal researchers in California had their homes' windows broken, cars scratched, and paint thrown on their houses and, in one case, a car and house were firebombed. In one incident, six masked intruders even attempted to invade an animal researcher's home during her daughter's birthday party. At one university, shotgun shells were repeatedly rammed into the mufflers of numerous school vans.

Some animal rights' terrorists focus attention on a corporation called Huntington Life Sciences, which provides a vast array of research and testing services that often involve animals. A group known as Stop Huntington Animal Cruelty (SHAC) frequently targets other corporations that do business with Huntington Life Sciences. The acts may be small, such as forcing a business to pay return postage on an empty letter, but they may also include firebombs and threats of physical violence.

Fighting for the environment

Ecoterrorists, like animal rights' terrorists, are less likely to participate in structured organizations and more likely to come together to form temporary cells for specific terrorist acts. The Earth Liberation Front (ELF) is one of the more prominent umbrella groups that take credit for terrorist acts in the name of the environment. For example, ecoterrorists may leave a sign at the scene by spray-painting the letters *ELF.* Or they may issue a statement through an environmental group sympathetic to ELF.

In the late 1990s, ELF firebombs across the western United States resulted in millions of dollars of damage to U.S. Forest Service buildings, lumber industry buildings, genetically engineered forest products, car dealerships, resorts, and housing developments. In operation "Backfire," one of the most successful anti–domestic terrorist investigations in U.S. history, the FBI and local law enforcement agencies identified the members of the cell responsible for many of these acts and, after many years of investigation, brought them to justice. Nonetheless, ELF and other environmental terrorists continue to strike. Some common tactics include:

- **Tree spiking:** Ecoterrorists drive railroad spikes into trees targeted for logging. If a chainsaw bites into a spike, a logger can be killed.

- **Monkey wrenching:** Ecoterrorists vandalize heavy equipment left at logging or construction sites.

- **Firebombing:** Ecoterrorists fill containers with fuel and then set them on fire with a delayed fuse.

- **Vandalizing SUVs:** Ecoterrorists target SUVs because they aren't fuel-efficient.

> ✔ **Targeting homes and property:** The primary targets are corporate officials deemed unfriendly to the environment, such as people who lead power and logging companies and the bankers who do business with them.

Since 2000, more than 140 ecoterrorist acts have occurred in the United States. One of the more severe attacks occurred in 2003 in San Diego. A five-story apartment building under construction was destroyed by a fire, resulting in damages of $50 million. A banner nearby declared, "If you build it, we will burn it, the ELFs are mad."

There may be significant crossover between ecoterrorists and animal rights' terrorists because they're frequently sympathetic to each other's causes. Training events in *direct actions* — a phrase terrorists use for specific acts — often involve people from both camps.

Targeting abortion

Since 2000, there have been approximately 26 attacks on abortion clinics in the United States. These attacks have involved explosive devices, gun shots into clinics, letters containing white powder (initially assumed to be anthrax), arson, and even car crashes into clinics.

Unlike animal rights' terrorists or ecoterrorists, antiabortion terrorists often act alone, seeking to shut down a clinic or make its operation unprofitable. Such terrorists may justify their actions by arguing that shutting down a clinic even temporarily prevents abortions, and every abortion prevented is a life saved.

It appears that the number of attacks on abortion clinics has diminished since 9/11. However, in 2009, a Kansas physician who performed late-term abortions (a particularly controversial procedure) was shot to death on a Sunday morning while attending his church.

One of the most notorious antiabortion terrorists is Eric Rudolph. He's perhaps best known for setting off a bomb at the 1996 Summer Olympics in Atlanta, Georgia, which killed two people. But he also bombed several abortion clinics across the South, killing one other person. His bombs were made of dynamite with numerous nails attached as shrapnel. Rudolph remained at large for over five years before a North Carolina police officer apprehended him in 2003 while Rudolph was rummaging through a garbage can. Rudolph pled guilty to all charged crimes and was sentenced to life in federal prison.

Acting out of hate

Hating someone isn't a crime. Nor does it constitute terrorism. But individuals and groups that harbor racist, antireligious, or homophobic views sometimes give action to their hate by committing violence against others, which is where hate crimes come in.

A *hate crime* is a crime committed because of the race, religion, or sexual orientation of the victim. Most states today have created separate crimes that punish violence more severely when it's motivated by hate.

Many hate crimes don't fit the strict definition of terrorism that I give you at the beginning of this chapter — for one, racist attacks often aren't driven by a desire to change governmental or social policy. A drunk white kid who strikes out at an African American woman in a convenience store, for example, is more likely just filled with hate. But some groups do advocate racist violence, and because they *are* attempting to achieve a social objective, they can fairly be considered terrorist organizations.

The FBI documented 7,624 hate crime incidents in the United States in 2007. About 64 percent of victims were targeted because of their race, ethnicity, or national origin. Seventeen percent were targeted because of their religious belief and 16 percent because of their sexual orientation.

Numerous groups in the United States espouse various views about one person's superiority over another person. The Southern Poverty Law Center (SPLC), a nonprofit organization devoted to fighting hate groups, has documented 888 active hate groups in the United States. Keep in mind, though, that the SPLC takes an expansive view of the term "hate group," including organizations opposed to illegal immigration, among others. Thus, inclusion on the SPLC list doesn't mean a group is a terrorist organization. But prominent in the list are numerous neo-Nazi organizations, various groups claiming affiliation with the Ku Klux Klan, and racist Skinhead groups. Some of these groups advocate for violent action against groups of people they hate.

These groups are becoming more sophisticated in their recruitment of members. They may use social networking sites on the Internet to reach out to like-minded youngsters. I've seen white-supremacist Web sites that contain video games in which a player can kill blacks or Jews. Clearly, these sites are designed to appeal to kids. In addition, there's a relatively large white-supremacist music industry. Bands that celebrate white-supremacist views may play at organizational rallies to draw recruits. Some hate groups even fill Easter eggs with racist propaganda and distribute the eggs on school yards.

Fighting Back against Terrorism

From a criminological perspective, it's worth noting that terrorism combines two elements:

- ✔ **Motivation:** A desire to strike out in violence to achieve a terrorist goal
- ✔ **Operational capability:** The people and the tools necessary to commit a terrorist act

To successfully fight against terrorism, you have to eliminate at least one of these two elements. In the following sections, I take a closer look at these elements and how the U.S. government is trying to combat them.

Eliminating terrorist motivation

All kinds of people desire significant change in governmental or social policy. But what leads them to use terrorism, and how can the U.S. government combat such extreme motivation? If I knew the answers, I'd have the formula for world peace. But even though no perfect answers have been discovered, society can gain some insight by looking at the last 30 years in the Islamic world.

Since about 1980 (coinciding with the creation of groups like Al Qaeda in Afghanistan and the rise of the Ayatollah in Iran), Islamic extremists have been pouring money and resources into reshaping the minds of Arab Muslims. For example, rich benefactors, such as Osama Bin Laden, have funded the creation of thousands of *Wahabi* schools — which teach Al Qaeda's fundamentalist view of Sunni Islam — with the goal of spreading Islamic law and dominance throughout the world. In addition, Islamic extremists have worked hard to build resentment throughout the Islamic world against the West, against Israel, and against moderate Islamic regimes that are supported by the West, such as Egypt and Saudi Arabia.

The result of these schools and this resentment has been thousands of people willing to carry suicide bombs and die to achieve their goal. (One of the tools used to motivate suicide bombers is the promise of 70 virgins in heaven for a *shahid,* or martyr of the faith.) Fighting this motivation is a challenge in the extreme, but, in the long run, success in the war on terror will depend on reducing the resentment and anger toward the West by using tools such as education and economic development.

Eliminating operational capability: Law enforcement's role

In the short run, the U.S. military and local, state, and federal law enforcement officials carry the burden of preventing terrorism. The 9/11 Commission (a group created by Congress to study the failure to stop the 9/11 attacks) identified some serious lapses in the fight against terror, but none is more important than the need for everyone involved in the fight to *share* information. Before September 11, 2001, not only did the Central Intelligence Agency (CIA) not talk to the FBI, but different branches within one agency didn't talk to each other. And federal communication with local law enforcement on the issue of terrorism was minimal at best.

As a result of 9/11, the federal government has significantly changed its strategy. Mechanisms for sharing foreign intelligence with federal law enforcement are now in place. Federal agencies communicate with each other much more. And significant inroads have been made in developing communication between local law enforcement agencies and their federal counterparts.

In particular, the development of *Fusion Centers* — state-based operations that "fuse" together personnel from many different agencies — is having a big impact on the fight against terrorism. In essence, Fusion Centers bring together intelligence personnel to share information among different agencies within a state. The goal is to break down the walls of communication between local, state, and federal law enforcement agencies so that the next 9/11 can be identified before it occurs. Today, if a patrol officer stops a suspicious person with a bag of ammonium nitrate (fertilizer that's also used in making bombs), the officer can call his Fusion Center to find out whether that person is a terrorist suspect.

While Fusion Centers help gather and analyze information, the FBI has taken the lead in conducting actual investigations. The FBI has made terrorism its number one priority and has put significant resources into its Joint Terrorism Task Force program (JTTF). This program, replicated throughout the country, combines police from numerous agencies into a single task force to investigate terrorist activities. These task forces are the primary investigative tool against terrorism within U.S. borders, and since 9/11, they've been very successful.

Despite the significant improvement in cooperation among law enforcement agencies, many challenges still exist. Trust, information sharing, and cooperation don't come easily in the world of law enforcement. Much depends on personal relationships, and given the fact that cops spend a lot of time with liars and crooks, building trust is a full-time, never-ending challenge.

Part III

Figuring Out Who Commits Crimes and Why

"Here are this month's crime statistics. I stole some numbers from last month's statistics, but it should still be pretty accurate."

In this part . . .

One of the central concerns of criminology is figuring out why people commit crimes. Over the years, many people have developed theories to try to answer this question. In fact, the number of theories of why people commit crimes sometimes seems to equal the number of criminologists. In this part, I discuss the major criminological theories and their applications in the real world.

Do most criminals act rationally after weighing the costs of crime versus the benefits? Is society ever to blame for driving an individual to commit a crime? Do mental diseases or even genetics factor into a person's attraction to a life of crime? I explore these questions and much more in the chapters that follow.

Chapter 11

What Factors Lead to Crime?

Criminal justice students and crime-show fans alike are fascinated with the reasons why people commit crime. This may help explain why authors like John Grisham and Dean Koontz and TV shows like *CSI: Crime Scene Investigation* and *Law & Order* are so popular.

There are many factors that influence the likelihood that someone will become involved in crime. In this chapter, I discuss some of the more interesting ones, including age, race, neighborhood, pop culture, genetics, and even weather.

Noting Personal Characteristics That Many Criminals Share

Here's what cops know from experience: Certain people in certain circumstances are more likely than others to get involved in criminal conduct.

One day a police officer and I were walking down the street when we saw a young man skateboard past us. The cop told me that when he sees a man in his mid-20s riding a skateboard, he can almost guarantee the man has drugs on him. From what he'd observed in his profession, the cop was making some additional, unstated assumptions about the skateboarder's personal characteristics:

✔ He probably doesn't have a car.

✔ He probably doesn't have a good job, or even any job.

✔ He probably doesn't have a wife and kids.

✔ He probably doesn't have a college degree.

✔ He probably participates in street culture, which is heavily associated with drug use.

Of course, police have to back up these kinds of generalizations (called profiling by people in the know) with evidence before they can bring any charges against someone. And police must be very careful to appropriately evaluate all available information before they compromise someone's rights with a generalization.

Unfortunately, *profiling* has become something of a dirty word in law enforcement because of its association with an unconstitutional practice known as *racial profiling*. Racial profiling is making assumptions about someone's likelihood to commit crime based solely on the person's race. See the "Race: Does skin color influence criminality, or is racism to blame?" section for more details about racial profiling.)

Despite this negative connotation, however, profiling is a crucial tool in the fight against crime because, as I explain in this section, certain personal characteristics do indicate that someone may be more likely to get involved in criminal activity.

Age: Seeing crime as a young person's game

According to the Federal Bureau of Investigation's (FBI's) arrest statistics, in 2007, 16 percent of arrests for violent crime and 26 percent of arrests for property crime involved people 18 years old or younger. As Figure 11-1 shows, the age at which someone is most likely to be arrested for any type of crime is 18 or 19. And as I point out in Chapter 3, arrest statistics may not paint a completely accurate picture, so juvenile crime is likely even higher than what this figure shows. One reason for the discrepancy is that juveniles who commit offenses are often returned to their parents without being formally arrested.

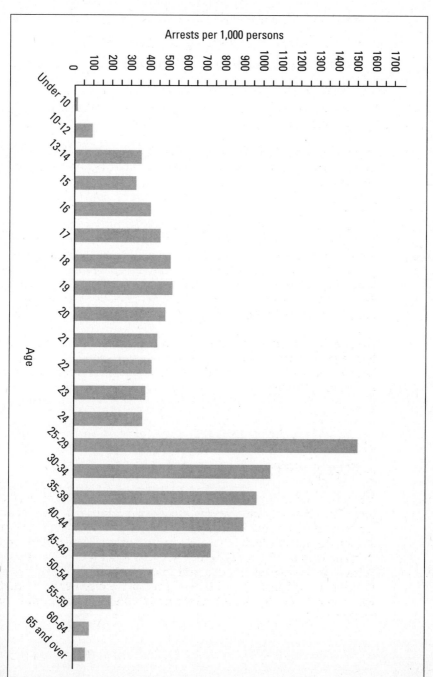

Arrests per 1,000 persons

Age

Figure 11-1:
The number
of arrests
made per
age group in
2007.

Source: Federal Bureau of Investigation

So, why exactly are young people more likely to commit crime than older people? Well, a few factors are at play here, including the following:

- ✔ As any old person (such as me) can tell you, the younger you are, the more energy you have. So, as people get older, they simply don't have the energy they once did to commit crimes.

- ✔ To be blunt, the younger you are, the stupider you are. Sometimes young people do dumb things that older, wiser people don't do. In particular, young people generally find delaying gratification or resisting temptation difficult to do. As a result, they're more likely to seek a quick thrill — perhaps by committing a crime — without weighing the risks or consequences.

Young people often make poor choices because they are assuming more responsibility and freedom even as their brains are still undergoing significant development. Recent studies have shown that an adolescent's brain doesn't fully mature until the person is between 22 and 25 (check out Chapter 14 for more on brain development and Chapter 22 for more on dealing with juvenile crime).

- ✔ As people get older, they're more likely to have families, which demand more stable lifestyles. Having a spouse and children means spending less time skateboarding with friends on the street and more time making a living and providing for your family.

Gender: Men take first place in crime

Which gender commits more crime is no mystery. In 2007, 75 percent of all arrests involved men. Men accounted for 82 percent of all violent crime arrests and 67 percent of property crime arrests.

When a woman goes to commit a crime, chances are high that she'll commit a property crime. In 2007, women committed slightly more embezzlement than men and were arrested for 44 percent of all fraud, 40 percent of all theft, and 38 percent of forgeries.

According to recent trends, women appear to be increasing their presence in the criminal community: Between 1998 and 2007, the overall crime rate for men dropped 6 percent, but the crime rate for women increased almost 7 percent.

As crime rates for men drop and rates for women rise, it seems very likely that sociological factors are at play. For example, as women gain more prominent professional positions, they have greater opportunity to commit embezzlement, which explains why the percent of women arrested for embezzlement increased by 30 percent between 1998 and 2007.

Nonetheless, men still take the prize for committing the most crime mostly because, quite simply, men are different from women. To a significant degree, the differences between male and female traits are the results of hormonal differences. For instance, men are generally physically bigger and more aggressive than women, and they often lack certain female-attributed traits, such as compassion, empathy, and the need to nurture — all traits that don't easily correlate with violating someone else's rights through crime.

Hormones aside, criminologists hotly debate why women commit fewer crimes than men. Some criminologists, including those who subscribe to feminist criminological theory, contend that the difference can be explained by how boys and girls are raised (see Chapter 15 for more on this theory). These criminologists argue that boys are trained to be physical, dominant, and more aggressive, while girls are rewarded for exhibiting stereotypically feminine virtues. (All I know is that, contrary to my best efforts, my daughter showed much greater interest in dolls and ballet than she did in football.)

Income: Does less money in your pocket lead to more crime?

The FBI compiles the Uniform Crime Report (UCR) after receiving crime-related statistics from police agencies across the United States. (Check out Chapter 3 for more on the UCR.) Unfortunately, the UCR doesn't contain information about the income of criminal offenders. However, it does track information about the location of crimes. And in doing so, it shows that typically lower-income regions, such as inner cities, have higher crime rates than more affluent areas, such as suburbs.

To explain the difference in crime rates between lower- and higher-income areas, criminologists have developed various theories, including the following:

- Police often spend more time in poorer areas. Therefore, they're more likely to arrest criminals in poorer neighborhoods than affluent businessmen in big, shiny offices.

- Lower-income areas often experience higher rates of drug use than more affluent areas, and drug use correlates to higher crime rates.

- The quality of schools is often lower where incomes are lower, and lower-quality education often leads to higher crime rates. (See the "Education: Higher degrees equal lower crime rates" section for more details.)

- In lower-income areas, people are often unable to land well-paying jobs, and people who don't spend their days working and earning money are more likely to commit crime.

> ✔ People who struggle with impulse control are more likely to live in poorer neighborhoods because they have a tougher time holding on to well-paying jobs. These same people are more likely to commit crime, too, because poor impulse control increases the chances that someone will commit crime.

I discuss these criminological theories in greater detail in Chapters 12 through 15.

In 1978, Charles Tittle, Wayne Villemez, and Douglas Smith conducted a significant study that looked at self-reporting of crimes by people in different social classes. (*Self-reporting* means the person who committed the crime reports on himself to the criminologist doing the study — not the cops!) The study concluded that there's little evidence that a person's social class influences crime statistics. However, other criminologists disagree, arguing that the study placed too great an emphasis on low-level offenses. They argue that although rich kids may be just as likely as poor kids to be caught drinking, shoplifting, and using drugs, lower-class neighborhoods have higher crime rates for serious felonies than upper-class neighborhoods.

The bottom line is that criminologists haven't been able to draw any definitive conclusions about income as a crime-causing factor; however, living in a low-income area does seem to correlate with higher crime rates.

Instead of looking at income levels, some studies have shifted the focus to parental control and discipline and have concluded that these factors are much more predictive of criminality than either income or social class. In other words, these studies point out that kids whose parents or other guardians watch them more closely and actively discipline them are less likely to grow up to commit serious crime, regardless of the neighborhood they live in. I discuss this theory of crime control in detail in Chapter 13.

Related to income, the section "A bad economy: Does recession lead to crime?" looks at the effects of the economy on criminality.

Race: Does skin color influence criminality, or is racism to blame?

In 2007, 28 percent of all people arrested were African American. The overall U.S. population is about 12 percent African American. The question of whether the disproportionate arrest rate for African Americans is the result of racial bias is an extremely sensitive one for communities, law enforcement, and criminologists. In fact, few issues in criminology have been the subject of more statistical studies than racism in law enforcement.

Consider the fact that African Americans had an even higher arrest rate — 39 percent — for all *serious violent* offenses in 2007. Is it possible that institutionalized racism means that blacks get arrested for serious violent crime much more often than whites? Many criminologists doubt that police under-investigate serious offenses, such as robberies, rapes, and murders, perpetrated by white criminals. These criminologists contend that racial bias in the criminal justice system is no longer highly prevalent and that the higher *arrest rate* just reflects a higher *offense rate* by African Americans.

In contrast, other criminologists attribute the disproportionate arrest rate to discriminatory processes that are ingrained in the U.S. justice system. These criminologists suggest that racism isn't overt today like it was decades ago. Instead, racism is institutionalized so that African Americans are more likely to be stopped and questioned, more likely to be arrested, less likely to receive bail, and more likely to receive longer sentences than similarly situated white people.

Minority communities often point out situations when police officers pull over African American or Hispanic people for minor driving infractions that seem unwarranted. Minority and civil rights' activists accuse police of pulling people over for "driving while black" or "driving while Hispanic." They assert that the police are racially *profiling* — assuming that an African American or Hispanic person is more likely to be engaged in criminal conduct than a white person.

Taking a closer look at racial profiling

Profiling can certainly be a useful technique in law enforcement because it helps police understand what kind of suspect to look for in connection with certain crimes. Some large agencies, including the FBI, even have profiling experts who look for personal characteristics that are common among people who commit a certain crime. For example, psychopathic murderers often have a history of juvenile delinquency, animal abuse, and fire setting.

Racial profiling, on the other hand, takes place when a police officer draws conclusions about someone based solely on race or ethnicity. Clearly, practicing racial profiling is illegal. Civil rights' organizations have filed numerous lawsuits over the last 40 years, alleging that police officers engage in such practices. For example, in 2008, the American Civil Liberties Union (ACLU) of Maryland entered a settlement with the Maryland State Police over allegations that state police pulled over men on the freeway because of their race. The state police department paid a cash settlement and agreed to hire an independent consultant to make sure the agency didn't engage in racial profiling.

Such lawsuits often end in *consent decrees*. A consent decree is an order from a federal court demanding that a police agency take a specific action. For example, an agency may be forced to monitor all its traffic stops to look for evidence of racial profiling.

These days, I'm not aware of any police agency that engages in racial profiling by policy. However, civil rights' organizations still fear that individual cops engage in the practice or that an unofficial culture within a police agency may encourage it. I know of at least one city that has responded to these fears by requiring its officers to hand out business cards after each traffic stop. Doing so makes filing a complaint against the officer easier for the citizen to do if she feels like the officer violated her rights. Many police agencies gather racial statistics from every traffic stop to look for signs or patterns of mistreatment of minorities.

Fear of civil rights' lawsuits has significantly changed police practices in many parts of the country. In one medium-sized town with an anti-law-enforcement reputation and a very small minority community, some police report that they're very reluctant to pull over someone from a minority community for fear of being sued. Although this situation is likely an overreaction, most cops do resent the assertion that they're racist. As a result, many communities have tension between their minority citizens, who believe they're being mistreated, and the police, who assert that they're just trying to do their jobs.

Examining cultural challenges

If institutionalized racism within the justice system can't explain *all* the disparity in arrest statistics, what can? Well, some criminologists believe that the amount of crime committed within any group of people reflects certain cultural challenges. For example, roughly 68 percent of African American children in 2005 were born to single mothers. This statistic reflects a significant, steady increase from the mid-1960s when the rate was only about 25 percent. (For comparison's sake, 25 percent of white children were born out of wedlock in 2005.)

The absence of a second parent in a home likely has an impact on income, educational opportunities, and the oversight and discipline of children. Single-parent families are more likely than two-parent families to be poor and live in higher crime areas, and, as a result, children in these families are at greater risk of joining youth with similar backgrounds in delinquent behavior. I discuss the negative impacts of poor neighborhoods, bad peer groups, and dysfunctional families on criminality in Chapter 13.

It's interesting to note that Asian Americans accounted for just under 1 percent of all arrests in 2007, although they represent about 5 percent of the U.S. population. Some criminologists explain this disparity using the *social disorganization theory*, which I discuss in more detail in Chapter 13. In essence, this theory holds that people living in a disorganized society (one with dysfunctional schools and high rates of vandalism and unemployment) are more likely to be involved in criminal conduct. According to this theory, Asian Americans don't commit as many crimes because Asian culture is highly structured and goal oriented.

Education: Higher degrees equal lower crime rates

The more education a person has, the less likely she is to commit a crime. But the education itself doesn't lead a person away from a life of crime. Rather, many crucial elements often accompany a good education, including the following:

✔ Better jobs

✔ The chance to live in better neighborhoods with better schools

✔ Perhaps less exposure to delinquents

Another important benefit of school is that it offers a great opportunity for juveniles to develop social bonds. Social activities, such as playing sports, playing in a band, or acting with a theater group, all build relationships that correlate with lower crime rates. Kids who drop out of school, on the other hand, are less likely to develop social bonds, at least in a noncriminal context.

Dropouts still look for social relationships, of course, but they're more likely to develop them with other kids who are marginalized from school. Thus, joining a gang, or just "hanging out" after school (when most crimes are committed), becomes an attractive alternative. Chapter 13 dives into this topic in greater detail.

Religious affiliation: The benefits of practicing a faith

The *hellfire hypothesis* suggests that religion decreases crime because believers fear being damned for misbehaving. I'm not sure how valuable this theory is, but studies have shown a correlation between *attendance* at religious services and a reduced likelihood of committing crime. People who make the effort to attend religious services are more likely to take seriously the teachings of their religions. And few religions advocate for the commission of crime. These studies may also reflect the value of an additional layer of social bonds that churchgoers develop.

Criminologists have also done studies on the differences in crime rates among religions. In general, Jews had the lowest crime rate, followed by Protestants. Catholics had the highest rate among religious affiliations. However, these distinctions have been criticized because, generally speaking, each of these groups consists of slightly different social classes. For example, Catholics have a higher percentage of new immigrants to the United States, as well as lower-income minorities. With these social differences in mind, some criminologists have concluded that social class is more meaningful in predicting criminality than which type of church a person attends.

Looking at the Impact of Societal Conditions on Crime

In this section, I discuss a couple of frequently cited causes of crime: pop culture (including movies, TV, music, and video games) and a bad economy. I also look at differences between city and country areas in terms of the number of crimes committed.

Pop culture: Inspiring violence through entertainment

In 2003, 24-year-old Ronell Wilson of New York City shot two undercover detectives in the backs of their heads, killing them. When police arrested him, they found in his pants pocket the following rap lyrics: "Leave a 45 slugs in da back of ya head. Cause I'm getting dat bread, ain't goin stop to I'm dead." In 2006, a jury convicted Wilson of various counts of murder and sentenced him to death. Was the fantasy life of gangsta rap a motivation for Wilson to kill the two detectives?

Ever since Elvis Presley first started gyrating his hips, people have complained about the impact of pop culture on youth. But medical science didn't begin to study whether pop culture makes kids more violent until the mid-1970s. Recent studies have estimated that the average child will see more than 18,000 murders and 250,000 acts of violence on TV and at the movies before he or she graduates from high school. And this statistic doesn't even touch the influence of violent video games and song lyrics.

What's the effect of being exposed to violence in pop culture? Numerous studies have shown that children, who are still developing their value systems and learning how to solve problems, may become desensitized to violence after so much exposure. They may also come to see violence as an appropriate way to resolve conflict, and, perhaps as Ronell Wilson did, they may come to identify with fictional violent characters. Certain conduct, such as shooting cops in the back of the head, may come across as cool.

I have to point out, though, that most kids who watch violent TV shows and movies, play aggressive video games, and listen to misogynistic music don't engage in criminal violence. But a growing body of research seems to indicate that some kids are at greater risk for turning to crime when they're exposed repeatedly to such media.

A bad economy: Does recession lead to crime?

When the United States goes into a recession and people lose their jobs in large numbers, does the crime rate rise? It seems logical that unemployed people would be more likely to steal or commit other crimes just to survive. However, the evidence doesn't support this assertion. The truth is that criminologists don't know exactly what the economy's impact on crime really is.

While the U.S. economy prospered in the 1960s, the nation's homicide rate rose 43 percent. Yet, in the mid-1990s when the U.S. economy was again prospering, the nation's crime rate began to fall.

When looking at what causes crime, criminologists have so many variables to consider that they simply can't isolate the economy as a cause. Figure 11-2 shows the complete lack of correlation. The fact that the national economy changes nationally may be one explanation of this lack of correlation. For example, a recession, more or less, hits all 50 states. Crime trends, on the other hand, tend to occur locally. Murder rates in St. Louis may be near record-high levels at the same time that they're dropping in Atlanta.

Here are two opposing but fairly logical theories that attempt to explain the relationship between the economy and crime rates (note that neither theory has a lot of statistical support):

✔ Unemployed people, especially young men, have more free time, which can lead to mischief, criminality, or even illegal jobs, such as selling drugs.

✔ Severe economic downturns, like the Great Depression, bring families together, which results in a decrease in crime.

Another possible connection is that higher crime rates may actually lead to higher unemployment. For example, a 19-year-old man convicted of burglary will find it very difficult to get a job when he finishes his sentence. The higher the crime rate in a certain area (and the more 19-year-olds convicted of crime in that area), the more unemployed people there are. So, in a way, high rates of school dropouts, broken families, and other causes of crime may actually hurt the economy.

One conclusion that criminologists *have* been able to make about economy and crime is that, generally (but not always), for every 1 percent increase in the unemployment rate, the rate of burglaries goes up 2 percent. But given all the discussion among politicians and media pundits about the relationship between the economy and crime, it's interesting to see that the rhetoric isn't based on much evidence.

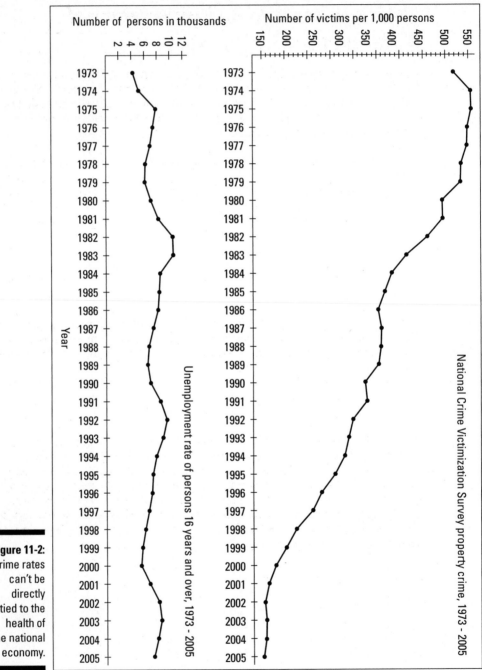

Number of persons in thousands

Number of victims per 1,000 persons

Year

Unemployment rate of persons 16 years and over, 1973 - 2005

National Crime Victimization Survey property crime, 1973 - 2005

Figure 11-2:
Crime rates can't be directly tied to the health of the national economy.

Source: Bureau of Justice Statistics

Your zip code: Identifying regional differences in crime rates

Crime rates vary depending on where you live within the United States. Contrary to what you see on TV about the "mean streets" of northeastern cities, the Northeast is the safest place to live, followed by the West and then the Midwest. The South has more crime per capita than any other region. Figure 11-3 shows you what I mean.

The South has consistently had higher crime rates than any other part of the country (although in 2007, the West actually had the highest *violent* crime rate). The regional differences in crime rates across the United States, which have been fairly consistent over time, have led some criminologists to conclude that regional culture must play a role in the commission of crime.

Beyond just regional differences, crime rates also differ depending on whether you live in the city or the country. Generally, as the population density increases, so does the crime rate, a fact that's particularly true for violent crime.

But it's not just the crime *rate* that differs from rural to urban areas. The cultural values that impact law enforcement differ, too. In my experience in my own state, folks who live in the country seem to value independence and self-reliance very highly. Thus, rural police may be more likely than city police to believe that someone used a gun in self-defense. (I've heard the following statement about a homicide victim in a rural county: "He was a guy who needed killin'.")

These cultural and value differences may be slowly disappearing, however. As cable and satellite TV access has expanded in the past 20 years, pop culture has become thoroughly available in rural communities as well as in the city. And as drug traffickers become more sophisticated, many rural communities have been fully exposed to the negative effects of narcotics, too. In fact, because rural areas often lack even basic drug treatment and law enforcement resources, the impact of drug crime in rural areas may even be greater than it is in big cities.

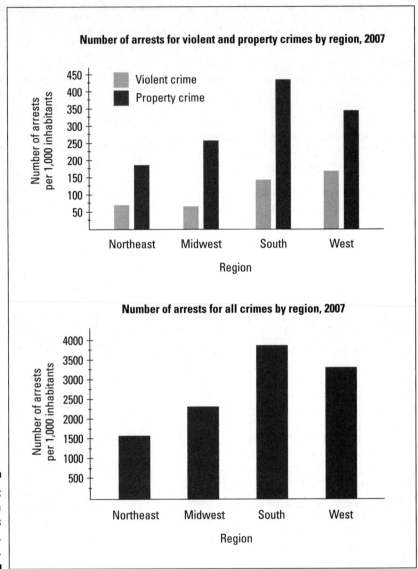

Source: Federal Bureau of Investigation

Figure 11-3:
Per-capita
crime rates
in each U.S.
region.

Gun control as crime control?

A heated criminological controversy deals with whether gun ownership can or does reduce crime. On the one hand, criminologists who favor *gun control* — laws regulating or restricting the possession of firearms — point to the fact that guns are involved in a high percentage of crimes. For example, in 2005, 71 percent of all homicides involved firearms. These criminologists contend that by making guns more difficult to obtain, society can reduce their availability and, thus, reduce their use in crime. An example of gun control in action is the *Brady Law,* which requires a five-day waiting period before a person may purchase a handgun.

On the other hand, some criminologists contend that gun ownership *prevents* crime. They point out that no study has shown a correlation between gun control and lower violent crime rates and that a person in possession of a firearm can actually prevent a crime simply by flashing the weapon. For example, in 2002 at the Appalachian School of Law in Virginia, a former student killed three people and wounded three others. Sounds like a good reason for gun control, right? Not exactly. Often not reported about the tragedy is the fact that two students ran to their vehicles, retrieved their personal guns, and confronted the killer, who then surrendered. Roughly 40 states have laws permitting citizens to carry concealed handguns if they have permits from a local law enforcement agency, and the violent crime rates in those states are no greater than the rates in states that don't permit the carrying of guns.

An eye-opening 1994 national survey conducted by Florida State University professors Marc Gertz and Gary Kleck found that people in the United States used a gun defensively as often as 2.5 million times in one year. The National Institute for Justice sponsored a follow-up survey published in 1997 that found the estimated number of defensive uses of guns to be somewhere between 1.5 million and 3.1 million a year.

In 2008, the U.S. Supreme Court declared that the 30-year-old law banning handguns in Washington, D.C., violated the Second Amendment of the U.S. Constitution. Proponents of gun rights point to the fact that while handguns were banned in Washington, D.C., its murder rate actually rose at the same time that the murder rate in the rest of the United States dropped. Strongly believing that gun possession deters crime, the town of Kennesaw, Georgia, went so far as to pass a city law *requiring* every household to own a firearm.

Studying the Impact of Atmospheric Changes

If "the moon is in the seventh house and Jupiter is aligned with Mars," are you more likely to rob a bank? Although the alignment of the stars may be of questionable value in studying crime patterns, it's clear that the date, time, and even weather play important roles.

Crime stats show that more crime occurs during the summer than in other times of the year. Here are some reasons why:

- Kids are out of school and have more free time. And you know what they say about idle hands — the whole devil's workshop thing.

- More people are outside interacting with each other (rather than sitting on their couches watching TV), which produces greater opportunities for conflict.

- People generally take vacations in the summer, leaving their homes for a week or two — and leaving them vulnerable to burglary. (If you were a burglar, would you rather be out on a nice July night, prowling around houses looking for an easy entry, or would you prefer to be out on a rainy, windy, 40-degree December night when every house is likely to be occupied?)

- Hot weather may lead to an increase in domestic violence as tempers turn short.

    Interestingly, *extremely* hot weather may decrease crime somewhat. For example, when it's too hot, the number of sexual offenses, such as rape, generally decreases.

Robberies are an exception to the summer-weather rule. More robberies occur in the winter, perhaps because winter offers more darkness to conceal criminal acts. Plus, the cold weather justifies wearing more clothes (which lets robbers conceal their appearances without raising suspicions).

Chapter 12

Regarding Crime as a Rational Decision: Rational Choice Theory

....

....

*O*ne of the core theories of criminology holds that, for the most part, criminals engage in a rational decision-making process when choosing to commit crime. This theory, called the *rational choice theory,* is at the heart of society's primary response to crime — which is putting criminals behind bars. Many people believe that when you punish crime sufficiently (through jail or prison), a rational person will choose not to commit crime.

In this chapter, I discuss the ramifications of the rational choice theory after taking a brief look at its forbearer, classical theory. I finish with a discussion on the limits of the theory.

Taking a Quick Tour through Classical Theory

In the late 18th century in many European countries, criminal justice systems were little more than collections of arbitrary laws unknown to the populace. Confessions by torture were common, and you could've been arrested for doing something you didn't even realize was a crime. Punishment was often arbitrary, excessive to the crime, and not based on any written law. Judges may even have had financial interests in the outcomes of criminal cases, which as you can imagine, made the punishments even more subjective.

An Italian man named Cesare Beccaria came to the rescue in 1764 when he published the world-changing essay known as *On Crimes and Punishments*. In this essay, Beccaria rebelled against the arbitrary nature of punishment and laid the foundation for the *classical theory* of criminology. Beccaria's utilitarian philosophy (and a key element of classical theory) is summed up in the following excerpt:

> *In order for punishment not to be, in every instance, an act of violence of one or many against a private citizen, it must be essentially public, prompt, necessary, the least possible in the given circumstances, proportionate to the crime and dictated by the laws.*

> — Cesare Beccaria

Beccaria sought to bring reason to punishment. He and other like-minded individuals succeeded magnificently, igniting a revolution in Western law. That revolution included doing away with torture, writing down the criminal laws and making them known to the populace, and adding the Eighth Amendment to the U.S. Constitution, which prohibits cruel and unusual punishment. In the United States, the principles that Beccaria and others (he can't have *all* the credit) promoted were ingrained in the Bill of Rights in 1791, just 27 years after they were first brought forward.

Although the call for proportionate punishment was a crucial part of classical theory, the theory also included another important element: the belief that individuals act purposefully to maximize their pleasure in life. The theory held that people will commit crimes unless they believe that the potential punishments outweigh the pleasures or benefits they gain from committing the crimes.

Calculating the Benefits and Drawbacks of Crime

Over time, classical theory evolved into its modern version called *rational choice theory,* which holds that criminals think about their actions, weighing the pros and cons (including the risks of punishment) and making decisions based on their calculations.

Analyzing risks and rewards

When you need to make an important decision like changing jobs or deciding where to go to college, you may sit down and write out the pros and cons on a piece of paper. You attempt to reason through each option to make the best decision. Most criminals don't engage in this level of rational thought before committing crime, but rational choice theorists contend that even though a criminal may not write out the pros and cons of a decision to commit a crime, he does go through a rational decision-making process. That is, he engages in a risk/reward or cost/benefit analysis by asking himself, "What are the risks and rewards of my actions?"

By saying that a decision to commit a crime is rational, rational choice theorists are *not* saying the decision is smart. In reality, rational decisions to commit crimes are likely based on faulty values and bad judgments, but they are, nonetheless, decisions made after weighing risks and rewards. For example, a person who steals an iPod clearly undervalues the property rights of others, but his decision may still be rational because he believes committing the crime will end not in punishment but in iPod possession.

What are some of the benefits that a person may get from committing a crime? Of course, the answer depends on the type of crime, but here are a few possibilities:

- ✔ Money or property
- ✔ Thrills and excitement
- ✔ Status among peers
- ✔ Revenge
- ✔ Dominance over others
- ✔ A bond with other criminals

Think about a teenage dropout who sees a super smart kid he knew in geometry class before he dropped out. The dropout decides to beat up the smart kid. At first glance, this choice seems irrational. What good can come from this action? Indeed, the dropout probably isn't consciously following a logical progression in his decision making; rather, his decision is partly subconscious. But when you break it down, here's what the dropout may be thinking right before he beats up the smart kid:

- ✔ I never liked that kid.
- ✔ He thought he was so smart.
- ✔ I felt dumb around him.
- ✔ I'm bigger and tougher than him.
- ✔ Now that we're out of the classroom, I want him to know what I felt like.
- ✔ I'm going to kick his butt.

The reward for committing this crime of assault is primarily a feeling of superiority and dominance over the smart kid. Of course, in making a rational decision, the dropout must also consider the costs or risks involved. For instance, if he's caught, he may be arrested for assault.

But what if there were no costs? Imagine a society without criminal laws. Everyone would have to fend for himself, and the only law would be survival of the fittest. The dropout's only fear would be that the smart kid may use his geometry prowess to get even.

In modern society, however, the existence of criminal laws provides the most likely risk or cost to the dropout. So before he decides to beat up the smart kid, he probably looks around for a teacher or other adult who could turn him in. Seeing no one, he assesses the risk as minimal and proceeds with the beating. He may also know that because he's under 18, the justice system can't treat him as an adult, so not much can happen to him even if he is caught. In essence, the dropout gets to feel dominant over the smart kid without much risk of negative consequences — at least in the short run.

Although the dropout's rational thought process is partly subconscious, rational choice theorists believe that a lot of crime involves the actual conscious weighing of risks and rewards.

Choosing the type and place of crime

Part of choosing to engage in crime is rationally choosing the *type* of crime to commit. For example, wanting to assert dominance over the smart kid, the dropout from the previous example doesn't just randomly start committing crime against anyone. He doesn't choose to burglarize the smart kid's house or steal his skateboard. Instead, he consciously chooses to commit assault.

Deciding *where* and *when* to commit a crime requires a lot of thought, too — perhaps more thought than deciding whether to commit the crime in the first place. After all, if you're going to commit a crime, you want to be successful. So burglars choose vulnerable homes or stores. Street-level drug dealers pick locations where customers are readily available and police are visible from a distance (so they can run before the cops get to them). Car thieves choose cars that are easy to take and can be sold (either whole or in parts) for the highest profit.

Choosing the time and place of a crime may be based on improving the reward of the crime or reducing the risk of being caught. For example, a robber usually chooses a location near his own home because he knows all the escape routes and, therefore, can reduce his risk of being caught. At the same time, however, the robber also wants the crime to be fairly easy to commit. It's a well-known secret that most criminals are extremely lazy and unwilling to make extra efforts, even when those efforts may mean increased rewards.

Factoring in personality and skills

Obviously, the personal characteristics of a criminal are tremendously important in influencing the decision to commit crime. For example, the ability to delay gratification often divides criminals from law-abiding citizens. Two people may equally desire an LCD television. One may choose to work for six months and save money to buy the TV. The other person, who can't stand to delay gratification so long, may decide to run the risk of being caught and steal the TV now.

Some people not only have personality traits that influence their criminal decisions but also develop skills that make criminal choices easier. For example, a significant problem with putting a bunch of criminals in prison is that they learn new criminal skills from each other, which they can use when they're released. A serial car thief may spend two years in prison, sharing a cell with a drug trafficker. During those two years, the car thief may learn how to conceal drugs in vehicles. When he's released, the car thief may decide to start trafficking heroin and cocaine.

Meeting the offender's needs

Basically, the benefit the criminal hopes to receive from a particular crime determines which type of crime he chooses to commit and how he decides to commit it. People who want goods or money generally commit property crime. For instance, if I simply want an iPod, I can steal it from my friend's backpack. But if I want an iPod *and* I want to show my friends that I'm fearless, I may go into an electronics store, grab one, and run out. In contrast, people who want to feel dominance over others are more likely to commit violent crimes. Someone who wants status in a street gang may look for an opportunity to use his gun against a rival gang, for example.

Generally, people who commit property crime don't cross over and commit violent crime because the punishment for violent crime is usually much higher. So property criminals, making rational calculations, choose to commit offenses that are less likely to cost them significant prison sentences. For example, a property criminal can choose to commit armed robbery (theft by force) of a jewelry store, or he can choose to break into the store at night and commit burglary. Because robbery is considered a violent crime with a much greater punishment, the property offender is likely to opt for burglary. Robbers, on the other hand, often want more than just property — they want the thrill, excitement, and danger of sticking a gun in someone's face.

Creating Rational Deterrents to Crime

Supporters of rational choice theory believe that if the risk of being caught is high enough — and the punishment is severe enough — most crime will be deterred. Before I jump into that discussion, however, I need to point out a few other deterrents to crime, including

- ✔ The disapproval of family and peers
- ✔ Moral or religious objections
- ✔ Recognition that, in the long run, the criminal life isn't rewarding

Society can benefit greatly from encouraging these deterrents; I discuss the impact of family and society in discouraging crime in Chapter 13. But the reality today is that society spends most of its resources for deterring crime on the threat of arrest and punishment in the justice system.

In this section, I take a look at the different ways society tries to deter people from committing crime through punishment.

Running the risk of being caught (and punished)

For the threat of arrest and punishment to be an effective deterrent to crime, potential criminals have to believe their chances of being caught and punished are high. So, how high is the risk of being arrested for a crime? Not very. As I discuss in Chapter 3, the Federal Bureau of Investigation (FBI) keeps statistics on the number of arrests for certain serious crimes and calculates the national rate — called the *clearance rate* — at which reported crimes are cleared by arrests of suspects. Unfortunately, most serious crime doesn't end in arrest. Figure 12-1 shows the 2007 U.S. clearance rates for a variety of offenses.

Note: These statistics don't include minor crimes, such as shoplifting, which aren't even reported to the police unless the suspects are caught. So the total clearance rate for *all* crime is actually much lower than it appears to be in Figure 12-1.

As you can see, serious violent crimes are solved at a much higher rate than serious property crimes, which means violent criminals face a greater risk than property criminals. Why the difference? For one, law enforcement agencies put a higher priority on solving violent crime, devoting significantly more resources to investigating rapes and murders than thefts and burglaries. In fact, in many communities, a police officer doesn't even visit your home to take a report when your home is burglarized. In addition, violent crimes, such as rape, assault, and robbery, often involve victims who are eyewitnesses (which means they can often describe or identify the criminal), while property crimes usually don't involve eyewitnesses.

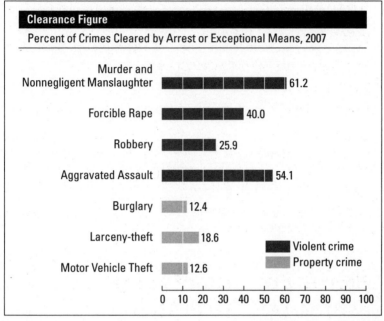

Clearance Figure

Percent of Crimes Cleared by Arrest or Exceptional Means, 2007

Murder and Nonnegligent Manslaughter — 61.2

Forcible Rape — 40.0

Robbery — 25.9

Aggravated Assault — 54.1

Burglary — 12.4

Larceny-theft — 18.6

Motor Vehicle Theft — 12.6

■ Violent crime
■ Property crime

0 10 20 30 40 50 60 70 80 90 100

Figure 12-1: The clearance rates for various crimes in 2007.

Source: Federal Bureau of Investigation

Based on the risk component of the rational choice theory, if state governments (and federal agencies) hired enough police officers (and other law enforcing agents), they'd be able to significantly increase the risk of being caught and, thereby, deter much more crime. So why doesn't the government do so?

The truth is, it has. Between 1992 and 2004, the total number of state and local police agency employees in the United States grew from about 841,000 to 1.1 million — an increase of 23 percent. During that time period, the national crime rate decreased significantly. For example, the violent crime rate dropped by more than half between 1992 and 2004. Of course, criminologists debate about the actual cause of this dramatic decrease in crime, and deterrence from greater police presence is just one of many theories. (See the next section for another potential reason: an increase in the length of prison sentences.)

Adding even more law enforcement personnel would cost U.S. taxpayers a lot of money, and society currently has many other ills calling for tax dollars. In addition, U.S. citizens highly value individual freedom and tend to distrust any government presence that's too dominant — the kind that would result from having a police officer on every street corner.

Increasing the severity of punishment

The fear of being embarrassed by an arrest is enough to deter many people from committing crime. (Just think of the mug shots that show up on TV when the latest celebrity is arrested and booked. Imagine having your friends and co-workers see you like that.) But in addition to embarrassment, the type and amount of punishment for a particular crime is very important in a criminal's risk/reward calculations.

Beginning in the mid-1990s, a movement spread across the United States to significantly increase the punishment for serious violent offenders. Prior to this movement, murderers were commonly released from prison after ten years — sometimes even less. As a result of this movement, a typical sentence for a murderer today is life in prison. I discuss incarceration theories in detail in Chapter 21, but for now here's what you need to know: One major goal of the movement toward more severe sentencing was to deter violent crime. And some criminologists cite increased punishment as a reason for the dramatic decrease in violent crime since the 1990s.

An unintended result of this movement toward increased punishment has been the filling up of jails and prisons, which results in a lack of space for low-level offenders. Thus, serious offenders get longer sentences, but shoplifters, drunk drivers, or even wife beaters may not get any jail time at all. Judges try imposing other creative punishments, such as community service or fines, on low-level offenders, but if a criminal isn't deterred by the fear of arrest, this minimal punishment isn't likely to have much of an effect, either.

What about the ultimate punishment — death? I discuss this topic in detail in Chapter 21, but suffice it to say, criminologists, politicians, and citizens alike engage in a vigorous debate about whether the death penalty deters crime.

Aiming for speedy punishment

Some people believe that a long delay between the arrest and the imposition of a sentence negates the deterrent effect of punishment. Most defendants, for instance, aren't held in jail while they wait for their trials (or while they wait to plea bargain), so they're free to commit additional crimes before they experience any punishment. Criminals can rack up quite a few crimes before they ever see the inside of a jail cell.

In addition, most people — including criminals — rationalize their misconduct, and as more time passes after their arrest, they can persuade themselves that they weren't all that responsible for their crime. By the time sentencing rolls around a year later, many criminals have completely disassociated the punishment from their criminal conduct. Therefore, they feel that the punishment is unwarranted and, thus, resent their treatment.

Deterrence requires people to associate punishment with the crimes they commit. If criminals don't make that association, they're more likely to commit more crime in the future.

One of the criticisms of the death penalty is that long delays of 10 to 20 years from sentencing to execution mean that people don't fear being executed if they commit murder. (In Chapter 21, I discuss the death penalty in detail.)

Punishments throughout U.S. history

Today the primary means of criminal punishment is jail or prison. U.S. courts require certain minimum standards for inmates, including access to daylight and fresh air, exercise, protection from the elements, and quality meals. In the past, however, particularly before the passage of the Bill of Rights, society imposed some very different forms of punishment. Here are just a few that used to be popular:

✔ **Stocks and pillories:** Punishments involving stocks and pillories were slightly different from one another, but generally, stocks and pillories were wooden frames that held criminals in place so that other citizens could insult them and throw rotten food at them.

✔ **Public humiliation:** When criminals received this punishment, they had to wear clothes with big letters sewn on them, representing the crimes they'd committed. For example, a *T* stood for theft.

✔ **Whipping:** This punishment involved lashing someone on the back with a whip. The number of lashes depended on the seriousness of the crime.

✔ **Tarring and feathering:** This punishment involved hot tar being applied to the criminal's skin and then feathers being stuck on top of it. Criminals who received this punishment were then paraded around town. Tarring and feathering was more often a vigilante punishment than something imposed by a judge.

✔ **Burning at the stake:** A common punishment throughout history, burning at the stake was outlawed in England in 1790. (Contrary to popular myth, the Salem witch trials of the 1690s didn't end in the burning of witches, but rather in hangings — except one poor soul who was executed by having a pile of stones placed on top of him.)

✔ **Hanging, drawing, and quartering:** This punishment was used primarily in England for men who committed treason, but it was also used in Canada and may have once been used in New York (before the United States became a nation). The criminals were dragged to a location where they were hanged for a short period of time. They were then disemboweled and made to watch while their innards were burned. The criminals were then cut into four parts and beheaded. The body parts were placed around the country as a deterrent to other criminals.

Preventing the rewards

According to the rational choice theory, when you reduce the rewards for crime, or make the commission of the crime more difficult, reasonable adults are less likely to commit crime.

Society can employ many strategies to reduce the benefit of crime to criminals, particularly for property crime. Among private corporations, these strategies are known collectively as crime prevention or loss prevention. For example:

- ✔ Many retailers lock up items that thieves highly value, such as electronics and even baby formula. In addition, most retailers also have theft-prevention devices — which they attach to high-priced items — that set off an alarm when someone leaves the store without paying for an item.

- ✔ Most banks place a pack of dye next to their tellers, who put the pack in the middle of some cash when they're being robbed. The dye explodes some time later, turning the cash (and perhaps the robber) red.

- ✔ And, of course, the security industry makes billions each year by *hardening targets:* making buildings and businesses less vulnerable to crime through alarm and camera systems.

Examining the Limits of Rational Choice Theory

Understanding rational choice theory is tremendously important to understanding why someone may commit crime. But it fails to account for a number of circumstances that, as a budding criminologist, you simply can't ignore. I cover some of those circumstances in the following sections.

Considering humans who behave irrationally

When I was a child, I spoke like a child, I thought like a child, I reasoned like a child. When I became a man, I gave up childish ways.

— 1 Corinthians 13:11

This famous biblical saying is meant to inspire people to act wisely, but the truth is, adults often act unwisely, like children — or worse.

Sometimes people look at situations and say to themselves, "Screw it," and then dive right into criminal conduct. Humans often throw reason out the window. Imagine a cop responding to a 9-1-1 call of a man threatening his family with a knife. (Disturbingly, such conduct is common.) Trying to change the man's cost/benefit analysis by telling him he's going to prison probably isn't a good strategy. The man is acting irrationally, and the reason behind his conduct is likely one of the following:

- ✔ Drugs
- ✔ Alcohol
- ✔ Mental illness
- ✔ Extreme emotional distress

As I discuss in Chapter 5, some drugs, such as methamphetamine, can cause a psychosis in which a person acts completely irrationally and violently. Aside from such a physical reaction to drugs, addiction itself often drives people to commit completely irrational acts, such as running great risks for another quick fix.

Similarly, a person who's drunk usually exercises very poor judgment (you've probably seen this at some point). In 2007, 12,998 intoxicated drivers crashed their cars and killed someone. I bet that if asked today, every one of those drivers would say that their decision to drive drunk was dumb. By far, alcohol and drugs are responsible for more crime than any other factor, in large part, because drugs and alcohol cause people to act irrationally.

Mental illness also poses a significant challenge for cops on the street — and for policymakers, in general. It seems like society has more mentally ill people than ever before. Mental health facilities are overflowing, forcing many people with mental illnesses out on the street, where their irrational conduct can often lead to crime.

In 2005, for instance, more than 24 million adults (11 percent of the U.S. population) suffered from serious psychological distress, according to the Substance Abuse and Mental Health Services Administration. One reason for this high percentage may be the dramatic increase in drug use in the last 40 years. More and more medical evidence shows that mothers who use drugs or alcohol are more likely to have mentally handicapped children. And the National Institute on Drug Abuse reported in 2007 that six out of ten drug abusers also suffer from a mental illness. (In some cases, the drug abuse causes the mental illness.)

Of course, numerous other factors contribute to the development of mental illnesses. I discuss mental illness in more detail in Chapter 14, but suffice it to say that the mentally ill often act irrationally when they commit crime.

Seeing how crime often pays

Folks in law enforcement often joke about how they could make a financial killing by becoming criminals. If crime really does pay, a rational (if immoral) person may very well choose a life of crime.

As I discuss in Chapter 8, a lot of people make a lot of money committing crime (namely, in organized crime organizations). Every day, drug traffickers in the United States send millions of illegally earned dollars south of the border.

Society can try to affect a criminal's risk/reward analysis by decreasing the profits of crime or by increasing penalties. It can also try to address the moral shortcomings of its citizens who believe selling drugs is okay if they can get away with it. But as long as crime pays, even for just a handful of criminals, some people are going to choose to take the risk.

Dealing with the values gap

I know of a young man who wants to go to prison so he can move up in the hierarchy of his street gang. According to the rational choice theory, his conduct is perfectly explainable because he has something that he deems important to gain from committing crime. However, that *rational* explanation doesn't do society much good.

How did this young man come to place such a high value on his street gang status that he would be willing to give up several years of his life and go to prison for it? If society can begin to understand how a man comes to develop such values, perhaps it can prevent others from going down the same path. But that's an awfully big *if*.

Besides rational choice theory, criminologists have developed numerous other theories to try to explain why people engage in crime. I discuss these theories in the next three chapters.

Chapter 13

Looking at Society's Role in Crime

· ·

In This Chapter

▶ Connecting crime to decaying neighborhood structures

▶ Feeling the strain of not fulfilling society's expectations

▶ Observing how to become a criminal

▶ Keeping criminal impulses in check

· ·

As I explain in Chapter 12, rational choice theory is a prominent theory in the study of causes of crime. However, this theory fails to account for people's irrational decisions, and it doesn't explain how people develop values that lead them to make *rational* choices to commit crime.

In this chapter, I look at some prominent theories that focus more on society's role — and less on individual choice — in explaining why people commit crime. Keep in mind that most crime is committed by young people. The theories I discuss in this chapter attempt to explain how someone gets into crime in the first place, which almost invariably happens during the teen years.

Alone, none of these theories adequately explains why one person becomes a criminal and another doesn't. But, by understanding each theory, you can gain some great insight into what motivates human conduct. Perhaps you'll also develop an appreciation for just how difficult dealing with crime really is.

Introducing Social Disorganization Theory

The *Chicago School,* a school of criminological thought that developed in the 1920s, argues that a person's physical and social environments are primarily responsible for the behavioral choices that person makes.

A significant component of the Chicago School is *social disorganization theory*, a theory that sociologists Clifford Shaw and Henry McKay developed after tracking crime within different neighborhoods in Chicago in the 1920s and 1930s. Social disorganization theory emphasizes the connection between crime and the neighborhood structure. The theory argues that more crime occurs in neighborhoods that have fraying social structures, such as

- ✔ Poor schools
- ✔ Vacant and vandalized buildings
- ✔ A mix of commercial and residential property
- ✔ Changing ethnicity
- ✔ High unemployment

As social structures decay, families that can move out of the neighborhood do so, which further destroys the social ties that can help reduce crime. Conversely, in neighborhoods with good schools, little vandalism, low vacancy rates, and a stable population, social bonds are stronger and, as a result, crime rates are lower.

Shaw and McKay found that the areas of Chicago with the most crime were inner-city zones with large populations of new immigrants. During Shaw and McKay's studies, the immigrant populations of crime-ridden neighborhoods changed from mostly German and Irish immigrants to Italian immigrants.

Their social disorganization theory continues to play a significant role in U.S. social policy today as governments grapple with the same dynamics of inner-city crime and new immigrant populations. For example, efforts to encourage businesses to establish operations in poor neighborhoods and tax breaks for people who buy older, broken-down homes are attempts to revitalize neighborhoods and help them improve social bonds and community strength.

Studying Strain Theory

In general, a group of theories, called *strain theory*, contends that most people in society share the same goals of achieving wealth and success. But some people in lower classes don't have the same opportunities that their wealthier counterparts do, and, as a result, they get angry when they can't achieve their goals. This frustration, or *strain*, leads to crime. I take a look at the different variations of strain theory in the following sections.

Anomie theory

Anomie is another word for strain — it refers to the difference between what a person aspires to do and what he can actually achieve. When Robert Merton developed the anomie theory in 1938, he focused on the interplay between the following two concepts:

- ✔ Society imposes expectations or goals on its people — to make money and to be successful.
- ✔ Society approves only of certain ways to achieve these goals — go to school, work hard, and delay gratification, for example.

Merton contended that poorer classes lack real opportunities for making money and being successful according to society's standards, which leads to anomie, or strain, or frustration (take your pick). People who live in poor neighborhoods with bad schools and few positive role models are significantly disadvantaged compared to folks who live in better neighborhoods. At some point, people who are disadvantaged recognize that they can't achieve society's goals in the approved way, so they resort to crime to achieve success.

In modern times, Merton may argue that bling — in other words, the gaudy jewelry that people who are perceived to be wealthy in inner-city neighborhoods display and the Mercedes and BMWs that wealthy people from richer neighborhoods drive — demonstrates how strong and influential the social forces are that drive people to seek material success. The fact that drug dealers like to wear bling and drive nice cars shows that their concept of success is a significant motivator for their criminality.

Merton's theory has been very influential in criminological circles. But one criticism of the anomie theory and other similar theories is that most people raised in lower-class neighborhoods *don't* commit crime, and some people in higher classes *do* commit crime. So, lower-class frustration in failing to achieve goals may be an explanation for some crimes, but it certainly doesn't explain them all.

General strain theory

In 1992, Robert Agnew developed a variation of anomie theory, known as *general strain theory* (GST). GST focuses on the strain (or anomie) that people in *all* classes can feel — not just the lower classes. He contended that strain isn't just frustration over failing to achieve the goals that society imposes, but that strain includes many other issues, as well. For example, all classes (rich or poor) feel some of the following strains:

- ✔ The failure to keep up with the Joneses — to achieve what your neighbor has achieved

- ✔ The failure to live up to your own expectations

- ✔ The loss of positive influences, such as separating from your parents or moving to a new community where you have no friends

- ✔ The introduction of negative influences, such as delinquent friends, alcoholic parents, and child or spousal abuse

Because people who live in good and bad neighborhoods may experience each of these types of strain singly or in combination, GST seems to be an improvement on Merton's theory of anomie, which attributed strain mostly to the lower classes. However, GST still isn't an all-encompassing theory of criminality because it doesn't fully explain why many people who feel significant strain don't commit crime.

Institutional anomie theory

Institutional anomie theory contends that certain institutions play an important role in keeping people from fixating on material success, and, as a result, these institutions help reduce strain. Families and churches, for example, temper the desire for material wealth. They emphasize nonmaterial success, such as a good home life, close friends, and spiritual strength. These institutions also help people find ways to deal with strain without resorting to crime.

Unfortunately, fewer people are attending church these days, and families are much more fractured, thanks to high divorce rates and the increasing number of births out of wedlock. According to the institutional anomie theory, the lessening impact of these institutions is leading people to place more emphasis on material success. It also reduces their ability to deal with strain. As a result, more people turn to crime.

As positive institutions weaken, negative institutions may grow. For example, street gangs and drug-trafficking organizations may flourish. As these criminal groups become institutions in some neighborhoods, they pass on negative — not positive — values from generation to generation.

Subculture theories

A number of similar theories generally contend that subcultures that encourage values different from mainstream society frequently develop in lower-class neighborhoods (I discuss a few of these theories in this section).

Although hard work, education, and delayed gratification are society's preferred means for achieving success, failure to achieve middle-class success leads to strain in poorer areas. The subcultures that develop in these poorer neighborhoods promote different values, such as

- ✔ Instant gratification
- ✔ Violence
- ✔ Excitement
- ✔ Toughness
- ✔ Risk taking

Lower-class reaction theory

In 1955, Albert Cohen developed a subculture theory called *lower-class reaction theory,* which holds that as kids in lower classes fail to live up to society's expectations, they reject middle-class values and develop their own value systems. Doing so allows them to maintain their self-esteem.

For example, poor kids who develop status frustration because they don't do well in school may try to obtain status elsewhere, most likely among their delinquent, lower-class peers by drinking alcohol and using drugs, joining gangs, committing theft, or engaging in violence.

The lower-class reaction theory includes a strong dose of anomie because Cohen believed that the lower classes are frustrated at not being able to meet society's expectations.

Differential opportunity theory

In 1960, Richard Cloward and Lloyd Ohlin developed another subculture theory called *differential opportunity theory.* This theory is similar to Cohen's lower-class reaction theory because it, too, argues that lower-class juveniles who fail to live up to societal expectations often rebel and seek to participate in subcultures with distinct values.

However, Cloward and Ohlin also included a dose of social disorganization theory. They contended that kids in stable lower-class neighborhoods are more likely to find criminal role models who help them achieve some level of criminal success by apprenticing the kids into a variety of criminal enterprises.

But, in socially disorganized neighborhoods, where the population is constantly moving in and out and little stability exists, even role models for criminals are hard to come by. As a result, not even criminal organizations thrive, and kids fail to find any "successful" criminal group to join. Such kids may then turn to groups of thugs who primarily fight with other groups.

According to differential opportunity theory, delinquents in stable, lower-class neighborhoods develop values according to their possibility of achieving criminal success. In contrast, delinquents in disorganized neighborhoods develop values and maintain their self-images not through criminal business but by winning conflict battles with others.

Considering Social Learning Theories

Some criminologists contend that who you are and what you do is a product of your social interactions and that, essentially, you *learn* how to be a criminal — which is where social learning theories come in.

Differential association theory

In 1934, Edwin Sutherland developed *differential association theory,* one of criminology's most influential theories. He contended that crime isn't just a function of lower classes and that both the rich and the poor can become criminals, depending on whom they hang out with and what values and beliefs they learn. Sutherland believed that your families and close friends have the greatest impact on your behavior and that you're likely to learn your values from them. For example, if your dad grows marijuana in his basement and your mom sells the dope out the back door, you'll likely grow up to view selling drugs as an acceptable behavior.

The differential association theory contends that you not only learn the basics of committing crime but also all the rationalizations, excuses, and motivations that explain and validate crime. For example, a child raised in a family that grows marijuana may learn how to fertilize crops and harvest the highest-quality buds, but that child may also come to believe that

- ✔ Marijuana has medicinal properties that help people.
- ✔ Marijuana isn't a dangerous drug because it just helps people relax and have fun.
- ✔ Selling marijuana is one way to fulfill the American capitalist dream.
- ✔ Police and government officials are authoritarian jerks who strip people of their freedoms.
- ✔ You don't have to pay taxes for selling drugs because those taxes just go to the government to take away your liberty.

How close your association with criminals is makes a big difference, too. For example, a juvenile who spends a little time with some casual drug-using friends may experiment with drugs herself. But, because other friends and her family frown on drug use, she'll probably reject drug use at some point. On the other hand, if her mom and sister are prostitutes who also use and deal drugs, she's more likely to engage in enduring criminal behaviors.

Differential association theory isn't based on class difference. Thus, it helps explain crime committed by middle- and upper-class people, not just the poor. After all, many poor people adopt society's positive values — including hard work, thrift, and delayed gratification — and have happy, successful lives. In the same way, many wealthy people lie, cheat, and abuse drugs and alcohol — all behaviors that negatively impact their peers and family members.

In a nutshell, this theory contends that people become criminals if, from association with their family and peers, they learn behaviors that violate the law. The duration, frequency, and intensity of that contact influences just how much they learn.

Techniques of neutralization theory

Developed in 1957 by David Matza and Gresham Sykes, *neutralization theory* points out that people who commit crime actually fluctuate back and forth between criminal conduct and law-abiding conduct. They may buy groceries, pay for their gas, go to school, and otherwise engage in behavior that is acceptable in society. In fact, many criminals view themselves as normal members of society by rationalizing their criminal conduct. In other words, criminals *neutralize* society's anticrime values with their own excuses.

Matza and Sykes contended that a person may employ the following five basic techniques of neutralization after committing a crime:

- **Denying responsibility:** For example, a person who just abused someone may say, "It was an accident" or "It's not really my fault — my dad abused me my whole life."

- **Denying harm:** For example, a person who just bought or stole drugs may say, "Buying drugs doesn't harm anyone" or "I was just borrowing them — I planned to return them."

- **Denying a victim:** For example, a person who just stole someone else's car may say, "He had it coming" or "She can afford it."

- **Condemning people in authority:** For example, criminals often call authority figures hypocrites or corrupt jerks.

✔ **Appealing to a higher authority:** For example, a gang member may justify a gang shooting by saying that it was the only way to defend his fellow gang brothers.

According to neutralization theory, criminals may follow society's rules most of the time, but when they occasionally violate society's rules, they know how to justify their conduct (at least in their own minds).

Delving into Social Control Theories

Why doesn't everyone commit crime? It can be exciting because it often provides thrills and immediate gratification. *Social control theorists* believe that most people would commit crime if society didn't impose certain controls that keep them in line. These controls can be either internal (the ones you impose on yourself) or external (the ones that come from families and school, for example).

Containment theory

First proposed by Walter Reckless (what a great name for a criminologist!) and achieving prominence in the 1950s and 1960s, *containment theory* contends that social pressures and individual characteristics work positively and negatively to affect a person's behavior. Some pressures make a person want to commit a crime, while other pressures, called *containments*, make him want to obey the law. The following examples show you some external and internal pressures that often lead to crime and some containments that encourage law-abiding behaviors:

✔ **External pressures toward crime:**

- Bad neighborhood

- Little opportunity for education, employment, or success

- Delinquent friends

- Negative subculture, such as gangs

- Negative media influences

✔ **Internal pressures toward crime:**

- Lack of self-esteem

- Personality traits such as being easily angered or predisposed to addiction

✔ **External containments:**

  • Strong family support

  • Church involvement

  • Positive role models

  • Nondelinquent friends

✔ **Internal containments:**

  • Strong self-esteem

  • Ability to resist temptation and show self-control

Because these forces are constantly at work on all people (rich or poor), this theory can help explain why some kids in bad neighborhoods turn out as law-abiding citizens and why some kids in good neighborhoods turn out as criminals.

Social bond theory

Proposed by Travis Hirschi in 1969, *social bond theory* contends that social bonds — bonds to family, friends, and others — are what keep people from breaking the law. For example, my friends may reject me if I act on my impulses and steal a few cans of soda from the convenience store. If I didn't have any close friends, I may feel freer to steal the drinks.

As part of his social bond theory, Hirschi broke down these social bonds into four parts:

✔ **Attachment:** This refers to the bonds you have with other people (friends and parents, for example) and institutions (schools and churches). Someone with strong attachment to positive role models and institutions is less likely to engage in crime than someone who lacks such strong bonds.

✔ **Commitment:** This refers to the investment you have in mainstream society. For example, a person with a college degree has a greater commitment to society and more to lose by becoming a criminal than a high school dropout does.

✔ **Involvement:** This refers to the amount of time you spend on community activities, such as sports, drama, or volunteer work. Significant participation in societal activities helps build bonds with others and leaves less time for criminality.

✔ **Belief:** As its name implies, this refers to the extent to which you believe in the values society offers. Believing in the positive values of mainstream society reduces your likelihood to commit crime.

A person who strongly holds each of these four components is unlikely to engage in crime because they're much more likely to have strong social bonds. But, as each of these elements weakens, a person's social bonds weaken, too, and it becomes easier to engage in criminal acts.

Chapter 14

Can Your Mind or Body Make You a Criminal?

....

In This Chapter

▶ Trying to define a criminal appearance

▶ Considering the genetic link to crime

▶ Connecting the brain to criminal behavior

▶ Touching on mental illness and personality disorders

....

Genetics, early development, neighborhood quality, socialization, diet, brain chemistry, education, income, intelligence, social institutions, good and bad friends, and free will — in other words, societal and biological factors — all work together to make you a law-abiding or law-breaking citizen. In this chapter, I explore how criminologists have attempted to use biology, in combination with societal factors, to explain criminal behavior.

When you look through this chapter, keep in mind that the one clear thing about criminological theories is that *nothing* is clear. Crime has a myriad of potential causes that all work in conjunction with one another in varying ways and to varying degrees.

Biological Positivism: Trying to Link Appearance to Crime

An important approach to criminological theory involves the use of *positivism*, which is a fancy word that simply refers to the attempt to bring the scientific method to criminology. Positivists believe in objectively measuring cause and effect. Here I focus on *biological positivism*, which concentrates on the physical characteristics that may influence a person to commit crime.

The search for biological traits associated with criminality may have begun in the late 1880s with an Italian prison doctor named Cesare Lombroso. Lombroso developed a theory based on his own research that certain physical characteristics were associated with being a criminal. In other words, criminals often had a similar *look*. Lombroso's research was an early form of *profiling*, which in its modern form is a technique that police sometimes use to identify people more likely to commit crimes. I discuss modern profiling in greater detail in Chapter 11.

According to Lombroso, some signs of criminality included

- ✔ Big jaw and cheekbones
- ✔ Strangely shaped nose and ears
- ✔ Big lips
- ✔ Sloped forehead

Basically, all you have to do is picture an ugly mug from a 1930s gangster movie.

 Lombroso's work was extremely influential during his time, but it turned out to be mostly wrong. Although a few people have called him the "father of criminology," many modern criminologists bristle at the suggestion. In fact, many criminologists believe that because Lombroso's work was so well received (but poorly done), he set back the field of criminology many years. (Because science — even social science — builds on the work of previous generations, I think criticism of Lombroso's honest efforts are somewhat unfair.)

Wrestling with the Influence of Genetics

Is there a criminal gene that gets passed from generation to generation? As I explain in Chapters 11, 12, and 13, analyzing why someone commits a crime is incredibly complicated. So many variables come into play that isolating one particular cause, including genetics, is extremely difficult.

Even if genetics play a role in crime, that role clearly doesn't involve just one *crime gene*. Rather, a person may be genetically predisposed in varying degrees to certain activities or emotions, such as anxiety, aggressiveness, or even learning impairments, all of which can play a part in a person's decision to commit crime. (I discuss how poor education can indirectly lead to a greater likelihood of criminal behavior in Chapter 11.)

In this section, I touch on some of the work that scientists have done to try to determine whether genetics play a role in criminality.

Figuring out how parents influence criminal behavior

Many studies have shown that parents who are criminals are more likely to have children who engage in criminal conduct. However, this trend doesn't necessarily mean that criminality is genetic. Criminal kids may come from criminal parents for a variety of reasons, including the following:

- ✔ Kids learn criminal behavior from their parents.

- ✔ Criminal parents are poor parents who don't raise their kids well. For example, the parents may fail to teach appropriate ways to deal with anger.

- ✔ Criminal parents are less likely to emphasize the importance of education.

- ✔ Criminal parents may be more likely to allow kids to hang out with other delinquents, which reinforces criminal values.

To try to determine whether a genetic component to crime exists, criminologists have done a variety of studies involving adopted children. One such study by W. F. Gabrielli Jr., S. A. Mednick, and B. Hutchings in 1984 drew the following conclusions from a set of historical adoption data:

- ✔ 13.5 percent of adopted sons engage in criminal conduct when neither biological parents nor adoptive parents are criminals.

- ✔ 14.7 percent of adopted sons engage in crime when the adoptive parents are criminals but the biological parents are not.

- ✔ 20 percent of adopted sons engage in crime when the biological parents are criminals but the adoptive parents are not.

- ✔ 24 percent of adopted sons engage in crime when both the biological and adoptive parents are criminals.

Studies like this one seem to indicate that biological parents impact the criminal conduct of their children by the genes they pass down and that parental figures who raise children also impact criminal conduct through social learning and the environments they create.

Other studies have focused on the behavior of twins. Identical twins share the exact same genes, but fraternal twins share only half of the same genes. So if genetics play a role in creating criminals, you expect a greater correlation in criminal behavior between identical twins than between fraternal twins. Some studies have shown that identical twins are more likely than fraternal twins to share traits, such as suicidal tendencies, impulsiveness, and criminal antisocial behavior.

However, I must point out some valid criticisms of studies involving adopted children and twins. For one thing, samples are often small, which means a small error can have a significant impact on the results. Also, records such as whether a twin is truly an identical twin are often based not on blood tests but on less reliable assessments. Furthermore, keep in mind that twins are almost always raised in the same environment, so you can also explain the similarity in criminal behavior partly by the fact that the twins are raised by the same parents with the same social influences.

Nonetheless, evidence that genetics play an important part in determining whether a child is more likely to engage in criminal conduct seems to be mounting.

Creating criminals through evolution

Some people theorize that the most aggressive males in society are more likely to mate and, thus, to have more offspring than other males. Over time, through the process of evolution, the human population features more men with genetic predispositions to aggression — and, theoretically, predispositions to violent crime.

The scientific study of criminological evolution is very difficult. However, the interest in studying such theories — including the mating patterns of criminals, which may have long-term societal impacts — is growing. For instance, one argument in favor of longer prison sentences for violent criminals (at least among cops who deal with violent people on the street) is that a criminal can't procreate in prison. Because most violent crime is committed between the ages of 17 and 35, the same ages as peak sexual activity, longer sentences may reduce the number of offspring of violent offenders (and increase the chances of a shy criminologist getting a date).

Blaming the Brain

Many other factors besides genetics affect your brain function. In this section, I briefly introduce a few of these factors that may impact criminality.

Eating a poor diet

Yes, nutrition can impact crime, albeit indirectly. Human beings need all sorts of nutrients, including minerals and vitamins, for optimum health. Nutritional deficiencies can have many negative impacts on physical well-being and brain functioning. For example, if you have a nutritional deficiency, you may experience

✔ Difficulty learning

✔ The onset of attention deficit/hyperactivity disorder (AD/HD)

✔ Depression

As I discuss in Chapter 13, poor performance in school and impaired social relationships may be closely related to delinquency in youth. Similarly, AD/HD and depression also are linked to higher incidents of antisocial and delinquent conduct.

Several studies of children and prison inmates have shown that using dietary supplements, including omega-3 fatty acids (which are found in fish oil), not only produces general health benefits and improved performance in school but also can significantly reduce violent or antisocial behavior. Other studies show that low blood sugar, known as *hypoglycemia*, leads some people to more violent conduct.

The myth of the Twinkie defense

In 1978, a former cop, fireman, and city supervisor named Dan White murdered San Francisco Mayor George Mosconi and another city supervisor, Harvey Milk. Despite confessing, White was convicted of only voluntary manslaughter after his attorneys asserted a defense of *diminished capacity*. Essentially, they claimed that White was debilitated by mental illness and wasn't fully responsible for the crime. Under the weak sentencing laws of the 1970s, White was sentenced to fewer than eight years in prison and ended up serving only about five. (After the sentence was pronounced, the gay community of San Francisco erupted in protest because Harvey Milk was one of the nation's first prominent gay politicians.)

White's lawyers asserted that he was suffering from severe depression and that his life had begun to unravel before he killed Mosconi and Milk. A very small piece of testimony focused on how, as part of his depression, White stopped eating healthily and began eating junk food, such as Twinkies, HoHos, and Ding Dongs. The defense offered this evidence to show that White was depressed, and a psychiatrist testified that what a person ingests can impact his actions. But the focus of the defense was on how White's depression impaired his ability to *deliberate,* a requirement for a murder conviction in California.

A columnist for a San Francisco newspaper first mentioned the "Twinkie insanity defense" in passing. Shortly thereafter, other media picked up on the phrase. Within a few months, there was a nationwide outcry over the fact that someone could get off for a murder by claiming he ate too many Twinkies. Politicians joined in the misplaced outcry (no surprise) and eventually removed the diminished capacity law from the books in California.

The truth is White didn't avoid a murder conviction by asserting a Twinkie defense. He was convicted of a lesser charge because his lawyers persuaded the jury that his depression meant he shouldn't be held fully responsible for his crime. His eating of junk food, including Twinkies, was just a symptom of his depression. After his release from prison, Dan White committed suicide in 1985.

Grappling with the wrong brain chemistry

Obviously, the brain is an incredibly complex organ, dependent on numerous chemicals in the right amounts to function properly. Deficiencies in these chemicals can lead to all types of behavioral and emotional problems, including anger, aggressiveness, impulsiveness, depression, and difficulty dealing with stress.

Some people, whose tendency toward violence is difficult to control, may be prescribed certain drugs that help balance out essential brain chemicals. One such antipsychotic drug is *haloperidol* (brand name *Haldol*), which doctors also give to schizophrenics who suffer from delusions and hallucinations. Controlling criminal impulses in individuals with strong tendencies toward violence largely depends on getting them to regularly take their medications.

Having a low IQ

Early criminological theories found a link between intelligence and crime. However, this analysis fell out of favor until a 1977 study by Michael Hindelang and Travis Hirschi found that delinquents tended to have lower IQs than nondelinquents. This study also found that a lower IQ meant a person was more likely to be a *recidivist* (a criminal who commits another felony within three years of being released).

Since this 1977 study, many criminologists have argued that the link between IQ and criminal conduct is indirect. Lower IQ leads to poor school performance, which weakens ties to positive institutions and to society, which, in turn, leads to criminality. Kids with higher IQs are more likely to succeed in school and have more opportunities for jobs and income in mainstream society, which often leads them to commit less crime.

People also point out that IQ tests can be culturally biased, resulting in lower scores for lower classes or certain racial and ethnic groups. Such bias means that a person's class or race is a part of the IQ score, thus invalidating the link between IQ and crime.

Struggling with Mental Illness

In some cases, mental illness is a significant cause of criminal conduct. A few categories of mental illness actually excuse a person from criminal responsibility. (See Chapter 20 for a discussion of the insanity defense.) More commonly, however, people suffer from other impairments that may affect criminality but not excuse it.

The American Psychiatric Association has attempted to categorize most types of mental illnesses in its book called the *Diagnostic and Statistical Manual of Mental Disorders,* known as the DSM-IV (currently in its fourth edition). The experts who drafted the latest edition of the book break down mental impairments into five categories, or *axes.* Axis I includes the most serious mental illnesses that can form the basis for an insanity defense and excuse criminal conduct.

A serious discussion of the impact of mental illness is beyond the scope of this book. But the evidence is clear that people who suffer from illnesses such as paranoid schizophrenia or bipolar disorder can have a difficult time getting by in society.

Schizophrenia, for example, can be accompanied by delusions and hallucinations that lead people to commit crimes. If I have a hallucination that a TV newswoman is telling me the postman is trying to kill me, I may decide to kill the postman before he tries to kill me. For such a crime, the judge or jury would likely find me guilty but insane because I acted based on the hallucination. For more information about schizophrenia, check out *Schizophrenia For Dummies* by Jerome and Irene Levine (Wiley).

Dealing with a Personality Disorder

Psychiatrists and psychologists often distinguish serious mental illnesses like schizophrenia from *personality disorders,* which are rigid patterns of behavior and belief that differ markedly from society's expectations. Having a personality disorder doesn't provide a legal excuse for committing a crime. In other words, you can't claim the insanity defense just because you're diagnosed with a personality disorder.

A person may develop a personality disorder based on combinations of the factors I discuss throughout Part III of this book, including family influences, environment, diet, lack of attachment to institutions such as schools or churches, delinquent friends, brain chemistry, genetics, and drug and alcohol abuse.

The DSM-IV includes ten personality disorders, which are designated as Axis II conditions (as opposed to Axis I mental illnesses). Some personality disorders are associated with criminal conduct, including the following:

- **Antisocial personality disorder:** I discuss this disorder in detail in the next section.

- **Narcissistic personality disorder:** Obviously, this label describes a person who is narcissistic, but someone with this disorder may also lack empathy, be arrogant, and have a sense of entitlement.

✔ **Borderline personality disorder:** This disorder is characterized by extreme black-and-white thinking, mood swings, and difficulty functioning within societal norms. It's also associated with higher suicide rates.

✔ **Histrionic personality disorder:** Excessive emotionality and attention seeking are characteristics of this disorder.

✔ **Paranoid personality disorder:** A person who is paranoid, distrustful of others, hypersensitive, and quick to react angrily may have this disorder. (Don't confuse this disorder with paranoid schizophrenia, which is a very different condition that often involves delusions and hallucinations.)

Focusing on antisocial personality disorder

Antisocial tendencies are strongly linked to criminal behavior. However, a person who is diagnosed with antisocial personality disorder may never commit a crime, and many criminals don't have antisocial personality disorder.

According to the DSM-IV, a person with antisocial personality disorder generally demonstrates a "pervasive pattern of disregard for and violation of the rights of others." In the United States, approximately 3 percent of the male population and 1 percent of the female population suffer from this disorder.

Distinguishing psychopaths

Many people use the term *psychopathy* interchangeably with the diagnosis of *antisocial personality disorder,* but doing so is a mistake because most people with antisocial personality disorder aren't psychopaths.

A *psychopath,* as defined by leading expert Dr. Robert Hare, "is a remorseless predator who uses charm, intimidation, and, if necessary, impulsive and cold-blooded violence to achieve his ends."

The distinction between psychopathy and antisocial personality disorder is important because psychopathy has been shown to be a strong predictor of recidivism (the tendency to commit serious crime after being released from custody). A psychopath is three or four times more likely to reoffend after release from prison than someone else. However, criminologists haven't found any strong link between recidivism and antisocial personality disorder.

Furthermore, psychopaths are resistant to treatment regimens; in fact, they often become more dangerous after treatment as they learn how to manipulate the system. Studies have also shown that people diagnosed with antisocial personality disorder may grow out of their antisocial conduct and, after age 35, are less likely to engage in crime. Psychopaths, however, don't seem to age out of crime, at least not until their mid-40s.

Defining *antisocial*

Because the word *antisocial* is so prevalent in criminology, understanding how psychiatrists define it is useful. The Diagnostic and Statistical Manual of Mental Disorders, 4th edition (DSM-IV), includes the following criteria for antisocial personality disorder:

- Displaying a pervasive pattern of disregarding and violating the rights of others since the age of 15

- Experiencing *conduct disorder* (essentially violating the rights of others) before the age of 15

- Participating in conduct that isn't solely the result of a schizophrenic or manic episode

In addition, the person diagnosed must meet at least three of the following conditions:

- The failure to conform to social norms with respect to lawful behaviors, as indicated by repeatedly performing acts that are grounds for arrest

- Deceitfulness as indicated by repeated lying, use of aliases, or conning others for personal profit or pleasure

- Impulsivity or lack of planning ahead

- Irritability and aggressiveness as indicated by repeated physical fights or assaults

- Reckless disregard for the safety of oneself or others

- Consistent irresponsibility as indicated by the repeated failure to sustain steady work or honor financial obligations

- A lack of remorse as indicated by being indifferent to or rationalizing having hurt, mistreated, or stolen from another

What causes psychopathy? A 2008 study by Donald Lynam, Rolf Loeber, and Magda Stouthamer-Loeber followed 271 13-year-old boys from Pittsburgh, Pennsylvania, until they turned 24. The researchers found that

- Boys who scored low in psychopathy at age 13 were more likely to score high at age 24 if they were exposed to a lot of antisocial friends and if they experienced higher levels of physical punishment.

- Boys who scored high in psychopathy at age 13 remained high at the age of 24 regardless of the caliber of their friends and whether or not they were physically punished.

In other words, good friends and a good home life don't seem to moderate psychopathy in a kid. But bad friends and a bad home life can make psychopathy worse.

Other studies have shown that traits consistent with adult psychopathy are visible in children as young as 3 years old. This finding suggests that being a psychopath is more dependent on early development and genetics than on socialization as a teenager or adult.

Chapter 15

Critical Theory: Theories off the Beaten Path

*C**ritical criminology* — a fairly vague categorization that applies to a broad array of unconventional criminological theories — developed in the 1960s as a challenge to *conventional* criminology, which encompasses the theories I discuss in Chapters 12 through 14. In essence, conventional criminological theories all accept (to some extent) the normal societal power structures. Critical criminology, on the other hand, challenges these generally accepted power structures.

Many of the writings of early critical criminologists were based on Marxist philosophy. Marxist criminologists argued that government creates criminal laws to benefit the people who own the means of economic production — who happen to be the same people who exercise tremendous influence over the government. Because conventional criminology is often dependent on government funding for its studies, some critical criminologists think of mainstream colleagues who take government money for their studies as sellouts to "the man."

Today, a critical criminologist may subscribe to any of a number of different critical theories, but almost all of them focus on power structures and the conflict between the haves and the have-nots. These theories tend to argue that people in power use the economic and justice systems to control poor people, minorities, and women. In this chapter, I introduce several of the more prominent critical theories, including a couple that deal more with solving the crime problem than figuring out why it exists in the first place. Understanding these more radical theories is essential to having a complete grasp of the wide world of criminological theory.

Labeling Someone a Criminal

Labeling theory, which achieved prominence in the 1960s, essentially consists of the following two concepts:

- ✔ The people in power decide what conduct is deviant or criminal as a way to control others, including minorities, women, and the poor.
- ✔ The *act* of labeling someone a criminal makes that person a criminal — not the person's conduct itself.

In other words, the people in power decide which acts are crimes, and then they label anyone who commits those acts a criminal. For example, politicians may make the act of accepting political contributions from lobbyists legal for themselves but make accepting money for favors a crime (known as bribery) for low-level bureaucrats. In this section, I take a closer look at labeling theory and its weaknesses.

Changing someone's self-image

A significant component of labeling theory holds that labeling someone a criminal negatively affects her self-image and increases her chances of committing more criminal acts. In other words, how society reacts to a person's committing a crime can actually cause her to commit more crimes.

Criminologist Edwin Lemert developed the following two stages of labeling:

- ✔ **Primary deviance:** The first crime that someone commits
- ✔ **Secondary deviance:** The crimes someone chooses to commit after (and often because) society labels that person a criminal

People who have been labeled criminals may start to reject societal values and look for support from others who have also been labeled criminals or deviants. For example, kids who have been caught up in the criminal justice system may begin to associate with one another, form a gang, and engage in joint, antisocial activities because they share the criminal label.

Why all the fuss because of a label? Try this little experiment: Think back to something stupid or illegal you did in your youth that you got away with (underage drinking, for example, or smoking marijuana or shoplifting). What if you had been caught? How would your life be different today?

Because you weren't caught, you were spared the label of being a criminal and, along with that label, the stigma and potential downward spiral of secondary deviance. Had you been caught, you may have been kicked out of your high school band or sports team and suspended from school. In that situation, instead of helping you decide on a college, your high school counselor may have recommended that you consider a less-skilled profession. (Ditch digging, anyone?) With decreased educational and professional opportunities, you may have been less compelled to hold tight to society's values, and, as a result, your path in life may have taken a very different route.

I once worked with a deputy district attorney — an excellent and very skilled prosecutor — who was hired only after the elected district attorney determined that something he did as a teenager (breaking a storefront window) didn't result in any criminal charges. Had he been labeled as a criminal in his youth, he may never have become a successful and effective prosecutor.

Erasing the criminal label

Clearly, attaching a stigma to someone who commits a crime is a big part of criminal enforcement. The act of labeling someone a criminal is one of the most significant punishments that society can deliver. For this reason, you can be sure that society won't stop labeling criminals anytime soon.

For most people, though, being caught once is enough to discourage a criminal lifestyle. (They don't move on to the secondary deviance stage.) In these cases, does forcing someone to carry the stigma of a conviction around for the rest of her life seem fair? For many low-level crimes, such as damaging property, driving with a suspended license, or getting in a bar fight, most people probably say no.

Because lawmakers understand to some extent the impact that labeling someone a criminal can have on that person, many states allow for *expungement:* a process that wipes a criminal conviction off someone's record after a few years have passed. For example, in my home state, if a person is convicted of a misdemeanor, completes probation, and then avoids trouble for three years, she can ask a judge to remove the conviction and arrest from her record. Thereafter, when applying for a job, she can honestly answer that she has "never been convicted."

Another way the law acknowledges the impact of labeling is through *diversion programs.* Diversion programs often give people who have been charged with nonviolent crimes a chance to avoid conviction if they comply with conditions set by a judge. In a diversion program, for example, a woman charged with possession of cocaine can pay her court costs and perhaps complete some drug treatment, and, as a result, the judge doesn't enter a conviction against her. Thus, she doesn't have to bear the stigma of having been convicted.

Diversion programs are the law's attempt to prevent labeling people and unnecessarily harming their futures, as well as a way to avoid causing secondary deviance. These programs have been an excellent development in criminal law — when they're run correctly. (Incidentally, they also save courts and jails millions of dollars.)

Finding the theory's weakness

The first component of labeling theory — that people in power use crime labels to control the poor, minorities, and women — seems more difficult to support than the idea that the label can create the criminal. The vast majority of crimes are crimes that almost everyone agrees should be punished: theft, assault, driving while intoxicated, burglary, sex crimes, robbery, identity theft, and so on.

Passing laws to make these activities crimes and, thus, creating labels isn't an example of the ruling class sticking it to the poor. Instead, these laws serve as an example of society's attempts to control antisocial behavior, regardless of the skin color, gender, or income of the person committing the act.

A criminologist who subscribes to some other critical theory may respond to this argument by saying that the ruling class *applies* its criminal laws in a discriminatory manner. Hence, in the next sections, I move on to some of the theories that suggest discriminatory treatment of women, the poor, and minorities.

Exploring Feminist Theory

Critical feminist theory is actually a large group of theories linked by their focus on the power struggles between men and women. Generally, feminist theory holds that the following ideas are true:

 ✔ A significant cause of crime is the unequal power in society between men and women. Because men have most of the power, they can exploit women. This fact is particularly evident in crimes such as rape and domestic assault.

✔ In today's society, men are rewarded for their work outside the home, while women are encouraged to do unpaid housework or other undervalued jobs. Therefore, society's version of capitalism allows men to control the power and exploit women — a system known as *patriarchy.*

✔ Some men victimize women as a means of control. But as women assume greater prominence in society and in the workforce, their power increases, and, as a result, they're victimized less.

In support of this last point, feminist theorists refer to the fact that women in developed countries who have access to education and equal treatment in the workplace are less likely to be victims of assault, rape, or other gender-based crimes than women in developing countries are.

Another arm of feminist theory attempts to explain why women commit fewer crimes than men. As I explain in Chapter 11, men are arrested three times as often as women. According to feminist theory, the reasons for this difference include the following:

✔ Under the patriarchal system, women are more likely to be isolated in homes and taking care of a family. As a result, they lack the opportunity to commit crimes that powerful men enjoy.

✔ Men and women are socialized differently as kids. Society teaches girls certain values that help to keep them in powerless, submissive roles. As a result, they're less likely than men to engage in aggressive criminal conduct.

In the 1970s, some feminist criminologists predicted that as women took a more prominent role in the workforce, their percentage of crime would increase. And, as I explain in Chapter 11, while the crime rate for men has been dropping since 1998, the crime rate for women has been slowly rising.

Examining Leftist Realism: A Response to Law and Order

Some criminologists, known as *left realists,* reject what they perceive as the right-wing tilt of anticrime efforts in the last 30 years, including longer prison sentences for offenders and reduced funding for social programs. However, they also recognize that crime is a problem that society must take seriously. Violent criminals aren't just victims abused by society, as old-school Marxist criminologists may have argued. They're frequently dangerous people who must be locked up.

But, although left realists do recognize that society has an interest in holding criminals accountable for their crimes, they also see oppression in society, mainly in the struggles between the rich and the poor. Specifically, they believe the following:

- The poor are oppressed by capitalist forces.
- The poor are victimized by having to live in neighborhoods with high levels of crime.

Left realists attempt to identify realistic plans for dealing with crime that take into account *social justice* — a vague phrase that generally refers to the goal of taking a more holistic approach to dealing with crime. In other words, social justice involves fixing the problems in society that cause crime in the first place, such as improving neighborhood environments and reducing social class frustration.

Unlike some other critical criminologists, left realists don't view members of the law enforcement community as tools of capitalist oppression but rather as necessary servants of the public. Nonetheless, society must guard against potential discriminatory abuses by law enforcement.

Recently, one significant focus of the left realist movement has been on opening up police forces to citizen involvement and control. For example, some cities are appointing civilian oversight boards to handle citizen complaints of police misconduct.

By implementing civilian oversight boards and ideas such as community policing, which encourage police to work proactively with neighborhood groups, left realists hope to encourage police to use means other than violence to maintain social order. (I discuss the practice of community policing in Chapter 16.)

Marxism

Marxism had a strong influence on the development of critical criminology in the 1960s. Developed by Karl Marx, a 19th-century German economist, Marxism holds that society evolves through class struggle. Marxists believe that society will eventually evolve from capitalism to socialism as the working class rises up against the class that owns the means of production — essentially the people who own factories and industry. Marx and his cohort, Friedrich Engels, believed that the working class would inevitably revolt and overthrow the rich class in a revolution that would ultimately end in a classless society in which the state would own all property (in other words, the class revolt would end in communism).

The challenges of having civilians oversee police internal affairs

Many cities across the United States are hiring civilians to oversee citizen complaints of police misconduct. Other cities are appointing boards of volunteers to do the job. In part, this action is a response to the fact that police agencies investigate their own people through internal affairs departments. Civilians wonder whether coverups are taking place amidst these investigations. How do civilians know that the police sufficiently value the outsider's point of view in such investigations?

Police often resent this interference by civilians, arguing that a civilian can't fully understand what dealing with society's worst criminals day after day is like. (I know an officer whose superior verbally reprimanded him for prolific cursing around bystanders while ordering an armed robber to drop his gun. Fifteen years later, this officer still resents the discipline.)

In one city (that shall remain nameless to protect the people involved), a situation arose that highlights the challenges of bringing civilians in to oversee police. Police arrested a drug dealer after they received a tip from an informant. The drug dealer accused the arresting officer of stealing some cash and lying about the information from the informant. The civilian hired to oversee police misconduct investigations in that city demanded the name of the informant to determine whether the officer was lying. The identity of an informant is closely guarded by police in any circumstance. In this case, the informant actually worked for an officer in another police department. The police speculated that this drug dealer cleverly made the allegation of police misconduct to try to identify the informant so that he could violently retaliate against that informant later.

What's the proper course of action in this case? Should the overseer drop her investigation or pursue it? Should the police refuse to identify the informant? You can see some gray areas here, and the relationship between civilian overseers and police can get tense.

Making Peace

Borrowing from religious themes, *peacemaking theory* asserts that punishment and violence can't end crime. Only through peace — that is, compassion, love, and forgiveness — can society overcome crime. (Interestingly, one of the leading proponents of peacemaking theory, Richard Quinney, was a former Marxist criminologist in the 1970s.)

Peacemaking theory isn't so much a theory of what causes crime as a quasi-spiritual solution. It contends, like some religious faiths, that retribution and vengeance are improper motivations for punishment. By locking people up, society engages in the same acts as the criminal. Instead of looking for vengeance when punishing people for their crimes, society needs to build connections among people through concepts such as restorative justice (which I discuss in the next section) to overcome the crime problem.

In reality, society would have a hard time turning the other cheek when faced with a rapist or child molester. I don't know of any country that doesn't punish acts, such as assault, theft, rape, and murder, which are all universally recognized as crimes.

But, at the individual level, acts of peacemaking can be inspiring. In many criminal cases, a victim or his family members are given the opportunity to address the court. In news reports, you may have heard some family member scream at the defendant, "I hope you rot in hell!" But, in other cases, you may have heard the media report that a family member announced to the judge that he forgives the murderer and hopes that the murderer can forgive himself. You can become very close to the victim's family when you're trying a murder case. I've stood in a courtroom and watched this type of compassion on display, and I've been amazed.

Seeking Healing through Restorative Justice

Instead of locking someone up and throwing away the key, *restorative justice* seeks to make victims whole, hold criminals accountable, and bring healing to the community. You're probably thinking that this theory is a pretty ambitious one. Well, like peacemaking, restorative justice is less an explanation for why people commit crime and more an attempt to shift society from warehousing criminals to permanently solving the problem of crime.

Encouraging justice within a community

Many communities have implemented some form of restoration programs, particularly in dealing with juvenile delinquents. For example, some schools deal with delinquency by using a "court of peers." Peer programs like this one try to bring the victims and the offenders together in a community-based setting rather than in a real courtroom. The offender must take responsibility for harming the victim, the victim has the chance to repair the damaged relationship, and community members can participate as encouragers.

Although courts of peers may work in schools, the sheer volume of crime in today's society makes these kinds of time and labor-intensive programs difficult to implement on a broad scale. If society lived in small tribes, it could likely manage misconduct through community intervention; however, most people don't live in a true community. Often your neighbors are strangers, and the people you do know are spread all over town and even across the country.

I suppose you can argue that the constitutional right to a trial by jury began as a form of community involvement in the justice process. But, over time, the legal system has placed more and more procedural restrictions on criminal trials so that the opportunity for restorative justice by the jury has been eliminated. Today, jurors mostly determine guilt or innocence. They have no involvement with a victim, and they aren't allowed even to speak to a defendant.

But, as critics of restorative justice point out, society has put these procedural restrictions in place to protect defendants against governmental abuse, as well as mob rule. Before such procedural safeguards existed, rough justice through mobs or even excessive governmental enforcement was more common.

Nonetheless, many (perhaps most) state court systems have attempted some initiatives in the spirit of restorative justice. For example, diversion programs, which I discuss in the "Labeling Someone a Criminal" section in this chapter, are part of states' attempt to simultaneously make victims whole while not incarcerating or labeling defendants as criminals.

Such models of restorative justice can have an impact when an offender experiences remorse and feels an obligation to make things right for the victim and the community. But even the most ardent supporters of restorative justice acknowledge that some criminals are so dangerous and without remorse that society has to lock them up. Thus, thinking that imprisonment will someday go away is unrealistic.

One of the most ardent and effective supporters of restorative justice is Chuck Colson, a former aide to President Richard Nixon. Colson converted to Christianity around the time that he was convicted for his role in the Watergate scandal. After serving a prison sentence, he founded Prison Fellowship Ministries, a nonprofit organization that ministers the Christian faith to inmates, and has strongly advocated for community solutions rather than prison (except for violent offenders) for more than 30 years. From his personal experience, he contends that prison is dehumanizing and makes criminals worse citizens after they're released. Given that roughly two out of three inmates reoffend within three years of their release from prison, Colson clearly has a point.

Debating treatment versus incarceration

Although I find restorative justice admirable and think efforts to increase its use in appropriate circumstances are worthwhile, I have seen policymakers clamor for one kind of treatment or another instead of imprisonment, ostensibly in the name of restorative justice. These policymakers frequently do so without much evidence that a particular treatment works. "Treatment" becomes an anti-incarceration mantra, irrespective of its effectiveness. (Call me cynical, but because treatment is cheaper than incarceration, I think some policymakers just want to save money for their own pet projects.)

In my opinion, the widespread employment of restorative justice for many crimes depends on whether or not treatment providers can develop effective treatments for offenders and then prove their effectiveness through legitimate studies. And, as Colson may assert, it may also depend on more than a little divine help.

Part IV
Fighting Crime

In this part . . .

As long as some people choose to commit crimes, other people will work to prevent those crimes and to arrest the bad guys. In this part, I introduce you to the people who fight crime at both the local and federal levels. Then I share some insight into the processes that law enforcement officers use to try to solve crimes.

Chapter 16

Battling Crime at the Local Level

· ·

In This Chapter

▶ Figuring out how local law enforcement works

▶ Getting help from task forces and citizen cops

▶ Introducing theories about how to police effectively

· ·

About 17,000 police agencies operate in the United States, and the vast majority of them are city and county agencies that answer to local public officials and citizens. Yet, local agencies certainly aren't alone in the fight against crime: They're joined by federal agencies (which I discuss in Chapter 17), state police, university police, and airport police.

In this chapter, I keep the focus squarely on local law enforcement. So the next time you see a police officer or two patrolling your neighborhood, you'll have a better idea of what they're doing to keep your hometown safe.

Keeping the Streets Clean: The Players at the Local Level

Unless you actually work for a police department or a sheriff's office, the structures and jurisdictions may seem a bit murky. What's the difference between a police chief and a sheriff? How about a sergeant and a detective? If you can't answer with confidence, don't stress; I'm here to guide you through the specifics.

Distinguishing sheriffs from police chiefs

Most people don't know the difference between a sheriff's office and a police department. Here's how the jobs of a sheriff and a police chief differ:

✔ **Sheriff:** A sheriff is responsible for providing police services for an entire county. A sheriff is also often in charge of running the county jail, which is usually the primary local jail (although some police departments may have small holding facilities where they hold people before transporting them to the county jail).

Sheriffs are elected by the public. Some sheriffs may be outstanding cops, and others may just be good politicians. I knew someone who was a typewriter repairman before being elected as the sheriff of a small county.

The officers that work for a sheriff are called *deputy sheriffs.*

✔ **Police chief:** A police chief is the head of a police department, which typically is the law enforcement agency for a town or city. Frequently — and especially in small police departments — a person works his way up within the agency to be rewarded (or punished) with the position of chief.

In large cities, police departments often do nationwide searches for their chiefs. For example, Bill Bratton was superintendent of the Boston Police Department and commissioner of the New York Police Department before becoming chief of the Los Angeles Police Department in 2002.

Chiefs can also have names like *superintendent, commissioner,* and *director of public safety.* Officers that work for a police chief are called *police officers.*

Both cities and counties are referred to as *jurisdictions.* A jurisdiction is the region in which an agency has authority. In a typical state,

✔ Police chiefs have jurisdiction over their cities or towns.

✔ Sheriffs have jurisdiction over their counties.

✔ Chiefs of state police have jurisdiction over the entire state.

Contrary to what you may have learned from the legendary TV series *Hawaii Five-0* and its hero Steve McGarrett, Hawaii is the only state without a state police agency. Because more than one-fourth of the entire population of Hawaii live in Honolulu, the Honolulu Police Department is easily the largest law enforcement presence in the state.

Because cities are within counties, sometimes jurisdictional conflicts arise between police departments and sheriffs' offices. But, for the most part, sheriff patrols stay away from the city unless they're asked to help. As a result, sheriff's offices generally patrol the parts of a county outside the city limits.

Both police chiefs and sheriffs are responsible for all the administrative tasks of running a police agency: hiring and disciplining staff, controlling budgets, reporting to city and county officials, and taking the heat from the press and the public when things go wrong. Being a police chief or sheriff is a very demanding job.

Driving the streets: Patrol officers

The heart of any police department or sheriff's office is its cadre of patrol officers. For simplicity's sake, I refer just to *police* or *patrol officers* for the rest of this chapter. Unless I indicate otherwise, that reference also includes deputy sheriffs.

The vast majority of police in the United States patrol the streets in police vehicles. Their primary responsibilities are to

✔ Reduce the commission of crime with their preventive presence

✔ Respond to emergency 9-1-1 calls

✔ Identify and arrest criminals

✔ Enforce traffic laws and keep traffic moving safely

Roughly 80 percent of police departments in the United States require only a high school diploma to qualify to become an officer. (This number is somewhat deceiving, though, because larger agencies, which employ more officers, often require some level of college education.) In addition to education requirements, applicants usually must pass written and oral tests, receive an evaluation by a psychologist, and graduate from a police training academy.

A full-fledged police officer has to be *sworn* (meaning that he has to swear an oath to uphold the Constitution and the laws of his jurisdiction) before he can perform certain tasks. For example, a sworn police officer can legally carry a firearm, arrest someone, and write search warrant affidavits.

Many other people who work as government investigators aren't *sworn* and, therefore, can't perform these tasks. For example, a state health licensing agency may have a civil investigator who makes sure that beauty salons are properly licensed and follow all health codes. However, that investigator can't arrest someone or conduct a search (although he may be able to issue a citation or a fine).

In the old days, most patrol officers walked a *beat* — in other words, they focused on a specific neighborhood. Today only a few officers have that type of job (see the following section on community officers). Instead, most officers ride in cars and have a much wider area to patrol. As a result, more officers are available to respond to any given situation, and they can do so faster.

For example, when a report comes in of a convenience store robbery in progress, the closest patrol officer arrives first, but three more cars may quickly follow. This additional support can help in an arrest, a pursuit, or a search of the surrounding area for the suspect. (As gas prices rose to historic levels in 2008, some police departments actually ordered their patrol officers to park their cars rather than drive around.)

For every arrest or investigation, police officers must write a police report. This report details what an officer did during the investigation and identifies whom the officer interviewed. If an arrest is made, the police report is the primary means for the officer to communicate to the district attorney what the crime was and what evidence will help prove the crime. District attorneys rely heavily on police reports when deciding whether to file criminal charges.

Most police departments provide 24-hour police services, which means that officers work different shifts. An officer may work the same shift for six months and then switch to another. After all, retaining officers would be difficult if they had to work the night shift throughout their whole careers.

Focusing on neighborhoods: Community officers

Community officers are police officers assigned to specific areas within a jurisdiction to develop relationships with citizens in the area. These officers may walk a beat or ride a bicycle in their particular areas of patrol. They're usually assigned as part of a community policing effort, which I discuss in detail in the "Policing at the community level" section later in this chapter.

Having community officers requires a tradeoff. On the one hand, community officers may help develop neighborhood watch programs and hold community meetings to identify public safety issues, which, in turn, allows the community to address those issues before they become big problems. On the other hand, diverting some officers to community patrols means having fewer patrol officers in vehicles able to respond quickly to crimes that happen across town.

Community policing efforts over the last 30 years have been very successful at decreasing citizens' fear of crime.

Supervising patrol officers: Sergeants

In most police departments, a *sergeant* is the direct supervisor of patrol officers. He or she typically oversees five to ten officers and is promoted from being one of the troops. Not only does the sergeant supervise the officers and hand out assignments, but he also typically reviews and approves every police report his officers write. This task can be a challenge because busy officers write a lot of reports.

If you ever get the chance to ride along with a police officer on patrol (such an experience is cleverly called a *ride-along* by those in the know), ask to ride with the night-shift sergeant. The sergeant typically goes to wherever the action is — and most of the action is at night — so you'll see a lot of activity.

Investigating crimes: Detectives

When you watch a cop show on TV, odds are that the show depicts detectives (very unrealistically, I might add). In a nutshell, *detectives* are responsible for conducting investigations.

Although patrol officers respond to crime scenes, they usually don't conduct long-term investigations to solve crimes. The exception is in small police departments that don't have any detectives; in those departments, patrol officers must do everything, including conduct investigations.

Detectives — usually not in uniform — try to solve serious felony crimes. A detective responds to a crime scene and reviews physical evidence, such as fingerprints, blood spatter, and injuries. (Remember that the patrol officer is usually the first to arrive at a crime scene.) The detective also identifies witnesses and interviews them.

A shorthand way of referring to a detective, still used by old-timers, is *dick*. No kidding. Often, dicks specialize in certain types of crime and work in one of the following detective units:

- Robbery and homicide
- Drugs and *vice* (which primarily refers to prostitution)
- Property and financial crimes
- Gangs

In many departments, patrol officers rotate to the detective unit and then back to patrol. The idea is that rotation gives more officers the chance to learn how to conduct investigations, which leads to better officers throughout the department. In other agencies, detectives who display particular talent for investigations may stay detectives for their whole careers.

Drug and vice detectives are usually considered the "cowboys" of a police department. They often work undercover and use *informants* (citizens who have information about the conduct of criminals) to buy drugs, and they're involved in high-risk police actions, such as executing search warrants. For example, they may have to enter a home quickly before bad guys flush drugs and other evidence down the toilet.

Homicide is the most serious crime, of course, so many detectives view this assignment to be the most important among all detectives. But I've known both good and bad homicide detectives, as well as good and bad *narcs* (the nickname given to drug detectives).

Like patrol officers, detectives report to a sergeant (known, creatively enough, as a *detective sergeant*).

To become a detective, a patrol officer must seek a promotion. Often this process involves a written test and then *oral boards,* during which senior detectives ask questions of the candidate. Detectives usually earn higher salaries than patrol officers.

The skills that departments look for in selecting new detectives include the following:

- ✔ **Good communication skills:** One of the hallmarks of a good detective is the ability to interview suspects and get them to confess.

- ✔ **Attention to detail:** Proving a criminal case often hinges on just one key fact, which a good detective can identify.

- ✔ **Self-motivation:** Detectives are on their own a lot, so a good one isn't lazy.

Giving police officers special assignments

Police officers can be assigned many specialized duties within a department. Some assignments are considered plum jobs, while others (such as internal affairs) are less attractive. Some special assignments include

- ✔ **Accident reconstruction:** When someone dies in a car crash, a police department often assigns one or more specially trained officers to determine how the crash occurred and whether someone was criminally responsible.

- ✔ **Internal affairs:** The officers who work in internal affairs are essentially the police's police. When a police officer violates policy or even commits a crime, most medium-sized or large police agencies have officers who investigate such internal misconduct.

- ✔ **Computer forensics:** Specially trained officers with this assignment know how to retrieve evidence from computers and phones without altering that evidence.

- ✔ **Training coordination:** Police must undergo constant training on the law, firearms use, use of other physical force, driving, and many other topics. Most agencies have at least one person assigned to arrange for appropriate and necessary training. Large agencies may have an entire unit assigned to training.

- ✔ **Jail operation:** Sheriffs' offices are usually responsible for operating county jails, which means they need many people to perform the required jail tasks, such as controlling inmates and providing security. For more information about jail operations, turn to Chapter 21.

✔ **Bomb squad:** In 2007, law enforcement agencies reported 2,772 explosive incidents to the Bureau of Alcohol, Tobacco, Firearms and Explosives (ATF). That number includes both actual bombs and hoaxes. Specially trained police officers must respond to each incident with great care and neutralize the suspected bomb. (Although many incidents do turn out to be hoaxes, you can't underestimate the seriousness of this assignment. In 2008, a friend of mine, who served on a bomb squad, died while attempting to disarm a bomb in a bank.)

✔ **Gang enforcement officer:** Gang enforcement officers work in the world of street gangs. Their main duties are to prevent gang crime and to investigate it when it does occur. Gang officers do their job by developing expertise in gang culture and building relationships with gang members and informants.

Counting on civilian employees

Every police department depends heavily on *civilian employees,* or employees who aren't sworn officers. If you're interested in finding out more about a particular civilian job with a police or sheriff's department, check out Chapter 23. Here are some key positions that civilians fill in most departments:

✔ **Evidence technician:** This person receives evidence from a police officer, identifies it, records it in a log, and places it in a secure evidence room. This job is crucial because a sloppy evidence locker results in evidence being lost or mishandled, which, in turn, leads to criminal cases being dismissed.

✔ **Forensic specialist:** Many larger departments have their own forensic scientists who respond to crime scenes to retrieve evidence and then process that evidence in a lab. For example, a forensic specialist may receive a semen sample from a rape victim and conduct a DNA test to see whether the semen matches the suspect.

✔ **Secretary:** Patrol officers and especially detectives need someone to transcribe taped interviews, proofread police reports, arrange for travel, and do all the little things that help an organization work smoothly.

✔ **Parking enforcer:** A larger agency usually doesn't want its officers spending time writing parking tickets. But tickets are a good source of revenue, so some departments employ civilians to do this dirty job for them.

✔ **Crime analyst:** Analysts can identify crime trends from statistics, help detectives organize complex cases, manage wiretaps and phone record data, and much more. See the section "Adopting intelligence-led policing" for more information about the duties of an analyst. I highly value good analysts and believe this position is crucial to good detective work in the 21st century.

Greater than the sum of their parts: Task forces

Frequently, officers from different agencies band together in task forces to combat a particular type of crime.

In law enforcement, a *task force* is made up of officers from different agencies who focus on a certain type of crime, usually some type of organized crime. For example, because drug dealers work across jurisdictional boundaries, officers from different jurisdictions can be more effective by working together. Gang task forces are also common because gangs cross jurisdictional boundaries, too. Such task forces often include local, state, and federal officers.

A smaller agency may participate in a *major crime* task force. Unlike drug and gang task forces, members of a major crime task force usually don't work out of the same office. But when a murder or other violent felony occurs, the major crime team comes together to conduct the investigation because small departments often don't have enough qualified detectives to do a major crime investigation. By pooling resources, they can get the job done. (For instance, when a person commits a murder in Mayberry, Sheriff Andy Taylor isn't left only with Barney; he can also rely on the hot shots from Mount Pilot to help.)

Bringing in citizen cops: Reserves

Most police agencies rely on a cadre of citizen volunteers to handle many police functions. These citizens are known as *reserve officers* or *reserves*. Reserves may provide the following types of police services:

- Traffic and pedestrian control at parades
- Security at sporting events
- Desk duties, such as answering phones and taking complaints
- Transportation of prisoners

All reserves go through some level of training which varies from department to department. If they're properly trained, some reserves may also perform full law enforcement duties, including patrols and arrests. Reserves who can perform these duties usually have to work under the supervision of a full-time, paid officer.

Chances are good that the next time you go to a county fair or parade, the officer directing traffic will be a reserve. Say hi and thank him because he's probably standing out in the hot sun for free.

Thinking about Theories of Policing

A small branch of criminology studies complex theories of how police function in various societies, including Western, Islamic, European, Asian, and totalitarian countries. These criminologists may also study the sociolegal implications of how and why police exercise the force they do. Don't worry; I don't get into that type of discussion here.

In this section, I focus on three practical approaches to improving police work that police departments throughout the United States have adopted in varying degrees.

Policing at the community level

Over the last three decades, *community policing* has become a buzz phrase within law enforcement — kind of a generalized concept that many street cops don't fully understand, even as they participate in it. To help you better understand community policing, I want to take a quick look at how policing evolved in the 20th century.

Earlier in U.S. history, police were integrated into the fabric of society. They walked a beat, getting to know shopkeepers and families in a particular community. Police were responsive to the needs of the community and, in a democratic society, *worked* for the community. The police officer gathered information from the citizens and helped provide protection and all kinds of services. At least, this is the romantic, nostalgic view many people today have of how policing used to work.

On the down side, these police were highly susceptible to corruption and influence. By today's standards, they were relatively untrained and often resorted to street justice instead of enforcing laws by the books. As a result, a movement developed in U.S. policing away from this community-based model to a more efficient and professional crime-fighting model.

Eventually, this change led police to become more centralized with fewer precincts. Instead of trying to flag down the neighborhood cop for help, citizens were supposed to call the local precinct, which would then quickly dispatch a patrol car to the scene.

Over time, this change had several effects: Corruption decreased and police were quicker to respond to crime, but, at the same time, communities became more disconnected from police. Without a neighborhood officer in sight, the fear of crime grew. And amid the political tumult of the 1960s, many people grew concerned that officers were abusing their authority, and, thus, they became more distrustful of police.

Making way for community policing

In response, beginning in the late 1970s, police agencies and the politicians they reported to sought a new way of protecting communities. What arose was the concept of *community policing,* which is something of a compromise between the two historical approaches. Community policing is meant to reconnect police with the community, reducing fear and distrust, while also maintaining professionalism, integrity, and quick response to incidents.

Here are some ways that community policing plays out:

✔ Police departments create more precincts, or *substations,* so that people are aware of a police presence in their neighborhoods.

✔ In some urban areas, police departments reinstitute foot patrols. (Obviously, such patrols aren't practical in most parts of suburban and rural America.)

✔ Police hold regular community meetings with citizens to build relationships to help identify problems early on.

✔ Many police departments train their community officers in special problem-solving skills to remedy smaller issues without resorting to arrest.

Other public safety professionals have also adopted a community approach. For example, *community prosecutors* may handle some cases in a neighborhood courtroom and work with citizens to attack a specific crime problem through enforcement, prosecution, legislation, or other nontraditional approaches.

Understanding the challenges

The community policing model does have its problems, however. For one, it's a rather vague philosophy that can be tough for police and communities to understand. It places significant responsibilities on community officers to be involved in nontraditional police duties, such as community problem solving. Given that the vast majority of police agencies require only a high school diploma for their officers — and given that solving other people's problems is one of the most difficult tasks out there — the expectations for community officers can sometimes be too great.

Another challenge with community policing is getting the community involved. In surveys of community policing efforts, the citizens' knowledge of the program has been crucial in reducing levels of community fear. The citizens who are most likely to be fearful of crime — the elderly — are consistently the least likely to know about community policing efforts.

Yet another challenge stems from the fact that police are typically rewarded with promotions and status for good arrests, not for effective problem solving. Thus, altering police reward structures to somehow account for good community policing has posed problems, too.

Keeping in mind the positives

Community policing has been around since the late 1970s, so criminologists should be able to say whether it works or not, right? Not quite. As I explain in Chapter 3, reliable statistics about crime and crime fighting are very difficult to find. Generally, studies comparing departments that use community policing with departments that don't use it haven't shown a significant difference in the amount of crime in each community.

However, some studies have shown greater satisfaction among citizens with the police department's performance and decreased citizen fear of crime in neighborhoods where community policing is used. Another positive outcome is that community officers who have been specially trained in problem solving tend to report slightly greater job satisfaction over time than officers in more traditional police roles.

Fixing broken windows

In the mid-1970s, New Jersey embarked on a significant community policing effort to get officers to walk beats in 28 different cities. A review after five years concluded that crime rates hadn't dropped at all but that citizens in those cities *believed* crime rates had dropped and *believed* they were safer.

In a landmark article written by George L. Kelling and James Q. Wilson that appeared in the March 1982 issue of *The Atlantic,* the authors argued that people in New Jersey felt safer, in part, because the presence of police helped maintain public order. Cops walking a beat moved drunks, beggars, and drug addicts out of the communities. Likewise, those same cops closely monitored strangers and quieted disruptive teenagers. In general, the heightened police presence led to greater public order, which, however, wasn't reflected in crime statistics.

From this article developed the theory of policing known as the *broken windows theory.* This theory argues that a building with a broken window that isn't repaired will soon have a second broken window, and then a third, and so on. If vandals perceive that no one cares about the building, they'll attack it. But if the first broken window is immediately repaired, vandals are less likely to break another one. Lack of attention to minor issues like broken windows leads a community to spiral downward into greater issues. After all the windows are broken, vandals may be more likely to conclude that no one cares about the neighborhood, and, as a result, they'll attack the next building on the block. Ultimately, lack of attention to fixing problems leads to the destruction of neighborhoods. People feel less safe on the street, families move out, and, eventually, serious crime increases.

The New York City Transit Police put the broken windows theory into practice in 1990 by cracking down on people who weren't paying subway fares. New York police later expanded the program citywide and called it *zero tolerance*. They focused on low-level crime, such as public drinking, public urinating, and *squeegee extortioners* — people who dirty windshields and then ask for money to clean them. Rates of both low-level and serious crime fell significantly in New York throughout the 1990s, and many in the police department and the media hailed the zero-tolerance policy as the reason behind the drop.

As I note in Chapter 3, criminologists argue about why crime dropped so much in the 1990s. Critics of the broken windows theory point out that crime dropped nationwide during the 1990s, including in many cities that hadn't adopted any new theory of policing. Other studies have found little correlation between the implementation of a zero-tolerance policy and a reduction in serious crime. But the criticism has focused more on claims that policies such as zero tolerance reduce serious crime and less on the idea that attention to small problems (like quickly fixing a broken window) deters other low-level crimes and improves social order in a neighborhood.

Adopting intelligence-led policing

A third modern theory of policing is *intelligence-led policing*. This theory involves using information to direct police efforts and make police more effective. Since the terrorist attacks of 9/11, the intelligence-led policing model has received wide endorsement and encouragement from police organizations such as the International Association of Chiefs of Police. Nevertheless, most police agencies haven't adopted intelligence-led policing.

Noticing how intelligence can help

What is *intelligence* in terms of this particular theory? At the most basic level, it's sensitive information that may not be useable as evidence in a trial but that still points to criminal activity. For example, a woman tells an officer that her neighbor is up all night and has a lot of vehicle traffic at his house. She also says she overheard a visitor say something about buying cocaine. This information is criminal intelligence that helps a detective decide to open an investigation.

Intelligence can come from many sources, but the following are some of the most common:

- Tips and information from concerned citizens
- Information from informants, who are sometimes paid by police to get inside criminal organizations
- Intercepted jail communications, such as pieces of mail, notes passed between inmates, and recorded phone calls

✔ Surveillance of suspected criminals

✔ Undercover police operations

✔ A suspect's garbage

The components of effective intelligence-led policing are deceptively simple:

✔ A department establishes a method for collecting and storing information.

✔ An analyst compiles the collected information and makes sense of it.

✔ Police leadership uses the analyst's product to design crime suppression strategies.

✔ Police officers implement the strategies.

For example, citizens in a community complain to their city council about a gang problem. Police begin to collect information about gang members in their daily activities. One officer is called to a gang fight in a park. She identifies the gang members, documents how she knows they belong to a gang, and writes a police report about everyone involved in the incident. Over the course of several months, the police department sends every police report about gang activity to an analyst, who documents the gang membership and leadership, their territory, the crimes they commit, and the most dangerous members. The analyst then gives this information to leadership in the police department, which devises a strategy to conduct surveillance on three identified gang leaders whom the analyst deemed the most violent. Meanwhile, a group of social workers start a gang intervention program in the gang's neighborhood to target the nonviolent members to try to separate them from the gang lifestyle.

Aside from police reports, police also record valuable case intelligence in one of six regional intelligence databases, which are all connected via the nationwide Regional Information Sharing System (RISS). RISS is a federally funded program that provides secure, online databases in which police from different agencies and even different states can share their suspect intelligence. RISS is one of the best uses of federal dollars in law enforcement because it greatly improves the efficiency of investigations.

Taking a look at the challenges

Unfortunately, intelligence programs have a bit of a black eye in the law enforcement community. In the late 20th century, many police agencies tried to develop intelligence programs. But often these programs consisted of a unit of detectives who received information from other officers and did nothing with it. *Intel units,* as these units were called, developed a nationwide reputation as "black holes." Information went in, but nothing came out. As a result, other officers stopped feeding information into these units. Today, as some advocate this newer model for using intelligence, many people in police leadership remember the less-than-successful intel initiatives of the past and are resistant.

Here are some of the other challenges to the intelligence-led policing model:

✔ Most police agencies don't have analysts. Very few analyst training programs exist, and, as a result, the pool of qualified analysts is small.

✔ Most police agencies don't have a strategy for collecting information or compiling the information they have. Cops write reports of their activities, but the reports' purpose is just to document arrests and other incidents. These reports may go to the district attorney for filing charges, but the information isn't used for any other purpose. Also, most police departments don't train their officers to gather intelligence for later use by an analyst.

✔ Politicians who oversee police efforts fear the word *intelligence* because it conjures images of CIA operatives digging into citizens' private lives.

Despite these challenges, as police agencies improve their ability to gather information through the use of electronic databases and technology, I believe intelligence-led policing will be the most effective way to attack serious organized crime threats, such as gangs, drugs, property crimes, and terrorism.

Chapter 17

Tackling Crime at the Federal Level

· ·

· ·

Most people who work in the criminal justice system work for a local government (see Chapter 16 for more on local crime-fighting efforts). But federal officers (or *feds,* as many people call them) play a very significant role in the criminal justice process. Roughly 106,000 federal officers working for over 65 different federal agencies have the authority to make arrests and carry firearms anywhere in the United States. (Of course, not every federal officer can make an arrest for every crime. After all, you probably don't want the Bureau of Engraving and Printing Police doing major narcotics investigations!)

In this chapter, I focus on introducing you to some of the biggies in the federal fight against crime. I also explain how federal and local law enforcement work together to beat the bad guys.

Sorting through the Alphabet Soup of Federal Agencies

Perhaps no other profession is more filled with acronyms than law enforcement. With only two exceptions, every major federal law enforcement agency is referred to by a series of letters. (You get bonus points if you can guess the two exceptions before you read any farther.)

Federal Bureau of Investigation (FBI)

In 1908, under President Theodore Roosevelt, the U.S. Attorney General appointed 34 men as "special agents" for the U.S. Department of Justice. Although it had no formal name at this point, these special agents became known as the Bureau of Investigation. Their appointment was a controversial action because states believed that most governmental responsibilities should rest in the states' hands. Besides, very few crimes were considered federal at the time.

In 1910, Congress passed the Mann Act (technically called the White-Slave Traffic Act), which made transporting women over state lines for immoral purposes a federal crime. This act led to a quick expansion of the Bureau of Investigation. By 1917, the bureau employed more than 300 special agents.

In 1935, the agency's name was formally changed to the *Federal Bureau of Investigation* (FBI). Today, the FBI employs roughly 13,000 special agents and 30,000 people total.

The FBI is part of the U.S. Department of Justice, but the FBI director is specially appointed by the president of the United States and confirmed by the Senate. The director serves for a period of ten years. This ten-year term is supposed to remove the director somewhat from the political process (because the position doesn't change with each new president). The limit on each director's service is a direct result of the fact that J. Edgar Hoover became the veritable king of the FBI, serving as director from 1924 to 1972, when he died.

Every major U.S. city has an FBI *field office,* which is simply an office of FBI agents located outside the headquarters in Washington, D.C. Each field office of the FBI is run by a special agent in charge, known as a *SAC* (pronounced "sack").

The FBI's responsibilities

The FBI's role has changed dramatically through the years. For example, in the 1980s, the FBI was responsible for *counterespionage,* or tracking spies from other countries in the United States. At the same time, it was heavily involved in fighting organized crime, including the Italian Mafia in the United States. As the international drug trade exploded on U.S. soil in the 1980s, the FBI also took responsibility for part of the mission to fight the drug war. Plus, it played a large role in combating white-collar crime. As violent crime exploded in the late 1980s, the FBI added violent crime to its list of priorities. And, with the rise of the Internet in the 21st century, the FBI has taken on a significant role in combating computer crime.

But on September 11, 2001, the FBI's mission changed significantly. Today its primary mission is to protect the United States against terrorist threats. However, the bureau continues to be involved in other areas of crime, as well.

As of this writing, here are the FBI's top eight priorities, in order:

- ✔ Protect the United States from terrorist attacks.
- ✔ Protect the United States against foreign intelligence operations and espionage.
- ✔ Protect the United States against cyber-based attacks and high-technology crimes.
- ✔ Combat public corruption at all levels.
- ✔ Protect civil rights.
- ✔ Combat transnational/national criminal organizations and enterprises.
- ✔ Combat major white-collar crimes.
- ✔ Combat significant violent crimes.

A special agent's job

An FBI special agent has a much different role in fighting crime than most local patrol officers do. For instance, special agents don't enforce traffic laws, and they don't respond to 9-1-1 calls. And because the number of FBI special agents is so small compared to the overall crime threat in the United States, they typically don't become involved in an investigation unless it's very serious. Usually, they take part in longer-term investigations and gather evidence by interviewing witnesses, conducting surveillance, issuing subpoenas for records, going undercover, and *managing informants* (which means using citizens, and often criminals, to get inside a criminal organization to find out what's happening).

Many special agents participate in task forces that involve local police and other federal agents. For example, the FBI has set up Joint Terrorism Task Forces (JTTFs) throughout the United States, which are made up of local, state, and other federal agency officers, along with FBI special agents. The JTTFs investigate activities of terrorists. (See Chapter 10 for a detailed discussion of terrorism.)

The FBI also has jurisdiction over bank robberies, and these cases are another example where local police and the FBI attempt to work closely together.

Bureau of Alcohol, Tobacco, Firearms and Explosives (ATF)

Can you guess which types of crimes this bureau investigates? Formerly part of the U.S. Treasury Department, the *Bureau of Alcohol, Tobacco, Firearms and Explosives* (ATF) became part of the U.S. Department of Justice in 2002 (after the 9/11 attacks), and the word *Explosives* became part of its title. Because the bureau was known as the ATF for so many years, that acronym stuck.

The ATF got its start in 1920 during the era of prohibition; hence, it was called the Bureau of Prohibition. This agency employed Elliot Ness and his crew of agents nicknamed "the Untouchables," who took down gangster Al Capone in Chicago. After the government legalized alcohol in 1933, its agents became known as *revenuers* because they were responsible for enforcing alcohol tax laws and protecting tax revenue. In the 1950s and 1960s, the agency took on responsibility for regulating tobacco and gun crimes, as well.

Roughly 2,400 special agents and about 2,600 other employees work for the ATF today. The agency has several programs, each with its own responsibilities, including the following:

- ✔ **Firearms regulation:** Some agency employees are responsible for enforcing all gun regulatory laws, such as complying with the requirements of the federal firearms licenses. Employees in this program inspect gun sellers to make sure they're in compliance with such laws.

- ✔ **Arsons, explosives, and firearms investigations:** ATF special agents have the broad authority to enforce *any* federal criminal law. But their primary responsibility is to investigate federal crimes committed with explosives or firearms. To be clear, the ATF doesn't take over every criminal investigation that involves a gun. In fact, local law enforcement investigates the vast majority of violent crimes committed with firearms. However, the ATF often takes a lead role in investigations involving large-scale weapons trafficking (sometimes involving motorcycle gangs) as well as significant bomb cases. (See Chapter 8 for more on motorcycle gangs.)

  For example, the ATF played a prominent role in tracking the vehicle used in the 1993 World Trade Center bombing, which ultimately led to the arrest of the perpetrators.

  In 2006, the ATF investigated 3,445 explosive incidents that resulted in 135 injuries and 14 deaths. Of these incidents, the agency referred 745 cases for prosecution.

- ✔ **Alcohol and tobacco tax revenue:** Other ATF agents are responsible for investigating crimes that involve tobacco and alcohol *diversion* (which means smuggling to avoid taxes or other laws). Avoiding the tax on these products can lead to big money, and organized crime groups are frequently involved in diversion crimes.

For instance, criminals often try to sell cigarettes on the black market to avoid paying taxes and to make greater profits. The 2009 federal cigarette tax is $1.01 per pack, and some state taxes are much higher. For example, the cigarette tax in New York City totals $5.26 per pack. A criminal can sell a semitrailer full of cigarettes on the black market in New York for more than $3 million. (Don't try this scheme at home — selling cigarettes without paying taxes is illegal and can be dangerous to your health.)

Drug Enforcement Administration (DEA)

The *Drug Enforcement Administration* (DEA) is a part of the U.S. Department of Justice. DEA special agents enforce federal laws that deal with controlled substances. Although their responsibilities include regulating the pharmaceutical industry, they're primarily known as the federal drug cops, who take on large-scale narcotics-trafficking organizations. Richard Nixon created the DEA in 1973 in reaction to the growing national drug problem at the time. Today, the agency employs about 5,200 special agents. Most of these agents work in the United States, but some work in 63 other countries around the world.

As I discuss in Chapter 9, illegal drugs are the primary driver of organized crime in the world, so the DEA's mission is terribly important. However, like other federal agencies, the DEA has suffered significant funding cutbacks during the wars in Iraq and Afghanistan because so many U.S. tax dollars have been spent fighting wars overseas.

Because the drug problem in the United States is so large, and because the number of DEA special agents is relatively low, the DEA routinely partners up with local law enforcement via task forces. This allows local officers to receive temporary federal authority which gives them the ability to subpoena phone and Internet records under federal law. These and other benefits of federal authority can help local officers identify important evidence.

DEA special agents also work closely with federal prosecutors in U.S. attorney offices to try to dismantle big-time drug-trafficking organizations (known in the business as *DTOs*). This work often involves using mobile tracking devices, surveillance cameras, satellite and aeronautical imagery, and wiretaps. As I write this chapter, the DEA is working with state prosecutors in my office on two separate wiretaps to bring down heroin and cocaine organizations on the West Coast.

One of the most significant contributions the DEA makes to the U.S. drug enforcement effort is its worldwide access to intelligence about international drug-trafficking activities. A local police agency would never have access to this type of information.

Feds on the big screen

The storylines aren't always true to life, but seeing how various federal agencies are depicted in the movies can still be fun. Here are a few movies that portray federal agencies in all their glory:

The FBI:

✔ *Silence of the Lambs:* Jodie Foster plays a young FBI agent up against cannibal Hannibal Lecter. It features the grossest meal description ever — a victim's liver with fava beans and a nice Chianti.

✔ *Point Break:* Keanu Reeves stars as a new FBI special agent and former college quarterback who goes undercover as a surfer to catch Zen-like bank robbers — probably not a fair and honest picture of life in the FBI.

The Secret Service:

✔ *To Live and Die in LA:* William Peterson stars as a Secret Service agent who tracks counterfeiters and protects the president.

✔ *In the Line of Fire:* Clint Eastwood stars as a Secret Service agent who tries to make up for not saving President Kennedy.

U.S. Marshal:

✔ *The Fugitive:* Tommy Lee Jones plays a deputy U.S. marshal who tries to track down a fugitive, played by Harrison Ford.

The DEA:

✔ *Traffic:* DEA agents pursue a drug lord's wife, played by Catherine Zeta-Jones, who has taken over her husband's business.

Border Patrol:

✔ *The Border:* Jack Nicholson plays a dirty Border Patrol agent who tries to clean up his act.

Immigration and Customs Enforcement (ICE)

Immigration and Customs Enforcement (ICE) wins the award for best acronym. ICE is part of the U.S. Department of Homeland Security and was formed in 2003 in response to the terrorist attacks of 9/11. The Immigration and Naturalization Service, the U.S. Customs Service, and the U.S. Federal Protective Service merged to create ICE.

ICE's mission is not only to enforce immigration laws but also to target criminal networks and terrorist organizations that seek to exploit vulnerabilities in the U.S. immigration system, in the U.S. financial networks, along U.S. borders, and at federal facilities. ICE has over 17,000 employees.

Because of ICE's broad authority, an ICE special agent can be involved in a variety of criminal investigations, including human smuggling and trafficking, narcotics, immigration crimes, child pornography, gangs, financial crimes, weapons smuggling, and terrorism. In addition, the U.S. Federal Protective Service, which is part of ICE, is responsible for protecting federal agencies and buildings. The U.S. Federal Protective Service alone employs more than 2,000 federal law enforcement officers and has 15,000 contract security guards.

Because of the significant presence of foreign organized crime in the United States, the law enforcement community highly values ICE special agents. Frequently, the government can most easily deal with a foreign criminal offender by using a federal conviction for *illegal reentry* (which means an illegal second entry into the country). Illegal reentry is often much easier to prove than other more complex crimes that require more laborious state prosecutions — prosecutions that may not end with any significant punishment. (People prosecuted for illegal reentry almost always have a significant criminal record in addition to their immigration crimes.)

Secret Service

What, no acronym? The *U.S. Secret Service* is another part of the U.S. Department of Homeland Security. It was created in 1865 to fight counterfeit currency. (If you're of a certain age, you may remember that James West of the TV series *The Wild, Wild West* was a Secret Service agent.) Although the Secret Service was originally a part of the U.S. Treasury Department, it moved to the U.S. Department of Homeland Security after 9/11. The Secret Service has two missions:

- ✔ To protect visiting foreign officials and U.S. officials (most notably the president).

- ✔ To conduct criminal investigations to maintain the integrity of the nation's financial infrastructure. This responsibility goes well beyond investigating counterfeiting and includes almost every conceivable type of financial fraud and systematic identity theft.

There are 3,200 special agents with the Secret Service who conduct criminal investigations regarding threats to dignitaries, as well as significant financial crimes. There are another 1,300 Secret Service officers who wear uniforms and provide security for the White House, the vice president's residence, and foreign missions and embassies in Washington, D.C.

U.S. Marshals Service

For my money, there's no better job title anywhere than being a U.S. Marshal. Notice that *marshal* has just one *L,* a fact that everyone in the Marshals Service is quick to point out. In existence since 1789, the U.S. Marshals Service is the oldest federal law enforcement agency. It's a part of the U.S. Department of Justice. One U.S. marshal is appointed for each of 94 separate districts in the United States, and each marshal has deputies who work under him or her. More than 3,200 deputy marshals and criminal investigators work in this agency.

One of the most significant responsibilities of the Marshals Service is tracking down and arresting fugitives. In 2007, the service arrested more than 36,000 fugitives. (A *fugitive* is a person who is wanted for a crime and who has a federal warrant out for his arrest.)

Because the Marshals Service generally goes after the most dangerous felons, being a deputy marshal is a very challenging job. The Marshals Service also protects federal judges, transports federal prisoners, and runs the government's witness security program.

Internal Revenue Service (IRS)

The *Internal Revenue Service* (IRS) is part of the U.S. Treasury Department and employs more than 2,800 special agents. Obviously, IRS special agents focus on tax cheaters. But other police agencies often seek out IRS agents to be partners in complex financial investigations, too. Most cops don't enjoy digging through bank statements and tax records to find evidence of crime. Yet, some of the best evidence often comes from these financial documents, and IRS special agents are good at uncovering this valuable evidence.

Finding money that criminals have carefully hidden is important for one because doing so prevents criminals from benefitting from their crimes, but it's also important because law enforcement can often seize proceeds through a process called *forfeiture.* For example, a drug dealer may use his illegally gained profits to buy a Cadillac Escalade. If police can prove that the vehicle was bought with drug proceeds or that the vehicle was used to transport drugs, they can seize the vehicle, sell it, and use the money to pay for law enforcement costs.

For this reason, good financial investigators, including IRS special agents, can be worth their weight in silver (if not gold).

Other federal law enforcement agencies

As I mention in this chapter's introduction, over 65 federal agencies employ law enforcement officers. Each agency has enforcement authority related to its own area of expertise. For example, the Bureau of Land Management (which is part of the U.S. Department of the Interior) and the U.S. Forest Service (which is part of the U.S. Department of Agriculture) employ special agents who provide law enforcement services on federal land. Other significant federal law enforcement agencies include the Border Patrol, the U.S. Postal Inspection Service, the U.S. Capitol Police, and the U.S. Park Service. The U.S. Department of Homeland Security and the U.S. Department of Justice have, by far, the most federal law enforcement jobs.

Many federal agencies include offices of inspector general, which are responsible for catching misconduct by employees within their agencies. These offices often employ special agents who have full law enforcement authority and who can arrest agency personnel and others involved in crime.

Job hunting at the federal level

In this chapter, I focus largely on the responsibilities of special agents — are you interested in becoming one of these special agents? The minimum requirements for special agent positions differ widely, depending on the agency. For example, in most cases, the FBI requires a law degree or a four-year college degree in accounting, computer science, or electrical engineering. Other agencies prefer to hire people who have prior police experience. Physical restrictions often influence hiring, as well. For example, the Secret Service doesn't hire anyone older than 37 or anyone with eyesight worse than 20/60.

Most agencies require applicants to pass physical, written, and oral examinations, lie detector tests, drug-screening tests, and background investigations. After this initial screening process, accepted applicants normally must graduate from a basic training program. In the FBI, for example, each new special agent must go through a 17-week training course at the FBI Academy in Quantico, Virginia. Other agencies send their newbies to the Federal Law Enforcement Training Center, known as FLETC, in Glynco, Georgia.

If you're not into becoming a special agent, you can consider lots of other positions in federal law enforcement. Agencies need forensic scientists, legal assistants, and intelligence analysts, for example. Intelligence analysts, who are growing in importance, assist police by taking large volumes of complex information and making it understandable. They're often central to organized crime investigations because they provide the outline and structure of the organization while also managing wiretap and phone call records.

If you're interested in a career in federal law enforcement, visit the Web site of any agency that interests you to see the specific job duties and minimum requirements. A great place to look for actual job openings is the official job Web site of the U.S. government: http://jobsearch.usajobs.gov/.

Coordinating Federal and Local Efforts

The feds make up just a fraction of the total law enforcement presence in the United States. So, for feds to be effective, they often must work closely with local and state police organizations.

Working with local law enforcement

As I explain earlier in this chapter, most federal law enforcement agencies tend to work on the more significant cases. For example, an FBI white-collar crime unit won't even touch a case unless the amount of fraud is six — or more likely seven — figures.

Often, federal cases start as investigations by city or county detectives, who eventually realize that they're into something big and that they're going to need extra help. If local detectives have good relations with federal special agents in their areas, they may ask for federal help or even turn the case over to the feds. So, for practical reasons, good relationships between federal special agents and local law enforcers are crucial from both perspectives.

But the animosity between feds and locals that TV shows often depict has a basis in fact. This resentment can arise from several factors, including the following:

✔ Many federal law enforcement agencies move their employees around frequently. For example, a DEA special agent may live in four or five cities during her career. As a result, she can't develop special ties or commitments to the community in which she lives at any given time. For many special agents, building friendships and relationships with other police may not be a priority.

✔ Local officers can easily develop some resentment against feds, who take on only the *most* significant cases. Even a good, self-effacing federal special agent has to work very hard to avoid ruffling feathers and appearing arrogant.

✔ Many local officers don't perceive federal special agents as having much experience "working the street." That is, many federal agents don't start out as regular street cops, so they don't deal face to face with all the difficult and crazy issues that can help build *street smarts* — the ability to work in the seamy world of crime and still effectively gather evidence. So when a fed takes over a significant local case, local officers may not believe she earned it.

✔ Cops, in general, are some of the most sensitive people I know — and I don't mean that they cry during chick-flicks. Rather, they're extremely quick to perceive slights, and they often respond in-kind. As a result, feds and locals sometimes have a hard time getting along.

But to do their jobs effectively, feds need locals and locals need feds. Fortunately, the importance of the mission usually wins out over personal animosities.

Federal funding: Tapping federal resources to maximize effect

Local governments pay for the lion's share of the nation's law enforcement efforts (see Chapter 3 for more on the costs). But the federal government provides critical funding to extra law enforcement initiatives that can make a big difference.

For example, the Office of National Drug Control Policy (ONDCP), an agency run by the national *drug czar* (who reports directly to the president of the United States), heads up one of the government's most effective federal funding programs. This program is known as the High Intensity Drug Trafficking Area program (HIDTA), and it provides funds to local and state agencies to attack major drug-trafficking organizations. What makes HIDTA so effective is that ONDCP turns over the money to an executive committee of local and federal law enforcement officials who, working together, decide how to spend the money — instead of letting some Washington, D.C., bureaucrat (or worse, a politician) decide what to do with it.

Numerous other federal grant programs help local and state law enforcement. Some significant ones include funding from the U.S. Department of Homeland Security to fight terrorism and Community Oriented Policing Services (COPS) grants from the U.S. Department of Justice to fund community policing efforts (which I discuss in Chapter 16.) Other grants provide funding for bulletproof vests, overtime for intoxicated-driver-saturation patrols or drug investigations, gang interdiction programs, and just about any other worthy cause you can think of.

Most law enforcement initiatives beyond everyday police services depend, at least in part, on federal funding. As a result, most police chiefs and sheriffs know that they have to try their best to stay on good terms with their U.S. senators.

Chapter 18

Solving Crimes: The Process

. . . .

In This Chapter

▶ Investigating crime scenes and writing reports

▶ Talking to witnesses and suspects

▶ Handling evidence from crime scene to courtroom

▶ Using search warrants, electronic evidence, and lie detector tests

▶ Looking at fingerprints, DNA, and handwriting

▶ Analyzing blood stains and reconstructing accidents

. . . .

You've probably seen a number of different portrayals of criminal investigations on TV. Some seem realistic, but others just seem silly. Well, now it's time to find out what really happens during police investigations.

In this chapter, I focus on what police do *after* a crime is committed: how they conduct an investigation and how they use special scientific techniques to collect and analyze evidence.

Responding to a Crime Scene

Police become involved in crime in at least three different ways:

✔ In response to calls for service, such as 9-1-1 calls

✔ Through police observation, such as when an officer on patrol sees a mugging going down

✔ During police investigations, in which detectives build cases involving ongoing crime, such as identifying the members of a street gang involved in the sale of narcotics

The majority of crimes that local police deal with are reported through 9-1-1 calls — you can probably imagine the wide variety of calls that 9-1-1 dispatchers receive. Here's just a small sample of some common crimes that a patrol officer may be called to respond to:

- A traffic accident caused by a drunk driver
- A shoplifting incident at a grocery store
- A robbery at a local convenience store
- A domestic assault in an apartment complex
- A fight at a bar
- A burglary at someone's home
- A purse stolen from a gym locker room
- A naked mentally ill man walking down the middle of a highway (an incident I had to deal with as a new prosecutor)

The truth is police officers never know what they're going to face when they go to work. In this section, I describe the process police follow when they respond to a crime scene, from talking to witnesses to collecting evidence to writing reports.

Interviewing witnesses

Upon arriving at a crime scene (of domestic violence, for example), the first thing an officer has to do is check on the status of any victims to see whether they need medical attention. To ensure everyone's safety, the officer has to separate all parties involved and make sure no other violence occurs. Then the officer needs to figure out what's going on. The best way to do so is by talking to the witnesses.

Here are some things good interviewers do:

- **Make sure that everyone who may have seen something sticks around.** You definitely don't want to have a key witness walk away without being interviewed.

- **Write down the witnesses' names and addresses.** You may need to contact them later with more questions. Plus, you have to put this information in your police report so that the prosecutor can subpoena them as witnesses.

- **Separate witnesses before you interview them.** People are susceptible to suggestion. A witness may overhear what another witness says and subconsciously (or purposely) change her own statement.

  For example, a witness who actually only *heard* yelling from next door may start to believe that she *saw* the assault after listening to a few other witnesses give their accounts.

  I've seen witnesses who thought they saw something change their story later under cross-examination, so it's important for officers to separate witnesses while conducting interviews.

✔ **Don't ask leading questions.** A leading question strongly suggests the answer you're looking for. You want to allow the witness to tell *her* story, not yours.

For example, don't ask, "You saw the large man hit the victim with his fist, didn't you?" Instead, ask, "What did you see?"

To be honest though, sometimes asking a leading question is the only way to get information.

Interviewing witnesses seems relatively simple, but it can be very challenging. For example, what if a witness doesn't speak English? You may have to rely on someone present at the scene to translate for you, but you can't be sure of the accuracy of the translation. Another challenge is determining whether the witness is telling the truth. Does the witness have some bias that leads him to lie to you? Officers must assess situations very quickly and then just do the best they can.

Interrogating suspects

Now this is the stuff of great drama — it's no wonder why cop shows on TV frequently show suspect interrogations. On TV, interrogations usually occur in rooms with one-way mirrors while other cops watch. But in real life, interrogations are more likely to occur at crime scenes or in police cars.

Interrogation skills are extremely valuable to cops, and a good interviewer is valuable property in a detective unit. Although some people are better interviewers than others, most police officers spend a lot of time in training to learn interrogation skills. These skills are important for the following two reasons:

✔ A confession, which you often get in an interrogation, is just about the best evidence you can have.

✔ A suspect's provable lie, which you also get from an interrogation, is the next best type of evidence (because a person who lies is hiding something — probably guilt).

Because confessions can be so valuable as evidence, governments throughout history have sought confessions aggressively — sometimes too aggressively. For example, the "rubber hose" treatment is the old practice of beating a suspect with a rubber hose until he confesses. The U.S. Constitution contains protections against such coercive government practices. For instance, it says that a confession must be voluntary — not extracted by torture or coercion — to be admissible.

Miranda rights

Today when a suspect is *in custody* (which means the person reasonably doesn't feel free to leave the scene), if the police don't read the suspect certain rights (called *Miranda rights*), the suspect's statements aren't admissible in court. The U.S. Supreme Court came up with these rights in the 1966 case *Miranda v. Arizona.* If you watch TV at all, you probably already know these rights. The exact language can vary somewhat, but here are the basics:

✔ You have the right to remain silent.

✔ Anything you say can and will be used against you in a court of law.

✔ You have the right to speak with an attorney and to have that attorney with you during questioning.

✔ If you can't afford an attorney, the court will appoint one for you.

If a suspect says he understands his rights and still chooses to make a statement, the court presumes that statement is voluntary, and, thus, deems it admissible at trial. Some states require that a suspect in custody be *Mirandized* (meaning have his Miranda rights read to him) *and* that his statement be recorded for it to be admissible in court.

You may be wondering why anyone would ever agree to talk to the police. Well, imagine that you were wrongly arrested. You'd try to persuade the officer of her mistake, wouldn't you? Similarly, guilty people often try to fool officers by trying to act innocent. In other words, they try to talk their way out of the situation.

Gathering physical evidence

Although statements from witnesses and suspects can be great evidence, physical evidence can also make a case. I talk about some specific types of physical evidence in the "Using Special Crime-Fighting Tools and Techniques" section, but here I want to focus on how police go about gathering evidence.

For serious offenses, it's often important to photograph the entire crime scene. Police officers should try not to move anything until they've taken these preliminary photos. (I talk specifically about crime scene investigations in the next section.) While searching for evidence, if an officer finds something, she places it into a special evidence bag in a way that preserves any trace evidence, such as blood or fingerprints, that exists on it (see the "Looking for fingerprints" section later in this chapter for more details). The officer who seizes each piece of evidence marks the bag she puts it in and then seals it. The officer then stores the bag of evidence in a secured room, known as an *evidence room,* at the police department. Every police department has an evidence room where police store physical evidence while waiting for trial.

If the evidence needs to be checked for fingerprints, the keeper of the evidence room, sometimes known as the *evidence technician,* checks out the bag (and makes a note of this action in an evidence log). She then sends it to the crime lab. When the crime lab scientist breaks the seal on the bag, he makes a notation on the bag that he did so. After he tests the evidence, he places it back in the bag, seals it up, and sends it back to the evidence technician.

On the day of trial, the officer who originally seized the evidence comes to the evidence room and retrieves the bag. She takes the bag to court and gives it to the prosecutor.

Why do officers have to follow this process so carefully? Some evidence requires proof of a *chain of custody,* or proof that the evidence was in police custody the entire time from the moment police took it from the crime scene to the moment it appears in court as evidence.

For example, if a prosecutor who's trying a murder case wants to offer into evidence fingerprints found on a knife that police retrieved from the murder scene, he first has to prove that

- ✔ The knife that was tested in the crime lab for fingerprints was the same one that was found next to the murder victim.

- ✔ The knife wasn't touched by anyone from the time it was found until the time it was tested by the scientist in the crime lab.

To prove this chain of custody, the prosecutor has to call as witnesses the officer who seized the knife and the scientist who tested the knife.

Unlike the knife in the preceding example, some evidence doesn't require a chain of custody. For example, if an officer takes a photo of an assault victim's face, the prosecutor doesn't need to prove that the photo was kept secure in an evidence locker. The officer who took the photo just needs to testify that the photo "fairly and accurately" depicts the scene she photographed. In fact, the officer doesn't even have to testify if the victim can testify that the photo is accurate.

Writing a report

Every piece of information a police officer uncovers about an incident must be conveyed to the prosecutor, who ultimately decides whether criminal charges should be filed. (I discuss the prosecutor's role in more detail in Chapter 19.) The officer conveys that information by writing a police report.

Every police department has a standard form that allows the officer to input the following pieces of information:

- ✔ The type of crime under investigation
- ✔ The names and addresses of witnesses

✔ Witness statements and officer observations

✔ Suspect information, including descriptions of identifiers like height, weight, hair color, and tattoos

In addition, reports have spaces for recording other statistical information about the crime, such as

✔ Whether the crime was gang related

✔ Whether it was a *hate crime* (motivated by racial bias, for example)

✔ Whether a weapon was used

✔ Whether the suspect was under the influence of an intoxicant

✔ How much loss, if any, occurred

Writing a good report is a crucial skill that can have a big impact on whether prosecutors make good decisions about charging suspects. Reports that leave out crucial information, are confusing, or are poorly written can lead to problems or mistakes in the criminal justice system.

Officers write their police reports at the police station after they've arrested the suspects or issued citations. (Increasingly, officers don't arrest suspects but, instead, issue them citations — like traffic tickets — to appear in court at a later date.) While the officer is actually at the crime scene, she may use a tape recorder or (more likely) a notebook to record observations and witness statements. If the officer concludes that no crime was committed and doesn't arrest anyone or issue any citations, she probably won't write a report. But she will hang on to her notes in case they become important and perhaps document her actions in a department activity log.

When an officer is conducting an ongoing investigation, she probably doesn't write her report until after she develops enough evidence to make an arrest.

Using Special Crime-Fighting Tools and Techniques

Once upon a time — not that long ago, actually — fingerprints were considered cutting-edge technology. (I must confess that I've never found fingerprints to be that helpful. In my entire career, I've used fingerprint evidence only a couple of times.) But as science continues to march on, a slew of crime-fighting techniques have become available. These techniques can solve thousands of crimes. Unfortunately though, they don't always do so because police often don't have enough resources to take advantage of them. The truth is crime labs across the country are often dramatically underfunded.

WARNING!

The *CSI* effect

Is it possible to flick through your TV channels without seeing a show about crime scene investigations? If you haven't seen the original *CSI,* you may have seen *CSI: Miami, CSI: New York,* or a variety of other similar shows. But how accurate are these shows? And has their popularity had any impact on what happens in real-life courtrooms?

The answer to the first question is that these shows are highly inaccurate, just like most other TV dramas. Here's how:

- ✔ Murders aren't solved in an hour, and sometimes they aren't solved at all.

- ✔ Crime scene investigators don't interview suspects.

- ✔ Often, crime scene investigators are trained scientists, not police officers.

- ✔ Crime scene investigators don't shoot bad guys.

- ✔ DNA testing takes weeks or months, not 15 minutes, to process.

- ✔ Fingerprint evidence rarely is helpful.

- ✔ Forensic scientists rarely have model-like good looks.

- ✔ Crime labs are often dramatically underfunded, so most of the techniques you see on TV are used only in the most serious cases.

The answer to the second question is yes — these TV shows *have* impacted real-life courtrooms, and they've done so by raising jurors' expectations about forensic evidence. In 2006, the *Yale Law Review* reported that a poll of prosecutors in Phoenix revealed that 38 percent of prosecutors failed to convict in at least one case because jurors had unreasonably high expectations for scientific evidence.

For example, one Phoenix prosecutor referred to a case in which a cop saw a drug dealer throw away a baggie of drugs. After the trial, jurors told the prosecutor that they were concerned that the baggie wasn't fingerprinted, even though the officer *saw* the defendant throw it away. In other words, fingerprint evidence wasn't necessary in this case. The jury didn't know that there was a six-month backlog in the crime lab for checking for fingerprint evidence. (And if every baggie of dope was tested, the backlog would probably be six years.)

Today, because of *CSI* and shows like it, jurors expect forensic evidence, such as DNA, fingerprints, and microfiber analysis, for all crimes, even minor ones. When they don't get it, they question the thoroughness of police and prosecutors.

In this section, I explain a variety of crime-fighting techniques, from low-tech to high-tech, including good ole fingerprints.

Conducting crime scene investigations

Whether or not investigators carefully scrutinize a crime scene for evidence depends on the seriousness of the crime. In fact, some crime scenes aren't examined at all. For example, in many jurisdictions, police don't even respond to burglary scenes because they don't have enough officers or forensic scientists. In such cases, an officer just takes the report over the phone. In reality, police agencies reserve crime scene investigations for the most serious of crimes.

Crime scenes can contain all kinds of evidence. Some of it is obvious, such as a murder weapon or a kilo of cocaine. But even a kilo of cocaine must be tested by a scientist in a crime lab to prove that, in fact, it is cocaine and not some harmless substance like sugar. Evidence that's obtained specifically for court is called *forensic evidence.* So the cocaine itself isn't forensic evidence, but the test results that prove it's cocaine are. If you're fascinated by forensic science, check out *Forensics For Dummies* by Douglas Lyle (Wiley).

So how does an officer treat a crime scene to secure the best forensic evidence? The first officers to arrive at a crime scene search the location to make sure no bad guys are lurking in the bushes and to verify that any injured victims are being cared for. After securing the scene, the next step is to lock it down so that no one can alter any evidence, hence the yellow tape you see encircling crime scenes.

Unless a jurisdiction has a very small police force, detectives are called to the scene, and one detective is put in charge of the investigation. Here's what happens in the initial stages of an investigation:

✔ An officer or a crime scene investigator photographs the scene. The photographic evidence is crucial for both the prosecution and the defense because it allows everyone to see the crime scene, even after it has been cleaned up.

✔ Someone is put in charge of logging in the evidence (called the *evidence custodian*). Cops who find evidence photograph it where they find it and then bring it to the evidence custodian, who records the item and secures it for storage in the evidence locker. Much of this evidence doesn't need to be analyzed by forensic scientists. (For example, I had a case where old grocery receipts in a garbage can showed the purchase date of duct tape used in a murder. I didn't need a forensic scientist to tell me this info.)

Initially, it's very hard to know what evidence is relevant to the case. The basic rule is: When in doubt, bag it and tag it.

✔ Forensic scientists or investigators are called to the scene to look for scientific evidence. At a murder scene, for example, they want to try to determine the cause of death, how it was done, and, ultimately, who did it. Here are just a few examples of what a forensic scientist may look for:

- **Angles of bullets:** The angle of a bullet entering a wall can reveal the trajectory of the shot and, thus, the location where the shooter was standing.

- **Blood patterns:** The pattern of blood spatter can reveal where the victim was standing when struck, whether the blood came from a hard blow, and even whether the victim was alive during that blow. (Check out the "Studying blood stain patterns" section for more details.)

- **Duct tape:** Duct tape placed over a victim's mouth can be matched up with the end of the roll of duct tape found in the suspect's truck to see whether there's a match. (This is done through microfiber analysis.)

- **Shell casings:** The location and number of shell casings can reveal where the shooter was standing, how many shots were fired, and perhaps whether the shooter was acting in self-defense. Testing the shell casings can help identify the murder weapon, too.

Applying for search warrants

Except in rare emergencies, police cannot just come into your house and search it. The U.S. Constitution requires police to have *probable cause* (meaning that it's more likely than not that they will find evidence of a crime) before they can search your home. They also have to obtain a judge's approval for a search warrant. Sometimes this means waking up a judge in the middle of the night so that he can sign a search warrant. Of course, a person can consent to a search of his or her house, which means a warrant isn't needed.

Police can obtain a warrant to search a house, car, or any private property. Such searches are often treated like crime scenes, with an assigned evidence custodian and other officers assigned to conduct the search. However, for most search warrants, forensic scientists aren't called to the location.

The scope of an officer's search of someone's private property is limited by what the officer is looking for. In other words, police can search only for evidence of the crime they're investigating. For example, if an officer is looking for evidence of a stolen car, he can certainly look in the suspect's garage, but he probably can't look in a drawer in the suspect's clothes dresser.

The most common type of search warrant permits officers to look for evidence of drug crimes. Drug units regularly obtain warrants to search houses for drugs, cash, packaging materials, or records of drug activity. Needless to say, executing such search warrants can be very dangerous. Police never know what's waiting for them when they break into a criminal's house.

To listen to suspects' conversations (called a *wiretap*), police have to obtain a special type of search warrant order from a judge. Because of the significant privacy intrusion involved, a wiretap order is much tougher to get approval for than a regular search warrant. I discuss wiretaps in more detail in Chapter 8.

Analyzing computers, cellphones, and other electronic evidence

Today evidence is commonly found on high-tech devices. Anything that can store electronic data may contain evidence of a crime. In most circumstances, however, police need a warrant to search items such as computers, cellphones, and flash drives.

Even after a cop has a warrant, however, he doesn't just open a computer with a screwdriver and look for evidence (although I do know officers who have found drugs hidden inside computer consoles). And a cop can't just turn on a computer and start looking around at files. Everything he does alters the data. For example, when he opens a document, the computer records the specific time he opened it, so a jury can't know when that document was previously opened. (The jury may also question whether the document was altered.) If police searched computer evidence in this way, it likely wouldn't be admissible in court.

Therefore, it takes a specially trained forensic computer expert to retrieve electronic evidence. Typically, after the officer seizes the computer, the expert makes an exact copy of the hard drive. Then, using special software, she searches the copy without altering any of the original data.

Because cellphones are so common, and because everyone seems to be text messaging and taking photographs through cellphones, they can be treasure troves of evidence. But searching a cellphone is a challenging task. Each phone requires different search technology, and phone companies keep changing the designs. As a result, very few police experts can keep up on cellphone technology, so most small police departments have trouble taking advantage of this type of evidence.

Administering lie detector tests

Also known as a *polygraph*, a lie detector is a machine that measures certain biological responses in a person while she's being asked a series of questions. The machine measures the following:

- ✔ Heart rate
- ✔ Body temperature
- ✔ Blood pressure
- ✔ Skin conductivity
- ✔ Breathing rate

While connected to the machine, a subject has to answer a series of questions. The subject receives the questions in advance so she isn't surprised. Some of the questions are *controls,* meaning that they aren't the focus of the interrogation. A control question may be, "Is your name Barack Obama?" The officer conducting the test then compares the physiological responses during the control questions to the physiological responses during the important questions. If the subject's heart rate, body temperature, and other responses change during the important questions, the officer may conclude that the person is being deceptive.

Results from lie detector tests aren't admissible in court because there's great debate about their reliability — not to mention you can find numerous Web sites that claim to teach you how to defeat a lie detector test.

Defense attorneys sometimes use polygraph tests to try to persuade prosecutors that their clients are innocent. But their most important use in law enforcement is as an interrogation technique. A person under suspicion of a crime may be asked to take a polygraph test (he can't be forced to). A guilty person may do so because he wants to appear innocent. An innocent person may do so because he wants to be cleared. The test is an opportunity for the polygraph examiner to ask pointed questions about the crime and to use the test results to try to persuade the subject to "come clean." This is important because, although the test results aren't admissible in court, the statements of the subject taking the test can be admissible.

Ultimately, the test relies on the skill and experience of the polygraph examiner to interpret the meaning of changes in a person's physiological reactions. Thus, interpreting results is a subjective process, which may be another reason why polygraph results aren't admissible in court.

Looking for fingerprints

Look closely at the tips of your fingers. You see *friction ridges,* which help you hold on to things. The pattern of ridges is unique to you and makes up your *fingerprint.* If you pick up a glass right now, sweat and oil on your fingertips may leave a latent fingerprint on the glass. Fingerprints can be left behind at crime scenes or on evidence, and they can be powerful proof that a particular suspect touched a particular item.

Most fingerprints aren't visible to the human eye (hence the word *latent*), so police use various methods to locate prints. For example, at a crime scene, police may apply a special powder to various surfaces, which helps make prints visible. Or they may take an item from a scene back to the crime lab and use more sophisticated techniques to locate prints. One highly regarded technique is known as *vacuum metal deposition,* in which fine layers of gold and zinc are applied to the item; the metal attaches to minute fat molecules left in prints.

If a print is identified on an item of evidence, the scientist must have another print to compare it to. So, if police have a suspect, they take fingerprints from him and compare his prints to the ones from the crime scene.

Fortunately, there's also a nationwide electronic system that contains fingerprints of just about everyone who has ever been arrested. The system contains more than 47 million prints. This system, run by the Federal Bureau of Investigation (FBI), is called the *Integrated Automated Fingerprint Identification System,* or IAFIS for short.

When a person is arrested, his prints are taken and entered into IAFIS. Then, using computers, police can check prints from a crime scene against prints in the database. If a potential match is found, a trained fingerprint examiner does a comparison, looking for identical features in each set of prints.

Of course, using fingerprints as evidence does pose a few problems. For instance:

- ✔ Finding a perfect print is rare. For example, when you pick up a glass, your fingers rub against that glass. Instead of leaving a perfect print, you may leave a smudge or just a partial print, which is much harder to match than a full print.

- ✔ Most surfaces aren't perfectly smooth like glass, so they may not retain identifiable fingerprints.

- ✔ The comparison print may be less than perfect. After all, when someone is arrested, a local jail official likely takes his prints by applying ink to the arrestee's hands and rubbing those hands on a fingerprint card. Imperfect prints are common.

The bottom line is that retrieving good prints from an item of evidence and then comparing those prints with a faulty comparator can be a challenging science.

As I discuss next, advances in DNA analysis may make fingerprint evidence less and less important.

Testing DNA

DNA testing has become the mother of all forensic evidence. Expectations of DNA testing have progressed quickly: In the late 1990s, defendants regularly challenged its accuracy, but jurors today expect DNA to solve almost every crime.

DNA is short for *deoxyribonucleic acid*. It contains the genetic instructions for the development of every living thing — including you — and is present in almost every cell in your body. Its importance in criminal forensics comes from the fact that no two people have the same DNA (except identical twins, which could make for an interesting soap opera storyline). So if a criminal leaves behind some organic matter at a crime scene, DNA evidence can play a role in solving the crime.

Here are some of the most common sources of DNA evidence:

- ✔ Blood
- ✔ Semen
- ✔ Saliva
- ✔ Skin
- ✔ Teeth
- ✔ Hair
- ✔ Urine
- ✔ Perspiration
- ✔ Fingernails

Note that DNA evidence isn't always visible. For example, the handle of a baseball bat used in an assault may contain invisible perspiration. Cigarette butts may have saliva. Bed sheets may contain dried semen stains. A murder victim's fingernails may contain skin cells from the murderer.

Your DNA and mine are 99.9 percent identical. However, certain known regions of the DNA string do vary from individual to individual, and these sections are the ones forensic scientists compare.

Using DNA as evidence

Police, victim advocates, and medical professionals have systematized a lot of DNA evidence gathering. For example, a rape victim is usually asked to undergo a medical examination to look for evidence of blood, semen, or pubic hair, which may help capture the rapist. After police and medical professionals have collected items that may contain DNA, they store them in certain types of containers to preserve the evidence for later testing. In fact, following strict protocols and maintaining a chain of custody are crucial to accurate DNA testing. If the evidence becomes contaminated in any way, it loses all value. (Check out the "Gathering physical evidence" section for more on gathering evidence and maintaining a chain of custody.)

How is DNA used as evidence? Obviously, it can identify a suspect, as in a rape case. But DNA evidence can also place a suspect in a location where he claims not to have been. It can establish that a suspect held a weapon, and it can help police eliminate potential suspects. DNA has even been used in some cases to obtain the release of persons wrongly convicted.

DNA evidence is collected mostly in "person" crimes, such as serious assaults, rapes, and murders. Most policymakers consider the costs too high to do DNA analysis for common property crimes, such as burglary. However, a 2008 study by the National Institute for Justice found that gathering and using DNA evidence in property crimes doubled the arrest and conviction rates and helped identify the most serious of property offenders. Significantly, the study found that DNA evidence was twice as effective as fingerprint evidence in identifying suspects.

But DNA evidence isn't a cure-all. Even when police find DNA evidence and follow proper procedures for collecting it, they can still encounter challenges. For example, DNA samples can be mixed, meaning that DNA from at least two different people is found together. This situation is common during investigations of violent encounters, as you can imagine. After all, blood, saliva, and other body tissues can easily be intermingled. As another example, a hotel bedspread can contain DNA from a number of different people. (Trust me, you don't want me to elaborate on this point.)

DNA evidence can survive for 20 years or more. Many states are contemplating laws that require police to keep DNA evidence even after a suspect has been convicted. The argument is that as science progresses, that evidence may later help exonerate persons wrongly convicted. The long-term storage of biological evidence is certainly a headache for police agencies, however. It not only takes up space, but bloody evidence may contain diseases, such as hepatitis, which pose serious health risks for everybody concerned.

Compiling DNA samples

As with fingerprints, a forensic scientist working with DNA evidence must have a sample (an *exemplar,* as people in the know call it) with which to compare the DNA evidence from a crime scene. Obviously, if police have a suspect, they can require the person to give them a sample. You may recall federal officials taking a saliva swab from former President Bill Clinton to do a comparison with the stain found on Monica Lewinsky's infamous blue dress. But what happens when police don't have a suspect?

Most states maintain databases containing the DNA of convicted criminals. Individual states have laws that determine whose DNA profile must be stored in those databases — people convicted of certain crimes, for example, or even people who are just arrested but not yet convicted. After police take — and scientists analyze — the biological sample from the convict or suspect, they put that person's DNA profile in their state's database. The state databases are all connected nationally by an FBI system known as the *National DNA Index System,* or NDIS. Similarly, if DNA evidence is retrieved from an unsolved crime, that unidentified DNA profile may also be stored in the state database.

Once a week, a program known as the *Combined DNA Index System,* or CODIS for short, compares DNA profiles from unsolved crimes against the DNA profiles from convicted offenders. If there's a match, called a *hit,* the FBI notifies the state crime lab that submitted the DNA profile.

As of 2009, CODIS contained the DNA profiles of more than 6.7 million criminal offenders and more than 250,000 DNA samples from unsolved crimes. Since the program started in 1990, it has produced more than 85,000 hits. That's *a lot* of serious crimes solved.

But CODIS isn't problem free. DNA profiles take a lot of time to process, and most state and local crime labs don't have enough scientists to analyze all the biological samples and submit the DNA profiles into the database. As a result, many states have giant backlogs of biological evidence from convicted offenders and from unsolved crimes that haven't even been analyzed yet. In fact, a 2003 study found that 169,000 biological samples from rapes and 52,000 samples from homicides hadn't been processed or entered into the database.

If you want more information about DNA testing and evidence, the federal government maintains a great Web site at www.dna.gov.

Comparing handwriting

In criminal cases involving handwriting, such as forged checks or even phony suicide notes, police may ask an expert in handwriting comparison to look at the evidence. As with fingerprints and DNA, the examiner must have the evidentiary writing, known as the *questioned document,* and something to compare it with. Often police require a suspect to give a handwriting sample, known as a *handwriting exemplar.*

Also, like fingerprints and DNA evidence, the science of handwriting comparison has many challenges. Here are just a few:

- An intentional simulation can be hard to identify.

- Suspects asked to give handwriting exemplars may purposefully alter their style of writing to make the comparison more difficult.

- Drugs, alcohol, or even caffeine can alter how a person writes in a given circumstance.

Most importantly, however, handwriting examination is ultimately subjective. It depends on the experience and skill of the examiner, and these obviously vary from examiner to examiner. At least in my little world, requests for handwriting comparisons have always ended with the following words: "results inconclusive."

Studying blood stain patterns

Blood stain patterns can provide valuable evidence. Whole books are written on this topic, but, basically, you can tell an awful lot from a blood stain.

Blood stain experts essentially define three types of blood stains:

- **Contact transfers:** When a bloody knife transfers blood onto a surface, such as a kitchen counter, for example

- **Passive blood stains:** When blood drips or pools on a surface

- **Projected stains or blood spatter:** When blood is flung or sprayed onto a surface

Blood spatter is further broken down into low-, medium-, and high-velocity blood spatter. These terms refer to the speed of the item that caused the injury, not the speed at which the blood flew from the body. For example, something traveling at greater than 100 feet per second (like a bullet) causes high-velocity blood spatter, characterized by tiny droplets of blood. Low-velocity spatter results in larger droplets.

A good blood stain expert can tell you a *lot* about a bloody crime scene, including the following information:

- ✔ What type of impact caused the blood to flow
- ✔ Where the victim was when the blood flowed
- ✔ Where the suspect may have gone after committing the crime (based on drops of blood from a knife, for example)

Consider the low-velocity stain in Figure 18-1. This illustration reveals a *castoff stain* from a knife, moving from left to right in a curve. You can tell the direction by the elongated shape of the drops as you move farther to the right.

Figure 18-1:
The castoff stain from a knife.

Next, look at Figure 18-2, which shows a *drip stain.* Notice how the stain is round with scalloping all around the edge, indicating that it fell straight down.

Figure 18-2:
A drip stain that fell straight down.

Collecting cell tower evidence

Records of cellphone signals can be very valuable in placing a suspect in the vicinity of a crime scene. For instance, when you make a call with your cellphone, that phone generally sends a signal to the closest cell tower. For billing purposes, your cellphone company keeps records of which towers received which signals. (Of course, they want to be able to hit you with roaming charges whenever they can.) Police or prosecutors can obtain cell tower information through a subpoena or a court order and then use that information to prove that a suspect was near a particular location at a particular time.

I once prosecuted a man for child molestation. He claimed to have been in Florida, but records of his cellphone calls placed him in the Northwest during the week of the crimes. Of course, I still had to prove that he was the person making the calls.

Reconstructing an accident

One of the most valuable forms of forensic analysis involves the reconstruction of automobile accidents. Accident reconstruction is an extremely complex area, but basically, it involves examining all the evidence from a car crash to determine what happened. When a death occurs, for example, accident reconstruction allows law enforcement officials to determine whether someone should be charged with murder, manslaughter, or negligent homicide.

Here are just a few examples of how reconstruction experts can piece together what happened:

- ✔ Tire skid marks can show when brakes were applied, how fast a car was going, and whether the car was turning at the time of the accident.
- ✔ The location of a shoulder harness injury can show who was driving.
- ✔ Headlight examination can reveal whether the lights were on or not.
- ✔ The amount and type of vehicle damage can explain what happened to the car.
- ✔ Evidence of food in the car or a cellphone that's turned on can show that a driver may have been distracted.

The main drawbacks of accident reconstruction work is that it's time-consuming and expensive. Although it's often used in civil suits involving car crashes, in the criminal arena, it's usually reserved for traffic fatalities.

Part V
Prosecuting and Punishing Crime

The 5th Wave   By Rich Tennant

In this part . . .

When police arrest someone for a crime, that person's criminal justice experience is just beginning. In the chapters that follow, I explore what happens to someone after the arrest.

I start by introducing the key players involved in the prosecution phase and explain what type of work they do. I focus on the two options that face someone accused of a crime: a plea bargain or a trial. Next, I explore how the U.S. criminal justice system punishes people and why it does so. Finally, I show you how the system treats juvenile offenders — which is often different from the way it treats adult offenders.

Chapter 19

Seeking Justice: The Players and Their Roles

*U*nderstanding the U.S. justice system requires understanding the duties and responsibilities of the key players in that system. In this chapter, I discuss the roles of prosecutors, defense attorneys, and judges.

Prosecutors: Guardians of Safety

Prosecutors are government attorneys who seek to convict criminals. (I'm always surprised by how many people don't know that.) Like all attorneys, prosecutors must graduate from a law school and pass a state bar exam. A *bar exam* is a test that each state administers to ensure that every attorney knows enough to practice law competently.

The vast majority of prosecutors in the United States work at the local level. Prosecutors are usually organized in the following way: A local office has one prosecutor in charge, who is elected by the citizens or appointed by a politician such as a governor. That person may be known as the *district attorney* or the *county prosecutor*. Depending on the population of the jurisdiction, the district attorney may have any number of prosecutors working for her. For example, in 2009, Los Angeles County District Attorney Steve Cooley had 1,017 deputy district attorneys working for him. In contrast, the county prosecutor for Barry County in Missouri, Johnnie Cox, had just one assistant prosecutor.

As of this writing, 2,344 local prosecutor offices in the United States employ roughly 25,000 assistant prosecutors. Confusingly, although these offices are usually organized by county, they're considered to be part of their *state* criminal justice systems because they enforce state laws passed by their state legislatures.

At the federal level, U.S. attorneys — appointed by the president of the United States — play the role that the district attorneys play at the local level. At the time of this writing, there are 93 U.S. attorneys, and each one has an office with assistant U.S. attorneys who prosecute federal crimes. Many towns also have small municipal courts that handle low-level violations and crimes. City attorneys may prosecute these offenses. (See Chapter 20 for more information about municipal courts and the differences between the federal court system and the state court system.)

Charging crimes

So what do prosecutors do? One of their most important responsibilities is deciding whom to charge with a crime, and what crimes to charge. When you think about this responsibility, you realize just how serious it is. In all of U.S. society, only the prosecutor has the authority to start the process that ultimately can take away a person's liberty. Such authority can't be exercised lightly.

Typically, police make an arrest, write a report that explains the crimes committed and the evidence of those crimes, and then forward that report to the local prosecutor's office. The prosecutor reads the report and decides whether or not to file charges.

A police officer needs only probable cause to make an arrest. (*Probable cause* means that it's more likely than not that the person committed the crime.) But ultimately, a prosecutor has to prove that the person committed the crime by a much higher standard — *beyond a reasonable doubt.* (Check out Chapter 20 for the common legal definition of this standard.) So although the officer may have been justified in making the arrest, the prosecutor can conclude that the evidence isn't strong enough to obtain a conviction. In that case, the prosecutor declines to file charges.

Sometimes the prosecutor sends a note to the arresting officer asking for more investigation. For example, as a prosecutor, I may decline to file charges on an assault because I need evidence of an injury to prove the case, and the officer's report may not have said anything about an injury. I may choose to send a note to the officer offering to reconsider the charging decision if he can bring me a photograph of an injury or a statement from the victim explaining the injury.

When prosecutors do decide to file charges, they can do so in three ways:

- ✔ For *misdemeanors* (low-level offenses punishable by no more than a year in jail), the prosecutor usually drafts an *information* (a charging document that describes the alleged crime) and files it with the court. The defendant eventually receives this document so that he can see the crimes being charged against him.

- ✔ In most states, for *felonies* (serious offenses punishable by more than a year in prison), the prosecutor presents evidence to a grand jury that decides whether there's enough evidence to file charges. (The grand jury can also be used for misdemeanor crimes, but it rarely is.)

  What's a *grand jury?* It's a group of citizens who receive a summons from the local court just like regular jurors. But unlike regular jurors, they don't decide guilt. Rather, in a secret proceeding, prosecutors bring evidence before the grand jury, which then decides whether or not to file criminal charges. The only people allowed in such a proceeding are the grand jurors, the prosecutor, and the witnesses relevant to the case. There's no judge present. If the grand jury decides that there's enough evidence to file charges, it does so through an indictment. An *indictment* is pretty much the same thing as an information — a charging document that describes the alleged crime — except that the citizens of the grand jury (not the prosecutor) issue it.

  Why does the U.S. justice system have grand juries? Few other countries do. In the United States, the grand jury system is considered a check on prosecutorial discretion. The idea is that citizens won't allow prosecutors to abuse their authority and wrongfully indict people. But a well-known joke among defense attorneys says that a grand jury would indict a ham sandwich if the prosecutor asked it to. The joke reflects the fact that the prosecutor has a lot of influence over the members of the grand jury because the proceedings occur in secret. No attorney is present to argue on behalf of the defendant.

- ✔ Some jurisdictions don't use grand juries. Instead, prosecutors draft an information for felonies like they do for misdemeanors. Then, at a preliminary hearing, a judge determines whether there's enough evidence to continue the case. This hearing is different from a grand jury because a judge, the defendant, and his attorney are present, and the defense attorney gets to cross-examine witnesses. In the preliminary hearing, the judge fulfills the same function as the grand jury, making sure the prosecution has sufficient evidence to go forward with the case.

  Still other jurisdictions let prosecutors choose whether they use a grand jury or a preliminary hearing.

In Chapter 20, I outline the course of a criminal trial from plea negotiations, to motions to suppress, right up to the trial.

Helping with investigations

In addition to making charging decisions on standard criminal cases, more senior prosecutors may be directly involved with cops in ongoing investigations.

For example, most homicide investigations heavily involve a prosecutor because, ultimately, the prosecutor has to prove the case. Thus, the prosecutor helps make decisions like the following:

- ✔ Do the police have probable cause to obtain a search warrant?
- ✔ Are witness statements admissible or should the witness be reinterviewed?
- ✔ Is it worth the cost to send a detective to another state to interview a witness?

In addition to serious violent crimes, prosecutors are often directly involved in ongoing organized crime investigations with drug and gang task forces. In these investigations, the prosecutors help choose targets for the investigation, approve search warrants before they're given to the judge, and decide when to make an arrest after enough evidence has been found to convict the suspect.

Generally, however, handling the constant flow of new cases is too much work to allow most prosecutors to be seriously involved in ongoing investigations. So, usually, cops are left to investigate by themselves. Turn to Chapter 18 for a discussion about police investigations.

Weighing ethical responsibilities

Prosecutors don't represent individual clients. They don't even represent the victims in their cases, although they may be very sympathetic and helpful to victims. Prosecutors represent the *government*. This statement sounds kind of cold to a jury, so as a prosecutor, I liked to say, "I represent the *people*." (The United States is a democracy after all.)

Among all lawyers, prosecutors have a unique obligation to do the right thing. Most attorneys have an ethical obligation to zealously represent their clients' interests, even when doing so means helping a guilty person achieve an acquittal. But in representing the people of the United States, prosecutors are bound by ethical rules to seek justice, not just convictions. Practicing according to this ethical code means that

- ✔ Prosecutors can't hide evidence.
- ✔ If prosecutors come to believe a defendant is innocent, they must dismiss the case.
- ✔ Judges hold prosecutors to a much higher standard than they do other lawyers.

And this is the way it should be.

Fulfilling additional duties

Although the trial process takes up most of a prosecutor's time, a prosecutor's office usually has a number of other responsibilities, as well. Here are some of the more common ones in no particular order (keep in mind that not all prosecutors' offices have all these duties):

- Representing the state in delinquency proceedings against juveniles who engage in criminal conduct. (In Chapter 22, I discuss juvenile cases in detail.)

- Representing children's interests in family court. For example, this duty may include proceedings to terminate parental rights when parents appear to be unfit to carry out their parental responsibilities.

- Pursuing someone's commitment to a mental hospital if that person's mental faculties are so impaired that she's dangerous to society or she can't care for herself.

- Ensuring that victims' rights are protected from the moment charges are filed until sentencing, and even after that. (I discuss victims' rights in detail in Chapter 4.)

- Enforcing civil restraining orders against people who violate them. A *restraining order* is an order by a court for one person to stay away from another person. Often, people request this order after their romantic relationships break up. If a person violates a restraining order, a judge can find the violator in contempt of court and fine the person, or even put her in jail.

- Overseeing *multidisciplinary teams* that investigate issues like child abuse or elder abuse. A multidisciplinary team may include social service workers, police, medical professionals, and judges. The goal of these teams is to bring a holistic approach to problem solving. Frequently, prosecutors lead these teams.

- Enforcing child-support orders against parents who fail to pay child support.

- Reviewing all suspicious deaths in the jurisdiction.

- Providing legal training to law enforcement agencies.

- Representing the state at probation-violation hearings, which occur when a probation officer alleges a person violated a condition of probation and brings the person before a judge for hearing.

As you can see, a prosecutor may have a number of different responsibilities. This wide range of duties can lead to a friendly dispute between elected prosecutors and elected sheriffs about who is the *chief law enforcement officer* in the county.

Defense Attorneys: Guardians of Liberty

Given humankind's penchant for tyranny and abuse of individual rights, the role of the criminal defense attorney is one of the most important guarantees of freedom in the U.S. justice system.

You hear frequently about the importance of the right to free speech, the right to bear arms, and other constitutional guarantees. But every day the institution of the defense attorney guards against the almost-inevitable abuse of governmental power. And this job is no piece of cake. Criminal defendants are often an unsavory lot. Spending most of the work day with accused burglars, thieves, and rapists is a difficult job.

In addition to representing adult criminal defendants, defense attorneys often perform the following duties:

- Represent juveniles charged with crimes.

- Represent people accused of probation violations.

- Represent parents in family-law matters, such as the termination of parental rights.

- Serve on *justice improvement committees,* which are committees focused on improving the criminal justice system. For example, a judge, prosecutor, probation officer, and defense attorney may meet to figure out a way to create a drug court that efficiently deals with low-level drug offenders by providing them treatment.

- Represent criminal defendants when they appeal convictions to a higher court.

Often people can't afford to hire lawyers to perform these services, which is where the constitutional right to counsel kicks in.

Hiring a public or private defender

The Sixth Amendment to the U.S. Constitution entitles a criminal defendant to counsel after judicial proceedings have begun against him. Generally, this right means that when a defendant is *arraigned* (informed of the criminal charges that have been filed against him), he becomes entitled to an attorney. At the arraignment, if the defendant wants a court-appointed attorney, he fills out paperwork setting forth his financial situation. The vast majority of defendants are *indigent,* meaning they can't afford to hire their own lawyers, and, therefore, qualify for court-appointed lawyers.

In many jurisdictions, a government agency employs attorneys to represent defendants. These attorneys are often called *public defenders*. Frequently, however, the local government may contract with private attorneys to represent indigent defendants. Either way, the government is paying for an attorney to represent a criminal defendant's interest. If the defendant is ultimately convicted, as part of the sentence, most states require a defendant to pay back some or all of the cost of his counsel.

The amount the government pays these attorneys is often well below the market rate for attorneys. In other words, representing indigent criminal defendants isn't lucrative. As a consequence, many public defenders are new attorneys with little experience. The attorneys who make public defender work a career are often attorneys with strong personal convictions about the need to stand up and defend individuals against the potential for governmental abuse.

Some crimes are more likely to be committed by people who can afford to hire their own attorneys. For example, people all across the economic spectrum commit the crime of driving under the influence of an intoxicant. High-priced private attorneys can demand a $20,000 retainer to handle such cases, and many wealthy people pay this price. Similarly, people who commit white-collar crimes, such as fraud or embezzlement, often can afford their own expensive attorneys.

So, is there a difference in the quality of lawyering between low-paid public defenders and high-priced private attorneys? Would O. J. Simpson have been acquitted if he hadn't paid for his "dream team" of lawyers: Robert Shapiro, Johnnie Cochran, F. Lee Bailey, and Alan Dershowitz? Well, I've known some very talented public defenders, but, in general, like everything else in life, you get what you pay for.

The public lawyer's salary

Young lawyers often graduate from law school with over $100,000 in debt. Servicing that debt takes enough income to pay for the normal costs of living plus the debt payments. Unfortunately, for too many public attorneys, government salaries are just too low to cover all these costs. In Florida, about 19 percent of prosecutors and 22 percent of public defenders quit every year, primarily because the government salary is far beneath the salaries of private attorneys.

In Missouri, for example, a new public defender makes $37,296, and a seasoned vet can make a maximum of $76,285. In contrast, according to the Association for Legal Career Professionals, the median starting salary for first-year private attorneys was $113,000 in 2007. Of course, this statistic includes mega-firms that pay very high salaries. But even for small private law firms of between 2 and 25 attorneys, the median first-year salary was $67,000.

The moral is: If you want to make money, don't work for the government.

Like prosecutors, public defenders carry very heavy caseloads. As a result, they have the same pressure to resolve cases efficiently through plea negotiations. High-priced private attorneys, however, have the luxury of smaller caseloads that allow them more time to investigate possible defenses and prepare for trial. So, generally, a privately hired attorney will provide better legal services because he has more time to prepare, has more experience, and may (or may not) be a better attorney.

Facing ethical dilemmas

Because of the nature of their work, defense attorneys regularly face a number of sticky ethical issues. Every state has different ethical rules, but for the most part, they're similar. For example, ethical rules, in general, allow most attorneys to refuse to offer evidence that they reasonably believe is false. However, a *criminal* defense attorney can't refuse to offer the testimony of his client unless he knows *for a fact* that the testimony is false.

Here's just one example of a sticky ethical issue that defense attorneys across the country face on a daily basis (what would you do if you were in this situation?): Say you're a defense attorney in the middle of trial. Your client is charged with assaulting his wife, and he says he wants to testify in his own defense. He plans to testify that his wife fell in the bathtub and that she ended up with a broken nose because of that fall. You don't believe your client, but you don't know for a fact that he's lying.

In this example, because you don't know for sure that your client is lying, in many states, you would have an ethical obligation to put him on the witness stand — even though you don't personally believe him. So you can see the difficult decisions defense attorneys have to make every day.

Trial Judges: Overseeing the Justice Process

A *judge* is an attorney who has been appointed or elected to public office. Federal judges are appointed for life, but the term of office for state or local judges depends on local law. If elected, a judge typically has to run for reelection after four or six years.

Judges oversee all kinds of legal proceedings from tax court to bankruptcy law. In this section, I explain a judge's responsibilities in the criminal justice system.

Authorizing cops to search

Even before criminal charges are filed, a judge may become involved in a criminal investigation. For example, police usually need to obtain a warrant from a judge before they can conduct a search of a private location. (I discuss search warrants in Chapter 18.) Officers visit a judge in her chambers or even at her home in the middle of the night to obtain search warrants. They present an *affidavit* (a statement under oath) that sets out why the officers believe the location contains evidence of a crime. If the judge finds that there's probable cause to believe the place contains evidence of a crime, she signs a warrant authorizing the police to search there.

As you see again and again throughout the criminal justice process, the search-warrant requirement is a check on the potential for abusing government power. The U.S. Constitution requires an independent judge to authorize police to invade someone's private place in most circumstances.

If a judge approves a search warrant, she usually doesn't participate as the judge in the subsequent case (if charges are filed). In part, this is because the application for the warrant may contain information that won't be offered into evidence during the trial. In effect, the judge who approved the search warrant would know more than she should if she presided over the criminal case.

Judges also approve other law enforcement activities, including the following types of searches:

- Wiretapping someone's phone, house, or car
- Attaching mobile trackers to someone's vehicle
- Requesting information about a person's Internet activity
- Requesting cellphone records to show a person's location when making a phone call

Keeping cases moving

When a defendant is charged with a crime, a judge presides over every hearing in the criminal justice process (but it's not always the same judge). At the end of each step, the judge schedules the next step to make sure cases stay on track to get resolved. These pretrial hearings — not actual trials — take up most of a judge's time. Here are the steps that a judge presides over:

✔ **Arraignment:** This step occurs when the defendant hears the charges against him and is given the chance to apply for a court-appointed counsel. The judge's role in the arraignment is to make sure the defendant knows all his rights and to assign an appointed counsel if the defendant can't afford his own.

✔ **Release hearing:** If a defendant is being held in jail, his lawyer may ask the judge to set bail or reduce bail. *Bail* is the amount of money a defendant pays as a guarantee that he'll show up for the proceedings. If the judge finds that the defendant is a flight risk or a danger to society, she may set bail very high (such as $500,000) or even deny bail.

✔ **Settlement conference:** After the prosecutor gives the defense attorney a plea offer (if he decides to do so), both the prosecution and the defense attend a hearing at which the defendant can accept the offer, plead guilty, and be sentenced. If the defense rejects the plea offer, the judge schedules the case for trial.

✔ **Omnibus hearing:** A defense attorney requests an omnibus hearing when she believes that some of the prosecution's evidence may be inadmissible (check out Chapter 20 for more info on this hearing). The defense attorney files a motion to suppress the evidence (usually to suppress the fruits of an illegal search or the inadmissible statements of the defendant), and, at the hearing, the prosecutor calls witnesses to prove that the evidence should be ruled admissible. The judge ultimately makes the decision about whether the evidence in question is admissible at trial.

✔ **Trial:** If the case isn't settled during the settlement conference (or during last-minute plea negotiations), it goes to trial. During the trial, the judge acts somewhat like a referee, ruling on objections by the lawyers and keeping the proceedings moving. (See the next section for more details on the trial.)

✔ **Sentencing hearing:** If a defendant is found guilty at the trial or by pleading guilty, the judge presides over a sentencing hearing at which the defense attorney and prosecutors advocate for the sentence that they believe is appropriate.

For example, the prosecutor points out any previous convictions of the defendant, the value of any property damage or medical costs to victims, and any other facts that may be helpful to the judge in imposing the sentence. The defense attorney explains any facts that may persuade the judge to lessen the sentence, such as: The defendant has started a new job, he's sorry for what he did, or the crime resulted from his drug addiction and if he could just get some treatment, he'd stop committing crimes.

The judge then imposes the sentence. Many states have *determinate* sentences for serious offenses, which means the judge has little discretion and must impose a specific jail or prison sentence based on the type of crime committed and the number of prior convictions.

Presiding over a trial

One of the most significant issues up for discussion before a trial starts is whether the defendant wants a jury. The Sixth Amendment to the U.S. Constitution guarantees a defendant's right to a jury trial, but the defendant can choose to waive that right. If the defendant chooses to do so, the judge acts as the *trier of fact,* meaning that the judge decides whether the defendant is guilty. Having the judge determine guilt simplifies the trial process quite a bit. For instance, the prosecutor and the defense attorney don't have to pick a jury, a process that can take a lot of time. And the judge doesn't have to give instructions to the jury at the close of the case.

Besides saving time, having the judge act as the trier of fact also saves the trial participants some extra work. When a jury is involved, everyone has to be careful not to somehow prejudice the defendant. For example, in many states, a defendant has the right to change out of his jail clothes and into street clothes for a jury trial. The idea is that a jury may be more likely to think the defendant is guilty when he's wearing an orange jumpsuit. If the defendant waives the jury trial, the trial participants don't have to take such precautions. After all, the judge already knows whether the defendant is being kept in jail.

The bottom line is that a defendant's decision to waive the right to a jury greatly speeds up a case. For example, early in my career, I tried an entire shoplifting case to a judge in a half hour. If the case had involved a jury, the case would've taken all day.

Regardless of whether the judge serves as the trier of fact, she must preside over proceedings and rule on numerous issues that pop up during the trial. Here are some of the more common issues the judge has to address:

- ✔ **Should a potential juror be excused because she says she can't be fair?** Sometimes potential jurors have strong beliefs or life experiences that make them think they can't be fair to the defendant or the prosecutor. For example, a potential juror whose husband was killed by a drunk driver may not think she can be fair to a defendant charged with drunk driving.

- ✔ **Should witnesses be excluded from the courtroom?** Usually, *the parties* (the prosecution and the defense) don't want witnesses to hear what other witnesses testify about. The fear is that a witness may change her story after hearing other witnesses' accounts. Many states do, however, give a victim the right to remain in the courtroom.

- ✔ **Should certain evidence be admitted?** Although most judges like to resolve questions about the admissibility of evidence before a trial begins, more issues about the admissibility of evidence inevitably arise during the course of the trial, and the judge must decide them.

✔ **Should objections be sustained or overruled?** Lawyers object to opposing counsels' questions or procedures all the time, and the judge must apply a complicated set of rules, known as the *rules of evidence,* to decide whether to sustain an objection or to overrule the objection and let a witness answer a question. These rules govern the procedure of a trial. For example, the rules of evidence usually (but not always) prohibit the admission of hearsay evidence. So an attorney may object to a question that attempts to elicit an answer based on hearsay. (Giving a *hearsay* answer is simply testifying about what someone else said.)

✔ **When should breaks or lunch be taken?** Judges often have other business to take care of and, thus, have to take breaks to resolve it. Everyone else needs a break now and then, too. For example, a juror who smokes can get pretty irritable if she isn't allowed to smoke a cigarette or two during the day. And everybody needs to go to the bathroom.

✔ **After the lawyers are done presenting evidence, what instructions should the judge give to the jury about how to deliberate?** The jury must be instructed on how to select a presiding juror (also called *foreperson*), how to decide the precise charges, and what facts they must find to conclude the defendant is guilty.

✔ **Should the judge order dinner for the jury and make them deliberate into the night or have them come back the following day to continue deliberating?** After a jury begins deliberation, the judge is responsible for the care and feeding of that jury.

Sentencing the defendant

If the judge or jury finds a defendant guilty, the next step is sentencing. Usually, the judge imposes the sentence. One significant exception involves the imposition of the death penalty sentence, which the jury imposes. I discuss the death penalty in detail in Chapter 21.

For misdemeanors and low-level crimes, judges usually have a lot of discretion about what sentence to impose (a sentencing system called *indeterminate sentencing*). With indeterminate sentencing, the sentence can include a combination of the following:

✔ Fines

✔ Jail time

✔ Community service

✔ An order to have no contact with a victim

✔ An order to complete treatment, such as drug treatment or anger management

✔ An order to pay restitution to the victim

For these sentences, the judge usually puts the defendant on probation, and a probation officer makes sure the defendant complies with the orders.

If the crime is a serious felony, such as rape, kidnapping, or murder, many states take away the judge's sentencing discretion through laws that force the judge to impose mandatory sentences. This kind of sentencing system is called *determinate sentencing* because the sentence is already determined. For example, in Delaware, the offense of rape in the second degree carries a mandatory sentence of ten years in prison. The judge can't do much about that sentence.

The prosecutor may allege additional facts in the indictment that ask the trier of fact (the jury, or the judge if the jury is waived) to find additional facts that can lengthen the sentence. For example, in Missouri, a rape conviction carries a mandatory minimum five-year sentence. However, if the prosecutor alleges in the indictment that a deadly weapon was used in the rape, and the jury finds beyond a reasonable doubt that a gun was used in the rape, the minimum sentence becomes ten years in prison.

Mandatory minimum sentencing laws may have exceptions that allow the judge to impose lesser sentences, but these exceptions are often very limited. Minimum sentencing laws came into being, in part, as a check on perceived soft sentences by judges during the 1980s and 1990s when violent crime rates were very high. For example, in Oregon in the 1980s, a murderer could serve as few as 10 years in prison. In 2009, the minimum sentence for murder is 25 years.

Appellate Judges: Setting Legal Precedents

When a defendant is found guilty, he doesn't necessarily go quietly to jail and stay there. A defendant has the right to appeal his conviction. (The U.S. Constitution doesn't guarantee the right to appeal, but every state has passed laws that give criminal defendants that right.)

Each state has at least one appellate court, but most states actually have two levels of appellate courts:

- The first level must hear all appeals.

- The second level, known as the *supreme court* in most states and in the federal system, hears second appeals from cases already decided by the lower appellate courts. Supreme courts have the discretion to decide which appeals they want to hear.

State appellate judges are either appointed or elected. In the federal system, appellate judges are appointed by the president of the United States and serve for life. The job of an appellate judge is quite a bit different from the job of a trial judge.

Looking for procedural errors

I want to be clear that the state (in other words, the prosecutor) has very limited appeal rights. The state can appeal only *pretrial* rulings of a trial judge, such as a judge's decision to suppress evidence. After a trial starts, the state can no longer appeal any issue, which means that if a defendant is found not guilty, the case is over for good. The state can't appeal the not guilty verdict. The defendant, however, has much greater appeal rights. For example, if he is found guilty, he can still appeal.

Appellate judges don't hear evidence, and appellate courts don't have juries. Rather, the whole process is much more cerebral. (In fact, trial lawyers often complain about appellate judges working in their "ivory towers," not really knowing what life is like in the trenches.) Appellate lawyers write out their arguments, called *appellate briefs,* and give them to the appellate court. If the case is significant enough, the court may ask the lawyers to give oral arguments on the legal issues raised in the appellate briefs.

Appellate judges usually decide cases in groups. For example, three judges may decide an appeal. The three judges take a vote, and a judge on the majority side writes the appellate decision, called an *opinion.* State supreme courts usually have more than three judges that decide a case. And the U.S. Supreme Court has nine *justices* (another name for judges).

What exactly do appellate judges decide? Well, they don't decide whether a defendant is guilty or not guilty. Rather, they give great deference to the factual findings of a jury (or the judge if a jury was waived). For the most part, appellate judges decide whether the trial judge made any procedural errors.

For example, assume that a jury found a defendant guilty of stealing a six-pack of beer from a Quickie Mart. The defendant can't appeal the guilty finding, but he can appeal an evidentiary ruling of the trial judge.

For instance, if the trial judge admitted a confession by the defendant — ruling that the defendant wasn't in custody when he confessed to the crime so the police didn't need to read him his Miranda rights — on appeal, the appellate judges can conclude that the defendant was in custody because he was in a police car. Therefore, the trial judge made a mistake and shouldn't have admitted the confession into evidence.

One of the appellate judges then writes the appellate opinion stating that the defendant's confession should be suppressed because the police didn't read him his Miranda rights. The opinion ends by *remanding* the case, which means the appellate court sends the case back to the trial court for a new trial. At the new trial, the defendant's confession isn't admissible.

The written opinion of the appellate court is very important to the U.S. judicial system because the opinion serves as a legal *precedent,* which guides trial courts and lawyers about what the law means. Following up on the previous example, future trial courts will rely on the appellate court's decision and conclude that when a defendant is in a police car, he's probably in custody, which means that for his confession to be admissible in court, the police must first read him his Miranda rights.

Each state has hundreds of volumes of books containing appellate court opinions on thousands of different topics. Attorneys spend a lot of time reading these opinions to figure out what the law really is.

Wading through the final layers of appeal

Okay, so a jury decides the case, and then an appellate court upholds the guilty verdict, ruling that the trial court made no errors. Next, the state supreme court upholds the trial court. You may think the process is finally over. Not necessarily.

If a defendant believes his federal or constitutional rights have been violated, he can next appeal to the U.S. Supreme Court. This step is called filing a *writ of certiorari.* The U.S. Supreme Court accepts very, very few of these writs (although the famous *Miranda v. Arizona* decision was decided in the U.S. Supreme Court).

Even after the U.S. Supreme Court is done with a case, however, the case isn't necessarily over. A defendant who is still in prison can collaterally attack his conviction by filing a lawsuit that challenges the lawfulness of his imprisonment. For example, an inmate may seek a *writ of habeas corpus,* which is an order from a court ruling that an individual is unlawfully imprisoned.

The vast majority of lawsuits filed by inmates seeking a writ of habeas corpus claim that the inmates' defense attorneys provided *ineffective assistance of counsel.* In other words, the defendants' attorneys did such bad jobs in the courtroom that the defendants were probably wrongfully convicted. Inmates can file an infinite number of these lawsuits. Some inmates go overboard and file a lot, which clogs up courts.

But have you ever heard a lawyer complain that there are too many lawsuits?

Chapter 20

Finding the Truth: Pleading Guilty or Going to Trial

In This Chapter

▶ Looking for justice at the local, state, and federal levels

▶ Working toward a plea agreement

▶ Figuring out which evidence is admissible

▶ Following a case through trial

The U.S. criminal justice system includes local, state, and federal courts. The primary function of each court is to determine whether a defendant is guilty beyond a reasonable doubt. In this chapter, I briefly discuss each level of the court system and then walk you through a typical criminal case, from plea negotiations through trial.

Keeping It Local: Municipal Courts

Many towns and cities in the United States have their own laws and their own court systems. For example, a city council may pass laws against violations such as speeding and running a red light or even against some misdemeanor crimes like driving under the influence of intoxicants. At the local level, the police officer turns in her report to the city attorney, who acts as the prosecutor and decides whether to file charges. Someone who doesn't want to plead guilty can have a trial in front of a municipal court judge or justice of the peace (who's usually a local attorney working part-time as a judge).

Most of the crimes punished in municipal court are also crimes that can be punished in state court. So why do cities set up separate court systems? Because they get to keep the money they collect from fines. A municipal court can be a cash cow for a small town.

Keep in mind that you can't be prosecuted in municipal court for a crime and then prosecuted in state court for the same crime. Being prosecuted for the same crime twice constitutes *double jeopardy,* which the Fifth Amendment to the U.S. Constitution prohibits. So, if you're found not guilty of a crime, you can't face the same charges again even if the government finds some really good new evidence.

One large exception to double jeopardy exists. The federal government and state governments are considered different entities. So technically, you can be acquitted of a crime in state court but still be prosecuted for that same crime in federal court, or vice versa. This situation is known as the *dual sovereignty doctrine.* But as a practical matter, being tried for the same crime in both state and federal court almost never happens.

Movin' On Up: State Court Systems

In all states, the state court system does the heavy lifting. The vast majority of criminal charges in the United States are brought into state courts of *general jurisdiction,* which means they're trial courts that have the authority to hear a broad variety of matters — not just criminal cases. These courts go by different names depending on the state:

- ✔ District courts
- ✔ Circuit courts
- ✔ Superior courts
- ✔ Courts of common pleas

And just to keep things interesting, the trial court in New York is called the *Supreme Court.*

Every state court system is different, but, generally, they follow this pattern:

1. Charges are filed by the local prosecutor (usually a district attorney), and hearings are held in front of a *trial court* judge. Charges are brought based on violations of state law, passed by the state legislature.

   Of course, state courts have jurisdiction only over crimes committed in their states. Maryland state courts, for example, have no jurisdiction over crimes committed in, say, Virginia.

2. If a defendant is convicted, he can appeal his verdict to an appeals court. Each state has an *appellate court,* which decides whether errors were made in the trial court.

3. Many states now have two levels of appeals courts, so even if you lose your first appeal, you can appeal to an even higher court: the *highest state appellate court.*

4. After a defendant has exhausted his state court appeals, he may be able to appeal to the *U.S. Supreme Court* if he asserts that one of his U.S. Constitutional rights was violated. The case *Miranda v. Arizona,* which I discuss in more detail in Chapter 18, was a state court decision ultimately appealed to the U.S. Supreme Court; there it resulted in the Miranda rights we hear every night in cop shows on TV.

Affecting the Whole Nation: The Federal Court System

Federal courts deal with violations of *federal laws* — laws passed by the U.S. Congress. Typically, Congress passes laws that deal with only certain types of serious offenses that impact the nation as a whole. For example, there's no federal law against driving under the influence of intoxicants. So you can never be charged with a DUI in federal court. Also, most violent crimes and property crimes are taken care of in state court. So what exactly do the feds do?

Generally, the feds handle the types of crimes that federal law enforcement agencies investigate. (See Chapter 17 for a discussion of federal law enforcement.) These crimes include

- Acts of terrorism
- Serious drug trafficking (usually involving very large quantities of dope)
- White-collar crimes involving millions of dollars
- Serious computer crimes
- Weapons trafficking
- Immigration crimes
- Serious felonies on U.S. Indian reservations

At the federal level, the United States is divided into 94 districts. Each district has a U.S. attorney, who's appointed by the president; the U.S. attorney is the prosecutor at the federal level and brings charges against defendants. Each U.S. attorney, in turn, has assistant U.S. attorneys who, in reality, do most of the trial work and who file charges.

Each of the nation's 94 districts has its own U.S. district court, and each district court consists of a number of judges and courtrooms. The U.S. attorney in a district files charges in the district court, and a U.S. district court judge presides over a case just like a state court judge does.

U.S. district court judges are also appointed by the president, but the U.S. Constitution says that these judges are appointed for life (unlike the U.S. attorneys, who usually stay in office only as long as the president does).

Like in state court, defendants in the federal court system can appeal their guilty verdicts. They appeal to a U.S. circuit court, also known as a U.S. Court of Appeals. (The United States has 13 circuit courts, set up regionally.) Each circuit court has a number of judges who are appointed for life. When a defendant doesn't like the result after his first appeal, he can appeal again to the highest court in the land, the U.S. Supreme Court.

The U.S. Supreme Court consists of nine justices, each one appointed for life. The Supreme Court Justice is a very powerful position — I'm sure you've seen the intense political fights that surround the U.S. Congress's confirmation of presidential justice nominees.

Although the U.S. Court of Appeals has an obligation to take every appeal, the U.S. Supreme Court does not. In fact, it refuses to hear the vast majority of cases brought to it.

Negotiating a Plea Agreement

Note: Because the vast majority of criminal cases are processed in state courts, I use the language of state courts in the rest of this chapter. The procedures are fundamentally the same for federal and municipal courts.

In Chapter 19, I discuss the prosecutor's role in filing charges. But what happens after charges are filed? First, a defendant is *arraigned* in court, which means he's informed of the charges against him and given a copy of the charging document. This document is usually called an *information* or an *indictment.* (An *information* means the prosecutor is asserting the charges; an *indictment* means a grand jury instituted the charges. See Chapter 19 for a more detailed discussion.) Along with informing the defendant of the charges, the purpose of the arraignment is to provide him a court-appointed lawyer (if he can't afford his own). Most defendants request a court-appointed lawyer.

After a lawyer is assigned to the defendant, the key question at hand is whether the defendant will take a plea offer. In the vast majority of cases, the defendant does negotiate a deal with the prosecutor. A 2005 survey of state court felony prosecutions found that only 3 percent of felony cases were closed by jury trial. Of course, a defendant can also waive a jury and let a judge hear the case, but it's safe to say that more than 90 percent of criminal cases are resolved by plea agreement.

Typically, the prosecutor writes out a plea offer and gives it to the defendant's lawyer. The offer may have a deadline attached. On behalf of their clients, defense attorneys can accept offers, make counter offers, or do nothing.

Often, a defendant's lawyer will wait until the actual trial date approaches before answering a plea offer to see if the state's case gets weaker. Sometimes prosecution witnesses move away or just don't show up for trial. Other times the arresting officer is on vacation and can't make the trial date. So there's a constant tension between prosecutors and defense attorneys about whether plea offers will be accepted, countered, or rejected.

During negotiation, the prosecutor and defendant consider several different factors, which I discuss in the following sections.

Keep in mind that from the prosecutor's side, she should make reasonable plea offers — offers that are reasonably fair and that defendants are likely to accept. If prosecutors and defense attorneys couldn't agree on plea deals, the whole criminal justice system would break down. I don't know of any jurisdiction that has enough judges, lawyers, and courtrooms for every case to go to trial.

Determining the strength of the evidence

From the defendant's side, the most important consideration is how strong the evidence in the case is. The weakest cases (from the prosecutor's viewpoint) are the ones that go to trial. If a case is weak, the defendant has a good shot at being acquitted. If the defendant is clearly guilty, he's usually better off taking a deal.

The only time it makes sense for a defendant to go to trial when the state has a good case is when the defendant has nothing to lose. For example, if a defendant is facing a long mandatory sentence in prison even under the plea offer, he may roll the dice to see whether he can get lucky at trial.

Figuring out time in custody

Aside from the strength of the evidence, the next most important consideration is how much time in custody the plea offer contemplates. Obviously, defendants want to stay out of jail, so the two sides may negotiate over the amount of time in the plea agreement.

Negotiations over time in custody can get difficult when the crime calls for a *mandatory sentence*. A mandatory sentence means that if a defendant is convicted, whether he pleads guilty or is found guilty at trial, he must serve the entire sentence.

The presence of additional charges can make negotiations easier. For example, if a defendant is charged with attempted murder for shooting a gun into a house several times, the prosecutor may add additional charges, such as attempted assault or unlawful use of a deadly weapon. In the plea offer, the prosecutor can agree to dismiss these charges, which theoretically could carry additional prison time. By accepting this offer, the defendant at least gets some charges dismissed and reduces the risk of a lengthier sentence by pleading guilty to the attempted murder charge.

Considering victim compensation

As I discuss in Chapter 4, most states require that defendants compensate the victims for the losses the victims suffered. Prosecutors usually consider this compensation a high priority and don't negotiate it away. Sometimes, such as in theft scams of multiple victims, a prosecutor may reduce the number of charges if the defendant can come up with a bunch of money to help the victims recover from the crime. If the defendant doesn't bring the money up front, however, all the prosecutor can get is a court order for the defendant to pay money in the future, but, frequently, such orders aren't vigorously enforced.

Frankly, in such cases, I'd rather see a retiree get 70 percent of her life savings back than see a defendant spend an extra year in prison. And sometimes these are the tough choices that prosecutors must make in plea negotiations.

Working out probation conditions

If a defendant isn't sentenced to prison (and most defendants aren't), chances are he'll be put on *probation*. Probation means that for a certain period of time, a bunch of restrictions can be placed on him. If the defendant violates probation, he can be punished further. Prosecutors and defendants may work out probation options during the negotiations, but usually there are standard probation conditions that apply in most crimes. Some common probation conditions require that the defendant

- ✔ Perform community service
- ✔ Pay a fine
- ✔ Complete drug or alcohol treatment (if either one was involved in the crime)
- ✔ Complete anger management treatment (if anger was involved in the crime)
- ✔ Have no contact with the victim
- ✔ Pay back court costs
- ✔ Obey all laws

To avoid jail time, defense attorneys frequently offer that the defendant do community service. In many jurisdictions with limited jail space, community service is the primary sanction for misdemeanors.

Suppressing Evidence (Or Not): The Pretrial Hearing

As part of a plea agreement, the prosecutor often requires the defendant to give up his right to argue that evidence should be suppressed. Alternatively, if a defense attorney believes she has a good argument that some evidence is inadmissible, she may encourage her client to reject the plea offer and litigate the issue, which is where the pretrial hearing comes in.

The admissibility of evidence is determined in a pretrial hearing by a judge (no jury is involved). This hearing is sometimes called a *suppression hearing* or an *omnibus hearing*. In criminal law, two primary issues dominate omnibus hearings:

- ✔ Whether a search was lawful
- ✔ Whether the defendant's statements were voluntary

Of course, other issues are also litigated during omnibus hearings. If you're really interested in finding out what they are, maybe you're a good candidate for law school.

Determining whether a search was legal

Although the issue of police searches and seizures of property can be very complex (some people still struggle with it even after spending three years in law school), the U.S. Constitution basically prohibits police from searching a person or place except in these circumstances:

- ✔ The officer has *probable cause* to believe the location has evidence of a crime (meaning that the chance that evidence will be found there is greater than 50 percent) *and*

- ✔ The officer has a search warrant authorized by a judge (in which the judge agrees that the officer has probable cause) *or*

- ✔ There's a recognized exception to the warrant requirement.

  Many exceptions to the warrant requirement exist. Here's just one example: The search is *incident to an arrest,* meaning an officer who arrests a person can search that person for evidence of the crime or for weapons without getting a warrant from a judge (check out Chapter 18 for more on search warrants).

When a defense attorney believes a search may have been unlawful, she files a *motion to suppress* the evidence that was obtained from the search. A *motion* is simply a written argument filed with the court.

At the omnibus hearing, the prosecutor calls the police officer as a witness to testify about the actions he took. The defendant's attorney has a right to cross-examine the witness. If a judge agrees that the search was unlawful, he rules that the evidence obtained during the search must be *suppressed,* which means it isn't admissible at the later trial. The suppression of evidence often means the prosecutor can't prove his case and must dismiss it.

Taking a look at the confessions of a defendant

The other major area of criminal law that gets litigated in suppression or omnibus hearings involves defendant statements. Like search and seizure law, the constitutional right of a defendant not to incriminate herself can get very complicated. Here are a few of the more common scenarios that a judge may have to rule on:

- ✔ If a defendant was in *custody,* an officer must have read her the Miranda rights (right to remain silent, right to an attorney, and all that stuff) before the officer questioned her. (If she wasn't in custody, he need not have read the Miranda rights to her.) So the judge has to determine whether the defendant was in custody. Generally, being in custody means that a reasonable person wouldn't feel free to leave the scene.

- ✔ If the defendant was in custody and an officer read her the Miranda rights, the judge has to determine whether the defendant understood her rights and voluntarily waived them by agreeing to talk without a lawyer present.

- ✔ If the defendant was in custody, the judge has to determine whether the officer engaged in questioning or whether the defendant just voluntarily made statements without being asked any questions.

Each issue heavily depends on the facts in a particular circumstance. So testimony by police and perhaps the defendant are crucial to resolving these issues.

Facing a Jury (Or a Judge): The Process

After a defendant has rejected a plea offer and litigated all the issues about admissibility of evidence, the next step in the process is trial. Every case is presided over by a judge, but the defendant has the right to have a jury decide whether or not he's guilty. The defendant can also choose to waive the right to a jury and ask the judge to decide his guilt.

Choosing trial by jury or by judge

The Sixth Amendment to the U.S. Constitution provides that every defendant has "the right to a speedy and public trial, by an impartial jury." The framers of the Constitution considered the jury trial an important protection against governmental abuse.

But sometimes defendants waive their right to a jury trial and have a judge decide their case instead. A defendant's decision to have a judge decide his case depends on several factors. For one, judges are just like everyone else — some are tough, some are soft, some are good for a defendant, and some are bad for a defendant. Most defense attorneys know the judges in their courthouse, so they know which judges may help their defendant's case.

If a defendant draws a favorable judge, he may waive the right to a jury. Or, if the facts are particularly inflammatory, such as when a defendant is accused of molesting a child (an offense that can make jurors' blood boil), the defendant may waive the jury, hoping that a judge will do a better job of setting aside any passion or prejudice.

Selecting a jury

If the defendant chooses to have a jury trial, the next step is to select a jury. Each state determines who's eligible to be a juror. Typically, to sit on a criminal case, you must be a U.S. citizen, you must be 18 years of age or older, and you must not have ever been convicted of a felony. A large pool of potential jurors receives a jury summons in the mail, and these potential jurors are required to show up at the local courthouse. They sit in a waiting room, waiting to see whether a trial is going to happen. (Often, cases set for trial end in plea agreements at the last minute.)

If a case actually goes to trial, a judge's assistant comes to the waiting room and takes a large group of potential jurors back to the courtroom. At this point, the judge puts all the potential jurors *under oath* (meaning they swear to tell the truth). Then the judge, the defense attorney, and the prosecutor take turns asking questions of the potential jurors to see whether they can be fair and impartial. In truth, the defense attorney and the prosecutor are also looking for jurors who are more likely to be favorable to their side.

For example, a prosecutor may ask, "Has anyone ever had a bad experience with a police officer?" The prosecutor's purpose is to identify someone who may be less likely to believe a cop as a witness.

At the request of either attorney, a judge can excuse a potential juror who asserts that he or she can't be fair. In addition, the defense attorney and the prosecutor each have the right to remove a certain number of potential jurors. This process of removing potential jurors is officially known as exercising a *peremptory challenge.* For a 12-person jury, many states allow each side to challenge six potential jurors. The only restriction is that a prosecutor can't challenge a potential juror on the basis of the juror's race or membership in some other group, such as a group defined by gender or ethnicity.

Making opening statements

After the jury is selected, the next step in the trial is the *opening statement,* which is when each lawyer tells the jury what evidence he or she will offer during the trial. The prosecutor goes first, and the defense attorney follows. The opening statements aren't considered evidence.

At this point, the lawyers aren't permitted to try to argue or persuade the jury that they're right and the other side is wrong. Nonetheless, an effective opening statement can persuasively lay out the facts in such a way that a jury may start to believe one lawyer more than the other.

Personally, I believe the opening statement is the most important part of a jury trial. If I can get the jury to believe me during the opening statement, the jurors may almost be rooting for me as I lay out my evidence during the trial.

Proving the state's case

When the opening statements are finished, it's time to actually offer evidence. The state offers its evidence first because it has the *burden of proof.*

You've undoubtedly heard the statement, "The defendant is presumed innocent." In essence, this statement means that if neither the prosecutor nor the defense attorney offered any evidence, the jury would have to vote not guilty. That's because the prosecutor, on behalf of the state, has the burden of proof, and if he doesn't offer any evidence, he fails to meet that burden.

In law, there are generally three different levels (or *standards*) of the burden of proof:

✔ **A preponderance of the evidence:** This standard is used in civil lawsuits in which the *plaintiff* (the person who brings the lawsuit) has the burden of proof. Essentially, this standard means that the plaintiff wins the lawsuit if the jury finds that there's at least a 51 percent chance that the plaintiff is right.

✔ **Clear and convincing evidence:** This standard, which is slightly higher than "a preponderance of the evidence," is used in some types of legal proceedings, such as civil forfeiture of property (which I discuss in Chapter 8).

✔ **Beyond a reasonable doubt:** This standard, the highest burden of proof in law, is used in criminal cases. Here's a common definition of reasonable doubt that a jury may be given:

The defendant is innocent unless and until the defendant is proven guilty beyond a reasonable doubt. The burden is on the state to prove the guilt of the defendant beyond a reasonable doubt. Reasonable doubt is doubt based on common sense and reason and means an honest uncertainty as to the guilt of the defendant. Reasonable doubt exists when, after careful and impartial consideration of all the evidence, you are not convinced that the defendant is guilty to a moral certainty.

Conducting direct examinations

The state begins its case by calling a witness. The witness is placed under oath and asked questions by the prosecutor. This process is called *direct examination*. Except in simple cases, the prosecutor usually has to call a number of witnesses.

Direct examination isn't very difficult. Essentially, it's the art of getting the witness to tell a story about what she knows. Sometimes witnesses are scared or intimidated by court, and the direct examiner has to work a little harder. But to show how simple the process can be, here are a few of the most common direct-examination questions:

✔ What happened next?

✔ And then what did you do?

✔ Why did you do that?

Displaying physical exhibits

Sometimes jurors need to see physical objects (called *exhibits*) to help them make their decision. For example, photographs of a victim's face may help the jury decide whether the victim was assaulted by her husband. Other times a jury just expects to see an item like a murder weapon, whether it's crucial to the decision or not.

To allow a jury to see an exhibit, the lawyer must do the following:

✔ **Lay a foundation:** Laying a foundation means proving that the item is what the lawyer claims it is. For example, a lawyer may have to prove that the bullet he's offering into evidence was retrieved from the murder victim. To lay this foundation, the prosecutor would call as a witness the person who retrieved the bullet during the victim's autopsy.

✔ **Establish that the item is relevant:** The lawyer has to show that the exhibit is relevant to the case at hand. It wouldn't make sense to offer a gun into evidence in a drunk-driving case, for example.

The lawyer calls one or more witnesses and asks them questions to lay the foundation and to establish the exhibit's relevance. The lawyer then offers the exhibit into evidence. If the judge admits the exhibit into evidence, the jurors get to see it, and they get to take it with them into the jury room when they deliberate at the end of the trial.

Cross-examining witnesses

After the prosecutor has finished his direct examination of a witness, the defense attorney gets to cross-examine that witness. Unlike direct examination in which the lawyer asks open-ended questions, in cross-examination, the lawyer gets to ask leading questions. A *leading question* is one that contains the answer, so the witness just needs to answer yes or no.

Here are a couple of examples of direct-examination questions as compared to leading questions:

> ✔ Where do you live? (Direct)
>
> ✔ You live in Manhattan, don't you? (Leading)
>
> ✔ What happened next? (Direct)
>
> ✔ You then banged my client's head as you forced him into your police car, correct? (Leading)

Cross-examination is an extremely important right for the defendant. When done properly, it's the best defense against someone who lies or makes a mistake during direct examination. After all, placing someone under oath doesn't really prevent her from lying. But the fear of cross-examination does reduce lying, and if a person chooses to lie, cross-examination is the best way to expose it.

Putting on a defense

After the prosecutor has called all his witnesses and presented all his evidence, he stands up and tells the judge, "The state rests." At this point, it's the defendant's turn. But remember, the defendant doesn't have any burden of proof. This means the defendant doesn't have to offer any evidence. Frequently, at this point in a trial, the defense attorney will stand and say, "The defense rests also, your honor." This statement means the case is over.

Why would the defense attorney choose not to offer any evidence? Well, for one, she may think the prosecution's case was weak and that the prosecutor didn't prove the defendant's guilt beyond a reasonable doubt. Or, she may not have any evidence to offer. Ultimately, the decision isn't up to the defense attorney but to the defendant.

When a defendant decides to call witnesses, the lawyers' roles are reversed. The defense attorney conducts direct examination of the witnesses, and the prosecutor gets to cross-examine them.

Deciding whether the defendant should testify

One of the most important decisions a defendant and his attorney have to make is whether or not the defendant should testify. From the lawyer's perspective, it's often a mistake to have a defendant testify.

Cross-examination of a defendant often reveals weaknesses in the defendant's story and harms his credibility. But even though defense attorneys may try to persuade their clients not to testify, many defendants insist on doing so. Some defendants have extensive experience at fooling people and believe they can con a jury. Again, the decision ultimately belongs to the defendant.

Recognizing common defenses

When a defense attorney does call witnesses, she usually does so because she has a theory that explains the defendant's innocence. For example, her theory may be that the defendant was mistakenly identified, known as the "some other dude did it" defense. Or she may theorize that the police officer did a poor investigation and failed to look hard enough to find the evidence to clear her client.

Some defense theories are formally recognized by law. If a defendant asserts a formal theory after the prosecution has proved its case, the defendant actually has a legal burden to prove his defense. The following sections describe a few common legal defenses.

Self-defense or defense of another

It's a firmly rooted legal principle that a person is entitled to defend himself against a physical attack by another. Imagine, for example, that you shot and killed someone because that person was attacking you with a knife. Should charges be brought against you? Of course not — you were acting in *self-defense*. Similarly, you're entitled to defend an innocent third person against an imminent physical attack by another.

Every state has laws that recognize a person's right to defend himself or a third person. But there are limits. For example, if a person threatens to punch you, you can't shoot him. Or if a person says, "Tomorrow, I'm going to kill you," you're not entitled to shoot that person today.

The use of force in self-defense must be reasonable. You can use only the amount of force necessary to repel the attack, and the physical attack or threat of an attack must be imminent. Some states have laws that require a person under attack to escape, if he can. This is known as the *retreat rule*. Other state laws say you're entitled to stand your ground and don't have to retreat.

Smart prosecutors don't file charges when self-defense is a clear justification. However, if two guys are involved in a fist fight in a bar, and one pulls a knife and stabs the other, charges can be filed. The issues at trial would be the following:

✔ Did the defendant have an obligation to retreat under his state's law?

✔ Was it reasonable to use a knife to repel the attack?

Choice of evils

In some states, if you had no choice but to commit a crime, you may have a legal defense. Here's an example of when the choice of evils defense may apply. Your driver's license is suspended, so it's illegal for you to drive.

But your husband cuts off his hand with a table saw, and you drive him to the hospital. A police officer can arrest you for the crime of driving while suspended. But because you were forced to choose between letting your husband bleed to death and committing a minor traffic crime, a jury would probably acquit you. In fact, charges probably wouldn't be brought against you in the first place. This defense is very rare.

Alibi

With the alibi defense, the defendant asserts that he was somewhere else at the time the crime was committed. But it's not very persuasive for just the defendant to say so. He usually needs to bring in another witness — his *alibi witness* — to testify that the defendant was with him.

Many states require the defense to give advance notice to the prosecution of the use of an alibi witness so that the prosecutor isn't ambushed at trial and has time to investigate the alibi.

Entrapment

When the government induces a person to commit a crime, he has been *entrapped* and can assert this defense. Generally, this defense applies to undercover police work.

For example, some cops work undercover on the Internet to catch child molesters. If an officer pretends to be a 13-year-old girl and actively solicits an older man for sex, that older man can probably assert a defense of entrapment.

Insanity

Along with self-defense, insanity may be the most common legal defense. The theory behind it is that only people who understand what they're doing and who can control their behavior should be held responsible for their criminal conduct. States have different rules about what constitutes an insanity defense, but generally the rules require proof of one of the following:

- ✔ By reason of mental defect, the defendant was unable to distinguish right from wrong.
- ✔ By reason of mental defect, the defendant was unable to conform his conduct to the requirements of the law.

By *mental defect,* I don't mean a personality disorder. Many people who commit crimes have serious personality defects or even mental illnesses, but these defects don't excuse their conduct. The vast majority of people, despite their mental deficiencies, understand the difference between right and wrong. In Chapter 14, I discuss the distinction between personality disorders and mental illnesses in greater detail.

To constitute a legitimate insanity defense, the mental illness must be very severe. Paranoid schizophrenia is one of the mental illnesses most diagnosed in people asserting an insanity defense, because this disorder is usually accompanied by hallucinations or delusions. For example, if a person has a delusion that his neighbor is trying to kill him, his subsequent attack on that neighbor may be excused through an insanity defense.

Typically, a defendant must give advance notice that he's asserting an insanity defense. He does so only after his own psychologist or psychiatrist has evaluated him and concluded he was insane at the time of the crime. The state then has the right to subject the defendant to an evaluation by a psychologist or psychiatrist of its choice. Whether the defendant is found insane usually depends on the testimony of those mental health professionals. A person found insane isn't typically sent to prison but, if found dangerous, can be sent to a mental hospital.

In Chapter 14, I discuss brain function and mental illness as potential causes of criminality.

Hearing closing arguments

When both the state and the defendant have rested their cases, it's time for the closing arguments (also called the *summation*). The prosecutor goes first, followed by the defense attorney. In many states, the prosecutor then gets to give a rebuttal closing argument.

The point of the closing argument is to allow each side to make its best case for why the jury should convict or acquit. Unlike an opening statement, which is limited to describing what the evidence will show, during closing arguments the lawyers are much freer to comment on the credibility of witnesses and to argue the meaning of the law. However, the following restrictions limit what the lawyers can argue:

- The prosecutor can't comment on the defendant's refusal to testify. (Remember that defendants have the right to remain silent, and juries aren't supposed to draw any inference of guilt when a defendant exercises that right.)

- The prosecutor can't inflame prejudice or passion in the jury. For example, calling a defendant "an animal" has been ruled impermissible.

- Neither attorney can misstate the law or the evidence.

- Neither attorney can offer personal beliefs or personally vouch for the credibility of a witness. There's a fine distinction between commenting on the credibility of witnesses and offering personal beliefs. For instance, a lawyer can say that a witness lied, but she can't say, "I personally believe the witness is a liar."

Any of these missteps can result in an objection from the other party and possibly even a mistrial. A *mistrial* occurs when the judge believes that an error of such consequence has occurred that the jury can't ignore it and render a fair verdict.

Reaching a verdict

After the lawyers finish closing arguments, they're done. The judge now gives instructions to the jury about the rules they must follow and what they have to vote on. The instructions can be simple in a case with just one charge, but if the defendant is charged with multiple counts, the judge's instructions can be very complicated. The jury receives the elements for each crime and is reminded that they must find each element beyond a reasonable doubt.

Deliberating in private

After the jury is instructed, the jurors leave the courtroom and go into the deliberation room. The jurors are instructed not to talk to anyone about the case and not to read newspaper stories or listen to news reports about the case until they're done deliberating. In extremely high-profile cases, jurors may be *sequestered,* which means they're put up in a hotel and kept from having contact with anyone else until they're done deliberating.

The jury's first duty is to select a foreperson, who is also called *the presiding juror.* His or her job is to preside over the deliberations, take the final verdict, and deliver it to the court.

There's no set procedure for how a jury deliberates. Jurors are free to handle deliberations any way they want. I've seen juries conduct a preliminary vote and, if they're all in agreement, return a verdict within ten minutes. Generally, though, the more serious the charge, the longer the jury takes to deliberate.

Reaching a deadlock

In almost every state, the jury must reach a unanimous verdict. This means all 12 jurors must agree on a vote of guilty or not guilty. Sometimes, not all jurors can agree. This situation is called a *deadlock.* The foreperson may send a note to the judge explaining that they can't agree. Invariably, the judge tells them to keep deliberating.

Ultimately, if the jury can't reach unanimity, the judge finds that he has a *hung jury* (another word for deadlock) and declares a mistrial. Essentially, declaring a mistrial here is the equivalent of yelling, "Do over!"

Sometimes, a hung jury forces both sides to negotiate a settlement. Other times, if the vote looked bad for the prosecutor (such as 11–1 in favor of a not-guilty verdict), the prosecutor may just dismiss the case. But often, the court schedules another trial date, and everyone has to do it all over again. No one wants a mistrial, which is why the judge forces the jury to keep deliberating even after they first declare that they're deadlocked.

Asking jury questions

Frequently, juries come up with questions while they're deliberating. When they do, they pass their question to the judge via a note. The judge calls the lawyers into her chambers, and they all discuss how to respond to the question.

Personally, the best question I ever heard as a prosecutor was on a murder case. The jury asked, "Since we've found the defendant guilty of murder, do we need to consider the other charges?"

There's no typical question, however. Sometimes jurors don't understand their instructions and want a better explanation. Sometimes they want to hear a witness's testimony replayed. Sometimes they're hungry and want to order dinner.

Reaching the moment of truth

When the jury reaches unanimity on all the counts, they pass a note to the judge that says they've reached a verdict. The judge's clerk calls both lawyers and tells them to reconvene in the courtroom. The jury is brought into the room. The defendant is asked to stand. The foreperson either reads the verdict herself or hands it to the judge who reads it. Needless to say, it's a very anxious moment in the courtroom.

Not guilty doesn't mean "innocent"

Almost invariably, the media reports a *not guilty* verdict as "innocent" (such as in the headline, "Jury Finds O. J. Innocent"). Seeing headlines like this one is a pet peeve of mine because it's factually wrong. A criminal jury doesn't *ever* find innocence. What the jury finds is that either

✔ The defendant was guilty beyond a reasonable doubt *or*

✔ There wasn't enough evidence to find guilt beyond reasonable doubt so the defendant isn't guilty.

In other words, all you can conclude from a *not guilty* verdict is that there wasn't enough evidence to vote *guilty.* You may remember from the O. J. case that a later civil jury found that there was enough evidence to conclude that by the lesser standard of "preponderance of the evidence," O. J. did commit the murders. To me, the word *innocence* means that, conclusively, the person didn't commit the crime, and that's not what a jury finds.

Chapter 21

Punishing the Guilty: Why and How Society Does It

A s of June 2008, the number of people living in state and federal prisons and local jails in the United States was 2,310,984, or roughly 1 out of every 200 people. This rate is the highest in the world, followed first by Russia and then by a few countries in the Caribbean.

The U.S. incarceration rate has been growing steadily since the 1980s. Since 2000, it has been growing at an annual rate of 2.7 percent. The ramifications of a high incarceration rate are significant. The more people you lock up, the more tax dollars you need, the more hardships families of inmates experience, and perhaps the more hardened criminals you create. Thus, criminologists often decry the high rate of incarceration.

However, as the rate of incarceration has climbed, the overall crime rate has dropped. So the last 15 years seem to show that a greater incarceration rate may help lead to a reduction in crime, which means fewer victims and fewer societal costs associated with crime.

In this chapter, I explore different theories for why society locks people up, describe where society locks them up, and point out some of the challenges of running a prison system. I also wade into the debate about the death penalty.

Understanding Theories of Punishment and Incarceration

Since humans started committing crime, people have grappled with the question of what to do about it. Society's primary method for dealing with crime is restraint on liberty via imprisonment, or *incarceration,* although it also imposes fines and makes people perform labor (such as "community service"). Legislatures across the nation constantly debate the various theories of why and how society punishes criminals. In this section, I introduce the primary theories of punishment.

Seeking retribution, not personal revenge

Likely the oldest theory of incarceration, *retribution* holds that a person who commits a crime should pay some price, generally in proportion to the offense committed. This approach seems to fit society's sense of fairness: When you do something wrong, you pay a price equal to what you did.

Part of this theory is that punishment is necessary to maintain respect for the laws. If I received no punishment for stealing from the local grocery store, why wouldn't I do so? After all, everybody needs a free meal sometimes, right?

Also underlying the concept of retribution is the notion that, in a civil society, individuals shouldn't take revenge or seek personal retribution. Rather, the government is in a better position to consistently mete out the correct amount of punishment. In other words, society doesn't want victims to retaliate with violence, so it's in society's best interest for the government to take "revenge" on behalf of the individual.

Deterring future crimes

Deterrence is more of a utilitarian theory than is retribution. This theory holds that the existence of punishment prevents people from committing crime. For instance, knowing that I'll go to jail for 14 days for committing theft from the grocery store, I decide to pay for my six-pack of beer rather than steal it.

Obviously, this theory hinges on the belief that people change their conduct based on the threat of punishment. But as I discuss in Chapters 12 through 15, not all crime can be explained as being based on rational thinking. In other words, people may commit crime in the face of all reason, regardless of the punishment. And for people involved in organized crime, sometimes the punishment is just "the cost of doing business."

So why does the threat of punishment deter people from committing crime? Answering this question isn't just an intellectual exercise. Over the last 20 years, policymakers have dramatically increased sentence length for a number of offenses. So, is a long sentence more likely to deter crime? Or (as more and more people are arguing) is the certainty and swiftness of punishment more important than severity in deterring crime?

Some recent successful programs seem to suggest that immediate consequences may be more effective than delayed ones. For example, in Hawaii, a drug court program that immediately holds people accountable for failing urine tests has effectively deterred more violations than threats of longer but delayed sentences have done elsewhere.

Protecting society: Incapacitation

The *incapacitation theory* is based on the idea that when you lock someone up, you essentially keep that person from committing other crimes in the "outside" world. (Keep in mind, though, that the person can still commit more crimes in jail or prison.) So, by locking up a burglar, you prevent him from committing many more burglaries — thus, you protect society from the harm that comes from further theft by that person. (After all, burglars often don't stop at just one attempt.)

Generally, studies have shown that locking up violent offenders prevents the most harm to society. For example, sexual offenders are likely to commit numerous acts, and their acts have great costs to victims and society, so locking them up prevents them from continually harming new victims. Property criminals are also likely to reoffend, but their crimes carry much less cost to society.

Aiming for rehabilitation and restoration

The idea at the heart of the *rehabilitation theory* is that society provides treatment to criminals so they can be rehabilitated and released back into society — without committing future crimes. Strictly speaking, this theory isn't a theory of punishment. Rather, it's a kind of antipunishment that rests on the following assumptions:

- ✔ People can change.
- ✔ Society can identify the personal traits that lead a person to commit crime.
- ✔ Society can develop effective programs to change those traits in criminals.
- ✔ Criminals want to change (or society can make them change).

During the 1970s and 1980s, rehabilitation was a very popular theory. But the lack of widespread success in rehabilitating criminals led to greater emphasis on the other theories of punishment. Nonetheless, most prisons continue to operate significant treatment programs today. And as researchers increasingly use the scientific method to measure treatment success, the hope is that they'll make significant breakthroughs in effective treatment. I discuss treatment in more detail in the "Implementing treatment and education programs" section later in this chapter.

Combining the theories

In reality, nobody clings solely to one of these theories as the only reason for punishment. When deciding on how and why to punish criminal offenders, policymakers consider and adopt components of all these theories. For example:

- ✔ Society should provide effective treatment when it can.

- ✔ Society should keep dangerous offenders off the street.

- ✔ Society should provide a just punishment that fits the crime so vigilantes don't take justice into their own hands.

- ✔ Society should try to deter other people from choosing lives of crime.

Placing Defendants in Custody

After someone is convicted of a crime and sentenced, what happens to him? Jail? Prison? Something else? Well, it depends on the crime.

Before moving on, I want to make an important distinction. Very few people understand the difference between jail and prison. A *jail* is usually a county facility for incarcerating people who committed lower-level offenses for fairly short periods of time. A *prison* is usually run by a state (or by the feds) and is for housing inmates who committed more serious offenses for longer periods of time. Generally, a person convicted of a misdemeanor can go to jail but not to prison. And, generally, a person convicted of a serious felony goes to prison, not to jail.

Going to a local jail

Different categories of jails exist. The primary local detention facility is usually the county jail, operated by the elected sheriff for a county. The county jail is often the primary detention facility in the county. However, some police departments may have small jails, too, which are often referred to as *holding cells*. (Remember, sheriffs and deputy sheriffs usually work for the county; police work for the city.)

When a police officer arrests someone, he may take the arrestee to his own department and place her in the holding cell while he fingerprints and books her. Then, the officer may drive the offender to the local jail for an overnight stay. In many jurisdictions, however, the entire booking process takes place at the county jail.

Some police departments actually have larger jails, so they can detain inmates overnight.

Holding people before trial

What happens when a police officer arrives at the county jail with an arrestee? Today many (perhaps most) jails experience overcrowding, meaning that they don't have nearly enough jail cells to house all the criminals. So when a new arrestee arrives at a jail, a jail official, who may be known as a *corrections officer*, a *deputy sheriff*, or a *release officer*, must first decide whether to lodge or release the arrestee. Here are the two most important questions to consider when deciding whether to release an arrestee:

✔ Is the person a danger to society?

✔ Is the person likely to show up for his hearings?

For example, a person arrested for murder is considered both a danger to society and a flight risk, so, despite overcrowding, the jail official will find a bed for him. However, a person arrested for forgery isn't considered a danger to society (at least not for violent conduct). Such a criminal is much more likely to be released until arraignment. But if, for example, the forger has failed to appear for 15 previous cases, he may be considered a flight risk and, therefore, be lodged overnight.

When an arrestee is released, he's required to sign a release agreement, which has a number of conditions attached to it. Those conditions may require the arrestee to do the following:

✔ Post some bail. If bail is required, the arrestee is usually allowed to post 10 percent of the full amount. But if the arrestee flees, he may forfeit the full amount. For low-level offenses, bail usually isn't required.

✔ Have no contact with the victim (if there is one).

✔ Appear at the next scheduled hearing.

✔ Acknowledge that failure to appear at a court hearing can result in an arrest for the crime of "failure to appear."

What happens if a jail is completely full on Friday, for example, but Friday night, two gang members are arrested for murder? Jail officials can't release two persons arrested for murder. So they usually release less dangerous people who are already lodged in the jail. Most jails have developed complex formulas to help them decide whom to release when overcrowding becomes a problem. Where jail overcrowding is a serious problem, dangerous people are regularly released while awaiting their trial.

According to a U.S. Department of Justice study, in June 2008, there were 785,556 inmates in local jails, which were at 95 percent of capacity — meaning that many jails were filled to the rafters.

When a person is lodged in jail, his attorney may ask a judge for a *bail hearing,* during which the attorney asks that bail be set (if none was set previously) or lowered (if it was previously set too high for the defendant to post).

Punishing the guilty in jail

Although many people incarcerated in local jails are awaiting trial, jails are also used as destinations for convicted people. Usually, a person sentenced to jail is there for a misdemeanor or low-level felony.

A typical sentence in jail may be anything from a weekend to a year, but overcrowding can affect the length of time actually served. For example, someone who has served half his sentence for forgery may be released to make room for a person arrested for murder.

Heading to state prison

People aren't usually held in state prisons while waiting for their trials. Instead, people usually go to state prisons only *after* they've been convicted of serious crimes. In June 2008, 1,409,442 people were housed in U.S. state prisons, and 93 percent of them were men. About half of these people were in prison for violent offenses, 20 percent of them were in for serious property offenses, and another 20 percent were doing time for serious drug crimes. (A person doesn't go to prison for low-level drug offenses, typically.)

It's important to note, however, that today some states are paying county jails to house inmates who previously would've been sent to state prison. The reason is that jails are usually cheaper to operate because they provide fewer services to inmates, so states save money. (I describe the services typically provided in prison in the next section.)

State prisons are usually run by an agency called the state Department of Corrections. Most states have a number of prisons, and each prison may have different categories of inmates based on considerations like dangerousness and escape risk. The types of state prisons include

- Maximum security
- Medium security
- Minimum security
- Women's prison
- Work or boot camps (military-like programs that can reduce an inmate's overall sentence)
- Honor camps
- Youth correction facilities (technically not considered "prisons" because they house juveniles)

Obviously, a *maximum-security prison* holds the most dangerous offenders. It's built with many security features to prevent escape and to keep staff and other inmates as safe as possible. In contrast, a *minimum-security prison* or *honor camp* may have much less security. Inmates in such prisons typically aren't violent offenders and may be serving shorter sentences. A person with a short sentence is less likely to try to escape than a "lifer" (someone fulfilling a life sentence in prison) who has nothing to lose. In an honor camp, the inmate may be trusted to work outside the prison walls on his own and return back at the end of the day.

You may have heard people joke about "country club" prisons where people like Martha Stewart go. I can assure you that these minimum-security prisons are nothing like country clubs. But they do have less security for a good reason — maximum-security prisons are expensive to run. So a state can save a lot of money by placing nonviolent property crime offenders in less-expensive facilities.

General services in state prisons

Prison officials typically speak of the prison environment as a "city within a city." By that phrase, they mean that a prison has most of the services and activities of regular society. Here are just a few examples of the activities a prison must enable prisoners to do:

- Eat meals (on clean dishes)
- Take showers
- Have clean laundry
- Get haircuts
- Receive and send mail
- Go to church
- Work at jobs
- Go to school

> ✔ Exercise
>
> ✔ Take books out of a library
>
> ✔ Access healthcare

Most of these services, such as cooking, laundry, and running the library, are performed by inmates. But who else works in a prison? Obviously, *corrections officers* (or *prison guards,* as they were once called) are an important requirement. They're responsible for maintaining order and keeping things running smoothly in a prison. And, of course, you have prison administrative officials who manage operations. But a prison also needs just about every other type of service. For example, a prison must provide healthcare, so it needs doctors, nurses, and other medical technicians. So you see, a prison truly is a little city within a city.

Additional punishments within state prisons

When prison inmates violate rules, they're subject to punishment. Prisons typically have *disciplinary segregation units,* which are considered the "jails" of the prison. So when an inmate violates a rule or gets into a fight, he may be removed from his regular cell and placed in a segregation unit as punishment, where he loses the privileges that a well-behaved inmate enjoys.

When an inmate commits a serious violation, such as throwing feces on a corrections officer, he may be put in the prison's "prison," often known as an *intensive management unit.* Typically, an inmate loses all privileges and is isolated and confined to a cell. If you ever visit a prison, you'll notice that this unit is one of the bleakest places in the whole facility. People in this unit can be very dangerous — so much so that when they're moved to and from this unit, they usually have their hands and feet chained and are accompanied by at least two corrections officers. Inmates often refer to the intensive management unit as "the hole."

In addition to segregated disciplinary units, prisons also have special units for people in need of intensive psychiatric care or those who are at risk in the general prison population. These units are sometimes called *administrative segregation units* because inmates are segregated for administrative purposes and not for disciplinary reasons.

For example, corrections officers may decide to put an African American inmate in an administrative segregation unit for protection after learning that members of the Aryan Brotherhood, a white-supremacist prison group, have targeted him for killing. State prisons also have agreements with other states to exchange inmates for reasons of security. So the targeted inmate may even be moved out of state.

The majority of U.S. states allow the death penalty, which means that most state prisons also have a separate unit called *death row*. Death row units differ from state to state, but, generally, death row inmates are kept separate from inmates in the general population. As a result, their access to services is frequently quite limited. Death rows vary quite a bit, from California, where roughly 670 people sit on death row, to New Hampshire, where one person sits on death row (as of 2008).

Facing federal prison

The Bureau of Federal Prisons runs all the prisons in the United States for inmates convicted of federal crimes. There are no federal jails, so if you're convicted in federal court and sentenced to do time, you'll usually be sent to a federal prison. As of 2009, there were 115 federal institutions that housed about 165,000 inmates. (Another 40,000 federal inmates were housed in a variety of other settings, including private prisons, which I discuss in the next section.)

The federal prison system has a lot more money than most state prison systems. As a result, federal prisons experience less overcrowding and can hire more corrections officers. Even the food is usually better! The types of inmates in federal prisons may also be different from the state prison populations because state courts typically handle most violent crimes while federal courts more often handle serious drug-trafficking cases, immigration crimes, and major fraud.

Keep in mind, though, that federal prisons may also house inmates convicted in military court. And sometimes extremely violent offenders are convicted federally. For example, Timothy McVeigh, who killed 168 people by bombing the federal building in Oklahoma City, was convicted in federal court and lodged in federal prison until he was executed in 2001.

Like state prison systems, the federal system includes institutions with different levels of security, from a high-security prison in Victorville, California, to a minimum-security prison camp in Otisville, New York. What matters in prison life isn't so much the distinction between state and federal but rather the distinction between minimum-security and maximum-security facilities.

Serving time in Private Prison, Inc.

Since the 1980s, states and the federal government have looked to private corporations to help them house inmates. In 1984, the Immigration and Naturalization Service became the first government agency to lodge inmates with a private company, the Corrections Corporation of America, which now operates 60 different institutions and houses more than 75,000 inmates. This company claims to be the fourth-largest corrections system in America, behind the federal government and two large states.

Other large private companies in the corrections business include

- ✔ GEO Group, Inc.
- ✔ Cornell Companies, Inc.
- ✔ Community Education Centers, Inc.
- ✔ Management and Training Corporation

These companies may design, build, and manage entire prisons, or they may contract certain services, such as inmate transportation or education and treatment services. In June 2008, 126,249 inmates from state and federal systems were incarcerated in private prisons. This number was up from 90,542 in 2000. The southern states have by far the most inmates housed in private facilities.

Why privatize? Well, the primary argument is that private companies are more efficient and can run quality prisons for less than governmental bureaucracies. Keep in mind that the modern movement started during the Reagan era with its emphasis on privatization. A 2001 study by Montague and Erik based on a Federal Bureau of Prison survey in New Mexico found that private prisons were rated higher than government prisons in most categories.

However, some people, including criminologists and corrections officer unions, criticize the privatization of prisons for a variety of reasons. Here are just a few of the criticisms:

- ✔ Because a business's goal is to make money, these prisons have a strong incentive to cut corners, which means reducing inmate services. Doing so can place inmates and employees at risk.
- ✔ The close relationship between government and private corporations can lead to corruption. (Believe it or not, some politicians have been known to accept large contributions from private corporations.)
- ✔ Making a profit from imprisoning human beings doesn't seem morally right.

One of the key measures of the success of prison programs is the *recidivism rate:* the likelihood that an inmate will commit another crime and return to prison after being released. A 2003 study by the Florida Department of Corrections and the Criminology Department at Florida State University found no significant difference in recidivism for inmates in publicly operated prisons versus those in privately operated prisons.

Facing Challenges in the Prison System

Prisons are incredibly complex enterprises. Not only must management provide all the services I mention in the "Heading to state prison" section, but they must do so for people convicted of crimes.

Many prison inmates are physically dangerous, conniving, manipulating, and/or mentally ill. In other words, the normal level of trust that exists in open society can't exist in a jail or prison. In this section, I discuss just a handful of the many challenges of running a prison.

Controlling contraband

Anything that an inmate isn't allowed to possess is considered *contraband.* In most states, it's a crime for an inmate to possess certain types of contraband. As a practical matter, however, prisons rarely refer these cases to prosecutors because they would further clog the court system. Plus, prison management doesn't want to deal with the headache of transporting inmates out of the prison to local courts.

Here are some of the most common types of contraband:

- Drugs
- Cigarettes
- Chewing tobacco
- Cellphones
- Lighters
- Knives

Contraband is regularly used as barter within prison, or someone may extort another inmate for drugs or tobacco. One of the newer trends is using cellphones within prisons. Because normal prison phone calls are recorded, inmates try to use smuggled-in cellphones to conduct criminal activity outside of the prison walls.

So, if contraband is illegal, how does it get into prisons in the first place? Thousands of ways. After all, inmates are extremely creative people. Here are just a few:

✔ Visitors often aren't searched and are allowed to have physical contact (such as hugs) with inmates.

✔ Many volunteers work in prisons and bring in items such as books. A volunteer may not know that in the spine of a book is a small package of heroin.

✔ Friends who aren't in prison can throw items over prison fences into the yard, later to be found by inmates.

✔ Prison staff members are sometimes compromised and smuggle contraband into the prison for inmates.

Staff corruption is a particularly challenging issue for prison management. In many prisons, new corrections officers make very little money, and some of them can be paid off. Other staff members may become romantically involved with inmates, while still others are extorted.

In 2008, nine Federal Bureau of Prison workers were indicted for smuggling cellphones, heroin, tobacco, and a knife into prison. In that particular prison, a cellphone sold for $2,000 and a pack of cigarettes for over $100.

Contrary to what many people think, inmates *do* have access to money. The prison keeps an account for each inmate, into which relatives and friends can contribute money. Inmates can then use their accounts to purchase items from the prison commissary. But inmates generally don't get to carry cash, at least not lawfully, anyway. So inmates can pay for contraband in a variety of ways, including bartering or having relatives and friends on the outside exchange money.

Dealing with inmate violence

When a person is sentenced to prison, but before he's assigned a specific prison, he goes through an intake process in which he's evaluated to determine a variety of things, including the likelihood that he'll engage in violence. This process helps determine whether the inmate needs to be placed in a maximum-security prison or in a facility with less security. Considerations for which prison he should be placed in include

✔ The crime the inmate committed

✔ The inmate's criminal history

✔ The inmate's known membership in gangs or organized crime

- ✔ The presence of personality disorders or mental illness in the inmate

- ✔ Other characteristics that may lead to victimization in prison (such as being a child molester — because child molesters are often targeted for violence in prisons)

Identifying causes of violence

Although this intake process clearly does help reduce conflict and violence, prisons can still be dangerous places. Here are some of the most common causes of prison violence:

- ✔ Conflict between individual inmates

- ✔ Conflict between groups

- ✔ Race

- ✔ Status within a group

- ✔ Extortion of inmates

- ✔ Trade in contraband, including the collection of debts

- ✔ Resentment of authority and perceived abuse by authority

- ✔ Stress and oppression that may result from overcrowding or coercive actions

Racial bias and hatred are among the leading causes of violence in prisons. For example, tension between white-supremacist groups, black street gangs, and other groups like them — all of which are usually recognized in prison as *security-threat groups* — is behind much of the threat of violence in prisons. In fact, security-threat groups often grant higher status to members based on making one's "bones," which means assaulting a corrections officer or a member of a rival organization.

Getting creative with prison violence

As with smuggling contraband, inmates can be very creative in fashioning weapons. An inmate can rub a toothbrush handle against concrete to make a pointed stabbing weapon known as a *shiv*. Shivs are one of the preferred weapons because they're so easy to make. Inmates may even smear feces on such weapons to help create infections in the stabbing victims.

Smuggled metal with tape as a handle can also make an effective stabbing weapon or a set of metal knuckles. A heavy object in a sock, such as a bar of soap, can be dangerous when swung. And then there's the throwing of urine, human waste, or semen, which is particularly common when the violence is directed toward corrections officers.

Controlling the violence

Controlling prison violence is extremely difficult. Of course, super maximum-security prisons that lock inmates down for 23 hours a day can reduce violence. Although sometimes necessary, such an approach is extremely expensive, not to mention dehumanizing and harsh. (I've toured an institution in California that uses that approach, and it's depressing, to say the least.) Because most inmates eventually will be released, prison officials can't just isolate them while they're in prison and then expect them to successfully reenter society. Thus, this level of severe lockdown is reserved for the most dangerous criminals.

So how else can you control violence? Because prisons can't afford to have corrections officers everywhere, they tend to rely on a complex system of rewards and social controls. For instance, when an inmate behaves appropriately, he gains access to certain rewards, such as

- The choice of cells in a better cellblock
- The ability to lock his own cell
- A TV in his cell
- A better prison job
- Extended access to recreational facilities
- The ability to choose a cellmate

In addition, prison officials informally rely on a hierarchy in the prison that has a vested interest in reducing conflict. For example, I visited one prison where the "lifer's club" exerted a large amount of influence. Because these particular inmates were in for life, they generally wanted to maximize the benefits in prison, which meant coming down on individuals or groups who caused problems that may have reduced their privileges. In addition, people running successful businesses, such as smuggling contraband, don't want to upset the social order and risk their businesses.

Lastly, prisons have had success in dramatically reducing murder rates by placing stricter controls on gang leaders, who often direct violence in the interests of the gang. If the gang leader is isolated in administrative segregation, it's harder for him to order a "hit."

Implementing treatment and education programs

As I discuss earlier in the chapter, one of the core theories of punishment calls for society to help rehabilitate inmates. For the most part, rehabilitation occurs through treatment programs and education. Here are some common focuses of treatment and education:

✔ Alcohol and drug abuse

✔ Anger management

✔ Other mental health programs

✔ Job readiness

✔ Life skills

✔ Work skills

✔ Sex offender treatment

Thousands of treatment and education programs take place in prisons across the country. In fact, I can't even begin to discuss the scope and breadth of these efforts. But even with so many programs, it's important to note that one of the most significant issues surrounding treatment is figuring out how successful it really is.

According to one of the most important measures — recidivism rates — rehabilitation programs haven't been very successful at all. The most recent national study of recidivism rates found that, in 1994, two-thirds of released prison inmates were rearrested for felonies (not counting misdemeanors!) within three years.

For this reason and others, some politicians and law enforcement officials look at inmate treatment and education as a waste of money. After all, it's easy to say that an inmate committed a crime and, thus, deserves a hard, tough life in prison. But a California study concluded that nine out of ten of its prison inmates are eventually released back into society. In 2003, the state of Illinois found that an inmate's average prison stay lasted just 1.3 years. When these people get out of prison, society expects them to be successful, get jobs, and live crime-free lives, right? Well, education programs that help inmates earn GEDs or high school degrees or learn particular skills can help them transition to the real world and, ideally, reduce recidivism.

Sometimes, however, prison systems lack the funds for services that help people being released from prison during the transition period. For example, newly released inmates benefit greatly from getting help with paying security deposits (first and last months' rents), finding jobs, and making friends who aren't criminals. Unfortunately, when states face budget crises, corrections budgets are often the first place legislators look to cut back. Sometimes there are no government-sponsored transition programs at all and the only available services are those provided by underfunded, private, nonprofit organizations or groups of volunteers to help operate halfway houses or help with job placements or transitional counseling.

Critics of treatment and education programs rightly point out that evidence of their success is often questionable or nonexistent. Although some programs work, others don't, and prison officials often don't have enough evidence to decide which programs to keep. Plus, it's not just the programs that matter;

the quality and commitment of the corrections staff doing all the work play a big role in the effectiveness of treatment programs, too. In the coming years, my hope is that governments will spend sufficient tax dollars to identify successful programs through sound, scientific studies. In the long run, such efforts may reduce overall expenditures and lead to more successful rehabilitation efforts.

It's important for the criminal justice community to remember that inmates are human beings, entitled to certain minimum standards of decency and respect. Gandhi once said, "You can judge a society by how it treats its animals." But I believe how people treat their fellow humans, even those who violate criminal laws, is an even better barometer. Even from a purely utilitarian point of view, helping inmates successfully transition back to society makes the rest of society safer and saves money.

Covering the cost of imprisonment

In 2008, the United States spent approximately $50 billion on incarceration costs. This number is up from $38 billion in 2001 (not accounting for inflation). The most recent federal study of prison costs was done in 2001 by the U.S. Department of Justice Bureau of Justice Statistics. According to this study, total expenditures for corrections rose 145 percent between 1986 and 2001. (This stat *does* account for inflation.)

Although some states are more efficient than others, in 2001, the average annual cost for incarcerating one inmate was $22,650. Maine spent the most per inmate at $44,379 per year. (Maine also has one of the lowest incarceration rates in the country.) Alabama spent the least at $8,128 per inmate. Labor costs account for a lot of the differences in expenditures. Not surprisingly, prisons with high inmate-to-officer ratios are cheaper to run than prisons that employ many more corrections officers.

About three-fourths of all incarceration costs go toward running prisons; the remaining amounts go toward running juvenile incarceration programs (see Chapter 22 for more info on these programs) and probation and parole programs, which I discuss in the next section.

Placing Defendants on Probation

When a defendant is sentenced for a misdemeanor or a lower-level felony, the judge usually places that defendant on probation for a period of time.

Putting a defendant on *probation* allows a judge to create certain conditions that the defendant must comply with (or risk being punished more severely). Usually a defendant is assigned to a probation officer who makes sure the defendant complies with all the conditions the judge set forth. Here are some common probation conditions (though not all of them are always imposed):

- ✔ Complete a short jail sentence
- ✔ Successfully complete drug or alcohol treatment
- ✔ Pay all fines, court costs, and restitution to the victim
- ✔ Complete a certain amount of community service
- ✔ Finish anger management treatment or other mental health treatment
- ✔ Stay away from the victim
- ✔ Obey all laws

The probation officer's role

A *probation officer* (usually called a *P.O.*) must make sure the defendant (called the *probationer* or *parolee*) is complying with all the conditions of probation. Often, doing so means helping the probationer figure out how to comply. For example, a probationer who has lost his driving privileges may not be able to get to an alcohol treatment location, so the P.O. may help the probationer figure out how to take the bus there. P.O.'s also have the authority to conduct searches if they believe probationers are violating probation conditions. For example, if a P.O. believes that a probationer convicted of selling drugs is back in business, the P.O. can search the probationer's house without getting a warrant from a judge.

The difference between parole and probation

In most states, *probation* applies to lower-level offenses, such as misdemeanors. On the other hand, a person is likely to be placed on *parole* when he's released from prison. Essentially, parole is the same as probation. The parolee must comply with certain conditions or run the risk of being sent back to prison. Even so, he has the same right to a hearing as a probationer.

In some states, parole is called *post-prison supervision*. The parole officer performs the same role as the probation officer. In fact, in many states, a parole officer may simultaneously be a probation officer.

P.O.'s work for probation departments, which can be part of a county public safety agency, a sheriff's office, or even a state Department of Corrections. Each state is different. P.O.'s typically carry very heavy caseloads, which limit their ability to monitor their probationers. They may see each probationer once a month or less.

P.O.'s are the unheralded workhorses of the criminal justice system. You don't see a lot of TV shows about them, but a good, diligent P.O. can make a big difference in helping a probationer get out of the criminal lifestyle.

Probation violations and their effects

If a probationer gets caught violating a condition of probation, the P.O. or a cop can rearrest the probationer and bring him before a judge for a hearing on the probation violation. For example, a man convicted of burglary has a probation condition that requires him to obey all laws. So if the man gets arrested for driving while intoxicated, he'll face not only a DUI charge but also a probation violation on the burglary conviction.

Although probationers have the right to a hearing before a judge (as well as a right to a lawyer), as a practical matter, they usually work the matter out with their P.O.'s — at least for minor violations. In the DUI example, the P.O. may just recommend no sanction and that probation be continued, knowing that the probationer will separately be punished for the DUI charge.

Sometimes, however, the violation is more serious and can result in additional jail time. If the P.O. and the probationer can't work out a sanction, there has to be a hearing before a judge. A prosecutor calls witnesses to prove the probation violation, and the probationer's attorney has the right to cross-examine witnesses. This hearing usually follows a much less formal process than a real trial. (There's no jury, for example, and the judge determines whether the probationer violated the probation conditions.)

Debating the Death Penalty

No issue in criminal law is more contentious than *capital punishment,* otherwise known as the *death penalty,* which is why I devote an entire section to the subject.

Capital punishment is lawful in 35 states, which means in these states, the government can lawfully kill a person who has been convicted of certain types of murder. The federal government and the U.S. military also have laws for the imposition of the death penalty. As of 2009, the following 15 states (plus the District of Columbia) do *not* allow for the execution of a person as punishment for any crime:

- ✔ Alaska
- ✔ Hawaii
- ✔ Iowa
- ✔ Maine
- ✔ Massachusetts
- ✔ Michigan
- ✔ Minnesota
- ✔ New Jersey

- ✔ New Mexico
- ✔ New York
- ✔ North Dakota
- ✔ Rhode Island
- ✔ Vermont
- ✔ West Virginia
- ✔ Wisconsin

Only about 60 countries in the world still retain the death penalty and use it. (Some countries still have it on the books but haven't put it to use in many years.) Admission to the European Union (EU) depends in part on whether a country has outlawed the death penalty. Consequently, the only country in Europe that still allows the death penalty is Belarus. Other prominent countries that have abolished the death penalty include:

- ✔ Mexico
- ✔ Canada
- ✔ Australia
- ✔ New Zealand
- ✔ Brazil
- ✔ Israel

Still using the death penalty are most Middle Eastern countries, along with Japan, China, Cuba, India, and South Korea.

The crimes you can die for

Over time, the types of crimes that can be punished by death have changed. The first formal execution in the American colonies was in 1607 as punishment for mutiny. The second was in 1622 for theft. The vast majority of executions in the United States, however, have been for the crime of murder. Even so, in U.S. history, well over 400 people have been executed for the crime of rape.

Today the U.S. Supreme Court has essentially prohibited executions for any crimes except murder. In 2008, it ruled that a child rapist can't be executed because doing so would violate the Eighth Amendment to the U.S. Constitution, which prohibits cruel and unusual punishments. Essentially, the reason given was that the punishment would be disproportionate to the crime. Perhaps the only remaining crime on the books besides murder that can receive the death penalty is treason.

The rules of a capital case

The U.S. Supreme Court has set out some specific rules that a state must follow to impose a sentence of death. First, the murder trial must take place in two parts. In other words, there must be a trial to determine guilt for the crime and then a second penalty phase to make a separate determination of whether the defendant deserves to be put to death.

Penalty phase

During the *penalty phase,* a jury, not a judge, must decide whether additional *aggravating factors* that justify a death sentence are present in the case. These factors must be beyond just the crime of murder. Each state may identify its own aggravating factors, but it must do so in law, to avoid giving prosecutors or juries too much discretion.

Here are some common aggravating factors found in the criminal codes of many states:

- ✔ The defendant is a continuing threat to society.
- ✔ The murder was deliberate.
- ✔ The defendant killed two or more people.
- ✔ The murder was committed as part of an escape.
- ✔ The murder was of a witness, police officer, corrections officer, or judicial officer.
- ✔ The murder was of a child.
- ✔ The murder was accompanied by torture.
- ✔ The murder was for hire.
- ✔ The murder was committed in the course of committing another serious felony.

Mitigating evidence

In addition to deciding the existence of aggravating factors, a jury must also consider all *mitigating evidence* — evidence that argues against executing the defendant. Although aggravating factors must be set out in state law, mitigating factors are any factors that may persuade a jury to impose a sentence less than death.

Here are some common types of mitigating evidence:

- ✔ The defendant was under the influence of an intoxicant.
- ✔ The defendant suffered from a mental disorder at the time of the murder.
- ✔ The defendant is very young (or very old).

✔ The defendant was raised in a bad environment.

✔ The defendant was abused as a child.

✔ The defendant suffers from an organic brain disorder.

Essentially, the U.S. Supreme Court has said that anything is admissible as mitigating evidence if it may persuade a juror to spare the defendant's life.

Ineligibility categories

Certain *categories* of persons are ineligible for the death penalty, regardless of how bad their murder was:

✔ The legally insane

✔ Minors

✔ The mentally retarded

The Supreme Court has said that a person must be fully responsible for his crime to receive the death penalty, and because defendants in these three categories are somewhat less responsible, they're excluded from the death sentence. As a practical matter, however, whether someone is legally insane or whether someone is mentally retarded is often subject to vigorous challenge. If retardation or insanity isn't clear, a jury will be asked to make that determination.

After the defendant has been found guilty, and after the parties have conducted the second phase of the trial (the penalty phase), the jury is asked, "Should the defendant receive a death sentence?" The verdict must be unanimous for a person to be sentenced to death. If only one juror votes against death, the defendant won't be executed.

Appeals

After a jury has voted for a death sentence, the matter isn't over. Obviously, the defendant has the right to appeal any errors in the trial. Even when his appeals are done, he may collaterally attack his conviction, usually by claiming his lawyer was incompetent. (See Chapter 19 in which I discuss the appellate and habeas corpus processes.) Depending on the state, there can be more than ten levels of appeal over 20 years or more before a sentence is finally carried out.

The execution process

When an inmate's appeals and habeas corpus petitions have been denied, the process toward execution begins. Although each state is unique, generally, a final execution date is set. This step in the process often sets off another round of appeals and requests for clemency. For example, at this stage, a state's governor can *commute* (or change) a sentence from death to life imprisonment.

In 2003, Illinois Governor George Ryan granted clemency to all 167 people on Illinois's death row, reducing their sentences to "life in prison." He did so because he claimed the system was fraught with errors that had led to some wrongly convicted defendants. A firestorm erupted as families of many victims complained about the wholesale granting of clemency. (In 2006, Ryan was convicted of unrelated federal corruption charges.) This example of clemency was a rare exception, however. Usually governors don't commute sentences absent some unique political or compelling humanitarian reason.

As the execution day approaches, the inmate's attorneys may file additional paperwork with a court, sometimes asserting newly discovered evidence, to delay the execution.

Just before execution, in some states, the inmate is transferred from his cell on death row to another cell near the execution room. The inmate gets to choose a last meal and is entitled to meet with a prison chaplain or other clergy member.

All of the 35 states that allow the death penalty use lethal injections. At the appointed time, the inmate is strapped to a table. Witnesses, including relatives of the defendant, the victim's family, and a few chosen members of the media, are often allowed to attend. The inmate is allowed to make a last statement, and then IVs are inserted into his arms. An executioner in a nearby room starts the IV drip of several drugs, including a sedative, a muscle relaxant, and a drug to stop the heart. The inmate loses consciousness quickly, usually in about ten seconds, but a pronouncement of death may take five or more minutes.

Arguments for or against the death penalty

As of 2007, roughly 64 percent of the U.S. population favored the death penalty, while 30 percent opposed it. Only 6 percent were undecided. Where you stand on this issue will likely shape how you read this section.

Arguments about the death penalty can roughly be categorized into two camps: philosophical arguments and utilitarian arguments.

Philosophical arguments

Opponents of the death penalty argue on philosophical grounds that the death penalty

- Is cruel and inhuman
- Desensitizes the population to violence
- Eliminates the chance for the murderer to be rehabilitated

✔ Creates secondary victims — the family members and friends of the murderer

✔ Discriminates on the basis of race (because 41 percent of the inmates on death row are black, while only 12 percent of the U.S. population is black)

Proponents of the death penalty counter that the death penalty

✔ Satisfies society's need for retribution because a life for a life is a just sentence

✔ Helps a victim's family achieve closure

✔ Follows the will of the majority, which is essential for the legitimacy of any government

Utilitarian arguments

Utilitarian arguments relate to whether the death penalty actually serves some purpose or not.

Proponents of the death penalty argue that by executing a murderer, society prevents that person from committing future crimes, including murder. When a person isn't sentenced to death row, he becomes part of the prison's general population, where there's much greater opportunity for murdering someone else. Thus, the argument goes, by placing a person on death row, and by eventually executing him, the death penalty helps protect other inmates from him. It also eliminates the chance that the inmate may escape and commit other crimes.

I'm not aware of any study that has attempted to determine whether placing a person on death row helps save the lives of other inmates. It's interesting to note, however, that murderers historically have had a very low recidivism rate when compared to other violent criminals. Back in the 1970s and 1980s when murderers received less than life sentences, many were eventually released and didn't commit more crimes. Of course, capital murders are generally much more heinous than other murders, so it's quite likely that such murderers would be more dangerous than regular murderers.

Many studies have focused on the *deterrence effect* of the death penalty. The argument used by many proponents of the death penalty goes that if a person is actually executed, other citizens, fearful of being executed themselves, decide not to commit murder. A 2003 study by Professors Hashem Dezhbakhsh, Paul Rubin, and Joanna Shepherd of Emory University concluded that the arrest, conviction, and execution of one murderer can deter between 8 and 28 future murders. Other studies have concluded that executions do deter future murders but that they do so at a lower rate of 3 to 6 murders per execution. These studies have shown that pardons or commutations actually lead to more murders and that the deterrent effect may be reduced by delays in executions.

It's important to point out that other people hotly contest the methodology in these studies. In fact, opponents of the death penalty point to studies that show that in locations where the death penalty is imposed, there actually may be *more* murders. The argument is that by sanctioning killing (via the death penalty), the government creates a *brutalizing effect* or culture of violence among its citizens.

Another prominent argument against the death penalty contends that the death penalty is much more expensive than a life sentence. The additional costs include the extra security for housing a person on death row and paying lawyers, investigators, and court staff for all the additional appeals. Proponents of the death penalty counter that the lengthy appeals process can be shortened, reducing the costs.

Yet another argument against the death penalty is that innocent people can and have been put to death. This situation can occur because a jury may rely on faulty evidence or even because the defendant's court-appointed lawyer is incompetent.

Proponents of the death penalty respond by saying that defendants who receive a death sentence get more appeals than people who get life sentences. Thus, the chances of wrongly convicted people being exonerated are greater for the defendants who received death sentences. Further, modern science with its sophisticated techniques, such as DNA testing, has all but eliminated false convictions. (Check out Chapter 18 to find out how and when DNA testing comes into play in solving crimes.)

I offer no opinions, and I bet your opinion didn't change after reading this section, either, did it?

Chapter 22

Examining the Juvenile Justice System

*I*n 2007, more than 15 percent of all arrests reported to the FBI involved *juveniles,* or people under the age of 18. What should society do about kids who commit crimes (otherwise known as *juvenile delinquents*)?

In this chapter, I briefly discuss how juveniles have been treated in the criminal justice system historically. Then I move on to how the system deals with juvenile delinquents today and what the future may hold.

Taking a Look Back: The Historical Treatment of Juveniles

In the 1800s and before, juveniles above the age of 14 who committed crimes were generally treated as adults. Courts punished juveniles as adults, lodged them in prisons, and even executed a few of them. But in 1899, the officials of Cook County, Illinois, created the first juvenile court in the United States. The idea quickly caught on, and, within 26 years, 46 states had their own juvenile courts.

Why the sudden move to juvenile courts? Toward the end of the 1800s, more and more people started believing that children were less responsible for their conduct than adults and that they shouldn't be treated as adults.

The first juvenile courts were much less formal than adult courts in that they allowed judges broader latitude to gather information about the children from a variety of sources and to be more creative in sentencing. In effect, these juvenile courts acted according to the principle of *parens patriae* (meaning "parent of the people"), which is a doctrine that allows the government to care for the people who are incapable of caring for themselves. This principle continues to underlie juvenile courts to this day.

In the 1960s, political pressure from the left developed to provide juveniles with greater procedural protections — similar to what adults receive in criminal court. From the right side of politics came greater pressure to show that the perceived lenient treatment that juveniles received in juvenile court was actually working. As a result, the juvenile justice systems nationwide became much more formalized.

The U.S. Supreme Court decision in *In re Gault* (1967) held that juveniles had the constitutional right to certain protections, including the following:

- ✔ Notification of the charges against them
- ✔ Right to confront witnesses
- ✔ Fifth Amendment right not to incriminate themselves
- ✔ Notice of, and the right to, court-appointed counsel

Later court decisions granted additional rights to juveniles, including the following:

- ✔ To be convicted, juveniles must be found *responsible* (juvenile courts don't use the word *guilty*) beyond a reasonable doubt.
- ✔ Juveniles can't be tried twice for the same offense (under the double-jeopardy clause of the Fifth Amendment of the U.S. Constitution).

Within the last ten years — in part spurred by research into juvenile brain development — there has been a resurgence of interest in moving kids away from formalized, courtlike proceedings and into informal resolutions. I get into more on this debate in the next section.

Why Juveniles Are Treated Differently

How many stupid things did you do as a teenager? If you were a normal teenager, your answer is probably "a lot." As scientists continue to make advances in brain imaging, they see more and more that the brains of adolescents are far from mature. Teenagers often exercise poor judgment because physiological changes are still taking place in their brains.

Dopamine is a chemical produced in the brain that helps create the sensation of pleasure. A 10-year-old boy's brain produces dopamine when he skateboards, so he wants to skateboard more often. (Some illegal drugs dramatically increase the brain's release of dopamine, creating a *high*.)

As kids grow older, their brains may produce less dopamine for certain activities, which means they may have to engage in more risky behaviors to get the same pleasure they got from acts they enjoyed in preadolescence. So as a boy nears the age of 16, he may have to do riskier tricks with his skateboard to get the same dopamine release he got from simply riding his skateboard when he was 10. So he goes to the park and slides his board dangerously down the hand railing on some steep, concrete steps.

In addition to the changing dopamine levels, the *prefrontal cortex,* which is in charge of reasoning and impulse control, continues to develop throughout adolescence. In fact, it's the last part of the brain to mature. Often, it doesn't finish developing until a person is about 25 (which probably explains why few 45-year-olds appeared in the *Jackass* movies).

About 45 percent of violent crime arrests and 60 percent of property crime arrests are of people under the age of 25. Clearly, these numbers are the result of young people's faulty reasoning and lack of impulse control. Another factor that explains the extremely high rates of crime among juveniles is that, simply put, young people have more energy. Combine high energy with bad decisions and you get high crime rates.

Because of poor reasoning skills and a lack of impulse control, people under the age of 25 are also more likely to engage in drug and alcohol abuse, which, in turn, can negatively and *permanently* impact proper brain functioning, which can then lead to more crime in a vicious circle.

All this science confirms what most people knew all along: Kids don't exercise judgment the same way that adults do. And, thus, the criminal justice system shouldn't treat kids as being quite as responsible for their criminal conduct as adults.

Another significant reason why U.S. juvenile justice systems treat kids differently than adults is that they may be more treatable than adults because their brains aren't fully developed yet. Not only does society hope that a 16-year-old burglar will mature out of his crimes, but it also hopes that education and treatment will work better on the teenager than it does on a 35-year-old burglar.

In fact, a series of studies from the 1990s showed that the best intervention programs reduced *recidivism* (the rate of crimes committed after people are released from custody) among the most serious delinquents by an average of 12 percent. Such programs include providing employment and behavior modification counseling. This reduction may not sound like much, but given that it refers to the most difficult kids to reach, it's pretty significant.

For less serious delinquents, the most effective programs were the ones that were directly tailored to the individual juvenile and that focused on specific interpersonal skills and behaviors. For example, one-on-one counseling was successful for both serious and less serious delinquents. These studies support the idea that intervention and treatment can make a big difference with juveniles, which hasn't necessarily been the case with adults.

Walking through the Juvenile Justice Process

The juvenile justice system is essentially divided into the following two parts:

- One side deals with the kids who commit crime (juvenile delinquents).
- The second side, called the *juvenile dependency system,* deals with bad parents.

Not surprisingly, you often see a lot of overlap between the two parts because delinquents frequently come from bad home environments.

The juvenile dependency system tries to help parents get their acts together, providing training and education in parenting skills, as well as drug treatment. Usually a child welfare agency provides the dependency services to families. If the situation gets bad enough, this agency may ask a court to take kids away from parents, temporarily or even permanently.

Here I focus on the first part of the juvenile justice system: the delinquency process. In many ways, this system is similar to the adult criminal justice system. However, it uses different language to sound less scary and to reflect that the justice system treats kids differently than it treats adults. Also, the outcomes and the punishment of a juvenile can be quite different from what an adult receives. In this section, I walk you through the steps of processing a juvenile delinquent.

Speaking the language of the juvenile justice system

Typically, juveniles aren't convicted of crimes. In fact, they're not *convicted* at all. Although different states may use slightly different language, generally they follow the terminology I set forth here. (For comparison, I include the corresponding language for adult criminal court.)

Adult System	*Juvenile System*
Indictment or information	Petition
Plead guilty	Admit petition
Plead not guilty	Deny petition
Found guilty	Petition found true
Trial	Adjudication
Convicted	Responsible
Sentence	Disposition

So instead of filing an indictment, the prosecutor files a *petition* against a juvenile. The juvenile isn't charged with a crime; rather, in some states, the petition alleges that the "the petitioner committed acts which, if he were an adult, would constitute a crime."

The juvenile doesn't plead guilty but *admits* or *denies* the offense. If he denies the offense, the matter proceeds to an *adjudication* rather than a *trial*.

The juvenile isn't found guilty. Rather, the judge finds that the *petition is true* or that the juvenile is *responsible*. (There's no jury in juvenile court, so the judge makes all the decisions.) If the petition is found true, the juvenile is said to be *within the jurisdiction of the court*.

Finally, the juvenile isn't *sentenced*. Rather, the judge proceeds to *disposition*, where the judge decides whether to punish the juvenile, order counseling, order other treatment, or prescribe some combination of these options.

Introducing the key players

More people and programs are involved in the juvenile justice system than in the adult system, so before I get into specifics about how the system works, I need to identify the following key roles:

- ✔ **Juvenile department:** The juvenile department employs *juvenile counselors* (also known as *juvenile probation officers*), who work closely with kids to get them back on a law-abiding track. These counselors are directly involved with the juveniles almost from the moment of their arrests. So, right from the beginning, you can see a significant difference from the adult system, where probation officers don't get involved unless and until the defendant is convicted.

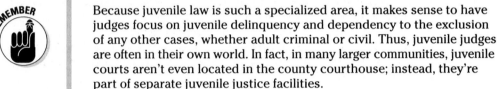

- ✔ **Prosecutor:** If a case is handled formally, a prosecutor usually files the petition and is responsible for proving the case in court (see the "Filing a petition — Or not" section for details on the difference between formal and informal cases). Prosecutors also plea bargain with the juveniles' lawyers and make recommendations to the court at the time of disposition.

- ✔ **Judge:** In many jurisdictions, the juvenile judge oversees the operation of the juvenile department and its counselors — quite different from what a judge does in the adult system.

Because juvenile law is such a specialized area, it makes sense to have judges focus on juvenile delinquency and dependency to the exclusion of any other cases, whether adult criminal or civil. Thus, juvenile judges are often in their own world. In fact, in many larger communities, juvenile courts aren't even located in the county courthouse; instead, they're part of separate juvenile justice facilities.

Because juvenile judges can specialize, they can also play a much more significant role in the lives of juvenile offenders than judges in criminal court do for adults. Juvenile judges have a lot of discretion in fashioning individualized sentences for kids. They also have much more authority over juveniles and can bring them back to court frequently to check on their progress.

- ✔ **Juvenile detention facility:** Typically, a juvenile detention facility (sort of like a juvenile jail) houses kids as they wait to go to trial. Sometimes the local juvenile department runs this facility, and sometimes the state runs it. Juvenile detention workers are more than just corrections officers; they're often responsible for assisting in treatment and even teaching basic lessons in life skills.

If, at the adjudication, a juvenile is found responsible for a delinquent act, the judge may require him to spend some time in the local detention facility, in the same way an adult can be sentenced to a local jail.

- ✔ **Private, nonprofit service providers:** Nongovernmental operations run by private, nonprofit groups may also provide treatment services, intervention programs, or temporary shelters for kids who have nowhere to go. For example, a kid may have an addiction to marijuana. In turn, the local juvenile department may contract with a drug rehabilitation program to provide treatment services for the kid.

Another important service of nonprofits is operating shelter programs. A *shelter* is a place to house juveniles who temporarily can't go home. For example, a kid arrested for a minor offense may have just one parent who happens to be a heroin addict and who has gone to inpatient treatment. The kid has to go somewhere, so he may be temporarily placed in a dormlike shelter.

Although these nonprofits are private, they usually contract with the juvenile department and are paid with government money.

✔ **Child welfare agencies:** Child welfare agencies deal with bad parents and try to protect kids from bad environments. Frequently, child welfare workers work very closely with juvenile counselors. After all, it doesn't do much good to help a kid, only to send him back to his heroin-using mom. So, ideally, child welfare and juvenile departments work together to develop programs to help entire families. I discuss this subject more in the "Facing probation" section.

✔ **Youth correctional facilities:** If a judge finds that the juvenile committed a serious act, he may send the juvenile to a state-operated correctional facility, which is the equivalent of an adult prison. However, the focus of youth correctional facilities is on providing the juveniles with an education, as well as various programs to help them reenter society. (In contrast, the focus of an adult prison is often just keeping the criminals off the streets while they do time for their crime.)

Arresting and detaining a juvenile

Unlike adults, kids can be taken into custody for *status offenses,* as well as for crimes. A status offense isn't a crime, but it's still considered misconduct when committed by a juvenile. The two most common examples of status offenses are curfew violations and truancy. In most states, police generally return kids who commit status offenses to their parents instead of holding them in a juvenile detention facility. Of course, if the parents are on drugs or have gone AWOL, the police have to do something with the kids. Typically, the police, a juvenile counselor, or a judge places the kids in short-term arrangements with foster parents or in a juvenile shelter.

If a juvenile is arrested for a serious-enough crime (such as a crime of violence), he may be held in the juvenile detention facility. Within 48 hours, he must be brought before a judge for a *detention hearing.* The judge decides whether the police have enough evidence to continue to hold the juvenile and whether it's in everyone's interest to do so.

In deciding whether holding the juvenile is the best option, the judge considers the child's history, whether there's a place to send the child, the seriousness of the offense, and the risk to the victim, among other factors. The judge also applies one of the most important principles in the juvenile justice system — the *least restrictive means* analysis — to the case. There's a very strong bias against holding kids in custody because it can be such a negative experience. (It's important to note that after being caught once, most kids never reenter the juvenile justice system. So it makes sense to spare them from the negative impact of incarceration). Therefore the judge looks for the least restrictive way to make sure the juvenile doesn't reoffend while waiting for his case to be resolved.

In most instances, when police arrest juveniles, they return them to their families rather than place them in detention. However, they're not off the hook.

Filing a petition — Or not

Regardless of whether a juvenile is detained for a crime or returned to his family, the next step in the system is to determine whether his case should be resolved formally or informally. *Formally* means that the prosecutor files a petition alleging the criminal acts and the case ends up before a judge. *Informally* means the case doesn't go to a judge. Instead, the kid's juvenile counselor tries to resolve the matter without making it a big deal. Most first-time offenses and lower-level offenses are handled informally.

As an example of how the process works, consider this situation: A 16-year-old boy is walking down the middle of a country road, causing cars to swerve around him. A deputy sheriff sees this behavior, arrests the kid for the crime of disorderly conduct, and takes him to his parents' house.

A juvenile counselor is assigned to the case and reviews the kid's history. The counselor sees that the kid has never been arrested. Because it's not a serious offense, she offers the kid the chance to treat the matter informally without going to a judge. If the boy admits that he did something wrong and agrees to perform some community service, the county juvenile department will wipe out any record of his acts.

But what if the deputy sheriff arrested the kid because he didn't like the kid's attitude, and the kid feels like he has been wrongly arrested? If he refuses to admit that he did anything wrong, the matter proceeds to formal adjudication. A prosecutor files a petition charging him with disorderly conduct, and the matter goes to a judge for an adjudication.

At the outset of a case, who makes the decision to treat a case formally or informally? It depends on the jurisdiction, but, generally, the best practice is a cooperative decision by both the prosecutor and the juvenile counselor. Often they have formal agreements that spell out how certain crimes are treated. For example, they may agree that violent felonies are always treated formally or that first-offense property crimes are always treated informally. Of course, if the kid isn't willing to admit some responsibility, the matter will end in formal adjudication, regardless.

In some states, even after a petition is filed, the case may not be formally adjudicated. The court may offer a *diversion program* or some type of contract between the kid and the juvenile department. In this situation, if the child admits his conduct and complies with some court orders, such as doing community service and completing treatment, the court may dismiss the case. In addition, the prosecutor and the juvenile's attorney may plea bargain and agree to an informal disposition.

Adjudicating a case

If a case is treated formally and the juvenile denies the petition, the case proceeds to an adjudication. This proceeding is pretty similar to an adult trial, except that the juvenile doesn't have the right to have a jury decide his case. He is, however, entitled to a court-appointed lawyer, who gets to cross-examine the prosecutor's witnesses and call witnesses on behalf of the juvenile. The prosecutor still has to prove the case beyond a reasonable doubt.

Just like in adult cases, juveniles may face allegations of numerous offenses, so the judge can find only part of a petition true. For example, a judge can find two allegations true (that a juvenile burglarized two homes) and, at the same time, find a third allegation untrue (that he sexually abused his 6-year-old sister).

The juvenile can also appeal his case to an appellate court if he or his lawyer believes errors were made during the adjudication. (See Chapter 19 for a discussion of the appellate process.)

In the juvenile system, however, what really matters is whether *any* allegation is found true. If the judge finds an allegation true, the juvenile is subject to the jurisdiction of the court. In other words, the judge has authority over the juvenile; he can do almost anything he thinks is appropriate to help correct the juvenile's delinquency. The hearing in which the judge decides what to do with the juvenile is called a *disposition*.

Proceeding to disposition

Juveniles aren't sentenced. Rather, the judge decides how to deal with the juvenile at the disposition hearing. Judges rely heavily on the juvenile counselor at this stage to provide information on the juvenile's education, family situation, prior delinquent acts, and impact of the offense on any victims. If the child welfare department is involved because of bad parenting, a social worker in charge of the case may also provide information to the judge. Of course, the prosecutor and the juvenile's own attorney weigh in, too.

Here are some probation options that judges can order:

- ✔ **Place the juvenile in custody in the local detention facility or the state youth correctional facility.** This order usually isn't a first option. Only after a kid has failed several times on probation is the judge likely to send him to a correctional facility.

✔ **Obtain a mental health evaluation.** This option may result in mental health treatment, a prescription for drugs, therapy for the juvenile, or even therapy for his entire family.

✔ **Conduct a substance abuse evaluation.** This order may result in mandatory drug testing, outpatient treatment, or inpatient treatment.

✔ **Conduct a sex offender evaluation.** Following this order, the judge may order treatment as appropriate.

✔ **Conduct an education evaluation.** Following this evaluation, a judge may order tutoring, placement in an *alternative education school* (which is a type of school for kids who struggle in a normal school environment), or special programs for learning disabilities.

✔ **Place the juvenile in foster care, a shelter, or an orphanage.** This option is possible when a bad family environment is a significant concern and the judge has jurisdiction over the parents as the result of a juvenile dependency case.

Facing probation

After disposition is completed, the hard work begins. The juvenile counselor works closely with the juvenile to carry out the judge's probation order at disposition. The judge will likely bring the juvenile back for regular status checks. If the juvenile is failing probation, such as committing more crimes or not showing up for treatment, the judge will modify the plan.

Frequently, juvenile counselors face challenges in coordinating a kid's probation with other governmental services that the kid or his family may be receiving.

For example, imagine that a 14-year-old boy who is persistently caught shoplifting and skipping school gets caught trying to set his neighbor's house on fire. His dad and the dad's live-in girlfriend are on disability and both sell methamphetamine for a living. The dad is on probation for a sex crime. The local prosecutor has brought an action to terminate the dad's parental rights. The boy's mom is in inpatient drug treatment. The boy's 16-year-old brother has also been caught in numerous offenses.

In a complicated case like this one, several government officials have an interest in the family.

One of the recent trends in juvenile justice is finding ways to develop greater coordination among all the different government agencies to make sure services don't overlap or conflict. The idea is to develop programs that engage entire families in reducing dysfunction and crime. As I've said before, providing a kid with a good intervention program and then returning him to a terrible home environment doesn't do much good for anyone.

Treating a Juvenile like an Adult

As violent crime by juveniles skyrocketed through the 1980s and 1990s, states passed laws allowing adult treatment for juveniles who committed certain serious offenses. Adult treatment means that the juvenile is tried in adult court with a jury, and, if found guilty, the juvenile receives the same sentence of incarceration as an adult. Often for these serious offenses, the sentences are long periods of mandatory incarceration.

All 50 states have some provision for this situation. In many states, the juvenile court has the discretion to decide which juveniles should be treated as adults. In other states, though, the court has no discretion; if a juvenile commits a certain offense, he *must* be treated as an adult. To be waived to adult court, the juvenile must be of a minimum age, usually 14 (although some states allow a waiver at a younger age). Some offenses that can receive adult treatment are

- ✔ Murder
- ✔ Attempted murder
- ✔ Manslaughter
- ✔ Rape

- ✔ Serious assault
- ✔ Armed robbery
- ✔ Arson
- ✔ Kidnapping

If a juvenile is convicted as an adult, he isn't ordinarily housed with other adults in prison. Rather, he is kept in a youth correctional facility until he reaches adulthood. Then, depending on the amount of time left on his sentence, he may be transferred to an adult prison.

I once tried a 17-year-old boy as an adult because he stabbed the boy he was babysitting 86 times and then set off down the street to find a girl to rape and murder. He was sentenced to life in prison after serving a period in a youth correctional facility.

There is one adult sentence that juveniles can't receive: a death sentence. See Chapter 21 for a discussion of the death penalty.

Eyeing Modern Trends in Juvenile Justice

Treating whole families by coordinating various government services has become a point of emphasis for juvenile courts across the country. However, such efforts depend on strong judges. After all, only judges have the authority to bring together various probation officers, welfare workers, and others to work in a coordinated fashion. Some jurisdictions have systematized this coordination by creating *family involvement teams* that bring a variety of services to dysfunctional families.

With the significant advances in brain development research, many people in the juvenile justice business are also questioning mandatory adult sentences for juveniles since their brains aren't fully developed until their mid-20s. One solution involves creating a *second-look program,* in which, after being convicted, a juvenile can be brought back to the judge for a sentence reduction if the juvenile is doing well on her education and treatment programs in custody.

Another significant issue facing juvenile justice systems across the country involves the use of detention space. The big question is, after arrest, which juveniles should be detained and which ones should be returned home or placed in shelters? Some facilities don't have enough space and, thus, are forced to release juveniles who may be dangerous to society.

For other facilities, the decision whether or not to release a juvenile involves an assessment of the risk that the kid will reoffend. Juvenile officers and judges weigh this risk against the knowledge that the effects of incarceration on kids are bad. Increasingly, courts are using a scientific process (rather than intuition and instinct) to assess the risk and decide whether to detain a juvenile or return her to her home.

Part VI
The Part of Tens

The 5th Wave   By Rich Tennant

"Ted and I spent over 120 man-hours together analyzing the survey data, and here's what we discovered: Ted borrows pens and never returns them, he intentionally squeaks his chair to annoy me, and, evidently, I talk in my sleep."

In this part . . .

I offer two short chapters in this part. The first one describes ten jobs that may interest you if you're considering a career in criminal justice. The second one explores ten unsolved crimes that almost everyone has heard of. Each crime created a media sensation when it was committed (even Jack the Ripper back in the late 1800s), and each one remains the subject of speculation today.

Chapter 23

Ten Jobs to Consider in Criminal Justice

*A*re you thinking about working in the field of criminal justice? Well, if you are, you've come to the right place! You can find all kinds of different jobs in this field. In this chapter, I give you the inside scoop on ten of the more important and interesting jobs to help you consider whether one of them is right for you.

Police Officer

Police officer is often the first job people think of when they're considering careers in criminal justice. But this job definitely isn't for everyone. And, if you think you know what the job is all about from watching TV cop shows, prepare to be disappointed.

To become a police officer, you must pass physical and psychological examinations. Many of the larger police departments also require at least a two-year degree from college. All departments require at least a high school diploma. After getting hired, but before starting on the job, most officers must go through a police academy that lasts an average length of 19 weeks. Police academies cover a variety of topics, including criminal law, police procedure, defensive tactics, firearms training, and *EVOC training* (emergency vehicle operator course). Then new trainees spend additional time on the street with training officers.

Where an officer works defines his job. For example, a deputy sheriff in a rural county may patrol hundreds of miles of remote highway. He may spend his time removing animal carcasses from the road and traveling several hours just to respond to a burglary call. In contrast, an officer in a large city may have daily contact with gang members and drug dealers. He may investigate shoplifting crimes from a department store and deal with mentally ill vagrants camped out in front of a nightclub.

The career path within a police department is quite broad. Some officers are happy to stay in patrol, enforcing traffic laws and responding to 9-1-1 calls, their whole careers. Others want to move up the ladder to become detectives or even chiefs of police. Lateral transfers by officers between departments are becoming more common. A department that hires a new recruit invests significant money in the training. (After all, the department pays an officer's salary while he goes to the police academy.) As a result, larger departments may try to hire experienced officers from smaller departments because the training has already been paid for.

Generally, the larger the department, the better the potential salary. A 2003 salary survey by the U.S. Bureau of Justice Statistics found that the average starting salary for the smallest police departments was $23,400, and the starting salary for larger departments averaged $37,700. Remember that a significant part of an officer's income can come from working overtime. For instance, officers frequently get overtime from testifying in court. The more arrests or traffic tickets officers write, the more likely they are to be subpoenaed to court. For the best pay, a career with a federal agency can net you a salary over $100,000 near the end of your career. Numerous federal agencies have criminal special agents; see Chapter 17 for some of the more prominent ones.

Local officers who are beneath the rank of sergeant are usually part of a labor union that negotiates on their behalf. Toward the end of their careers, many cops enjoy a significant benefit: Most departments allow officers to retire at the age of 50 if they have 25 years of service. As a result, a good officer has plenty of time to start a second career, sometimes with a different police agency. I know of many older cops who are double dipping, so to speak. They draw pensions from their first jobs while earning salaries from their second jobs.

But before you sign up for these benefits, remember that being a cop is an increasingly difficult job. For one, it places tremendous strain on family life. To stay safe, cops are trained to always control the situation, which means assuming a commanding role with potential criminals. For some officers, turning off this attitude at home is difficult. Not surprisingly, a high percentage of cops I know have had at least one divorce. Officers also frequently have to work different shifts, which means they work nights for awhile, then switch to swing shift, and finally switch to day shift. This type of schedule can be very difficult on family life.

Cops are increasingly under intense scrutiny from the media and civil rights groups. Life-or-death, split-second decisions are subject to endless second-guessing. Many departments hire civilian auditors who investigate allegations of misconduct in the public eye. If you have ever dealt with false allegations, you know how difficult they can be. Now imagine the investigation appearing in the local newspaper. With the expansion of the concept of community policing, the public increasingly calls on officers to be community dispute resolvers, a skill that few people — cops included — have in abundance.

It's not surprising that police departments across the country can't fill vacant positions. After all, the job has become more difficult, but the pay hasn't increased along with the duties. If you think I'm trying to talk you out of applying to be a police officer, well, you may be right. It can be a great job for the right person, but you need to think long and hard about the sacrifices you'll have to make.

Corrections Officer

A *corrections officer* works in a correction facility, typically a jail or a prison. Long ago, these officers were known as *guards*. But don't call a corrections officer a guard today — the least you'll get is a dirty look — because corrections officers may view it as demeaning.

Many (but not all) jurisdictions require corrections officers to attend some form of training academy. This training is much shorter and less burdensome than a police academy. In fact, many police officers start their criminal justice careers as corrections officers and then transfer after a few years.

Corrections officers can have a wide variety of duties, but, generally, they maintain order in a jail or prison. Corrections officers keep inmates on task, facilitate treatment and inmate work, and respond to security needs. The Florida Department of Corrections Web site (`http://fldocjobs.com/index.html`) offers detailed descriptions of the different duties of a corrections officer. Check it out for more information.

Corrections officers usually are members of unions, but their pay is generally lower than that of police officers. They may also be less likely than police to get overtime because they work regular shifts and rarely have to attend court.

Being a corrections officer holds many challenges. For one, you work in an environment with convicted criminals. Frequently, corrections officers aren't armed when they move among inmates because the inmates easily outnumber the officer and could take the weapon away. Consequently, corrections officers are at risk of attacks from inmates, which occur somewhat regularly, depending on the dangerousness level of the facility. Maximum- and medium-security facilities are more likely to have violent, assaultive inmates compared to minimum-security facilities. Physical attacks, stabbings, and human waste bombs (feces or urine thrown at someone) aren't uncommon. When a fight among inmates breaks out, corrections officers are on the front lines, as well, which can be quite dangerous, as you can probably imagine.

Working as a corrections officer in a prison or jail can be a hard job, but it can be a rewarding experience for the right person. Being a corrections officer is an excellent opportunity for a person with a high school degree to earn a decent wage and develop skills and a career.

Forensic Scientist

So you like to watch *CSI: Crime Scene Investigation,* and you think you have the model good looks it takes to solve murders in an hour. In truth, forensic scientists have a fascinating and very important job, but it's *nothing* like what you see on TV.

The word *forensic* means "developed for court," so a *forensic scientist* develops scientific evidence for court. Here are some of the key pieces of evidence a forensic scientist deals with on a daily basis:

- ✔ **Toxicology:** Identifying poisons and toxic substances at the crime scene can help scientists figure out what happened.

- ✔ **Controlled substances:** Scientists can use blood and urine analyses to find out whether defendants or victims were under the influence of any controlled substances.

- ✔ **Trace evidence:** Scientists analyze microscopic evidence for a variety of evidentiary reasons.

- ✔ **DNA:** Deoxyribonucleic acid (DNA), which is contained in almost every cell in the human body, is unique for each human being (except identical twins) and has become a tremendous crime-solving tool.

- ✔ **Fingerprints:** Each person (except for identical twins again) has a unique pattern on the end of his fingers that can leave behind prints at crime scenes; fingerprints can help scientists identify the perpetrator.

- ✔ **Firearms and ballistic analysis:** Determining whether or not a bullet came from a specific gun can help scientists find a shooter.

- ✔ **Blood pattern analysis:** Scientists can draw conclusions about what happened at a crime scene based on how blood stains look.

Applying forensics expertise to investigating a crime scene can be quite interesting; see Chapter 18 for a more thorough discussion.

Positions in forensic science usually require a bachelor's degree in a scientific field, such as microbiology or biochemistry. Some schools that have criminal justice programs also offer degrees in forensic science. People with these skills are in high demand, so the pay tends to be pretty good — $40,000 or more for a new graduate. But, contrary to what you see on TV, as a crime scene investigator, you probably can't carry a gun (unless you're also a certified police officer). Rather, job announcements usually say the physical requirements include "standing for prolonged periods."

Check out the American Academy of Forensic Sciences Web site for more information about the profession, including a list of available employment: www.aafs.org.

Computer Forensic Specialist

Usually a police officer who has received specialized training in retrieving evidence from computers, cellphones, and other electronic gadgets without altering the data holds the position of *computer forensic specialist.* However, some agencies are moving toward using *non-sworn personnel* (which just means people who aren't police officers). To become a computer forensic specialist, you must first receive certification from one of a few recognized training programs, such as the two-week course developed by the International Association of Computer Investigative Specialists — known in the business as IACIS. After you receive your certification, you must continue to stay up on current computer evidence trends, which means frequent training. Thus, you may have to be just a little geeky to enjoy this work.

Keep in mind that with the proliferation in child pornography, computer forensic specialists have to look at some particularly disturbing evidence, including numerous images of children being sexually molested.

People with computer forensic skills are in high demand both within the criminal justice system and elsewhere. Civil law firms and corporate security companies are increasingly using people with these skills to gather evidence for lawsuits or to discipline or terminate employees who misuse their computers at work.

A degree in computer technology, or at least some computer course work combined with a criminal justice degree, may help pave the way for employment in this field. Salaries of computer forensic specialists are typically the same as for detectives in police departments.

Crime and Intelligence Analysts

Crime and intelligence analysts are becoming crucial to the fight against organized crime and terrorism. But before you can understand how important these analysts are, you have to understand the difference between the two:

- ✔ *Crime analysts* usually do statistical analysis of community crime problems. For example, they may map crime locations to find hot spots for a city, which allows police chiefs to redirect officers to high-crime areas. (I've also seen police departments use their crime analysts for not much more than basic statistical gathering.)

- ✔ *Intelligence analysts* take intelligence, which is basically raw information, and put it in a usable form for cops. For example, a gang unit may ask an intelligence analyst to find out what's going on with a particular gang. The analyst may collect all the police reports that refer to that gang and try to identify all the members and their roles within the gang. Using that information, the intelligence analyst may create a link chart showing the relationship among all the gang members. This can help the police decide which gang members their investigation should focus on. This kind of work is the basis for the intelligence-led policing model I discuss in Chapter 16.

An analyst works closely with cops during ongoing investigations, suggesting whose phone records to subpoena or whom to conduct surveillance on. An analyst is absolutely crucial to any wiretap investigation.

Analysts are extremely important to the fight against terrorism, so the feds have recently been snapping up analysts across the country. Hence, today there appears to be a real shortage of qualified analysts. Because there are different levels of analysts, and because an analyst can work for a local, state, or federal government, the potential salary varies greatly. But a seasoned federal analyst can make over $100,000.

How do you become an analyst? Only a couple of schools in the United States offer programs in crime or intelligence analysis. If you don't plan to seek a degree in criminal intelligence, you should speak to a detective in your state to find out which agencies employ analysts. Often, a few agencies employ most of a state's analysts. After you identify those agencies, you can approach them specifically to find out about their hiring requirements.

The School of Criminal Justice at Michigan State University has an intelligence program and a useful Web site that includes an excellent policy paper on the intelligence process by Professor David L. Carter. Check out `https://intellprogram.msu.edu/Index.php` for more info.

Probation Officer

A *probation officer* is a criminal justice professional with some law enforcement authority whose primary job is supervising convicted criminals (called *probationers*) whom a judge puts on probation. As I discuss in Chapter 21, a probation officer makes sure a probationer is complying with all the conditions that the judge imposed, such as

- ✔ Going to drug treatment
- ✔ Obeying all laws
- ✔ Staying away from victims
- ✔ Completing community service

A probation officer, usually called a P.O., also serves as a counselor for the convicted person, giving guidance on living a crime-free life. If a P.O. believes her client is doing something wrong, she can submit an allegation of a probation violation to the judge. The P.O. then has to testify about the violation. P.O.'s have a lot of direct contact with convicted people, which often means they have to deal with antisocial and mentally ill folks. Even so, the job can be a rewarding one because, as a P.O., you can have a lot of influence over your probationer.

In the way of career progression, you won't find much — other than managing other probation officers. Usually, probation officers work for a local government, but federal courts and some state agencies also employ P.O.'s. A federal P.O. position usually requires a bachelor's degree and two years of experience, but the salary is good, ranging from about $40,000 to $75,000. (In contrast, at the state level in Indiana, for example, a local P.O. starts at about $27,000 and tops out at around $51,000.)

Juvenile Counselor

In most jurisdictions, a *juvenile counselor* is basically a hybrid of a corrections officer, a probation officer, and a treatment counselor — except that he only works with kids. Juveniles, like adults, commit crimes and sometimes need to be locked up. (By *juveniles,* I mean kids ages 13 to 18, typically.) But the justice system treats kids who commit crimes a lot differently than it treats adults. Although juvenile counselors are responsible for the safety and security of kids who are locked up in juvenile detention centers, they also have a much greater responsibility for providing treatment and teaching behaviors that hopefully will help the kids get along in society.

In terms of security, juvenile counselors have to search kids for contraband and impose discipline when a kid violates rules. Counselors also may develop and supervise work and study programs, as well as recreational activities. They work directly with kids to correct antisocial behavior and teach skills that help kids get by in society. Often this part of the job includes teaching basic life skills like hygiene and housekeeping. Counselors may have to lead group counseling sessions in which a bunch of kids talk about their issues on a specific topic. In addition, juvenile counselors frequently must deal with kids who suffer from mental illness or severe personality disorders.

This job is extremely challenging, but it also carries the potential for changing lives. To do this job well, you must have a thick skin and a compassionate heart. (This descriptor seems to apply to most of the jobs I present in this chapter.) Some of the people I admire most work in juvenile corrections.

Qualifications for this job depend on the jurisdiction. In many states, you need a bachelor's degree in a field such as social work, psychology, or criminal justice. But other jurisdictions provide entry-level jobs in which you can get a start with an associate's degree.

Regarding career development, a juvenile counselor can move up within an administration and supervise other counselors and even oversee an entire facility.

Crime Victim Advocate

As I discuss in Chapter 4, a *crime victim advocate* has to have a real heart for people who have been victimized by crime. Most victim advocates tend to be women because most crime victims who need services are also women. A victim advocate may help a woman who has been beaten by her husband obtain counseling or temporary shelter for her family in a safe place. The victim advocate may help someone get funds to help pay for medical costs or lost wages that resulted from a crime. The job requires not only compassion but also a thick skin to continue to provide empathy, as well as valuable services, over the long haul.

An associate's degree or bachelor's degree in social services or a related field can be a big help in landing a job in this field. However, you can gain valuable experience as a volunteer or as a lower-paid employee of a nonprofit agency that provides services, such as a domestic violence shelter, to victims. Developing skills in dealing with victims of domestic violence, rape, child abuse, or other violent crimes can help you get a better-paying advocate job without getting a college degree.

Legal or Law Enforcement Secretary

Defense attorneys, judges, prosecutors, and detectives all need skilled clerical staff to prepare documents, keep calendars, and do the thousands of daily tasks that help keep any office running. These clerical workers are called *legal secretaries,* and they can make up to $80,000 a year in a large civil law firm. In government service, however, the pay is much less.

I've seen secretaries in private law firms who come very close to practicing law because the lawyers they work for rely on them so heavily. Judges need secretaries for the same reasons as regular lawyers. And detectives need people to type up police reports and do other necessary tasks, such as organize evidence, manage schedules and travel arrangements, and otherwise keep the detectives out of trouble.

Numerous technical colleges across the United States specialize in legal secretary work. Another way to get into the field is by taking a lower-paying word-processing job in a law enforcement agency. Because there's always a demand for quality legal secretaries, if you distinguish yourself, you can quickly move up to a legal secretary position.

Sometimes good legal secretaries develop such an interest in the law that they move into the job of *paralegal,* which is a position that can pay more and that has more responsibility for quasi-legal work.

Court Reporter

Traditionally, a *court reporter* sat in a courtroom and typed out the statements of all the parties via a stenotype machine. But many courtrooms today use digital recording to record statements. In these circumstances, court reporters often operate the equipment, monitor the recordings, and take notes to help identify the speakers. And, frequently, the court reporter has to create a transcript of the event. For example, after a case is concluded, an appeal typically follows, and the appellate lawyers and judges need a transcribed written document to reflect the testimony in the case.

Court reporters also play important roles in civil cases for *depositions* (out-of-court hearings in which lawyers question witnesses). Thus, court reporters typically work for one of two types of employers: a local, state, or federal court or a private court-reporting business.

A number of schools provide training in the use of stenotype machines and other skills related to court reporting, and some states may actually require you to become certified to perform court-reporting duties. The following organizations provide certification:

- ✔ The National Court Reporters Association
- ✔ The United States Court Reporters Association
- ✔ The American Association of Electronic Reporters and Transcribers

The salaries of court reporters are often consistent with those of good private-firm legal secretaries. For example, the median salary in 2006 was around $45,000.

Chapter 24

Ten Notorious, Unsolved Crimes

C hances are you've heard of all, or at least most, of the cases I talk about in this chapter. Be honest: Just about everyone is fascinated by unsolved crimes like these famous ones. I bet more than a few detectives out there think they know who the bad guys are, but, to date, no one can say with complete certainty who dunnit.

The JonBenet Ramsey Murder

In 1996, the murder of child beauty queen JonBenet Ramsey developed into a national media obsession. On the day after Christmas in Boulder, Colorado, Patsy Ramsey discovered that her 6-year-old daughter was missing. The Ramsey family found a ransom note demanding $118,000 for JonBenet's return on their staircase. The dollar figure was the exact amount that JonBenet's father had received as a bonus the year before. The note said not to call anyone, but Patsy Ramsey didn't listen; she called family, friends, and the Boulder Police Department. John Ramsey, JonBenet's father, made arrangements to pay the ransom, but during a search of his basement, police and John Ramsey found JonBenet's body, covered with a white blanket, in the wine cellar.

An autopsy revealed that JonBenet's skull suffered severe blunt trauma and that she was also strangled. A tweed cord and the broken handle of a paint brush were used in the strangulation. Part of the paint brush was later found in Patsy Ramsey's art supplies.

According to the autopsy, JonBenet had eaten pineapple just hours before her death, and a photograph taken the day of her disappearance showed a pineapple in the kitchen with a spoon in it. However, neither parent remembered feeding pineapple to JonBenet.

Police found no sign of forced entry in the Ramsey house, but a broken basement window was unsecured. A blood sample found on JonBenet's underwear proved to be a mixed sample — from at least two different people. A DNA test done in 2003 revealed that some of the blood came from an unknown male.

In 2006, a 41-year-old man from Alabama, who was being held on child pornography charges in California, confessed to murdering JonBenet. However, when his DNA didn't match the sample found in the blood on JonBenet's underwear, police decided not to charge him. After all, no evidence placed him in Boulder at the time of the murder.

In 2008, the local district attorney announced that new DNA testing had established that the blood found didn't match any of JonBenet's family members.

Patsy Ramsey died of cancer in 2006 and was buried next to her daughter in Georgia.

To this day, no one knows who murdered JonBenet Ramsey.

The Sam Sheppard Case

Supposedly the inspiration for the 1993 movie *The Fugitive* (although the movie's creators denied any connection), the Sam Sheppard case was the 1954 equivalent of the O. J. Simpson murder trial in terms of national media attention. Dr. Sam Sheppard was accused of murdering his wife in the early morning of July 4, 1954. Sheppard claimed that a bushy-haired man knocked him unconscious and killed his wife. The murder, which occurred in a suburb of Cleveland, Ohio, came to trial in the fall of 1954.

During the trial, prosecutors revealed that Sheppard had had a three-year affair with a nurse, a fact that the prosecution asserted was his motive for killing his wife. Sheppard testified in his own defense, saying that he was sleeping downstairs when he awoke to his wife's screams. He ran upstairs, where a bushy-haired man attacked him and knocked him out. Evidence presented at the trial showed that Sheppard had broken teeth and cuts on his neck, which, according to the defense, proved he was assaulted. Sheppard said he woke up and chased the bushy-haired man outside, only to be knocked out again. Witnesses testified that they saw a bushy-haired man in the vicinity of the Sheppard house on the day of the murder.

Sheppard was convicted of second-degree murder and sentenced to life in prison. Shortly thereafter, his mother committed suicide and his father died of cancer. After Sheppard spent ten years in prison, the U.S. Supreme Court ordered a new trial, noting that the original trial took place in a "carnival atmosphere" and that the judge had failed to sequester the jury and instruct them not to watch TV or read newspaper stories about the case.

Three days after his release from prison, Sheppard married a woman he had been corresponding with from prison.

Sheppard was retried in 1966 and was represented by famed defense lawyer F. Lee Bailey (who was later part of O. J. Simpson's "dream team"). Sheppard didn't testify at his second trial, and the jury acquitted him.

Sheppard later wrote a book called *Endure and Conquer,* returned briefly to the practice of medicine, and even did a stint as a professional wrestler under the name of "the killer." Sheppard died in 1970 of liver failure. Just six months before his death, he married his wrestling partner's 20-year-old daughter. His first wife's murderer was never found.

The Zodiac Killer

A serial killer known as "the Zodiac" terrorized northern California in 1968 and 1969 but was never identified. The killer gave himself this name in letters he wrote to the media. In his letters, the Zodiac killer claimed to have killed more than 37 people, but, to date, only 7 victims have been identified as being his (and 2 of them survived to tell their stories).

After murdering two people in December 1968 and then murdering another and injuring a fourth in July 1969, the Zodiac killer called the Vallejo Police Department and took credit for both attacks. After that call, three newspapers received letters in which the Zodiac killer took credit for the murders. Each letter contained one-third of a 408-symbol code that supposedly revealed his identity. The killer demanded that each letter be printed in the newspapers or else he would drive around and kill other people. The newspapers eventually published the letters. The killer sent a fourth letter, in which he identified himself as "the Zodiac" for the first time, to the *San Francisco Examiner* in August 1969. The next day, a husband and wife team cracked the 408-symbol code (apparently for fun), but, unfortunately, it didn't reveal the killer's name.

In September 1969, the Zodiac killer approached a couple who was picnicking at Lake Berryessa. He wore a black executioner-style hood and a white bib that depicted a circle with a cross in the middle. After tying up both victims, he attacked them with a knife. The killer left after writing the circle and cross symbol, as well as the dates of the prior murders, on the couple's car. (See Figure 24-1)

Figure 24-1: The symbol of the Zodiac killer.

Twenty-seven miles from the scene, the Zodiac killer called the Napa sheriff's office from a pay phone to report the murders. He left the phone off the hook, and when police arrived at the scene, they found both victims still alive, although one eventually lapsed into a coma and died. The police were able to lift a palm print, but, unfortunately, the print never helped prove anything. One of the victims was able to give a detailed description of what happened, but that description didn't get the police anywhere, either.

In October 1969, the Zodiac killer killed a cab driver in San Francisco. In November, he mailed a 340-character code to the media. To date, this code still hasn't been cracked. Another attack, consisting of a kidnapping and eventual escape by the victim, may have occurred in Modesto in 1970, but the victim's inconsistent story led many people to question its truthfulness.

The Zodiac killer (or crackpots pretending to be the Zodiac killer) continued to send letters to the media through 1974, taking credit for previously committed murders in Southern California. Even after 1974, some letters continued to come, bearing resemblances to the Zodiac killer's handwriting, but police couldn't confirm the authorship. To date, the identity of the Zodiac killer has never been discovered, although every few years, someone claims to have finally determined the Zodiac's identity.

The Murder of Robert Blake's Wife

Robert Blake was a child actor in some of the *Our Gang* short movies from 1939 to 1944; he also starred as a murderer in the 1967 movie *In Cold Blood* and won an Emmy for his TV series *Baretta*. In 2000, Blake married his second wife, 44-year-old Bonnie Bakley, who had been dating Christian Brando, the son of Marlon Brando, at the same time. When she became pregnant, she told both Blake and Brando that they were the father. Blake eventually married Bakley after DNA tests confirmed that he was, indeed, the father. Her marriage to Blake was Bakley's tenth marriage.

On May 4, 2001, Blake took Bakley to an Italian restaurant in Southern California. After dinner, while she was sitting in their car parked on a side street, she was shot in the back of the head and died. Blake told police that, at the time of the shooting, he was returning to the restaurant to retrieve his gun, which he had left there. No restaurant employees recall seeing him return.

Blake was arrested a year later when two stuntmen came forward and said that Blake had tried to hire them to kill his wife. In 2005, a jury acquitted Blake of murder. The district attorney reportedly called the jurors "incredibly stupid."

In a civil suit filed by Bakley's children, Blake was later found liable for Bakley's death and was ultimately ordered to pay $15 million. Blake declared bankruptcy.

The Murder of Seattle Prosecutor Tom Wales

On October 11, 2001, in the fashionable Queen Anne Hill District of Seattle, Assistant U.S. Attorney Tom Wales was gunned down in his home. An 18-year veteran prosecutor of white-collar crimes, Wales was also active in a Washington gun-control organization known as Washington CeaseFire. He had actively supported a state law to require trigger locks on guns, although the law ultimately went down in defeat.

At about 10 p.m., Wales was working on his computer and checking e-mails — his nightly habit — when a shooter fired at least three shots through Wales's basement window. An elderly woman next door heard the shots and called 9-1-1. A neighbor saw a lone gunman walk quickly away from the scene and got into a car parked underneath a tree. At the time of the murder, Wales's ex-wife and son were in Europe.

An investigator associated with the case said that Wales's murder was close to being the perfect murder. The shell casings and the bullets were the only physical evidence police recovered at the scene. From this evidence, the Federal Bureau of Investigation (FBI) was able to determine that the killer used a .380 Makarov pistol with an after-market barrel. More than 2,000 of those barrels had been sold, and the FBI attempted to track down the owner of each one.

Originally, the FBI focused on possible gun-rights activists. However, over time, the focus shifted to a man whom Wales had prosecuted previously. Wales had indicted a commercial airline pilot accused of falsifying documents related to a helicopter business. Wales ultimately had to dismiss charges when the government's expert witness changed his testimony. The pilot filed a suit seeking over $100,000 in attorney costs, but the suit was dismissed. The pilot wasn't known to own a Makarov pistol, but he had been known to fire a handgun into the ground at his home. On the night of the murder, the pilot attended a movie with a friend near Wales's home and then made a phone call from his own home 20 minutes after the murder. Investigators concluded that the timeline would've been fairly tight to commit the murder but that the pilot could've left the theater, gone to Wales's home, fired the shots, and returned to his home to make his phone call.

In 2006, when the story had begun to lose public interest, someone sent a letter to the *Seattle Times*. The letter was from an unemployed man who claimed to have been hired by a woman to kill Wales. The letter recounted a number of accurate facts, but each one centered around information that had already been released to the public about the murder. An investigator associated with the case said he didn't think the letter was authentic.

The FBI continues to offer a $1 million reward for information that leads to an arrest and conviction of the person responsible.

The D. B. Cooper Hijacking

The day before Thanksgiving in 1971, a man going by the name of Dan Cooper and wearing a dark suit and tie got on a Northwest Orient flight going from Portland, Oregon, to Seattle, Washington.

After the flight had taken off, Cooper slipped a note to a stewardess (they called flight attendants stewardesses in those days). She thought he was giving her his phone number, so she slipped the note into her pocket. Cooper leaned over and told her that she should look at the note because he had a bomb. The note demanded $200,000 in unmarked $20 bills and four parachutes when they landed in Seattle.

The plane circled over Puget Sound while the FBI gathered together the money and parachutes that Cooper had requested. While waiting, Cooper drank bourbon and soda.

Eventually, the FBI notified the flight crew that the money was ready, and the plane landed in Seattle. Most of the bills given to Cooper were printed in 1969 and began with the serial letter L. The FBI recorded all the serial numbers. After the money and parachutes were delivered to the plane in a remote location on the tarmac, Cooper released the 36 passengers and one of the flight attendants, keeping the pilot and three other crew members onboard.

After the plane was refueled, it took off again and Cooper ordered the crew to fly to Mexico City at a very low altitude of 10,000 feet with the landing gear down. Cooper and the crew discussed the destination, and, after concluding that they couldn't get to Mexico, they decided on Reno, Nevada, instead. Cooper ordered the pilot to keep the plane unpressurized. After the entire crew was in the cockpit, Cooper opened a door and jumped — that was the last time he was ever seen.

At the time Cooper jumped, the plane was flying through a heavy rainstorm over southwest Washington. As a result, the U.S. Air Force jet that was following the hijacked airliner couldn't see Cooper when he jumped. Searches of the projected landing area by hundreds of police and U.S. Army troops revealed no evidence of Cooper.

Soon thereafter, the FBI interviewed a man in Portland named D. B. Cooper. A media miscommunication led to the name D. B. Cooper becoming the name the hijacker was known by.

In 1973, the *Oregon Journal* newspaper began publishing the serial numbers of all the $20 bills, offering a reward of $1,000 to the first person who brought forth a bill. The goal was to try to trace the money back to the hijacker. Despite intense national interest, no bill was found until 1980. An 8-year-old boy found $5,880 in $20 bills near the Columbia River on the Oregon-Washington border. The money proved to be part of the ransom given to Cooper. The boy was allowed to keep half the money.

The FBI ultimately concluded that Cooper probably didn't survive his jump, reasoning that he certainly wouldn't have left behind that much money. In 2007, the FBI revealed that it had accidentally given Cooper a "dummy" chute that was inoperable, along with the two operable chutes. That chute wasn't left behind on the plane and may have been the one he strapped to his back and jumped with.

Nonetheless, a number of suspects sprang up in later years, including a copycat hijacker who hijacked a plane and asked for $500,000. This man, Richard McCoy, Jr., was arrested and convicted, escaped from prison, and then died in a shootout with police.

The Black Dahlia Murder

In 1947, a young woman from Massachusetts named Elizabeth Short, who had lived a rather ordinary life, was murdered in Los Angeles in a gruesome attack in which her body was cut in half and drained of blood. Each cheek was slashed from mouth to ear, and she was left with her hands over her head. The media most likely nicknamed Short the "Black Dahlia" after her murder because she wasn't known by that name during her lifetime.

Hundreds of police participated in the largest investigation Los Angeles had seen in 20 years. Police treated everyone who knew Short as a possible suspect. Because of the intense media coverage, more than 50 people confessed to the murder.

Some people believed that the murder was related to other gruesome killings around the country, including some in Cleveland and Chicago. Despite the intense interest, however, no serious suspect was ever identified.

The Jack the Ripper Killings

In 1888, in a poor region of London, England, a serial killer brought terror to the city over the course of at least three years. He not only killed prostitutes, but also gruesomely mutilated their bodies and cut out their organs.

Hundreds of letters from the purported killer were sent to police and newspapers, including one that came with a human kidney. Police considered most of the letters to be fraudulent. However, police treated one letter that contained a promise to "clip the lady's ears off" more seriously when, three days after they received it, a murder victim was found with her ear partially cut off. This note identified the killer as Jack the Ripper. Police published the letter, hoping someone would recognize the handwriting, but no one ever did.

In response to the police's failure to capture the murderer, a vigilante group known as the Whitechapel Vigilance Committee formed. It patrolled the streets looking for the killer and petitioned the government to raise the reward.

After two brutal murders, a bloodstained piece of clothing belonging to one of the victims was found in a tenement stairwell. Near the clothing was a chalk writing that read, "The Jewes are the men that will not be blamed for nothing."

Religious tensions were very high at the time, and some people believed this note was an attempt by Jack the Ripper to create greater tension and start a riot. Others theorized that the chalk writing had no relation to the bloodstained clothes and that their proximity was just an accident. A third theory is that Jack the Ripper himself was sending an anti-Semitic message.

Although he wasn't the first serial killer in London, Jack the Ripper was the first one to kill after newspapers became widely read throughout the country. As a result, Jack the Ripper caused terror throughout England.

The Disappearance of Jimmy Hoffa

On July 30, 1975, Jimmy Hoffa, the former president of the International Brotherhood of Teamsters, a large labor union known to have ties to organized crime, disappeared — never to be seen again.

Hoffa became president of the Teamsters in 1957. In 1964, he was convicted of attempting to bribe a grand juror and was sentenced to 15 years in prison. In 1971, President Nixon commuted his sentence with the agreement that Hoffa would stay out of unions for ten years. When he disappeared, Hoffa was planning a lawsuit that may have put him in position to reassume his authority of the Teamsters. He was last seen in the parking lot of a restaurant in a Detroit suburb.

In 2004, the public learned that a man had previously claimed to have killed Hoffa while serving as a hit man for the mafia. The man identified a house in Detroit where he supposedly drove Hoffa and killed him. However, DNA testing of male blood found in the house showed that the blood wasn't Hoffa's.

When I was in college, my school's football team played a game in Giants Stadium in New Jersey, where many people believed that Hoffa had been buried in cement in one endzone. However, during an episode of the TV show *MythBusters,* testing with underground sonic technology disproved this belief (to my disappointment).

In the last ten years, numerous people have claimed to know something about the disappearance of Hoffa, whom many believed was deeply associated with Italian organized crime. However, to date, his body has never been recovered, and the circumstances of his death have never been confirmed.

His son is now president of the Teamsters.

The Murders of Tupac Shakur and Notorious B.I.G.

Gangsta rap is closely associated with violence, at least in its lyrics and themes. But its true nature came to life on March 9, 1997, when Notorious B.I.G., also known as Biggie Smalls — and by his mother as Christopher George Latore Wallace — was gunned down in a drive-by shooting in Los Angeles.

Wallace was born in New York and grew up among drug dealers. His debut rap album, *Ready to Die,* placed him in the center of the East Coast hip hop scene, which, at the time, was in the midst of a feud with West Coast rappers.

Wallace had been in a dispute with famed West Coast rapper Tupac Shakur. Shakur, a former rapping associate of Wallace, accused Wallace of being involved in a 1994 robbery during which Shakur was shot several times.

In 1995, Shakur joined Death Row Records — a West Coast–based production company that was a direct competitor of East Coast rappers.

In 1996, Shakur released a song called "Hit 'em up" in which he claimed to have had sex with Wallace's wife. Thereafter, an intense rivalry ensued between Shakur and Wallace. On September 7, 1996, Shakur was shot multiple times in a drive-by shooting in Las Vegas. He died six days later. Wallace denied involvement and claimed to be in New York at the time.

Six months later, while Wallace was stopped at a red light, a Chevy Impala pulled up, and an African American male dressed in a blue suit with a bow tie pulled out a 9mm handgun and filled the rapper's car with bullets. The shooter hit Wallace four times, and he died almost immediately. A double album was released 15 days after his death, and it became number one on the album charts.

To date, neither murder has been solved.

Index

• *M* •

• *N* •